# ANIMAL OPPRESSION AND HUMAN VIOLENCE

CRITICAL PERSPECTIVES ON ANIMALS: THEORY, CULTURE, SCIENCE, AND LAW

Critical Perspectives on Animals: Theory, Culture, Science, and Law
Series Editors: Gary L. Francione and Gary Steiner

The emerging interdisciplinary field of animal studies seeks to shed light on the nature of animal experience and the moral status of animals in ways that overcome the limitations of traditional approaches to animals. Recent work on animals has been characterized by an increasing recognition of the importance of crossing disciplinary boundaries and exploring the affinities as well as the differences among the approaches of fields such as philosophy, law, sociology, political theory, ethology, and literary studies to questions pertaining to animals. This recognition has brought with it an openness to a rethinking of the very terms of critical inquiry and of traditional assumptions about human being and its relationship to the animal world. The books published in this series seek to contribute to contemporary reflections on the basic terms and methods of critical inquiry, to do so by focusing on fundamental questions arising out of the relationships and confrontations between humans and nonhuman animals, and ultimately to enrich our appreciation of the nature and ethical significance of nonhuman animals by providing a forum for the interdisciplinary exploration of questions and problems that have traditionally been confined within narrowly circumscribed disciplinary boundaries.

*The Animal Rights Debate: Abolition or Regulation?* Gary L. Francione and Robert Garner
*Animal Rights Without Liberation: Applied Ethics and Human Obligations*, Alasdair Cochrane
*Animalia Americana: Animal Representations and Biopolitical Subjectivity*, Colleen Glenney Boggs
*Experiencing Animal Minds: An Anthology of Animal-Human Encounters*, edited by Julie A. Smith and Robert W. Mitchell
*Being Animal: Beasts and Boundaries in Nature Ethics*, Anna L. Peterson
*Animals and the Limits of Postmodernism*, Gary Steiner

# ANIMAL OPPRESSION AND HUMAN VIOLENCE

## Domesecration, Capitalism, and Global Conflict

David A. Nibert

COLUMBIA UNIVERSITY PRESS     NEW YORK

Columbia University Press
*Publishers Since 1893*
New York   Chichester, West Sussex
cup.columbia.edu
Copyright © 2013 Columbia University Press

Library of Congress Cataloging-in-Publication Data
Nibert, David Alan, 1953–
   Animal oppression and human violence : domesecration, capitalism, and global
conflict / David Nibert.
      p. cm. — (Critical perspectives on animals: theory, culture, science, and law)
   Includes bibliographical references and index.
   ISBN 978-0-231-15188-7 (cloth : alk. paper) — ISBN 978-0-231-15189-4 (pbk.) — ISBN
978-0-231-52551-0 (e-book)
   1. Animal welfare—History.   2. Domestication—History.   3. Pastoral systems—
History.   4. Animals and civilization—History.   5. Human-animal relationships—
History.   I. Title.

   HV4731 . N53 2013
   179'. 3—dc23

                                                                2012030357

COVER IMAGE: JACK DELANO © CORBIS

References to websites (URLs) were accurate at the time of writing. Neither the author
nor Columbia University Press is responsible for URLs that may have expired or changed
since the manuscript was prepared.

In my opinion the true and healthy constitution of the State is the one which I have described. But if you wish also to see a State at fever heat, I have no objection. For I suspect that many will not be satisfied with the simpler way of life. . . . Then we must enlarge our borders; for the original healthy State is no longer sufficient. Now will the city have to fill and swell with a multitude of callings which are not required by any natural want; such as the whole tribe of hunters . . . and *swineherds*, too, who were not needed and therefore had no place in the former edition of our State, but are needed now? They must not be forgotten: and there will be animals of many other kinds, if people eat them.

Certainly.

And living in this way we shall have much greater need of physicians than before?

Much greater.

And the country which was enough to support the original inhabitants will be too small now, and not enough?

Quite true.

Then a slice of our neighbours' land will be wanted by us for pasture and tillage, and they will want a slice of ours, if, like ourselves, they exceed the limit of necessity, and give themselves up to the unlimited accumulation of wealth?

That, Socrates, will be inevitable.

And so we shall go to war, Glaucon. Shall we not?

Most certainly, he replied.

—Plato, *The Republic* (2:373)

For Julie and Taylor

# CONTENTS

Acknowledgments    **ix**

Introduction    **1**

1. Nomadic Pastoralism, Ranching, and Violence    **9**

   The Rise of Nomadic Pastoralism    **13**
   Military Use of Domesecrated Animals in Agrarian Society    **18**
   Domesecration and Mongol Violence    **24**
   Violence and Hunger in the Middle Ages    **31**
   Violence and Warfare in the Pre-Columbian Americas    **34**

2. Domesecration and the Americas    **43**

   Animal Oppression and the Invasion of the Americas    **45**
   Expansion of Commercially Driven Ranching    **51**
   Ranching Violence and Destruction in Brazil    **56**
   Domesecration, Human Oppression, and the Rise of Capitalism    **61**
   The Spanish Invasion of the Philippines    **65**

3. Ranching and Violence in North America    **70**

   Crop Damage, Conflict, and Warfare    **71**
   Commercial Ranching and Violence    **76**
   Ranching Expansion and Indigenous Displacement    **82**
   Reign of the "Cattle" Kings    **86**

4. Domesecration in the Western Plains    **92**

   Expropriation of Western Lands    **96**
   The Bloody Western Bonanza    **103**
   Growing Levels of Animal Oppression    **108**
   Ranching in Canada    **120**

5. Capitalist Colonialism and Ranching Violence    126

British Invasion of Australia and New Zealand    133
Rancher Dominance in Latin America    142
Domesecration in Africa and the European Invasion    154

6. Social Construction of the "Hamburger" Culture    171

Corporate Engineering of Public Consciousness    175
Federal Policy and "Meat" Production    180
The Rise of Fast Food    185
The "Hamburger" Culture and Entangled Violence    188

7. The "Hamburger" Culture and Latin America    196

Hunger and Environmental Degradation    200
Repression and Poverty    203
"Low-Intensity" Terrorism    205
Domesecration and the Devalued    212
Global Ranching and Oppression in Oceania and Africa    216

8. Domesecration and Impending Catastrophe    223

Contemporary Ranching and the Oppressed    224
Growing Global Consumption of Domesecrated
Animal Products    233
CAFO Explosion    236
Misuse of Finite Resources    240
Looming Regional and International Conflict    242
The Potential Global Influenza Pandemic    247
The Growing Pandemic of Chronic Diseases    252

9. New Welfarism, Veganism, and Capitalism    259

Veganism as a Global Imperative    261
Transcending the Capitalist System    266

Notes    273
Index    321

# ACKNOWLEDGMENTS

Several people provided helpful comments and suggestions on parts of the manuscript, including Bill Winders, Michael Greger, Dennis Smith, Becky Crabtree, and Helen Masterman-Smith. Both Taylor Ford and Randy Shields read over the entire manuscript, providing valuable comments and suggestions. Special thanks to Gary Steiner, Gary Francione, Peggy Hanna, and Tracey Smith-Harris and John Sorenson for their support and encouragement. My inspiration for this project came in no small part from my close friendships with Chase, Zach, T. T., Karl, Twinkle, Callie, Bailey, Palma, and Mariah. This work would not have been possible without the patience and support of my spouse, Julie Ford, whose insightful comments and remarkable editorial skills were indispensable.

# ANIMAL OPPRESSION AND HUMAN VIOLENCE

In 1896, Frank Wilson Blackmar, who later would become president of the American Sociological Association, wrote:

> The *domestication* of animals led to a great improvement in the race. It gave an increased food supply through *milk* and the flesh of animals. . . . One after another animals have rendered service to *man*. They are used for food or clothing, or to carry burdens and draw loads. The advantage of their *domestication* cannot be too greatly estimated.[1]

A year earlier, the Harvard professor of paleontology and geology Nathaniel Southgate Shaler wrote similarly:

> In the group of continents termed the old world . . . there were many species of larger mammals which were well fitted for *domestication*, the advance of social development went on rapidly. . . . It is hardly too much to say that civilization has intimately depended on the subjugation of a great range of useful species. . . .
>
> The possession of *domesticated* animals certainly did much to break up . . . [the] old brutal way of life; it led to a higher sense of responsibility to the care of the household; it brought about systematic agriculture; it developed the art of war; it laid the foundations of wealth and commerce, and so set *men* well upon their upward way.[2]

Such long-held views about the role of other animals in human civilization have been widely accepted as obvious and unassailable. However, as Michael Parenti observes, "the most insidious oppressions are those that so insinuate themselves into the fabric of our lives and into the recesses of our minds that we don't even realize they are acting upon us."[3] This book offers a different point of view, one much neglected by academia. The thesis of this book is that the practice of capturing and oppressing cows, sheep, pigs, horses, goats, and similar large, sociable animals for human use did not, as Shaler put it, "set *men* well upon their upward way." Rather, it *undermined* the development of a just and peaceful world. The harms that humans have done to other animals—*especially that harm generated by pastoralist and ranching practices that have culminated in contemporary factory-farming practices*—have been a precondition for and have engendered large-scale violence against and injury to devalued humans, particularly indigenous people around the world.

Over the past ten thousand years, human lives and those of other animals have been shaped indelibly and tragically by the priorities and interests of elite groups in their societies. Those customs and practices that serve their interests include the much-touted process of "domestication" of other animals, from which human civilization and advancement allegedly sprang. Cultural representations and even much scholarly discussion long have mainly supported and preserved societal practices that serve the interests of the most powerful—and the practice of exploiting other animals is no exception.

The perspective on human treatment of other animals promoted by Blackmar and Shaler once stood alongside similarly anachronistic racist, sexist, and other proclamations by scholars and social commentators. Such beliefs have been ameliorated somewhat over the years, changed by decades of social-justice activism but also by the needs of the capitalist system. Profound institutionalized discrimination against women and people of color, for example, was inconsistent with increased profit taking and the expansion of capitalism.[4] But while the eventual prohibition of legalized human enslavement and some amelioration of sexist policies and practices furthered the expansion of capitalism, the lucrative exploitation of other animals continues and today remains one of the most profitable of industries. Not surprisingly, support for objectification and utilitarian use of other animals still is ubiquitous, well into the twenty-first century. For instance, current history textbooks contain statements such as: "*Domesticated* animals, especially *cattle*, yielded *meat, milk*, and *hides*. Food surpluses made it possible for people to do things other than farming. Some people became artisans and made weapons and jewelry that were traded with neighboring peoples."[5] Such reflexive pronouncements by scholars are commonplace.

A relatively recent work that supported this benign view of "domestication," one rooted in the speciesist writings of scholars like Blackmar and Shaler, is Jared Diamond's popular 1997 work *Guns, Germs, and Steel*.

Diamond suggests that human use of other animals facilitated the development of the collective knowledge that fostered human advancement.[6] This point of view was buttressed by the 2011 book *The Animal Connection* by Pat Shipman, who maintains that human use of "living tools" throughout history furthered human development and our capacity for caring.[7]

The moral-philosophical position inherent in the works of writers from Blackmar to Shipman is one in which the exploitation of other animals serves the interest of human society and the ethical implications of the suffering experienced by other animals are simply ignored. Such traditional representations of history and human society—in lectures, printed works, and documentaries that are widely used in school and university classrooms—deny the personhood and subjectivity of other animals, who are simply reduced to "biota."[8] The profound bias in this view presents the exploitation of other animals as normal and necessary; at the same time, *challenges* to the conventional view—works that speak to the interests of other animals and that reexamine the consequences of their use by humans—are widely regarded as prejudiced, unscientific, and flawed.

The tendency for the academy in capitalist society to reflect dominant ideological positions has been noted by, among others, the sociologist Thorstein Veblen. He observed in 1918 that while the scholar "is guided in effect by a meretricious subservience to the extra-scholastic conventions, all the while . . . *he* must profess an unbiased pursuit of the infusion and diffusion of knowledge among *men*."[9] Other writers have questioned scientists' very ability to conduct unbiased, value-free scholarship and suggest that intellectuals and teachers who present themselves as unbiased are participating in academic dishonesty. For example, as Robin W. Winks observes, "the tendency is for historians to examine a concept derived from popular culture and, especially when they feel that the concept has essential validity, to put little or no explicit distance between themselves and the popular manifestations of the idea they are examining."[10] Similarly, the sociologist Alvin Gouldner writes:

> If sociologists ought not express their personal values in the academic setting, how then are students to be safeguarded against the unwitting influence of these values which shape the sociologist's selection of problems, *his* preferences for certain hypotheses or conceptual schemes, and *his* neglect of others? For these are unavoidable and, in this sense, there is and can be no value-free sociology.[11]

Most contemporary scholarship pertaining to the relationship between humans and other animals reflects what the scholar and social critic Michael Parenti refers to as society's "background assumptions":

> Our tendency to accept a datum or argument as true or not depends less on the content and substance of it than it does on how congruent it is with the background assumptions we already have. But those background assumptions are of course established by the whole climate of opinion, the whole universe of communication that we are immersed in constantly, which is why dissidents learn the discipline of fighting and developing their arguments from evidence, while those who work within the safe mainstream work a whole lifetime with unexamined assumptions and presumptions.[12]

This book's perspective also is distinct from popular opinion and mainstream scholarship in presenting most human use of other animals, past and present, as *violence*—as the unethical and chauvinistic treatment of the other inhabitants of the planet. Increasingly, ethologists are reporting that other animals, including those relegated to the socially constructed position of "farm animal," are sentient beings with emotional lives, strong preferences and desires, and profound social bonds. However, the individuality and personality of each is ignored by the humans who benefit from their mistreatment and death. Rosamund Young observes, "Animals and people can appear to lose their identities or become institutionalized if forced to live in unnatural, crowded, featureless, regimented or boring conditions."[13] Much has been written about the sentience, consciousness, and mindedness of other animals, however, and this book is not an elaboration on that ongoing scholarship,[14] nor will it add to the critical reviews of the traditional arguments that have been used to legitimate the oppression of other animals.[15]

This book is a comparative historical analysis that examines recurring patterns of the oppression of significant numbers of large animals for food and resources by elites in different societies and at different points in history and discusses how this form of oppression led to invasion, conquest, and other harms. While the historical periods and regions are unique, they are not beyond comparison. The focal point of this study is the process commonly referred to as animal "domestication" and how this practice caused large-scale violence, destruction, and disease epidemics. Specifically, it will compare the ways that such use of other animals in different societies—as instruments of warfare, forced laborers, or rations and other resources—has *enabled* widespread violence. This work also will review the ways in which such use of other animals has *promoted* harm. These include damage from the need to expropriate the land and water necessary to maintain large groups of animals, the amassing of military power resulting from animal exploitation, and the pursuit of economic benefit from the use or sale of animals. The widespread violence and destruction engendered by such uses of large numbers of "domesticated" animals encompasses both the violence experienced by the animals and the ways in which this harm has been entangled with related forms of violence against free-living animals and groups of devalued humans. These include invasion, conquest, extermination, displacement, repression, coerced and enslaved servitude, gender subordination and sexual exploitation, and hunger. Accompanying such violence have been deadly zoonotic diseases that have contributed to the destruction of entire cities, societies, and civilizations. Finally, as the practice of oppression and the impediments to effective moral challenges to the practice are closely tied to the material interests of elites, special attention will be given to the relationship between animal "domestication" and the development and expansion of the capitalist system. A primary assumption of this work is that oppression—of both humans and other animals—is entangled with and motivated by the desire for material gain, especially by elites. Moreover, for institutionalized oppression to occur, it must be supported by state power and justified through ideological manipulation.[16]

This book takes a historical-materialist approach to the practice of animal oppression and the ensuing, pervasive violence of pastoralism, traditional ranching, and today's intensive factory farming.[17] This historical review emphasizes systemic factors and does not focus on the agency of individual human and animal actors. This is not to suggest that individual-level actions—and resistance to oppression—are insignificant, but a satisfactory treatment of this important subject is beyond the scope of this book.[18] However, it will try to recognize what the scholar E. P. Thompson asserted should be acknowledged in historical works: "the quality of life, the sufferings and satisfactions, of those who live and die in unredeemed time."[19]

Finally, it is important to recognize that public acceptance of the profitable oppression of other animals has been socially engineered in no small part through the creation and ubiquitous use of reality-defining words and expressions that disparage or objectify other animals. As William Kornblum puts it, "A culture's language expresses how the people of that culture perceive and understand the world and, at the same time, influences their perceptions and understandings."[20] Walter Lippmann noted, "For the most part we do not see first, and then define, we define first and then see."[21] Accordingly, throughout the text the phrase "other animals" often is used instead of simply "animals," to highlight the fact that humans also are animals—a truth that frequently is obscured in order to advance a powerful ideological divide that furthers terrible acts of oppression.

Moreover, in an effort to reject language that objectifies and devalues others, words such as "cattle," "poultry," and "livestock" are placed in quotation marks throughout the text, to underscore the usually overlooked ideology and values built into those terms and to reduce the likelihood that such disparaging terminology will be comprehended in the conventional sense. Words that represent parts and body fluids of other animals as mere commodities, such as "meat," "wool," "milk," "dairy," and "eggs," similarly facilitate a psychological-social detachment, in which the reality of the lives and deaths of other animals is masked and the animals themselves become what Carol Adams calls "absent referents."[22] This practice of placing certain language in quotes also is used in the cases of words such as "slave," "peon," and "peasant" that serve to devalue groups of humans and of male pronouns used where references to both women and men are implied. Moreover, terms such as "master" and "owner" that are euphemisms for oppressors or oppressive practices also will be set in quotes. When such terms appear in quoted material, they are placed in italics. While some readers may find this device awkward at times, it is very important, in any work that strives to address oppression, to avoid language that supports or legitimizes oppressive arrangements. To this end, the term *domesecration* will be put forward as a necessary replacement for "domestication" in chapter 1.

Chapter 1 of this book opens with humankind's transition from foraging systems of subsistence to hunting and then discusses agricultural society and the large-scale violence and warfare that was enabled and promoted by nomadic pastoralist and ranching practices. Chapter 2 examines the Spanish and Portuguese invasion of the Americas, incursions made possible by the oppression of horses, cows, and pigs as resources and as instruments of war, as well as the deadly effects of infectious diseases resulting from crowding together oppressed animals. Chapter 3 reviews the broader European colonization of North America and the lethal conflicts with Native Americans that resulted from the intruders' ranching of cows, pigs, and horses—violence that expanded with the emergence of commercial ranching operations. Chapter 4 focuses on ranchers' and enslavers' violent expropriation of Texas, the U.S. confiscation of half of Mexico, and the ensuing war against indigenous peoples and other animals of the Western plains that permitted the development of vast ranching operations.

Chapter 5 looks at the role ranching played in nineteenth-century European colonialism in other parts of the world—including the British takeover of Ireland, rancher invasions of many parts of Africa, and the British colonization of Australia, New Zealand, and Tasmania—and the tragic consequences for indigenous people and other animals there. Chapter 5 also examines postindependence Latin America, where powerful, landed elites—disproportionately ranchers—undermined attempts at democracy and perpetrated widespread violence in order to maximize profits from the export of ranching products. Chapter 6 reviews the rise of corporate capitalism in the United States and the development of the fast-food industry, the creation of "hamburger culture," and the push for expanded "meat" consumption. Chapter 7 examines the effect of "hamburger culture" on conflict and violence in Latin America, where the United States and international financial institutions helped expand greatly both ranching and feed-crop production. We will see that the recurring general pattern throughout this history—conflict and entangled violence produced by elite-controlled pastoral and ranching systems—has varied somewhat in different regions but has increased in complexity with the growth of capitalism. Chapter 8 discusses the global risks linked to the enormous contemporary expansion of intensive ranching operations and the vast increase in global consumption of animals as food. We will see that, in fact, "domestication" not only has undermined the development of a just and peaceful world but also presents one of the most significant threats to future stability, peace, and justice. In chapter 9, brief consideration will be given to the counterproductive nature of most contemporary animal advocacy and the obstacles that the capitalist system creates to achieving a just and nonviolent world.

# NOMADIC PASTORALISM, RANCHING, AND VIOLENCE

This essentially egalitarian relationship disappeared with the advent of *domestication*. . . . The human becomes the overlord and master, the animals his servants and slaves.
—James Serpell, *In the Company of Animals*

Thus, looked at in a long-term perspective, what seems to characterize the history of the Eurasian landmass is not the opposition between sea power and continental power but the opposition between sedentary areas and nomad invasions.
—Gérard Chaliand, *The Art of War in World History*

The political history of civilized Eurasia and of Africa, in fact, consists largely of intermittent conquest by invaders from the grasslands, punctuated by recurrent rebellions of agricultural populations against subjugation to the heirs of such conquerors.
—William H. McNeill, *The Great Frontier*

On December 8, 1237, the city of Riazan, some 125 miles southeast of Moscow, came under siege by 120,000 Mongol warriors. Mongol engineers and forced laborers surrounded the fortified city with a wooden palisade to prevent anyone from escaping and to provide cover for archers and artillery. The residents of the city watched in terror as the invaders completed the construction of the fence in nine days. On the tenth day, the bombardment began. On December 21, after five days of catapulting rocks and raining arrows on the populace, the Mongols stormed the city with scaling ladders, battering rams, and firebrands. The invaders set fire to the city and began an indiscriminate slaughter. Riazan's residents were disemboweled, impaled, drowned, set afire, and flayed alive; young women and nuns were systematically raped before they were killed. A handful of survivors were permitted to escape for the purpose of spreading the word of the Mongol horror.[1]

Why did such a terrible incident in Eurasia—and countless others like it in various ways—occur? Such violent and destructive practices cannot simply be written off as being part of human nature. For most of our time on the earth, the members of the human species lived relatively peaceably and survived by sharing resources obtained by foraging and gathering. Early humans, considered by some to be the "earliest affluent society,"[2] generally had abundant resources and were able to meet their subsistence needs while leaving time for leisure, play, and social activities. The reliance on foraging and the importance of sharing for the welfare of the group resulted in "minimal inequality in power and privilege."[3]

This early form of communal, egalitarian human society was undermined by the onset of organized hunting of other animals, which began no earlier than ninety thousand years ago—and probably much later.[4] The practice of stalking and killing animals increased the propensity for violence among human hunters, and the status of men in society began to be associated largely with their skill and success at hunting other animals. At the same time, the status of women declined; they came to perform more of the daily tasks and child care, while men cultivated their skill at stalking animals.[5]

The course of world history again was altered dramatically roughly ten thousand years ago, when humans living in the Middle Eastern region of Eurasia began to practice rudimentary plant cultivation, an early form of agriculture referred to as horticulture, in which humans used digging sticks to hoe small plots of land. In comparison with the lifestyles of foragers, early agriculturalists faced hard physical labor and increased risks to their welfare. While food production still required the efforts of most members of society, early horticulture generated a small food surplus, allowing a few individuals to live off the labor of the majority. The first such individuals were most likely priests, go-betweens who communicated with the gods who provided the conditions necessary for a good harvest. The priests collected much of the agricultural surplus as offerings to the deities and stored it in temple centers under their control. The priests' power and control grew as they became early directors and administrators of agricultural production. This form of economic production began to create unequal and increasingly exploitative human relations.

Early agriculture also increased the divide between humans and other animals. In some parts of the world, humans turned from hunting to capturing and controlling the reproduction of several species of other animals in order to exploit them as food and other resources. While foraging had resulted in a varied diet, "agriculture restricted food sources to highly specific crops or animal flesh/milk, the constant supply of which was never guaranteed due to the possibility of drought, crop failure, parasitic infection or infectious disease."[6] The practice of animal exploitation was most pronounced in Eurasia, with its populations of several highly social mammals, such as cows, pigs, goats, sheep, and horses. The term widely used to refer to this practice, "domestication," has come to reflect what is largely regarded as the "providential inevitability," the much-touted human-animal "partnership."[7]

Today, based on the growing body of work by ethologists and biologists about the profound mindedness and emotional life of other animals,[8] we can assume that, for the most part, the other animals' experience of capture, enslavement, use, and slaying was one of suffering and violence. While much of their treatment unquestionably was in the form of direct physical violence, the animals' systemic enslavement and oppression also resulted in their inability to meet their basic needs, the loss of self-determination, and the loss of the opportunity to live in a natural way—an indirect form of violence referred to as "structural violence."[9] Archaeological findings of the remains of early enslaved other animals provide evidence of their suffering. Generally, examination of the remains of animals held captive thousands of years ago reveals bone pathologies resulting from physical trauma, poor diet, chronic arthritis, gum disease, and high levels of stress.[10] For instance, excavations from 8500 BCE revealed bone deformities in enslaved goats and cows that provided "some indication of stress, presumably due to the conditions in which these early *domestic* animals were kept."[11] Remains of sheep and goats from the early Bronze Age show a marked decrease in bone thickness, reflecting calcium deficiencies "resulting from the combined effects of poor nutrition and intensive milking."[12]

While most definitions of "domestication" do not reflect the experiences of these highly sentient beings, the following definition by Pierre Ducos does reflect the objectification of other animals inherent in the term.

> *Domestication* can be said to exist when living animals are integrated as objects into the socio-economic organization of the human group, in the sense that, while living, those animals are objects for ownership, inheritance, exchange, trade, etc., as are other objects . . . with which human groups have something to do.[13]

This definition, put forth in 1975, attempted to acknowledge the oppression inherent in this form of animal exploitation. However, contemporary representations of the term overwhelmingly reflect hegemonic notions of "domestication" as a benign partnership. In reality, the "domestication" of highly social animals—which developed out of hunting them—was no partnership at all but, rather, a significant extension of systemic violence and exploitation. The emergence and continued practice of capturing, controlling, and genetically manipulating other animals for human use violates the sanctity of life of the sentient beings involved, and their minds and bodies are desecrated to facilitate their exploitation: it can be said that they have been *domesecrated*. *Domesecration* is the systemic practice of violence in which social animals are enslaved and biologically manipulated, resulting in their objectification, subordination, and oppression. Through domesecration, many species of animals that lived on the earth for millions of years, including several species of large, sociable Eurasian mammals, came to be regarded as mere objects, their very existence recognized only in relation to their exploitation as "food animals" or similar socially constructed positions reflecting various forms of exploitation.

One of the harms experienced by countless other animals as a result of domesecration was their increased vulnerability to infectious disease. The growing practice of confining ever-larger numbers of domesecrated animals in crowded conditions facilitated the mutation and spread of infectious, multiple-host-species pathogens; these diseases then infected the animals' captors, whose own permanent settlements and increasing population density furthered the transmission of the infections. Indeed, "most and probably all of the distinctive infectious diseases of civilization transferred to human populations from animal *herds*."[14] Diseases that humans contracted from the confinement and exploitation of large groups of other animals included smallpox, tuberculosis, measles, influenza, and malaria. This result of domesecration would have catastrophic consequences for countless humans and other animals as time progressed.

Eventually, early horticultural societies in Eurasia began to exploit the labor of cows and horses for agricultural production, a practice that led to the rise of what is frequently referred to as "true agrarian" societies. The difference between horticulture and agrarian societies was that while the former relied upon human labor for plant cultivation, the latter exploited animals by harnessing them to plows. The use of animals to pull plows facilitated the cultivation of larger areas and increased the number of people available to labor on other projects. This form of exploitation of other animals allowed for the emergence of a professional warrior or military class, which served to protect surplus food and other valuables from raids by outsiders—and to stifle dissent among soil cultivators, laborers, and artisans who were being exploited by the elites.

In sum, for most of human existence we lived in relatively peaceful egalitarian societies. It was only with the emergence of domesecration and agricultural society—the much acclaimed "Neolithic revolution" presented largely as a monumental step forward in human development— that social elites and large-scale violence and warfare came into existence. This transformation created a vastly different world for humans and other animals, a momentous departure from the "original affluent society."

## The Rise of Nomadic Pastoralism

The violence and suffering associated with domesecration and the exploitation of the human masses by agrarian elites was soon supplemented by another powerful cause of misery. Roughly eight thousand years ago, people migrated to the Eurasian steppes, the semiarid plains that ranged from Eastern Europe to northern China, and began to practice nomadic pastoralism. Unlike agriculturalists, nomadic pastoralists relied almost entirely on domesecrated animals for food and materials, and they routinely migrated in search of fresh pastures and sources of water. These early nomadic pastoralist societies comprised numerous associated patriarchal clans in which a man's power and status were linked to the number of domesecrated animals under his control.

Individuals in such societies can accumulate wealth in the form of *herds*. Further, they must defend their property. It's not easy to swoop down and make off with a horticulturalist's sweet potatoes, but *cattle* and horses must be guarded. This is usually the job of armed men (women and children are more likely to be given *herding* responsibilities for smaller animals, such as *poultry*, sheep and goats). Given that tending and guarding the *herds* are male responsibilities, men tend to dominate these societies. In fact, in some *herding* societies wealthy men acquire harems of women just as they do horses, *cattle* or camels. Men without *herds* are left to serve as hired hands, often with little prospect for advancement. In some societies this servant-hood develops into hereditary slavery.[15]

Pastoralist elites frequently increased the number of domesecrated animals under their control by raiding the rivals with whom they competed for optimal pasture and water resources. To facilitate raiding and to maintain possession of the other animals under their control, nomadic pastoralists became highly militaristic and eventually came to use horses as instruments of war. The enslavement of large groups of domesecrated animals, such as cows, goats, horses, and sheep, depleted the grasslands, which became desertified after intensive grazing. The migrations of the nomadic pastoralists from the Eurasian steppes—caused by drought, resource depletion, or warfare with other pastoralists—brought them into competition with agriculturalists for land. "The hostile migration of the mounted nomads accompanied by huge flocks of sheep and herds of horses into settled land signaled disaster for the farmers and their crops."[16]

While the enslavement of large groups of domesecrated animals necessitated migration and invasion, there was another motivation for conquest: settled, plant-based societies had manufactured and luxury goods that nomadic groups could not produce. "The greed for luxury or manufactured goods beyond the reach of their simple economy has repeatedly driven the pastoral peoples to ride out of the steppes and plunder the fields and cities of their sedentary and civilized neighbours."[17] Over the course of military campaigns, "many fields of crops, harvests, and farms were damaged or burned."[18] Women, especially those taken from conquered societies, were treated as possessions and enslaved as concubines and servants by men with high status. While some invasions were genocidal in nature, in other instances invading pastoralists settled in conquered areas and, as the new ruling elites, imposed their own values and culture.

It is likely that when pastoral nomads in substantial numbers successfully invade an area previously settled only by farmers, heavy interference in the population growth of the latter will result. Areas previously under cultivation will be used for pasture, if necessary acquired by force. A reduction in the number of farmers at saturation and an increase in that of the pastoralists will follow. Further disruptions of the farmers' political and social system will ensue. . . . Farmers are now the socially inferior group.[19]

Similarly, V. Gordon Childe observed:

A tribe of pastoralists, for instance, may conquer the land of a *peasant* community. They will leave the *peasants* on the land, and even protect them from other enemies, on the condition that they pay a tribute of farm produce. . . . These form a sort of landed "aristocracy," a class living off the tribute of *peasants*. The system is familiar . . . it was widespread in antiquity.[20]

It was the use of oppressed horses as vehicles of transportation that gave the pastoralists the ability to make "hit-and-run" raids, the capacity to travel great distances, and the power to lay siege to entire cities.

Riding meant that warring groups could strike militarily over vast distances with rapid movements that could be followed up by migrations, or by speedy retreat if more convenient. Nomadic groups were further able to settle in resource-rich niches in otherwise indigenously populated habitats. At the local level raids and looting gained new importance as they could be carried out quickly and efficiently, initiating a new age of warring and shifting territoriality. . . .

A mobile, warring, ideology prevailed, spurred by the need to move the *herds* between resource rich valleys, often separated by large stretches of less fertile arid grasslands, imposing a long-term trend towards mobility.[21]

For long-distance raids, each warring pastoralist was accompanied by a string of captive horses, mostly females. The *milk*, blood, and flesh of horses were used as nourishment, and fermented horse *milk* was consumed as an alcoholic beverage.[22]

The horse gave . . . [the nomadic pastoralist] speed, range and mobility. He could choose the place and time for battle, ambush his prey, and escape to the steppe in short order. . . . To develop these advantages the nomad kept not one horse but strings of them, affording him fresh mounts on demand. A string of horses was also an inexpensive addition to the nomad's equipment, for the horses could freely graze on the open steppe. Thus, as long as there were enough horses and sufficient pasture, the nomadic life promised adventure and wealth to the pastoralist and threatened confiscation and domination to settlers.[23]

This exploitation of animals, horses in particular, permitted pastoralists in what is now southern Russia to begin violent incursions into Europe, an area occupied largely by tribal farming communities, as early as six thousand years ago. The cultural symbols of these early pastoralist invaders, generally referred to as Kurgans, were the dagger and battleaxe, and they "glorified the lethal power of the sharp blade."[24] Waves of pastoralist invasions are believed by some to have molded the violent and expansion-prone cultures of the West and increased the role of animal exploitation in the developing European economies.[25] Childe referred to the collapse of plant-based communities and the increasing adoption of pastoralist economics and culture as the "late Neolithic crisis." Some scholars maintain that the development in some areas of Eurasia of transhumant pastoralism (the localized, seasonal transference of domesecrated animals from one grazing area to another) was cultivated in part as a strategy for fleeing from invading armies.[26] Marija Gimbutas, a leading scholar on the Kurgan invasions, writes:

> This transformation was initiated by the pastoralists of the Eurasian steppe whose success lay in their extraordinary mobility and advantage of weaponry. The stratified patrilinear social structure of these small, agnatically-linked *herding* units was superimposed over the egalitarian substrate of Old European agriculturalists. The shift to large *stock breeding* was only one symptom of the Kurganization process. The steppe people brought in new male deities of the sky, war and hunt. Solar signs, weapon-carrying gods, and ritual roles of the horse, boar and dog replaced Old European symbols connected with the mother creator and lunar symbolism.[27]

There is evidence that several largely egalitarian, women-centered communities in ancient Europe and their cultural and religious practices were destroyed by the steppe pastoralists:

In order to consolidate their economic and political power, Indo-Europeans would have to totally destroy the social structure and culture of older societies; religious, economic and political systems were inextricably tied. The overwhelming tendency towards egalitarianism and community needed to be undone. . . . If this system were not destroyed, the invaders would have had a much more difficult time securing exclusive rights to power and prestige. Consequently, as the leaders and the property system changed so did religion and the relationship between the sexes. Due to continued contact with the Indo-European invaders, the political, economic and spiritual authority of women was decimated by the 15th century BC.[28]

Pastoralists related to the Kurgans but located in mid-central Asia expanded southward, invading southern Eurasia about 2,500 years ago, while pastoralists on the eastern steppes menaced China. Over the centuries, such pastoralist peoples as the Scythians, the Huns, the Goths, the Turks, the Mongols, and the Manchus ravaged and terrorized Eurasian cities, stole valuables, and displaced, massacred, or dominated the inhabitants. It was not uncommon for pastoralists to obtain wealth by exacting tributes from threatened cities or extorting payments through their control of trade routes. Nomadic pastoralists' devaluation of nonpastoralists and people who cultivated the soil was evident in the social stratification they established in the regions they conquered and ruled.

Most pastoral nomads who originated in the Eurasian steppes and expanded from them seem to have shared a tendency to caste formation, as observed historically in Greek, Roman and Indian societies. This may have been a trend already present among the steppe pastoral nomads, or it may simply be a likely development whenever there is confrontation between pastoral-nomadic invaders and previous agricultural settlers. Under such conditions, systems of social stratification are the probable outcome. In extreme cases the fate of previous settlers has been annihilation or enslavement; but less extreme forms of serfdom or other modes of political control are more common. The generation of genetically closed segments of society ordered hierarchically, as bona fide castes are, is one form of societal evolution of which the strict Indian model represents an example.[29]

In agrarian society, control of the land was an important goal of elites and, similar to nomadic pastoralists, control and ownership of large numbers of domesecrated animals led to wealth and power. However, even the most powerful agrarian societies were vulnerable to nomadic pastoralist invasions—and the Roman Empire was no exception.

## Military Use of Domesecrated Animals in Agrarian Society

Like elite males in nomadic pastoralist society, the wealth and power of elite landowners in Roman agrarian society were linked to their control over large numbers of domesecrated animals and the land and water needed to sustain them. However, elite agrarian landowners raised and sold large groups of other animals for profit, a practice referred to in this book generally as "ranching." In Rome, "ranching paid off better than any other kind of agriculture," but to produce great profits it "had to be conducted on a large scale and on large estates."[30] Ranching was a favored investment for members of the Roman Senate because they could function as absentee landowners, delegating the management of their estates while living in Rome. For Roman ranchers, like their pastoralist counterparts, control of land and water was extremely important—and it was frequently acquired at the expense of others. For instance, in the early days of the Republic, many yeoman-soldiers required to participate in long military campaigns were unable to maintain their farms and were forced to sell and join the ranks of the impoverished. Much of their land was converted to pasture.

"As ruined farmers were selling out, the upper classes were in the market for properties on which to establish large estates manned by the *slaves* that Rome's conquest had also created in record numbers in order to produce cash crops—principally *cattle*, wine and olives—for new urban markets like Rome itself."[31] "Large tracts of land outside of the city-territories were in the hands of rich men, who kept on them great *herds* of *cattle*. . . . The labour employed for tilling the soil and *herding* the sheep was probably both slave and free labour (furnished by small tenants) for the fields, almost wholly *slave* labour for the pastures."[32]

Roman ranchers also used other methods to acquire grazing lands. "They bought up farms cheaply from peasants unable to pay their taxes, or took them over for bad debts, or even by armed force without any legal process."[33] According to one writer of the period, if a farmer refused to sell his land, the takeover could be accomplished by "sending into his green corn [ancient term for wheat and barley] by night a *herd* of lean and famished *cattle*, with wearied necks, who will not come home until they have put the whole crop into their ravenous bellies; no sickle could make a cleaner sweep."[34] The Roman ranchers' use of these and other illegal and violent methods to acquire land, supported by the state, was devastating for grain cultivators.

> The grain growing communities waged a bitter struggle against the *cattle* entrepreneurs whose *herds* swept across their land and invaded their common pastures; but they usually had to give in to this speculative economy, backed as it was by money and influence. In Southern Italy, agriculture was thus pushed gradually into the background by an extensive, all-conquering pastoral economy that despoiled the land.[35]

Wealthy landowners with extensive ranching operations often viciously oppressed enslaved humans, as seen in an ancient account of a Sicilian rancher:

> There was a certain Damophilus, a native of Enna, a man of great wealth but arrogant in manner, who, since he had under cultivation a great circuit of land and owned many *herds* of *cattle*, emulated not only the luxury affected by Italian landowners in Sicily, but their troops of *slaves* and their inhumanity and severity towards them. He drove about the countryside with expensive horses, four-wheeled carriages, and a bodyguard of *slaves*, and prided himself, in addition, on his great train of handsome serving-boys and ill-mannered parasites.
>
>   Both in town and at his villas he took pains to provide a veritable exhibition of embossed silver and costly crimson spreads, and had himself served sumptuous and regally lavished dinners, in which he surpassed even the luxury of the Persians in outlay and extravagance, as indeed he outdid them also in arrogance. . . .
>
>   Purchasing a large number of *slaves*, he treated them outrageously, marking with branding irons the bodies of men who in

their own countries had been free, but through capture in war had come to know the fate of a slave. Some of these he put in fetters and thrust into slave pens; others he designated to act as his *herdsmen*, but neglected to provide them with suitable clothing or food.[36]

Humans occasionally rebelled against the elites who had enslaved them, and domesecrated animals also struggled against their exploitation. The resistance of *oxen* (mature, castrated cows) to enslavement is seen in the following passage drawn from the works of the Roman writer Lucius Iunius Moderatus Columella: "The breaking-in regime is based on severe physical restriction of the animals by tying them to horizontal posts set above a stall 'in such a way that their ropes give very little play.' If they are very *wild* and *savage*, they must be kept like this for thirty-six hours to expend their fury."[37] To force a cow to pull a plow:

Here again, the animal is broken in by stages, first pulling the plough over tilled ground. Columella points out that this laborious process can be speeded up where you have *oxen* already trained, and then goes on to describe the system followed by his own farms, where the untrained *ox* is yoked with a fully trained one; a particularly obstinate animal is put into a triple yoke between a pair of veterans, and is thus forced willy-nilly to obey the orders.[38]

While the final destination of some cows was the tables of the Roman elite, the fates of many were entwined with the violence perpetrated by the Roman military. Like the nomadic pastoralists, Rome could conquer other peoples because its armies frequently were sustained by eating the domesecrated animals forced to accompany the military expeditions.[39] "The armies of the Republic while on campaign were supplied with fresh *meat* in the form of *cattle*, which transported itself on the hoof. Ancient armies were generally accompanied by *herds* of *cattle*, so much so that the sound of *cattle* could mislead the enemy into thinking that an army was marching along."[40] Sustained occupation of other territories was made possible by the importation of cows or by expropriating captive cows from the vanquished, as the Romans did in Britain.[41]

Horses also were exploited as instruments of war by the Roman army. Roman legions were accompanied by mounted archers and a plate-armored "cavalry." Rome's reliance on horses to boost its military power increased as the empire was threatened by the nomadic, pastoralist-based Persians, who waged war from atop the back of horses. Besides the cavalries attached to legions, "by the first century A.D., the Roman army also included 80,000 mounted auxiliaries."[42] Roman armies also were accompanied by mules, donkeys, and, in desert campaigns, camels, who were exploited as instruments of war and forced into service as "pack animals." "There are a remarkable number of occasions attested in which all the Roman army's water needs, and other supplies, were transported overland by pack-animals. In 108 B.C., in order to supply the siege of Thala in Numidia, Caecilius Metellus brought all the army's provisions and water to the site on *pack animals*."[43] "The longer a campaign went on the more animals would perish through disease, over-use, or poor treatment, and these were in the main replaced from civilian *stocks*."[44]

The exploitation of other animals furthered Roman aggression in other ways as well. The skins of domesecrated animals were used extensively in the body armor of Roman soldiers, and the tents that sheltered soldiers required even more.

> Each standard-size tent required about 42 panels, whereas a centurion's [professional officer's] tent took up to 168 panels of *leather*. Two panels would require a calf *hide* that included the back, neck and belly of the animal. If this is used as a base to calculate the amount of calves required to outfit the western frontier army of approximately 200,000 men, it is estimated that one and a half million calfskin panels cut from the *hides* of 750,000 calves were required.[45]

Not only did Rome's exploitation of cows facilitate its aggression, but the acquisition of cows also became a primary reason for many Roman incursions. "War booty taken by the Romans from Greece and in Asia Minor consisted mainly of men and *cattle*."[46]

> During the wars of conquest [the leaders of the Roman Army] increased their wealth. Large numbers of men and *cattle* fell into their hands. When cities were looted, they had the larger share of the booty. They returned to Italy with their "belts" (or, as we should say, pockets) full of money, and, if they did not dispose of them at once, with gangs of *slaves* and *herds* of *cattle*. . . .

The influx of money, *slaves*, goods of different kinds, and *cattle* from the provinces stimulated the economic life of Italy.[47]

Captured cows were prominent in the parades featuring successful generals returning to Rome from imperialist adventures. "Hundreds of thousands of people lined the city's streets, while musicians blew continuously on trumpets and horns. The parade opened with the standards of the victorious legions. Next came the spoils of war: baskets filled with coins and jewels, *herds* of *cattle*, and especially prisoners and their weapons."[48]

While Rome's might was built on the oppression of other animals, this powerful agrarian society itself eventually was overrun by nomadic pastoralists. These pastoralists, including the Goths, largely were forced into their invasion of Roman-held land by the more powerful Huns, who in turn had been forced by drought to migrate to Gothic territory. "The respect these Gothic tribes had for Roman legions was great, but far greater was the terror with which they viewed the wild fantastic *horsemen* from the distant plains of Central Asia who had suddenly appeared in their midst. It was this heart-piercing fear that forced them to break through the Roman outposts and sweep over the Roman provinces."[49] Weakened by war with the mounted Persian soldiers to the east, by decadence and corruption, and by troubles with food production brought on by significant overgrazing and soil deterioration,[50] Rome could not withstand the pastoralist invasion.

> From Central Asia came the forces that overthrew the Roman Empire. . . . It was the settlement of the Germanic peoples of the Roman Empire that caused the break-up of the old system. The Goths made the first serious inroads into Italy and Southern France, and into portions of Spain and Africa. The Suevi and Vandals occupied the remaining portions of Spain and Africa. The Burgundi moved into central France, and the Angles and the Saxons took over the portion of Britain which had once been a Roman colony.[51]

Invasions by Goths, Alans, Vandals, and other nomadic pastoralist societies facilitated the fall of the Roman Empire in the fifth century CE, and the replacement of cultivated fields with pasture led to deprivation and displacement. It has been estimated that "in the first five centuries after the fall of Rome the population in the former western Roman

Empire fell to half its original numbers,"[52] and the privileged pastoralists levied tributes on those who remained.

The suffering experienced by domesecrated animals oppressed by nomadic pastoralists and aggressive agrarian societies such as Rome was compounded by disease, which developed and spread because of the animals' forced groupings. Over the centuries, tens of millions of domesecrated animals, usually kept in crowded conditions, suffered terrible deaths from "animal plagues." One such disease, rinderpest—a form of measles with symptoms comparable to smallpox—caused the deaths of millions of cows and other animals; the disease frequently was transmitted through military campaigns.

> In Europe, as Charlemagne conquered the Scandinavians on the Elbe and Weser c. 800, "So great was the pestilence of *oxen* in this expedition that scarcely in the whole army did one remain, but all perished; and not only there, but a plague among animals, causing a dreadful mortality, broke out in all the provinces conquered by the Emperor," following in Italy immediately after his crowning in Rome as Emperor. This clearly seems to have been rinderpest despite the fact that it was accompanied by many human deaths as well . . . . Spreading to France in 801, it was possibly introduced with plundered *cattle* from Benevento in Italy.[53]

Elites were often quick to believe that devalued human groups were responsible for the plagues, and scores were scapegoated and murdered in retaliation. In the ninth century, many of the accused were "tied to planks and thrown into rivers to drown."[54]

Pastoralists terrorized Eurasia for centuries during the Dark Ages. Attila the Hun led an invasion of Europe in 450. His trademark was throat slitting. Tamerlane, a fourteenth-century Turk who invaded much of central and western Asia with Mongol support, had pyramids built from the skulls of his tens of thousands of victims. Torture was the fate of many of the leaders of the societies conquered by pastoralists. For example, Mongol invaders placed Russian princes under wooden platforms, where they were suffocated by the weight of the victory feast. Other victims had boiling liquefied silver poured into their eye sockets until they died. Some pastoralists enjoyed having the skulls of murdered leaders fashioned into drinking cups.[55]

The fierce existence of these pastoral nomads, whose way of life depended on the violent oppression of other animals, also can be seen in their social organization and cultural practices. Some, like the Huns and Scythians, "slit the throats of the chief's wives and servants on his tomb, such deaths numbering in the hundreds and [even] reaching a thousand."[56] Clans frequently fought and raided one another; the strongest would acquire more captive animals and take women as possessions while enslaving young males and putting them to work controlling domesecrated animals. Moreover, nomadic pastoralist societies were more likely to promote hereditary enslavement than any other societal type.[57] The advantages of hereditary enslavement for the oppressors and its similarity to the enslavement of other animals are noted by David Christian:

> To make *slaves* more amenable to control, they were often separated at birth from their families. And, like *domesticated* animals, many were deliberately kept in a state of infantile dependence that inflicted a sort of psychic amputation on them—they remained like children, and their helplessness made them easier to control. Both animals and human *slaves* could be controlled best if kept economically and psychically dependent on their *owners*.[58]

## Domesecration and Mongol Violence

One of the most destructive leaders of pastoralist societies was Chinggis Khan, who was born into a society of nomadic pastoralists in Mongolia in the thirteenth century. Chinggis Khan forged an alliance of Mongolian tribes and set out to conquer the world. In his rampage across northern China and southwestern Asia, he burned hundreds of towns and cities and slaughtered entire populations.[59] One period observer stated, "They pursue men like *game* . . . they slay them and take from them everything."[60] Chinggis Khan is reported to have stated: "The greatest pleasure is to vanquish your enemies and chase them before you, to rob them of their wealth and see those dear to them bathed in tears, to ride their horses and clasp to your bosom their wives and daughters."[61]

Chinggis Khan could be merciless; his army massacred many of the inhabitants of the areas he invaded, sparing for enslavement only selected craftsmen, artists, scholars, and women. In campaigns in northern China, for example, prisoners were forced "to fight in the front ranks against their own compatriots"[62] or face mass executions. The intensity of Chinggis Khan's aggression is glimpsed in a description of his attack on people resisting Mongol domination in Persia, what is now Iran, in 1220.

> The Mongols retaliated by sending in a huge army on a campaign of extermination. The army proceeded systematically to reconquer the country, besieging and taking each city with remarkable speed. The Mongols possessed a sophisticated knowledge of siegecraft and ample equipment, having for one siege 4,000 scaling ladders and 4,000 siege engines, including some adapted to throwing pots of burning naphtha over the walls into the besieged city.
>
> The Mongols overcame their inadequate ratio of force needed to subdue the space and population of the huge country because they never left garrisons in captured towns: they killed or drove away all the population, leaving "neither a cat nor a dog." The prisoners, artisans and men of military age, which they took with them, increased the strength of the Mongol army in the assaults. The unwilling conscripts cooperated, though they faced serious danger assailing the fortifications, because they knew that certain death awaited them if they failed to fight. These prisoners supplied most of the casualties in the combats and few of them survived.[63]

While the oppressive treatment of other animals as food, transportation, and weapons both enabled and promoted such invasions, countless free-living animals—some regarded as threats to the domesecrated animals controlled by the pastoralists—were terrorized and killed in the training of pastoralist armies. Perhaps the most terrible method of military training, the type preferred by Chinggis Khan, was the battue. The battue, a form of "hunting" in which free-living animals were boxed in by pastoralist armies and driven to a small area to be massacred, sometimes lasted as long as three months. A massive military exercise covering many miles of territory, the battue also was used as an exercise in discipline by Mongol leaders.

> On the last day of the drive, the Mongol army became a huge human amphitheatre with thousands of terrified animals crowded into its arena. Throughout the drive it was forbidden to kill, but it

was more than just a point of honor that none of the animals should escape; if any man allowed even the smallest of them to pass through the line, both he and his officer were severely punished. At first it would have been hares and deer that tested the soldiers' agility, but as the numbers of animals grew and the predators in their midst became as terrifying as the army, it would have been the *wild* boar and the wolf packs that tried their courage.[64]

Although almost no one chronicled the experiences of other animals during this era, the fear and resistance of those trapped by the Mongol hunts is evidenced by their daring efforts to break free of the contracting Mongol enclosure. A Persian historian who witnessed one such spectacle did make a point of noting the "cries and commotion" that came from the other animals that were trapped.[65]

The protocol for the murdering of the other animals that were trapped reinforced the stratified nature of the pastoral society. The first kill was made by Chinggis Khan, in the presence of his "wives" and "concubines." Khan's generals followed, and the carnage continued until the men with the lowest status had their opportunity to kill. The entangled oppression of the human and animal victims of Mongol invasions was noted implicitly by William H. McNeill: "The Mongols came as a horde of fierce and barbarian warriors, prepared to treat their human victims as they treated animals rounded up in their great annual hunts; *domesticating* or slaughtering them as circumstances might dictate."[66]

In another example of how the fates of humans and other animals were entangled with pastoralist violence, Alexander Monro writes of Chinggis Khan's conquest of northern China:

> At Wulahai the Mongols offered the city's mayor a deal, say the annals. If he would hand over every cat and bird inside the walls, the invaders would end their siege. The animals were rounded up and handed over to the Mongols, who attached flammable material to their tails and set them alight. Terrified, the cats and birds fled home. In the flames and confusion that ensued, the Mongols stormed in.[67]

In Chinggis Khan's violent sweep through Central Asia, millions of humans were brutally murdered. For example, in what is now Turkmenistan and northern Afghanistan an estimated seven hundred thousand people were killed. A million were slain on the Afghanistan-Persia border and yet another million in the conquest of Persia.[68] Preoccupied with increasing the number of domesecrated animals and the land needed to sustain them, Chinggis Khan was convinced only with difficulty not to convert all of northern China into pastureland. The importance of domesecrated animals in enabling and promoting the Mongols' invasion and violence is punctuated by the Central Asian specialist Denis Sinor, who writes: "it would appear to me that Chinggis Khan's often quoted intention to raze the cities of north China and transform the land into pasture was dictated by an accurate assessment of the military needs rather than by sheer destructive barbarism."[69] The enormous level of Mongol violence continued under the rule of Chinggis Khan's sons and grandsons, including Batu Khan, who led the massacre of Riazan described at the beginning of this chapter. After conquering Russia, the Mongol army turned to Eastern Europe, laying waste to Polish villages and towns and destroying Kraków. Their invasion of Hungary was equally devastating; approximately sixty thousand Hungarian soldiers died trying to defend their land. Subsequent Mongol armies brought terror and suffering as they swept from Eastern Europe to the Pacific Ocean and from Siberia to the steppes of Mesopotamia.

In some cases, the invading nomadic pastoralists, including some Mongols, settled in conquered areas and encouraged the expansion of agriculture. "This made them the mortal enemies of their distant cousins . . . who retained their nomadic habits accompanied by a passion for raiding and looting."[70] Nomadic pastoralists who became heads of state viewed themselves as superior to the people who worked the land. They retained aspects of their former nomadic identities and cultivated associations with those with whom they identified.

> The heads of states in many instances were themselves of distant nomadic origin. The memory and the social relations of the steppe and the desert were kept alive by a constant stream of aristocratic migrants seeking employment as military officers and administrators from the centralized states which derived their huge tax-revenue from the labour of peasant agriculturalists. Without a defined relationship with the rest of Asia, nomads cease to be nomads.[71]

Tensions between pastoralists who dominated empires and those who survived by raiding and looting were sometimes settled by policies that exploited others to the mutual benefit of the aggressors. For example, Ghazan Khan (1271–1304) put the issue to nomadic warriors in the following way:

> I am not on the side of the Tazik [Iranian]. If there is a purpose in pillaging them all, there is no one with more power to do this than I. Let us rob them together. But if you wish to be certain of collecting grain and food for your tables in the future, I must be harsh with you. You must be taught reason. If you insult the . . . [Iranian], take their *oxen* and seed, and trample their crops to the ground, what will you do in the future?[72]

Not all nomadic pastoralists over the past six thousand years were as destructive of plant-based societies as the invading khans. However, conflict was still the inevitable result of the pastoralist invasions, as food and water had to be provided to large numbers of domesecrated animals.

> The Bible contains numerous examples of conflict situations that are directly attributable to the practice of raising *livestock*, including contested water rights, bitter competition for grazing lands, and friction between agriculturalists and nomadic *herdsmen*. The more settled agricultural communities deeply resented the intrusion of nomadic tribes with their large *herds* of *cattle*, sheep and goats. . . . Aside from the threat to the crops themselves, large *herds* of *livestock* caused much damage to the general quality of the land as a result of overgrazing. It was ostensibly for this reason that the Philistines, whose primary agricultural pursuits were corn and orchards, sought to discourage nomadic *herdsmen* from using their territory by filling in many of the wells in the surrounding area.[73]

It was not only direct pastoralist violence that took the lives of so many humans and other animals but also infectious diseases, derived from domesecration, that spread throughout Eurasia. One such illness, smallpox, emerged as one of the ancient world's most dreaded plagues; it took countless lives from Britain to Africa to Japan. Nomadic pastoralists and the armies of large agrarian states frequently were transmitters of infectious disease. For example, it is believed that Hun nomadic pastoralists brought smallpox to China during a devastating invasion around 250 BCE; Roman soldiers returning from Asia are believed to have brought the disease back with them to Rome, where it took millions of lives between 180 and 165 CE.[74] And the Mongols are thought to have been primarily responsible for the spread of the bubonic plague in the fourteenth century. Reflecting on fourteenth-century China, William H. McNeill writes:

> The combination of war and pestilence wreaked havoc on China's population. The best estimates show a decrease from 123 million in about 1200 (before the Mongol invasions began) to a mere 65 million in 1393, a generation after the final expulsion of the Mongols from China. Even Mongol ferocity cannot account for such a drastic decrease. Disease assuredly played a big part in cutting Chinese numbers in half; and bubonic plague, recurring after its initial ravages at relatively frequent intervals, just as in Europe, is by all odds the most likely candidate for such a role.[75]

The leading explanation for the pandemic that struck Eurasia in the mid-fourteenth century was that Möngke Khan, a grandson of Chinggis Khan, sent his armies through the desolate Gobi Desert, where they came into contact with other animals that carried fleas harboring the deadly microbe Yersinia pestis, a bacterium that manifested in the form of the bubonic plague. The disease was spread by the Mongols, who killed marmots and used their skin and hair for garments. Infected fleas that survived on these garments and on the stocks of marmot skin and hair that were bundled and sent along trade routes for exchange were likely carriers of the deadly microbes. In 1346, the Mongol leader Kipchak Khan Janibeg was trying to drive disfavored Italian traders from the town of Caffa, on the Crimean Peninsula, when his army began to collapse because of disease. Refusing to leave the city intact, the Mongols began catapulting the corpses of their dead into the city. With the residents of Caffa weakened and hungry from the siege, the disease quickly spread. Several ships thought to be free of the disease set sail for Italy, but the plague traveled with them and soon spread to northern and western Europe. The Black Death, as the disease came to be known, is believed to have killed more than two hundred million people by the end of the fourteenth century, and more perished from intermittent outbreaks up through the 1800s.[76] Although infected fleas on European rats actually spread the disease, Jews and cats were blamed for the outbreak, and many were displaced or killed.

From this historical vantage point, the idyllic-sounding, romanticized term "pastoralism" should actually be seen as "a subsistence strategy often associated with territorial expansion, social stratification, and military aggressiveness."[77] The course of world history for both humans and other animals was shaped indelibly by the violence, trauma, and sharply stratified human societies that bore the imprint of domesecration, especially as it was practiced by nomadic pastoralists. Much of human history has been forged out of this predatory subsistence strategy, which was well "adapted to the fierce and cruel habits of military life."[78] The violence and oppression experienced by humans and other animals was closely intertwined. The enslavement of large numbers of domesecrated animals compelled the expropriation of land and water used by other humans, driving large-scale invasions and warfare.

The Mongol pastoralists, like many nomadic pastoralists before and after them, "altered the course of history and left it scarred."[79] Reflecting on the devastation wrought by the Mongols in just the thirteenth and fourteenth centuries, James Chambers writes:

> Russia was torn away from Europe, and when the Mongols abandoned it after two hundred years it was feudal and backward. Poland and Hungary were so devastated that they never emerged to play a part in the renaissance that followed in the west. Bulgaria, like Russia, was isolated and then fell to the Ottoman Turks, whom the Mongols had driven out of Khwarizm and who were one day to stand on the banks of the Danube as the Mongols had done. The lands that once nurtured the great civilizations of the Persians were returned to the desert and they have never recovered. Wherever the Mongols rode they left an irretrievably ruined economy and wherever they ruled they left a petty, self-important aristocracy and an exploited *peasantry*.[80]

China suffered terrible casualties from the Mongol invasions, with "over 60 million people dying or failing to be replaced."[81] In the seventeenth century, the human population of China dropped by twenty-five million after the invasion of the Manchu pastoralists.[82] Virtually all of

Eurasia "felt the influence of this patrilineal, sexually punishing, male-dominated, warlike, and essentially wasteful cultural tradition."[83]

## Violence and Hunger in the Middle Ages

The violent incursions of the nomadic pastoralists and the animal-supplied and -driven armies of Rome and other large agrarian states unquestionably had a significant effect on Eurasian social, cultural, and economic development. Bernard Bachrach observes:

> Perhaps the greatest significance for the early Middle Ages of the commitment to use animals and especially to use horses in warfare was the huge cost to the society. . . . Each horse consumed on average the wheat equivalent that could sustain four fully active agricultural or construction workers. In light of these data it must be concluded that economic development in the highly labor intensive economy of pre-Crusade Europe was severely retarded by the apparent willingness to use horses in warfare.[84]

Medieval rulers devoted considerable land to raising and pasturing horses. The kings of the Franks frequently used slaves to work on "royal stud farms," while mules and "oxen" continued to be used "to draw carts and wagons for the use of royal forces."[85] The entangled nature of the oppression of devalued humans and other animals is also seen during this period in the practice of medieval rulers requiring "serfs" and "peasants" to serve as mounted soldiers.[86]

Even the Vikings, whose raids terrorized much of Europe, relied heavily on horses beginning in the tenth century. Before they began to use horses, Viking assaults were largely hit-and-run raids by ships on coastal communities. However, their increased use of horses as laborers and instruments of war, load bearers, and mounts permitted incursions deeper inland and even periods of domination. In many instances, Vikings raided the populations of horses controlled by those they attacked, and their cargo ships were constructed to carry not only horses but also expropriated cows and sheep.[87]

As did "peasants" who occasionally rebelled against their exploitation, over the centuries domesecrated animals continued to chafe against their oppressive conditions and treatment at the hands of humans. This defiant behavior, often ignored by historians, did not escape the notice of every human observer over the course of history. For instance, writing of the Romans' use of cows to facilitate their domination of the British, the historians Towne and Wentworth note: "Roman domination of England lasted from the first to the fifth centuries. During this time, and for centuries after, 'rugged individuals' of the bovine species continued to fend for themselves in field and forest. They were . . . foraging for themselves and defying sporadic attempts at *domestication*."[88] "As the forests were cleared and humans multiplied, *wild cattle* became increasingly scarce,"[89] and pasture used for domesecrated animals became more degraded. For example, during the Middle Ages Spain "was seriously overgrazed, Spanish forests had been wantonly cut and burned, and vast areas of the nation were reduced to desert and semi desert."[90] Continued grazing of domesecrated animals "damaged arable interests and led to shortages of food,"[91] and farmers struggled against the rapacious practices of the sheep ranchers.

> This situation was aggravated by the fact that sheep posed an even greater threat to the land than *cattle* because they clipped grass closer to the ground, sometimes tearing it out by the roots. The Spanish sheep *owners'* guild known as the Mesta dominated Spain's political affairs for several centuries (A.D. 1200—A.D. 1500) and was the source of much internal strife within that country. The Mesta's sheep not only destroyed pastureland by overgrazing but were also allowed to rampage through cultivated fields. The *peasant* farmers could hardly expect the monarchy to rectify this injustice since sheep raising dominated medieval Spanish commerce and was the government's principal source of revenue during this period.[92]

Over the course of several hundred years (700–1500), the Spanish forced the Moors out of the Iberian Peninsula, land that the Moors were using in part to graze sheep and cows. After this *reconquista*, the Spanish monarchy awarded large estates in the reclaimed areas to military officers, who began large ranching operations for themselves. The skin of cows was in heavy demand both in Spain and in other parts of Europe, and many of the soldier-entrepreneurs found ranching cows to be very profitable.

In addition to the harms that accompanied nomadic pastoralism, ranching, and the reliance on domesecrated animals for sustained and successful military campaigns, other less direct but equally devastating forms of violence resulted from domesecration: human hunger and malnutrition. For example, during the dominance of Rome and continuing after its collapse, the eating of other animals was largely confined to the affluent and the military, and such consumption was viewed as a luxury and sign of elevated social status. "The gluttony of the rich provided a marked contrast to the restricted dietaries [sic] of the poor."[93] Interestingly, because the European population was significantly decreased by the Mongol-spread plague of the fourteenth century, historians expected to see an increase in the overall quality of life as wages increased because of labor shortages and a surplus of plant-based foods. However, the economic historian Karl F. Helleiner suggests that an increase in pastoralist and ranching practices during this period instead brought greater hunger and susceptibility to disease. The shift to greater pastoralism led to

a partial "decerealization" of Europe in favour of animal *husbandry*. However, given a certain level of agrarian technology, five or six times as much land is required for the raising of one calorie of animal food as is needed for the production of one calorie of vegetable food. It follows that whatever relief from pressure of population on land was afforded by the initial demographic slump must have been partly offset by that change in the pattern of consumption and production. This hypothesis helps to explain an otherwise puzzling fact, namely that the later Middle Ages should have suffered scarcely less than previous centuries from dearth and famine, even though *man's* per capita supply of fertile land was undoubtedly much higher in this period. These subsistence-crises invariably engendered epidemic outbreaks, and may thus have been among the chief factors responsible for the high mortality rates of late-medieval times.[94]

One contemporary observer noted the relationship between the feasts of animal flesh and the scarcity that resulted. "[People] dissolutely abandoned themselves to the sin of gluttony, with feasts and taverns and delight of delicate viands. . . . Everything came to unwonted scarcity and remained long thus. . . . There were grievous and unwonted famines."[95]

## Violence and Warfare in the Pre-Columbian Americas

With domesecration and enslavement of large mammals being a primary factor in much of the widespread, large-scale violence in Eurasia, it might be expected that there would be less violence in a region of the world that did not have populations of large, domesecrated animals: the pre-Columbian Americas. With the exception of llamas and alpaca in some parts of South America, there were no large, social mammals in the Americas for many thousands of years. In the absence of other animals who were large and controllable and whose exploitation would enable and promote massive wars, invasions, and death from infectious disease, what then was the level of warfare and disease among people in the Americas?

Initial accounts by fifteenth- and sixteenth-century Europeans of large-scale warfare among the peoples of pre-Columbian North America were exaggerated; these reports were based on the recorded observations of conquistadors and colonizers who sought an ideological justification for invasion and genocide. More reliable evidence comes from physical anthropologists who have studied settlement artifacts and burial sites. In North America, although there is evidence of conflict among indigenous peoples and a few examples of a village's destruction have been found, the archeological evidence largely suggests that pre-Columbian warfare was limited to small-scale raiding, sniping, and ambush. The numbers of deaths by violence were relatively low, and evidence of total devastation of an enemy population is rare.[96] A common explanation for the warfare that did exist in pre-Columbian North America is competition for resources.

> Instead of fighting over ownership, which really did not exist in native mentality, the most common form of conflict was raiding activity. Raiding helped accumulate wealth, material resources, and goods for a tribe. Raiding helped provide new tribal members as well; when people were captured in a raid, they were often adopted into the tribe. There was also a more subtle function. By obtaining goods from other tribes, those who participated could share those rewards with others who were less fortunate in their own tribe. That helped raise the standing of the less fortunate and often made it possible for them to continue to spread the wealth by having

enough resources to participate in future raids. Without disrupting tribes' traditional places on the land, warfare helped ensure tribal success, gave men in the community chances to prove their bravery, raised their status, and contributed to tribal health and wealth, while simultaneously preserving a balance between local native powers. . . .

Destroying the enemy completely could effectively devastate both tribes as the balance of people, supplies, goods, and resources often depended on war itself. If one of those tribes disappeared, their resource supplies also disappeared, leaving the future needs of the surviving tribe unfulfilled.[97]

The primary subsistence pattern of most pre-Columbian North American societies was horticulture, combined with the hunting of free-living animals. The violence involved in the hunting and killing of other animals most likely exacerbated intersocietal violence and the elevated status of hunter-warriors. While the status of a man in a nomadic pastoralist society was tied to the number of domesecrated animals in his possession, the status of a pre-Columbian male was based on his reputation as a successful hunter and combatant. Still, in the absence of large and sociable other animals to exploit, the level and magnitude of warfare in pre-Columbian North America were nothing like the massive destruction and enormous loss of life seen in Eurasia.

One might suggest that the absence of large-scale violence and destruction may have been the result of a smaller human population rather than the absence of large, domesecrated animals. It is true that pre-Columbian North America did not have the large human populations generated by animal exploitation in the agrarian systems that existed in Eurasia. However, sophisticated horticulture did give rise to sizeable population centers and extensive trade networks. A number of scholars suggest the pre-Columbian human population was much larger than once thought. For example, Gary Nash notes:

It is now believed that the pre-contact population north of Mexico may have been as high as 10 million, of whom perhaps 500,000 lived along the coastal plain and in the piedmont region accessible to the early European colonizers. Even if the most liberal recent

estimates are scaled down by half, we are left with the startling realization that Europeans were not coming to a "virgin wilderness,"
as some called it, but were invading a land which in some areas was
as densely populated as their homelands.[98]

The three most studied pre-Columbian empires from Mexico through
South America are the Maya, the Aztecs, and the Incas. These horticultural societies "achieved a level of technological advance comparable to
that of early agrarian Mesopotamia and Egypt,"[99] largely without having
to rely on large, domesecrated animals. The Mayan civilization stretched
from what is today the Yucatán region of southern Mexico to Guatemala.
It is estimated that at one time the Mayan population in southern Mexico alone was between eight and thirteen million, most living in grand
cities with elaborate architecture and fine works of art.[100] The Mayan city
of Tikal was designed with wooded groves and gardens that separated
residences, and a sophisticated system of irrigated food gardens permitted population concentrations comparable to midsize cities in the United
States today. The Maya made impressive astrological observations, developed sophisticated calendars, and created a complex system of hiero-
glyphic writing.

Politically, Mayan society was fragmented and characterized by numerous rivalries. While there is some evidence of infrequent, all-out destruction of rival cities, "for the most part, however, the Maya probably waged
war for economic gain through tribute and the control of trade routes."[101]
Thanks to the reliance on advanced horticulture, most wars were waged
only after harvest, during the dry seasons. Because of the high status ac-
corded to combatants, armies were disproportionately made up of elite
males and reinforced by conscripted militias. In the absence of other animals to exploit as instruments of war or as "meat on the hoof," Mayan
armies usually were forced to carry their own provisions, severely limiting
the "duration and spatial extent of Maya campaigns," which most likely
lasted "two weeks or less."[102] Warfare among the Maya provided captives
for religious sacrifice and forced military alliances and in later periods was
motivated by economic need exacerbated by climatic and agricultural
downturns.

Following the decline of the Maya, in pre-Columbian Mexico the
Aztec Empire emerged. The Aztec city Tenochtitlán was magnificent and
larger than any city in Europe. Almost all of the more than sixty thousand

houses had large rooms and gardens and were decorated with flowers. Although densely populated, the city's streets and arboretums were neat, clean, and maintained by public workers. Fresh spring water was provided by a complex aqueduct system. Beneath towering, ornate pyramids, tens of thousands of buyers and sellers came daily to a central gathering and marketplace, where officials "enforced laws of fairness regarding weights and measures and the quantity of goods purveyed."[103]

> It's gone now, drained and desiccated in the aftermath of the Spanish conquest, but once there was an interconnected complex of lakes high up in the Valley of Mexico that was as long and as wide as the city of London is today. Surrounding these waters, known collectively as the Lake of the Moon, were scores of towns and cities whose population, combined with that of the outlying communities of Central Mexico, totaled about 25,000,000 men, women and children. On any given day as many as 200,000 small boats moved back and forth on the Lake of the Moon, pursuing the interests of commerce, political intrigue, and simple pleasure.[104]

The grandness of the Aztec cities was built in part on military expeditions that focused on territorial acquisition and tribute and were "justified at least theoretically by the need for supplying the gods with an adequate diet of human hearts."[105] "The Aztecs made war for defense, revenge and economic motives, which were inextricably confused with the needs for sacrificial victims requisite for proper adoration of their gods. Thus in warfare the great aim was to take captives, but behind this religious goal lurked the less holy urges of political and economic expediency."[106]

However, these militaristic incursions were limited. Like the peoples of North America and the Maya, the Aztecs did not have large numbers of domesecrated animals, whose need for pasture and water would have promoted massive warfare and in turn made it more viable. Also like the Mayans, because of the requirements of food production the Aztecs waged war only after the harvest, when food supplies for campaigns were available and when the spoils of war would be greatest. The movement of an invading force was a difficult exercise, and Aztec "military campaigns were short-term, logistical nightmares. Most culminated in a single battle before the supplies ran out."[107]

Having no *beasts of burden*, the warriors had to carry their own food with them. Due to the governmental system, wherein each town was independent, the armies did not dare live off the country for fear of inciting revolt and also because most communities lacked the food to sustain a large body of men. Thus, prior to a war, negotiations had to be made where supplies could be concentrated and allies brought together at a point as near as possible to the zone of attack. Usually a single battle decided the issue, since the attacking force could not maintain itself in the field for more than a very few days.[108]

On some occasions, the Aztec armies relied upon human porters or could demand foods from tributary towns within the empire but, in general, the range of the army beyond the radius of the empire was approximately thirty-six miles.[109]

Open fighting, the difficulty of keeping up extended campaigns, and the informal character of the military force were factors that stultified the development of tactics or strategy. In battle, the howling mob that represented the collective strength of one group tried to rout the yelling horde of their adversary, and the first to run lost the battle. Captives were taken, tribute imposed, the temple burned, and the defeated group was then left alone again.[110]

The Aztecs rarely sought to destroy local tribes or city-states but instead aimed to develop the conquered region as a source of tribute. In some instances, ritualistic warfare was pursued to obtain captives and to hone or demonstrate the warriors' skill.

The War of Flowers was undertaken to satisfy this yearning when no active campaign was in progress. In this incongruously named ceremonial combat the best warriors from several states met in a very real battle, so that feats of arms could be accomplished and captives taken to satisfy the hunger of the gods. . . . If a warrior were captured he met the most glorious of deaths in direct sacrifice to the Sun. If he lived he gained renown. If he were slain, he was cremated, an honor reserved only for fighting men, and passed on to the special heaven where warriors dwell.[111]

In pre-Columbian South America, the Inca Empire, the largest of the American empires, was preceded by complex civilizations that had existed in the Andean highlands and western coastal regions four thousand years before the Inca reign. The Incas relied heavily on cotton for clothing and other textiles and grew beans and squash. These ancient peoples lived in highly populated areas, shared multistory residences, and "lived under remarkably egalitarian political conditions."[112]

However, the Inca Empire of the thirteenth through fifteenth centuries came to be ruled by a small group of elites who oversaw the construction of impressive cities such as Machu Picchu and Cuzco, which housed sophisticated monuments and were built with stone masonry. Cuzco's central plaza accommodated up to one hundred thousand people, and clear streams running through the city were used for bathing and recreation.

Like the Maya and Aztecs, the Inca campaigns of territorial acquisition were conducted in the agricultural off-season; large numbers of farmer conscripts were mobilized to present a show of overwhelming force to potential adversaries. "Messengers sent by the Inca commander would offer favorable terms of surrender: compliant subject elites received gifts and could expect to retain or enhance their status, while communities were allowed to keep many of their resources. . . . The general principle was to be generous with those who capitulated, and to punish those who resisted harshly."[113]

Overall, "the Incas negotiated dominion over many societies while shedding little blood"; however, "a few especially redoubtable societies fiercely resisted Inca rule for many years."[114] The Inca elite's establishment of the most extensive empire in the pre-Columbian Americas was attributable in part to its exploitation of enslaved llamas and alpacas—the only large, social animal species in the Americas. "Llamas played a crucial role in the Incan imperial system,"[115] and large numbers were forced to accompany military campaigns. As in Eurasia, struggles over grazing land and water resources by those who controlled domesecrated llamas and alpacas contributed to long-running "quarrels and even wars over pastures," and these conflicts between numerous South American groups "were utilized by the Inca to advance their dominion."[116]

While llamas and, to a lesser extent, alpacas were not exploitable as instruments of war, their enslavement enabled warfare by their use as "pack animals" and rations. "The [Incan] state owned hundreds of thousands of llamas and on occasion individual pack trains could include thousands of animals."[117] However, the empire's cultivated populations of llamas were incapable of carrying heavy weights long distances, and llamas would "refuse to budge when tired."[118] When llamas were no longer needed as porters or no longer able to function as such, they were killed and used as food by armies traveling long distances. The Incan state stored llama and alpaca flesh as dried and salted *charqui* in state warehouses in the cold Andes ranges, providing provisions for military campaigns. As in other parts of the world where domesecrated animals have been exploited as food, in South America—with the exception of the Incan army—the flesh of llamas was consumed disproportionately by the elites.[119] Similar to the Roman distribution of *booty*, Incan elites distributed llamas captured during military campaigns to high-ranking soldiers. By the fifteenth century, in part because of the exploitation of llamas and alpacas, the Inca Empire covered much of the coastal area of South America and included an estimated twelve million people, many of whom lived in large urban areas.

In sum, the peoples of the pre-Columbian Americas were capable of creating sophisticated social, economic, and political systems without the enormous reliance on domesecrated animals seen in Eurasia. Because of the relative absence of large, sociable other animals, the Americas did not experience large-scale and turbulent invasions comparable to those of the "great hordes" from the steppes that ravaged Eurasia. Moreover, epidemics of infectious disease such as those that took millions of lives in Eurasia appear to have been rare events in the pre-Columbian Americas.

This brief examination of the use of domesecrated animals in Eurasian history and a comparison with the pre-Columbian Americas reveals that the exploitation of other animals by both nomadic pastoralists and large agrarian societies contributed substantially to extensive violence and destruction—for example, the Mongol massacre at Riazan in the thirteenth century. For thousands of years, nomadic pastoralists used domesecrated animals as instruments of war, as laborers, and as food and other resources—exploitation that *enabled* mobile, stratified, militaristic societies to invade and conquer sedentary peoples. Moreover, the exploitation of large numbers of domesecrated animals *promoted* large-scale violence between humans, because of the need for fresh grazing land and water sources to sustain them. Such exploitation also facilitated the acquisition and concentration of power and wealth that accrued from both conquest and the trading or selling of domesecrated animals.

The reliance on large numbers of domesecrated animals also made possible the rise of powerful agrarian societies such as Rome, where other animals not only were exploited as agricultural laborers and as a source of food but also enabled and promoted warfare waged to increase the power of Roman elites. Successful military campaigns were made possible through an enormous level of violence against domesecrated animals, who were exploited as instruments of war and as laborers or killed to provide rations, shelters, and apparel for soldiers.

The violence and trauma experienced by domesecrated animals in Eurasia were deeply entangled with large-scale human displacement, enslavement, genocide, subjugation, sexual exploitation, and, frequently, hunger—all during a highly formative period in the history of the region. In addition to the extensive violence enabled and promoted by the oppression of other animals, the confinement of growing numbers of domesecrated animals near human population centers led to the mutation and spread of infectious diseases that took tens of millions of lives.

With the wealth and power that resulted from the ownership of domesecrated animals, it was, by definition, largely elites who held control over and ownership of large numbers of other animals. From the high-ranking soldiers in the Mongol armies to the wealthy members of the Roman Senate, elites used their power to establish the state policy necessary to ensure their continued disproportionate hold over the sources of wealth, including domesecrated animals.

Certainly not all organized violence, warfare, disease, and human subjugation in early Eurasia were attributable to domesecration. There were other factors that promoted the violence and conflict that plagued Eurasia for thousands of years. Competing religions, quests for political or economic dominance, principles of honor, and revenge all certainly contributed. However, it is unlikely that the extensive and deadly destruction and disease that occurred over thousands of years there could or would have taken place without domesecration. The actual history of domesecration and its effects thus is far different from the traditional representations, such as Blackmar's assertion that "the *domestication* of animals led to a great improvement in the race." While Roman and other agrarian elites and nomadic pastoralists such as the Mongols of the thirteenth and fourteenth centuries are credited with creating trade routes and with some impressive cultural development, these achievements came at an incredibly high cost for the inhabitants of the earth. (And the possible social and cultural achievements that could have taken place in the absence of the widespread violence and brutality linked to domesecration can only be imagined.)

In Europe during the Middle Ages, elites' exploitation of domesecrated animals led to continual warfare and the disproportionate use of arable land for grazing and feed production instead of for the cultivation of plant-based food, a "decerealization" that contributed to hunger, malnutrition, and the spread of disease. The increasingly precarious feudal society in Europe desperately needed an influx of wealth and resources, and many elites—including Spanish ranchers—looked to the Americas. And as the Europeans, well schooled in the violent use of domesecrated animals, invaded the "new" hemisphere, the continents that previously had experienced a comparatively lower level of violence and disease would soon see unprecedented conflict and devastation.

# CHAPTER TWO

# DOMESECRATION AND THE AMERICAS

Europeans were very prone to shed blood. The cult of prowess among them sustained a ready resort to violence in defense of personal and collective honor. As a result, in confrontations with people less well armed than themselves, Europeans seldom hesitated to inflict death and destruction on their foes, sometimes with only trivial provocation. Such ferocity descended from barbarian traditions and derived ultimately from patterns of life on the steppe.
—William H. McNeill, "European Expansion, Power, and Warfare Since 1500"

The *Indians* would have been ignored had they willingly surrendered their lands and not interfered in any way with the precious *cattle*.
—John Hemming, *Red Gold: The Conquest of the Brazilian Indians*

The cowman's heritage, first forged in the flames of Spanish conquest, . . . [was] brought across the sea to support a fabulous empire dedicated to bold men and grazing *herds*.
—Glenn Vernam, *The Rawhide Years*

Centuries before the European colonization of the Americas, tens of thousands of people lived on several of the Canary Islands, off the northwestern coast of Africa. The inhabitants of the islands, the Guanches, had lived in relative isolation for hundreds of years and survived on beans, peas, barley, wheat, and domesecrated goats and pigs. Little is known of these people except that they struggled against invasions by the French, Portuguese, and Spanish in the early fifteenth century. In the last quarter of the fifteenth century, Spanish elites became relentless in their quest for control of the Canaries, a region where they could establish sugar plantations and extensive ranches. The defeat of the Guanches was made possible largely by the use of horses as instruments of warfare. The Guanches "had never seen any animals as large as horses nor any which carried men on their backs and obeyed orders in battle."[1] In the face of relentless attacks by Spanish "cavalry" forces against a population weakened and diminished by deadly diseases of animal origins, Guanche resistance ended. The survivors were enslaved, and many were put to work on sugar plantations; their expropriated lands were used to graze cows, sheep, and pigs. As enslaved Guanche laborers died from Spanish oppression, they were replaced with enslaved people from West African societies. The violent conquest of the Guanches was a harbinger of similar deadly violence soon to come to the Americas, violence enabled and promoted by the exploitation of domesecrated animals.

The conquest of the Canaries and the use of the new land for ranching and other profitable practices were important steps for the fifteenth-century Spanish aristocracy. Like other feudal elites in Europe, whose lifestyles were based on the exploitation of devalued people and on the use of other animals as instruments of war, laborers, and food, their privileges were threatened by a stagnating economy. The feudal elite had invested little of the wealth squeezed from exploited humans and other animals into agricultural innovation. For the "peasants" who actually cultivated the land, the expropriation of their harvest provided little motivation for them to increase productivity. Topsoil depletion was contributing to a decrease in agricultural production, a problem that was compounded by periods of bad weather. Many who profited from ranching in Europe were running out of pasture, largely from overgrazing. Declining food resources and malnutrition rendered the European population even more vulnerable to disease, and elites faced a diminishing supply of human laborers who, through a series of revolts, were demanding greater compensation. From the revolts of Italian artisans in 1378 to English "peasant" uprisings in 1381, oppressed "people responded to the devastation of their lives."[2] With such pushes for social change, European history was at a pivotal point. Conditions were unfavorable for the emergence of a new, elite-dominated political-economic system, and the rise of capitalism would be unlikely without the escalation of oppression and the infusion of new resources and wealth. It was thus only with violent conquest and colonization, especially in the Americas, that the capitalist system came into being.

## Animal Oppression and the
## Invasion of the Americas

The history of humans and other animals was influenced profoundly in the fifteenth century when the "cavalries" of the powerful Turkish Ottomans, with their nomadic pastoralist origins, conquered the Middle East and took control of overland trade routes. The resulting decline of the trade in spices and other luxury items compounded an already deteriorating quality of life for European elites. Portuguese rulers began a search for maritime routes to India and China, hoping to achieve the economic dominance that would fall to whoever controlled the trade in luxury goods. Initially, the Portuguese found their way around the Horn of Africa and established oceanic routes to India, where they took control of the spice trade, creating greater wealth for Portugal's elites. However, even Spain's takeover of the Canary Islands and Portuguese control of new oceanic routes could not generate enough wealth or resources to fuel the rise of capitalism in Europe. The quest by elites to transform the stagnating feudal economy to a more powerful and wealth-producing system of exploitation remained closely linked to the oppression of domesecrated animals; however, the possibilities for expanding ranching operations in Europe were very limited. Vast new regions were needed—areas where land, humans, and other animals could be exploited as new resources, cheap labor, and profitable cash crops. The necessary expansion soon would be made possible by the invasion of the Americas.

> The precarious western perches of the range-*cattle herders* by 1500, while peripheral to the Old World and clearly endangered, placed them in an ideal position to profit from the discovery and colonization of the Americas. They would not, after all, be driven into the sea, but rather cross it and find vast new, less contested domains in which to tend their *herds* the old ways. At almost the last moment, a reprieve had come. Thus it happened that the *cattle* cultures of the Old World's Atlantic fringe were transplanted to both North and South America early in the colonial era.[3]

Domesecrated animals from Eurasia first were brought to the Western Hemisphere by Christopher Columbus, who happened upon the islands that came to be known as the West Indies in his attempt, funded by the Spanish elites, to find a shorter oceanic route to Asian markets. From the start, the Spanish lodgement that Columbus forged was precarious and "hung by a thread for the first decade until a *breeding herd* of *cattle* had been established."[4]

Columbus soon recognized how dependent the virgin settlement was on the *lowly* cow. On January 30, 1494, in a letter to the King and Queen (Ferdinand and Isabel), he cited " . . . the great need we have of *cattle* and *beasts of burden* both for food and to assist the *settlers* in their work," and then continued: "Plantings are far less than are necessary (for the support of the colony) . . . we had so few *cattle*, and these *cattle* were so lean and weak that the utmost they could do was very little." . . . Their Majesties agreed in principle to this appeal and said they would do what they could to send more *cattle*. They demurred, however, when Columbus made the suggestion, evidently to reduce the cost involved, that the *cattle* to be sent over should be paid for by sending back . . . *slaves* (Carib *Indians*).[5]

Columbus forced many of the native human inhabitants of Hispaniola (the island comprising what is now Haiti and the Dominican Republic) to search for gold; others were bound and sent to Europe as *slaves*, as Columbus suggested, to fund continued invasion and plundering. When Native Americans resisted this domination, the Spanish—like Chinggis Khan—"attacked with ferocity. Massacre became the means of conquest, terror the method of control."[6] A young priest, Bartolomé de las Casas, witnessed Spanish treatment of the Native Americans firsthand and recorded the atrocities on Hispaniola in his appeals to the Spanish elites.

The Spaniards . . . came with their *horsemen* and well armed with Sword and Lance, making most cruel havocks and slaughters among them. Over running Cities and Villages, where they spared no sex nor age; neither would their cruelty pity Women with childe, whose bellies they would rip up, taking out the Infant and hew it in pieces. They would often lay wagers who should with most dexterity either cleave or cut a man in the middle, or who could at one blow soonest cut off his head. The children they would take by the feet and dash their innocent heads against the rocks, and when they were fallen into the water, with a strange and cruel derision they would call upon them to swim. Sometimes they would run both Mother and Infant, being in her belly quite through at one thrust.

They erected certain Gallows, that were broad but so low, that the tormented creatures might touch the ground with their feet, upon every one of which they would hang thirteen persons, blasphemously affirming that they did it in honour of our Redeemer and his Apostles, and then putting fire under them, they burnt the poor wretches alive.[7]

As the Spanish invasion continued, "cargo manifests of vessels departing from Spain for the Indies often listed *domestic* animals such as horses, *jackasses* [male donkeys], *cattle*, sheep, goats, chickens and pigs."[8] Spanish ships departing from the Iberian Peninsula traveled first the nine hundred miles to the Canary Islands, now an important stepping stone to the West Indies, to obtain supplies and domesecrated animals before the remaining 2,500-mile voyage.

The journey was highly traumatic for the animals. Horses and cows were placed aboard ships in slings lifted by hoists. Once aboard, they were placed in hammocks with their feet hobbled for the sixty-day passage. When winds fell and travel was slow, and "when water began to run short and all fodder had been consumed, the *livestock* went overboard."[9] Domesecrated animals experienced terrible suffering, and "shipping losses were high."[10] "Horses were certainly the most difficult to transport across the Atlantic, and a high proportion died on the voyage."[11] Still, the number of domesecrated animals in the West Indies grew as the successful invasion proceeded. "As conquest proceeded from island to island and then on to the mainland, settlements and colonization were always secured by a base of *cattle*. As the conqueror's habitations became stabilized, the surplus from his *herds* spread out to virgin lands and founded *wild* populations which supported future advances."[12]

Las Casas related the horrific treatment of Native Americans on these islands:

In the year 1509, the Islands of St. John and Jamaica that look'd like fruitful gardens, were possessed by the Spaniards, with the same bloody intentions, as the others were; for there they also exercised their accustomed cruelties, killing, burning, roasting men, and throwing them to the dogs, as also by oppressing them with sundry and various torments in the Gold Mines as if they had come to rid the earth of these innocents and harmless creatures, of whom six hundred thousand were murdered in these two Islands . . . .

In the year 1511, they went over into the Island of Cuba, . . . inhabited with an infinite number of people, where the humanity and clemency of the Spaniards was not only as little as it had been in other places, but their cruelty and rage much greater. . . .

Sometimes it would happen, that a Band of Spaniards ranging abroad would light upon a mountain where the *Indians* were fled for protection from their cruelty, where they immediately fell upon the *Indians*, killing the Men, and taking the Women and Virgins captive; and when a great company of *Indians* pursued them with weapons for the recovery of their Wives and Children, they resolv-ing not to let go of their prey, when the *Indians* came near them, immediately with the points of their swords ran the poor Women and Children through the bodies. Upon which the wretched *Indians* beating their breasts for grief would now and then burst forth in the words, *O perverse men, O cruel Spaniards, What will ye kill helplesse women?*[13]

The trauma and deprivation resulting from the Spanish barbarity no doubt made indigenous peoples even more vulnerable to the infectious zoonotic diseases brought by the invaders. It is estimated that one-third to one-half of the indigenous people on the island of Hispaniola alone died from a smallpox epidemic, and it and other diseases spread through-out the Caribbean islands.[14]

After the indigenous peoples largely were purged, Cuba and other is-lands became a strategic location for the breeding and holding of animals. "There was nothing less than the wholesale substitution of an animal population for a human one."[15] Domesecrated animals raised in the Carib-bean and used as instruments of war and as food made mainland invasion possible. Moreover, "an export trade to Spain in *hides* and *tallow* devel-oped at an early date from Hispaniola, Porto Rico and Cuba, and was im-portant in providing a steady income for the colonists while they were building up their settlements as a springboard for further conquests."[16]

The Spanish invasion of what is now Mexico was just as brutal as its conquest of the Caribbean. In 1518, Hernando Cortés set out with heavily armed soldiers and captive cows to invade the mainland, resulting in a "genocidal siege" producing between 120,000 and 240,000 human casualties.[17]

> Two crowded years of war and cunning were required to conquer the region. Montezuma II was killed in 1520. More than a year later, after three months' siege, Tenochtitlan was taken. Cortés was made governor of New Spain, and the building of a new world began . . . .
> While some invading Spaniards "saw only the glitter of Aztec gold," like many of the conquistadors with Iberian ranching roots, Cortés "foresaw a *cattle* industry."[18]

> Among the earliest to bring *cattle* directly from Spain to the mainland was Hernando Cortés . . . who was not only a soldier but a rancher de luxe—recognized as such by King Charles, who assigned him vast estates and conferred upon him the unique title of Marquis of the Valley of Oaxaca. . . .
> Cortés introduced a novel practice to the range *cattle* business. After conquering the Aztecs, he branded his *Indian* prisoners on the cheek with the letter "G," for Guerra, or "war." Many of them were impressed into service as *herdsmen* for Cortés and other ranchers.[19]

Acting as cruelly as the Eurasian nomadic pastoralists and with a level of greed reminiscent of Roman ranchers, Cortés physically branded both enslaved humans and other animals as his property. "Within a decade of Cortés's arrival, *cattle* ranches had proliferated on the mainland of Mexico and along the Gulf coast."[20] Horses, cows, pigs, and sheep were transplanted from the *haciendas* of Spain to the plateaus and valleys of Mexico.[21]

Large-scale ranching of domesecrated animals provided "the accumulations of capital which made possible the large-scale mining of precious metals,"[22] and the successful acquisition of large amounts of gold and silver relied on the forced labor of other animals and indigenous peoples. In the early 1500s, the Spanish began forcing enslaved Native Americans to mine for gold in New Spain, and by midcentury significant silver ore deposits had been found near Zacatecas. Countless Native Americans and animals died from overwork or succumbed to disease, and many died from exposure to large amounts of mercury, which was increasingly used as part of a method for extracting silver from its ore efficiently. Large silver-mining areas required the exploitation of great numbers of domesecrated animals, and many were forced to power smelting-furnace bellows. The furnaces were fueled by lumber that animals carried over long distances; cows, horses, mules, and donkeys also transported processed silver to port. Many more were killed and their bodies used for food and to create candles and various textiles, such as sacks, to be used in the silver industry. The increasing availability of large numbers of enslaved oppressed animals allowed for the increased oppression and death of enslaved people, who, as surface deposits became depleted, were forced ever deeper into the earth. "Without cheap and plentiful candles, mining could never have been carried on as extensively as it was."[23]

The entangled oppression of exploited humans and other animals also played a primary role in another key revenue-creating export from the Americas: sugar. Spanish sugar plantations in the Caribbean, Brazil, and tropical New Spain required considerable labor power from exploited humans and other animals to clear forests and undergrowth, dig canals, and build mills. Once constructed, the mills required year-round labor for growing, harvesting, and processing. "The engenhos [sugar mills] needed constant supplies of *oxen* for the carts and mills, as well as *tallow* for candles and *meat* for employees and *slaves*."[24] As soil depletion in many areas led to reduced production, additional animals were required to meet the growing demand for fertilizer. While there is little record of the experience of the other animals exploited in sugar production, historians note that the mortality rate of cows exploited as laborers in *engenhos* was high.[25] Some witnesses, similar to las Casas, did take the time to document human oppression. One observer wrote, "The work is insufferable. The workers are always on the run and because of this many *slaves* die. The *owners'* profits were huge. This sweet bears a heavy load of guilt, for the *owners* commit so many sins."[26] Revolts by enslaved sugar-mill laborers in Latin America were frequent, and thousands sought sanctuary in the same mountainous areas where escaped domesecrated animals had fled.[27] Few enslaved humans were ever safe from their oppressors—nor were the fleeing animals, especially cows. Groups of "hide" hunters developed a brutal method of capturing and killing the fleeing, terrified cows: they were stopped by a long, bladed pole thrust into their hamstrings, then skinned once brought to the ground.

## EXPANSION OF COMMERCIALLY DRIVEN RANCHING

Increasingly, the body parts of domesecrated animals were becoming leading revenue-producing exports; cow skins, horns, and body fat sent back to Europe created profits "equaling or exceeding in value sugar and other plantation crops."[28] Between 1530 and 1540, "Española [another name for Hispaniola] shipped up to two hundred thousand" cow skins annually.[29] By the 1560s, "Española income from her imports probably amounted to about 640,000 pesos annually from sugar and 720,000 from hides."[30]

"During the period 1620 to 1665 *hides* accounted for 75 percent or more of the total value of exports to Spain."[31] By 1625, an estimated 1.3 million cows were in New Spain alone,[32] and tens of thousands were driven to mining areas, where they were killed and their bodies used for food and resources in the gold and silver mining performed by enslaved laborers.[33] "The spread of *stock* ranching was undoubtedly a major cause of depopulation in central New Spain, and overgrazing the principal cause of the soil erosion which has plagued Mexico ever since."[34]

> In the Panuco region alone, a native Huastecan population of perhaps one million in 1520 dwindled to about twelve thousand by 1532 as a result of disease, warfare, starvation, and *slave* export. *Cattle* ranching is not compatible with dense settlement, and the *Indian* die-off allowed virtually the entire tropical coastal plain to lie open for large-scale *herding* within no more than a half-century of the Conquest.[35]

The commoditization of the body fat and skin of cows encouraged even greater increases in the numbers of animals and the further expropriation of lands that had been used by free-living animals and indigenous peoples. And, as with the invasions of settled communities by Eurasian nomadic pastoralists and Roman legions, the Spanish invasion frequently resulted in hunger for the conquered people.

> The peoples of the high civilizations lived chiefly on a vegetable diet, so anything radically affecting their croplands radically affected them. The Spanish, anxious to establish their pastoral Iberian way of life in their colonies, set aside large sections of land for grazing,

much of it land that had once been cultivated. And the *livestock*, in this new continent where fences and shepherds were so few, often strayed into *Indian* fields, eating the plants and trampling them. As New Spain's first viceroy wrote to his king about the state of affairs around Oaxaca: "May your Lordship realize that if *cattle* are allowed, the *Indians* will be destroyed." Many people went malnourished, weakening their resistance to disease; many fled to the hills and deserts to face hunger in solitude; some simply lay down and died within the sound of the lowing of their rivals. The history of this phenomenon is clear in Mexico, and we have good reason to believe that parallels are to be found elsewhere in the Americas.[36]

Smallpox, most likely transmitted to New Spain by Cortes's army, proceeded southward through Central America and infected the Inca state by the middle of the sixteenth century. Throughout the entire region, hundreds of thousands of indigenous people also perished from measles, mumps, influenza, and typhus, all diseases derived from domesecration. Many of these deaths unquestionably were facilitated by the hunger and malnutrition caused by the incursion of ranching and the consequent weakening of the indigenous peoples' immune systems.[37] Survivors struggled to exist under the domination of a growing pastoralist/ranching economy. "*Cattlemen* . . . apparently pre-empted the best land without any vestige of a grant or other legal title and grazed animals with no provision for corrals or *herders*."[38]

"By the 1570s, some ranches had 150,000 head of *cattle*; 20,000 was considered a small *herd* and its *owner* a man of no importance. After touring the country, the French explorer Samuel de Champlain reported ranches 'stretching endlessly and everywhere covered with an infinite number of *cattle*.'"[39] Commercial exploitation of sheep, also carried over from Spain by enterprising conquistadors, created more wealth for Spanish elites and led to further instances of entangled oppression. By 1571, New Spain had eighty large textile mills "in which *Indians* were driven, often to the detriment of their health."[40]

As with the military campaigns of the Romans, cows and other domesecrated animals continued to be "driven in droves in the train of advancing Spanish forces to provide them with readily available *food*."[41]

Francisco Vásquez Coronado, in a ruthless march for gold, forced thousands of animals on a trek during which hundreds of Native Americans were killed. His 1540 incursion into what is now New Mexico, Arizona, Texas, Colorado, and Kansas was made possible by the forced accompaniment of 6,500 animals—goats, sheep, cows, and horses—"to provide *mounts* and *meat* for his fellow conquistadores."[42]

In his own 1540 foray from Florida into what is now the southern United States, Hernando de Soto dealt viciously with people from the Chickasaw nation who tried to take some of the pigs de Soto was using to fuel his incursion. Native Americans suspected of taking pigs who were not murdered outright were sent back to their villages with their hands cut off. Women were abducted as "slaves" to serve de Soto and his lieutenants, and others had collars chained around their necks and were forced to carry the invaders' provisions. One chronicler of de Soto's murderous expedition noted the vicious ways that he dealt with a group of Native Americans when their leader did not surrender himself: "Of those made captive, the Governor sent six to the Cacique [leader], their right hands and their noses cut off, with the message, that, if he did not come to him and apologize and render obedience, he would go in pursuit, and to him, and as many of his as he might find, would he do as he had done to those he sent."[43]

In 1598, Juan de Oñate, the son of a wealthy Zacatecas conquistador and silver baron, organized an attempt to settle what is now New Mexico, an area roughly one thousand miles north of the limits of Spanish control. His entourage included a "cavalry," eighty-three wagons, and seven thousand "*head* of animals."[44] When a community of Pueblos resisted Oñate's heavy-handed demand for supplies, Oñate's forces attacked "with devastating results. They killed some five hundred men and three hundred women and children, and enslaved about five hundred survivors, condemning adult males among them to have a foot severed."[45]

As in the Spanish invasion of the Canaries, horses became important "instruments of conquest in Mexico and Peru by terrorizing the *Indians* who had never before seen such animals."[46] The historian Carlos Pereyra notes, however, that while the use of horses was very significant in the Spanish Conquest in Latin America, "the *hog* was of greater importance and contributed to a degree that defies exaggeration."[47] The oppression of pigs and other animals was deeply entangled with the oppression of Native Americans.

Pigs naturally multiplied more rapidly than *cattle* in the New World, and droves of these animals and of *sheep on the hoof* were an important element in provisioning the expeditions of the Conquistadores. It is nevertheless surprising that Gonzalo Pizarro, on an eastward expedition from Peru in 1541, was able to take with him four to five thousand pigs, only eleven years after the country had been entered by the Spaniards.[48]

As was true of other areas of the Americas invaded by the Spanish, destruction in Central America occurred with deadly speed.

The Spanish conquest and colonization radically and rapidly transformed Central America. In two converging waves and in only forty years (from 1502 to 1542), single minded captains avid for instant wealth and the social recognition it conferred carried Spanish arms from one end of the isthmus to the other. . . . Ravaged by smallpox, measles, pulmonary plague, and other Old World diseases to which they were not immune, racked by internal dissension, and mesmerized by the strangeness and historic violence of the invading culture, native communities offered little effective resistance to this double-headed invasion. Populations plummeted. In Panama, the once populous confederation the Spanish called Cueva were obliterated within a few decades. The number of estimated native tributaries in early New Spanish Nicaragua declined from 600,000 in 1520 to 6,000 in 1560–70. . . . At first, the native labor supply seemed infinite, so little effort was made to mitigate suffering and death. Tens of thousands of native *slaves* were exported to richer parts of the rapidly expanding Spanish empire.[49]

Many Native Americans who were not killed, enslaved, or felled by disease faced starvation. Lands they had used for crops were expropriated by Spanish ranchers who "engulfed land which the *Indians* did not farm any given year but which constituted the indispensable reserve in their field-to-forest rotation. Occupation in this reserve imperiled the continued productivity of the fields left in *Indian* hands and thus also the *Indian* population which lived off that land."[50]

Six-sevenths of the population of Native Americans in Central America were lost between 1519 and 1650.[51] "Spanish haciendas, with their *herds* of *cattle* and sheep and fields of wheat, were located in the country-side where the *Indians* had been more successfully conquered and sub-dued."[52] As in other conquered areas, enslaved people from Africa were brought to replace the dwindling supply of Native American laborers and forced to control domesecrated animals and work in mines and on plantations. By 1575, there were 8,630 enslaved people from Africa working just in what is now Panama.[53] During the colonial period, extensive "cattle" ranching spread into what is now Guatemala, Honduras, Costa Rica, Nicaragua, and Panama.[54] Soon, Nicaragua "became the most important *cattle* region in Central America,"[55] and "*beef, hides* and *tallow*" were its primary exports from the 1600s until the mid-eighteenth century.[56]

In what is now Bolivia, enormous deposits of silver ore were found in the 1540s around Potosí, a largely desolate and arid region. Much of the silver that flowed into Europe during the period came from this area; the operation was so huge that "even though *tallow* was extremely cheap, in the early seventeenth century 300,000 pesos a year was spent on candles for the Potosí mines."[57] The Spanish forcibly relocated large numbers of Native Americans from the Bolivia region and Peru to work the Potosí mines. These forced laborers were required to remove 1.25 tons of silver ore a day, which had to be carried and pushed up through a maze of small tunnels in hundred-pound bags until it was delivered to a main tunnel. "In the first decades of this system, four out of five miners died in their first year of forced employment in the mines."[58] Most died from overwork, respiratory disease, or mercury poisoning. As in New Spain, successful mining operations also required an enormous level of animal exploitation, including the use of tens of thousands of llamas and mules for transport. "The llama and alpaca populations diminished as spectacularly as the *Indian* population after the conquest; and the reasons were the same: disease and brutal exploitation."[59] Countless mules and other animals died from the relentless pressure to power the furnaces, and the need for furnace fuel and stamp mills resulted in vast deforestation, which led to the death and displacement of countless free-living animals. Ranchers claimed the lands of the displaced Native Americans who had been forced into the mines and devoted it to raising the increasingly large numbers of domesecrated animals whose exploitation was essential for profitable mining.

## Ranching Violence and Destruction in Brazil

As in Mexico, Central America, and Bolivia, large groups of domese-crated animals were "an important instrument of the European occupation of the land in Brazil."[60] Land became available to the Spanish and Portuguese colonizers through the collapse of the population caused by disease and genocide and by the forcible relocation of survivors to sites where they could be taxed, their labor exploited, and their "souls saved." Portuguese colonizers in the northern coastal areas of Brazil initially re-strained their consumption of cows as food because the animals' labor was essential to power millstones used to crush sugarcane. "Thus there was a concentrated effort to promote *cattle* raising in the coastal mead-ows of the northeast, not despite but because of the devotion of that area to sugar."[61] Ranchers expanded their drive for land and water, and indig-enous peoples resisted.

> By 1590 *pioneers* moving north from Bahia [with assistance from the royal government] had broken the back of *Indian* resistance at Sergipe, and soon *herds* of *cattle* browsed in its grasslands. At the mouth of the São Francisco River, whose valley was to become the greatest corridor into the interior, the Bahian *cattlemen* met the *cattlemen* moving south from Pernambuco, each group a vanguard of the sugar plantations spreading laterally along the coast.[62]

> In many cases the owners of the engenhos or other members of their families also became ranchers. Sesmarias [large estates] in the sertão [backlands] were quite large, sometimes exceeding a hundred thousand acres, and by the close of the seventeenth century there were landholdings in the backlands larger than whole provinces of Portugal. Great ranching families might run more than twenty thousand *head* on their lands.[63]

Both Portuguese and Spanish invaders cultivated vast numbers of cows, and their skin "formed one of Brazil's staple exports throughout the colonial period."[64] As was true of competing pastoralist societies in Eurasia, raids for domesecrated animals were common among the rival Spanish and Portuguese colonizers, who sought to increase their wealth by confiscating captive animals from one another's occupied territories.

"Since many of the soldiers in the frontier campaigns were irregulars, they found their payment in the form of *livestock* sacked from the enemy."[65]

As in Mexico, hundreds of thousands of cows, pigs, sheep, and horses were driven great distances to be used as food and materials in the mining areas of South America. While surface mining for gold in Brazil was better than underground work, enslaved human workers still led a miserable existence:

> The work was still hard and bad for the health. *Slaves*, and the occasional Whites to be found physically laboring, shoveled and bent for long hours, sweating in the sun but with legs and feet chilled by the water in which they generally stood. One physician at the time observed that the contrast laid the workers open to "very severe pleurisies, apoplectic and paralytic fits, convulsions, pneumonia, and many other diseases." Washing did not consist simply of digging up stream beds and panning material in wooden bowls. Where possible, dams and channels were used to divert water from streams and rivers so that it flowed over promising strata, washing gold particles (or diamonds) free. This hydraulic work was arduous; and dams were known to break. *Slaves* were expected to last as useful workers for only seven to twelve years.
>
> The swelling mine populations of the interior took a great deal of feeding, and of supplying in general. . . . The *cattle* raisers . . . responded readily to the challenge, sending great numbers of *cattle* on the hoof, and quantities of salt *beef*. Live *cattle* also carried their *hides* with them; and *leather* had multiple uses in gold extraction and everyday life in the mining towns.[66]

Brazilian gold mining increased the demand for the flesh and labor power of cows, and the number and size of ranches inevitably grew. As coastal areas increasingly came to be used for the cultivation of sugar and tobacco, pastoralists pushed inland, seizing control of pastures adjacent to riverbanks and watering holes. Native Americans resisted the driving of tens of thousands of cows into their homelands.

> Ranchers, some of them also planters or related to planter families, and their *herdsmen* pushed their *cattle* out along both banks of the

São Francisco River and by 1640 there were over 2,000 corrals in the region. The history of much of the interior of the north-east can be summarized as exploitation, extermination of the *Indians*, large land grants, and the establishment of *cattle* ranches.[67]

Peter Bakewell notes:

As in Northern Mexico, native people of Brazil reacted fiercely to the bovine incursions. . . . Resolute *Indian* resistance to the spread of ranching punctuated the second half of the seventeenth century. . . . Colonial governors of the region, driven to distraction by these risings, called in seasoned bandeirantes from São Paulo to suppress them. With much violence the job was done.[68]

The violence included innumerable raids, campaigns, and massacres against the indigenous human populations of South America as ranching spread throughout the area. Chronicling the decimation of Native Americans in Brazil, John Hemming writes, "The native resistance to this *cattle* invasion was one of the most important stages in the conquest of the Brazilian *Indians*."[69] Noting the spread of ranching into the northeastern *sertão*, Hemming writes:

The reaction of most of these tribes followed a similar pattern . . . initial welcome, awe at the stranger's technology, military success and religious conviction; gradual realization that the settlers' motives were land and labour; armed resistance rather than submission on these terms. . . . Some *Indians* were needed to *herd* and drive the *cattle*, but generally the *Indians* would have been ignored had they willingly surrendered their lands and not interfered in any way with the precious *cattle*.[70]

The experience of one Native American society in Brazil, the Tapuia, is illustrative of what happened to many groups:

By 1680 the Tapuia of the Bahia hinterland were finally subdued. Some may have retreated southwards, melting into the forested hills of the interior of Ilheus; others were settled in aldeias [villages]; but many were simply destroyed or sold into slavery in other parts of

Brazil. Their lands were rapidly colonized. *Cattle* ranches spread westward to the São Francisco, and then north-westwards on the far side of that river. . . . The *cattlemen* had no sentiment about the moral need to treat *Indians* well. They helped themselves to *Indian* lands and, when possible, *Indian* women.[71]

Writing on his vanquishing of a village of Paiacú people who resisted ranchers' expropriation of their lands, the army officer Manuel Navarro grounded his ideological rationalization in religious beliefs. He bragged of his massacre of hundreds of people and lamented that some had escaped.

"On the fourth day of this month [August 1699] God was pleased to grant us a victory so fortunate that, totaliter [*sic*], it must be attributed to His divine omnipotence rather than to our limited forces." His only regret was that the tribe's "baggage"—its women and children—had been waiting in the undergrowth and had time to flee during the massacre of their men. "When we reached the *baggage* it was too late. Of those we did catch, the infantry's share was some 320 *head*. . . ."[72]

The internal warfare that existed at relatively low levels during the pre-Columbian era, described in chapter 1, grew significantly after contact with Europeans, further increasing Native Americans' suffering. This occurred for two reasons. First, the Spanish and the Portuguese frequently exploited indigenous rivalries and rarely launched military campaigns without indigenous auxiliaries from rival or conquered groups. Second, widespread death from disease was often believed to be caused by rival societies, leading to warfare and the taking of captives to replenish diminishing populations. The increased intensity of violence between indigenous groups after European contact has been referred to as a process of "warrification."[73]

By the early eighteenth century, Brazil was sending hundreds of thousands of individual cow skins to Lisbon.[74] The exploitation of the labor power of mules also increased significantly and, by 1826, twenty thousand mules were raised and sent from southern Brazil to São Paulo alone.[75] In an area of Brazil in what is now the state of Piauí, there were an estimated 578 ranches by 1772, "some of incredible size (one was twice the size of

Lebanon). . . . Slaves did much of the work on the ranches alongside free people of color."[76] The economy of the region was referred to as a "society of *leather*," and "great ranches often left much of their land unused and refused to rent or sell it in order to assure themselves of sufficient pasturage and an adequate supply of labor," by denying access to alternative employment opportunities.[77] By the mid-eighteenth century, the state of Pernambuco alone had twenty-seven *tanneries* staffed by hundreds of enslaved people.[78]

Ranching incursions extended deep into Peru and Chile and on to Patagonia, the southern region of the continent. Exports of animal skin and hair became the mainstay of these economies. The Spanish elite granted large tracts of land—land already occupied by Native Americans and countless other animals—to a few families to raise cows in what is now Uruguay. Cows were brought to Venezuela in the 1540s, and by 1640 their population was an estimated 140,000; the skin of cows was the leading export.[79] In 1750, only "thirty ranching families controlled much of the Venezuelan grasslands."[80] In Argentina, eighty thousand cows were killed for their skins around Buenos Aires in 1619, and by 1719 one observer estimated the number of cows in the southern pampas at forty-eight million.[81] Buenos Aires was exporting 150,000 cow skins a year by 1770.[82] While thousands of enslaved workers were forced to extract gold for the Spanish in Chile, Andre Gunder Frank notes that "at no time did the value of Chile's gold export exceed that of her *tallow* export."[83]

The Catholic Church played both an ideological and an economic role in the conquest of Latin America. "It was the Spanish Crown's idea that religion might be the most effective means of pacifying the Indians and winning them over as allies in the conquest of new lands and the exploitation of riches. The Jesuits introduced both education and *cattle* ranches into the disputed territory."[84] John Hemming observed, "Hard on the heels of each conquest came the missionaries [who used their] reputation as shamans and their knowledge of native psychology to overawe *Indian* allies and enemies."[85] Jesuit and Franciscan missions "were economic as well as spiritual institutions,"[86] and they held large numbers of cows throughout much of the Americas. At these missions, "*cattle herding* became an important economic activity for profit and for indoctrinating the *Indians*."[87]

In parts of northern New Spain (what is now Texas, New Mexico, California, and Arizona), enterprising priests converted conquered Native Americans and promoted the cultivation of large numbers of captive cows, creating a group of powerful Franciscan "cattle" barons. Spanish priests were among the first to pressure Native Americans in New Spain to tend to enslaved cows by riding on the backs of horses, and the Spanish gave *vaqueros* (*cowboys*) spurs to control horses by inducing pain. As in other conquered areas, Native Americans also were assigned the terrible tasks of killing, skinning, and butchering domesecrated animals.

Missionaries also used enslaved laborers from Africa to work their vast ranching estates and staff their sugar plantations.[88] One of the largest ranchers of the era was a Jesuit priest, Father Kino, who supplied cows from his nineteen ranches to expeditions and for settlement attempts. Missionaries "always traveled with their regular quantity of horses, mules and *cattle*, without which the spread of Christianity would have been literally impossible."[89]

In New Spain, when mining yields and profits declined at the end of the sixteenth century and northern migration increased, "the advance was made by *stock-breeders*, looking for new pastures to feed their enormous *herds*. *Stock* breeding, not cultivation, thus provided the 'cutting edge' of the northward Spanish advance."[90] By the end of the seventeenth century, there were more than one million domesecrated cows in California alone, and as cow skins were exported for profit, considerable revenues accrued to the Catholic Church and to Spanish elites.[91] Increasing numbers of free-living cows, who had escaped confinement and control, were living in New Spain; hunting them down "became a popular sport among Spanish *Cavalrymen* and local residents."[92]

## DOMESECRATION, HUMAN OPPRESSION, AND THE RISE OF CAPITALISM

The widespread plundering and violence by Europeans in the Western Hemisphere provided much of the wealth and resources necessary to transform the stagnating feudal order into a new elite-dominated economic system—capitalism. Spanish and Portuguese ranchers, merchants, and elites increased their wealth through the sale of ill-gotten commodities from the Americas, especially the skins, hair, and fat of other animals; sugar; and precious metals. By 1600, gold and silver from the Americas already had increased the supply in Europe eightfold, and control of silver and gold eclipsed land as the primary source of wealth and power in Europe. Spanish shipments of silver from the Western Hemisphere passed "into the coffers of financiers in Antwerp, London, Lisbon, the Hague, and Geneva, thus backing the increasing amount of species needed to fuel the growth of a western European commercial bourgeoisie."[93] Fueled as it was by the entangled oppression of enslaved humans and domesecrated animals, the Bolivian mining area of Potosí became "the first city of capitalism, for it supplied the primary ingredient of capitalism—money. Potosí made the money that irrevocably changed the economic complexion of the world."[94] Precious metals came to represent a standardized form of capital that quickly established the foundation "for the new merchant and capitalist class that would soon dominate the whole world."[95] Writing in the middle of the twentieth century, the historian Walter Prescott Webb romanticized European elites' plundering of the Western Hemisphere, a region that he referred to as the "frontier."

> The frontier furnished the setting for and supplied the matrix from which capitalism grew. It furnished the substance with which capitalism works; it supplied the gold and silver which facilitated exchange; and it gave the room for constant expansion which seems so necessary in a capitalist economy. . . . It was this American treasure, and it alone, that reversed the long descent of prices, and sent them slanting upward to such heights as to constitute a revolution.[96]

The powerful in Spain used much of their violently expropriated wealth to finance equally violent attempts to conquer Europe. Spanish elites spent a fortune on firearms alone; with the new market demand, gun manufacturers emerged. "Significantly, it was the mechanisms of capitalism and the spirit of bourgeois enterprise which fulfilled the need. Though there would be much starvation and depopulation among humans, guns continued to be fruitful and almost always well fed."[97] The wealth taken so viciously from the Americas and used to fund European warfare eventually led to Spain's decline, and its wealth passed into the hands of British, Dutch, and French elites, who used it to build and provision modern navies and armies—forces they would use to create mayhem around the world in the pursuit of profit.

The enormous influx of silver soon reduced its value, leading to inflation and prompting the land-rich, cash-poor aristocracy in Europe to look for ways to increase funds. Many sought to replace unprofitable feudal cultivation practices and used their land instead to raise sheep, whose hair was fueling the growing textile industry in Britain and the Netherlands. This more lucrative enterprise required the displacement of "peasants," whose exploited labor long was the primary source of aristocratic wealth. Increased grazing led to the conversion of the "commons"—land traditionally shared by many members of rural communities for a variety of subsistence purposes—from communal to private property. This conversion, known as the enclosure movement, occurred first in Britain and was replicated in other parts of Europe, with support and enforcement by area governments.

With the gradual breakup of the feudal order in Europe and the migration of people from agricultural areas to the growing cities, the labor power of the displaced cultivators increasingly became a commodity to be sold for wages. At the same time, the profit-driven enclosures increased the numbers of other animals who were exploited for their hair and flesh, supplementing the hundreds of thousands of animal skins and sheep hair imported from the Americas. Many people displaced and forced to work as wage labor were hired into the animal-based textile and "leather" industries. By the close of the seventeenth century, commerce based on making products out of animal skin and hair was one of the major industries in Britain and employed large numbers of newly created wage laborers.[98]

Some people paid to work with the skin of domesecrated animals were employed in "light leather" crafts, often through the putting-out or cottage system, a practice in which laborers worked at home at a piece rate. The light crafts, as opposed to shoemaking and the like, were considered unskilled work, and businesses in seventeenth-century London kept wages as low as possible by employing women and children. No doubt responding to criticism of their treatment of workers, in 1697 glove manufacturers in Worcester defended themselves by characterizing their underpaid employees as "decrepit and unfit for any other employment."[99]

The inflationary effects of the influx of silver and gold from the Americas had other significant consequences. The purchasing power of laborers declined significantly, in some areas by as much as two-thirds, requiring workers to devote as much as 75 to 80 percent of their wages to food alone.[100] Moreover, the importance of gold from West Africa was eclipsed by the supply from the Americas. With increasing labor demands from plantations, ranches, and mines in the Western Hemisphere, the most lucrative export from Africa soon became human beings, and thus the terrible transatlantic "slave" trade began to grow.

All the while, the raising and killing of cows and pigs for food in Europe enabled the militaristic naval expeditions that facilitated European domination of the world. For example, the Netherlands' successful colonization efforts relied on a strong naval force, which in turn relied on domesecrated animals.

> The *meat* supply on long voyages consisted largely of salt *beef*. The best results in respect of both keeping qualities and taste were obtained by salting down fine-fibred *meat*. This was one of the reasons why Danish *oxen*—especially those from Jutland—were in demand in Dutch towns. In the first half of the seventeenth century over 2,000 *cattle*, annually, were slaughtered for the victualling of the East Indian fleet alone. The requirements of the great war fleets were of a comparable order of magnitude. . . . Much of Europe's trade in the sixteenth and seventeenth centuries so to speak centred upon filling the belly and slaking the thirst.[101]

Many cows were "not much more than skin and bone" after being driven many miles to export destinations, so upon arrival they were allowed to eat and regain profitable body weight before they were killed. Consistent with the historical pattern, it was the elites who held firm control and "ownership" of large numbers of domesecrated animals.

> In most places the princes and noble landowners asserted that the rearing of *cattle* for export was their exclusive privilege. They demanded the right of pre-emption over the *peasants'* young *bullocks*, thus enabling prices to be held down and the lords' own profit increased accordingly. . . .
>
> The heyday of the *cattle* trade coincided with the golden age of the nobility. This is evidenced by the many examples, in Hungary, Poland and Denmark, of large incomes from *cattle* being lavishly dispensed upon the construction of stately homes and the maintenance of great households and a high standard of living.[102]

Meanwhile, Spain intensified its invasion of Florida in the sixteenth century and sent cows and other animals to facilitate the survival of the colonizers at St. Augustine. Widespread ranching operations were established by the early seventeenth century, and there was predictable resistance when domesecrated cows and pigs damaged Native American crops.

> The desire to expand Florida *beef* production was so great that some ranchos were maintained at government expense; however, when *Indian* hostilities erupted in the 1640's, the expansion of ranching was temporarily discouraged by the Spanish Crown. . . . It was believed by some authorities, including the king of Spain, that part of the *Indian* unrest was the result of roving *herds* of unfenced *livestock* owned by the rancheros. *Cattle*, horses and *swine* were constantly trampling over the *Indian* grain fields. There, of course, was no fencing for keeping *cattle* out of fields. True to the Hispanic tradition, the rancheros felt no obligation to limit the movement of their *stock*. . . . Spanish soldiers finally quelled the rebellion, but reprisals by the soldiers left a legacy of hatred among the *Indians*.[103]

## THE SPANISH INVASION OF THE PHILIPPINES

The Spanish conquest of the Philippines—and its contrasts with the situation in Latin America—supports the thesis that colonization was much more likely to involve large-scale violence when invasions involved expanding ranching operations. After Ferdinand Magellan's sixteenth-century expedition to circumnavigate the world arrived in the Philippines, he became involved in regional rivalries and was killed in 1521. Successful Spanish colonization did not occur until 1565, when López de Legazpi arrived from New Spain with both infantry and "cavalry" forces. Outside of the resistance of one regional ruler, initial Spanish control of the Philippines was established with relatively little use of direct violence.

Elites in Spain hoped the colonization of the Philippines would bring significant new revenues. "The geography of the islands, however, was not conducive to ranching of the type known in Mexico, and *cattle* raising never became extensive. Nor did mules or sheep thrive in the environment."[104] Moreover, the relative absence of precious metals meant there was no need for large numbers of domesecrated animals to sustain substantial mining operations. The Philippines' value to Spain largely was confined to facilitating direct Spanish access to spices, silks, porcelain, and other luxury goods from China, which were exchanged for silver from the Americas.

The Spanish did exact labor and tributes from indigenous Filipinos for supplies and to create a luxurious life for its elites there, and there was some resistance and violence. Missionaries dispatched to "Christianize" the indigenous population began limited ranching operations for local provisions. "Among the numerous *peasant* revolts, mention can be made of the unsuccessful uprisings during the years 1745–56 when [indigenous peoples from many towns] fought for the restoration of communal land which had been taken over by missionaries for *cattle* raising."[105]

Unlike in the Americas, though, the Spanish did not develop exports based on animal exploitation or require large-scale ranching to sustain major mining or plantation operations in the Philippines. With the exception of indirect violence through the spread of infectious disease from the domesecration of animals, these islands did not see the sort of large-scale carnage, displacement, and malnutrition that likely would have followed the development of extensive ranching operations. The demographic collapse of the indigenous population in the Philippines therefore was substantially less than what resulted from the Spanish colonization of the Americas. In the areas of the Philippines most affected by Spanish colonization, the indigenous human population declined at a rate of three to one, compared to roughly twenty-three to one among indigenous peoples in the Americas.[106]

Of course, while invasion with the intent to establish ranching operations almost certainly will produce conflict, violence, and displacement, such results also can occur in the absence of ranching. For example, during the period in which domesecration enabled and promoted invasion of the Americas beginning in the late fifteenth century, the same European powers also launched violent invasions of areas of the globe that offered other valuable resources but few ranching opportunities. In 1511, for example, the Portuguese sacked the port town of Malacca on the west coast of the Malay peninsula, killed the local population, and established control of the lucrative spice trade. The Dutch East India Company, asserting control of the spice trade by the early seventeenth century, invaded the Javanese port of Jakarta in Indonesia in 1619, burning down houses and displacing the populace to establish a fortress from which to maintain regional control. Two years later, the company violently took over five local islands where nutmeg was grown; "some 15,000 people were killed outright, left to starve in isolation, or otherwise taken into slavery in Jakarta."[107] It went on to gain control of the trade in other spices, such as cloves and pepper, by controlling production in its territory and destroying other cultivation areas to guarantee high process and profits. The violence in the region, although enabled by the use of domesecrated animals as provisions, was not promoted directly by the invasion of ranching operations. Of course, no small part of the lucrative spice trade was driven by the desire of the affluent in Europe to make "meat," especially that preserved by salt, more palatable.

As with the nomadic pastoralists and agrarian elites in Eurasia before them, the Spanish and Portuguese invaders' use of domesecrated animals in the Americas both enabled and promoted large-scale destruction, violence, displacement, hunger, and human enslavement. Indeed, without the use of domesecrated animals first as essential provisions and soon thereafter as instruments of war and laborers, the European conquest of the Americas very likely could not have occurred—and, even if it had, there would not have been the relentless expansion for grazing areas that caused so much conflict. Furthermore, as much as the direct exploitation of domesecrated animals contributed to the conquest, successful invasion might not have been possible without the devastation and disorganization among the indigenous peoples caused by smallpox and other infectious zoonotic diseases brought by the Europeans. In many cases, the destruction of Native American fields and crops to create grazing areas led to "decerealization," malnutrition, and the people's increased vulnerability to infectious disease.

And, again similarly to the domesecration-related violence in Eurasia, a great deal of the bloodshed in the Americas was motivated by the desire to acquire land and water sources necessary to graze large numbers of animals; such large-scale violence did not occur in the absence of extensive ranching operations in the Philippines. Entire civilizations in the Americas were invaded, robbed, and destroyed, and much of the expropriated land was converted to pasture. As in Eurasia, the conquered, displaced people became easily exploited, if not enslaved, laborers. However, in part because of the lack of nomadic pastoralism in the Americas and the absence of large agricultural societies deeply grounded in domesecration, the manner in which domesecrated animals were exploited there and the resulting violence took somewhat different forms than had been typical in early Eurasia. Unlike in many of those earlier domesecration-enabled invasions, the Europeans who came to the Americas seldom sought merely to establish themselves as local elites to rule over and force tribute from subjugated peoples. Rather, the rancher-invaders from Spain and Portugal wanted and achieved an enormous expansion in the overall number of domesecrated animals. Many of the invaders concentrated on the material rewards brought by the limitless expansion of commercial ranching, and animal skin, body fat, and hair grew as profitable exports.

European ranchers in the Americas achieved an expansion in the number of domesecrated animals such as nomadic pastoralists like Chinggis Khan or the ranchers of Rome never even dreamed. The expropriation of vast amounts of land for grazing permitted large populations of animals, whose presence in turn necessitated constant invasive and violent forays for the acquisition of fresh grazing areas and water sources. At the same time, growing numbers of horses, cows, mules, and other animals were indispensable laborers on sugar plantations and in mines. The use of the body parts of domesecrated animals as resources, especially for candles and as food—as dried, salted "meat" for enslaved humans—was crucial in making mining and sugar enterprises practical and cost effective. These profitable operations—frequently financed initially by the sale of the skin of other animals—in turn played a substantial role in the acceleration and expansion of the terrible transatlantic trade in human "slaves."

The immeasurable violence and oppression experienced by both humans and other animals in the Americas and the accompanying terror, trauma, and deprivation created the enormous wealth necessary for the development of mercantilism and the rise of the capitalist system. Inflation-producing imports of large quantities of ill-gotten gold and silver into Europe forced many landed aristocrats there to enclose the commons for the purpose of raising sheep for cash, a practice more profitable than traditional sharecropping arrangements. Huge numbers of families were compelled to migrate to urban areas and to sell their labor in order to survive; many were exploited by "leather," "wool," and other growing industries controlled by the emerging capitalist class. The fates of the indigenous human populations in the Americas, the growing numbers of people captured in Africa for sale as "slaves," and the new European proletariat all were thoroughly entangled with those of the domesecrated animals exploited by elites on both sides of the Atlantic.

While the Spanish and Portuguese elites and nascent capitalists found wealth and power in the vast expansion of ranching operations and the entangled oppression of humans and other animals mainly in Central and South America, the British, Dutch, and French elites also relied on domesecrated animals in their quest for material gain in North America.

# CHAPTER THREE

# RANCHING AND VIOLENCE
# IN NORTH AMERICA

Your *hogs* and *cattle* injure us, you come near us to live and drive us from place to place. We can fly no further, let us know where to live and how to be secured for the future from the *hogs* and *cattle*.
—Nanticoke spokesperson

The fifteen animals which stand compressed, with their heads thrust upward, awaiting the stroke of fate, express their emotions in the language natural to them and the noise is great.
—James Parton, "Cincinnati"

Much as Christopher Columbus's efforts to establish a beachhead in the Caribbean remained precarious until the use of enslaved cows and other animals made the conquest possible, so it was with the European invasion of North America. Thirty years after the Roanoke colony disappeared in 1607, the struggling colonizers at Jamestown experienced famine and significant loss of life. By 1625, some 4,800 of the six thousand who arrived since 1607 had perished from malnutrition.[1]

In "New England," as in "New Spain," European investors became aware of the need to send domesecrated animals to support successful colonization. And, again as for the animals forced onto ships by the Spanish and Portuguese, the ocean journey for other animals enslaved by the British and the Dutch was a miserable and frequently deadly one.

Confined to dark, fetid stalls below decks, *livestock* struggled to keep their footing as ships rose and sank with ocean swells. During the storms their terrified *bellows* and *squeals* added to a cacophony produced by lashing rains, howling winds, creaking timbers, and human shrieks and stammered prayers. A distressingly large number of animals perished at sea.[2]

One passenger aboard a Massachusetts-bound ship noted that "half of our cows and almost all our *mares* and goats" had suffered death during the voyage.[3] By 1634, there were twenty colonies in the Massachusetts Bay area, and they exploited 1,500 cows for subsistence.[4] The Dutch colonized what is now the Wall Street and Brooklyn shore and were killing four thousand cows a year by 1694.[5] Like their Spanish and Portuguese counterparts, early British and Dutch colonizers relied heavily on bread and salted "meat" until they developed better methods of storing vegetables for winter consumption. Male cows and horses frequently were exploited as "draft animals" to pull plows and wagons, and those who resisted were labeled as "lazy." One period "expert" recommended binding the feet of the "offenders'" so they would not be able to rise and eat or drink, thus "encouraging" compliance.[6]

Unlike the Spanish, who early on used methods reminiscent of Chinggis Khan, the colonizers of North America initially were less violent toward indigenous peoples than they were to other animals. With only a limited number of domesecrated animals available and needed for immediate subsistence, and in the absence of the precious metals whose mining required animals as rations and laborers, European investors in North America initially focused on the revenues to be gained from exporting the skin and hair of free-living animals, especially beavers and deer (of which Native Americans became valuable suppliers). Much of the skin and hair of beavers, for example, was fashioned into hats that were worn by the wealthy and privileged in Europe as a sign of their elevated status. The trade in animal skins "provided the initial stimulus for permanent European occupation of North America."[7]

## CROP DAMAGE, CONFLICT, AND WARFARE

As the numbers of domesecrated animals in North America grew, colonists began to brand them as personal property and then release them temporarily to seek food where they could. Predictably, Native Americans complained that "free-ranging" cows and pigs were damaging their crops, and violence usually followed. In many instances, Native Americans killed cows and pigs that came into their areas of cultivation in search of food. British colonizers, in retaliation for the loss of their "property," struck back violently. "In terms of the sheer numbers of incidents involved, nothing brought *Indians* and colonists into contact more frequently than *livestock*."[8] For example, there was violent conflict from 1622 to 1632 between Virginia-area colonists and a confederacy led by Powhatan, as Native Americans began attacking plantations and killing as many of the domesecrated animals as they could. Governor Francis Wyatt admonished colonists to defeat the indigenous population, stating, "our first work is expulsion of the savages to gain the free range of the country for the increase of *cattle, swine,* etc."[9]

In Maryland, one rancher continually drove cows and pigs in the direction of a Native American settlement "as if they were artillery, intending to inflict widespread devastation,"[10] and conflicts over domesecrated animals were a major factor leading to war between British invaders and the Pequots in Connecticut. "The English developed a tactic of warfare used earlier by Cortés . . . , deliberate attacks on noncombatants for the purpose of terrorizing the enemy."[11] "In May 1637 the English . . . launched an astonishingly brutal assault on a Pequot fort that left hundreds of *Indians* dead, including many women and children. Shortly thereafter, the conflict ended with the Pequots defeated and Connecticut open for further settlement by colonists and their *cattle*."[12]

Dutch colonizers also relied heavily on oppression of other animals in their forays into North America. Like the other colonizers, they made special use of cows and pigs to promote their expansion. One contemporary observed: "As the [Dutch] *cattle* usually roamed through the woods without a *herdsman*, they frequently came to the corn of the *Indians* which was unfenced on all sides, committing great damage there; this led to frequent complaints on their part and finally to revenge on the *cattle* without sparing even the horses, which were valuable in this country."[13] In 1643, a Dutch landholder who was opposed to retaliation against the Native Americans poignantly described his countrymen's actions:

When it was day the soldiers returned to the fort, having massacred or murdered eighty Indians, and considering they had done a deed of Roman valor, in murdering so many of them in their sleep; where infants were torn from their mother's breasts, and hacked to pieces in the presence of their parents and the pieces thrown into the fire and in the water, and other sucklings, being bound to small boards, were cut, struck, and pierced, and miserably massacred in a manner to move a heart of stone. Some were thrown into the River, and when the fathers and mothers endeavored to save them, the soldiers would not let them come on land but made both parents and children drown—children from five to six years of age, and also some old and decrepit persons. Those who fled from this onslaught, and concealed themselves in the neighboring sedge, and when it was morning, came out to beg a piece of bread, and to be permitted to warm themselves, were murdered in cold blood and tossed into the fire or the water. Some came to our people in the country with their hands, some with their legs cut off, and some holding their entrails in their arms, and others had such horrible cuts and gashes, that worse than they were could never happen. . . . After this exploit, the soldiers were rewarded for their services, and . . . Governor Kieft thanked them by taking them by the hand and congratulating them.[14]

Like other North American colonizers, the European inhabitants of "New Netherland" plundered countless free-living animals, including elk, rabbits, bears, squirrels, wolves, wild cats, minks, otters, beavers, geese, and numerous species of fish as "game" and "bearers of fur." The enormous increase in violence perpetrated against free-living animals—violence prompted by European companies—also increased warfare among indigenous peoples. "The land-based *fur* trade contributed to predatory raiding, resulting in more intensive long-distance slavery and violence, which may indicate more extensive conflict after European influence began. . . . As predatory raiding increased, so did the availability of trade goods, including [human] *slaves*."[15]

In the mid-1600s, in an effort to monopolize the trade in animal skin and hair, the Iroquois Confederation waged war on other indigenous societies in the Great Lakes region. In this intense and bloody conflict, called the "Beaver Wars," the British backed their trading partners, the Iroquois, with guns and supplies against the Algonquian-speaking societies who supplied the skins of other animals to the French. While fighting between Native American societies traditionally had been confined mainly to limited raids and skirmishes, the pursuit of animal skin and hair for profit resulted in full-scale invasions and mass killings and pursuit of refugees. The survivors of the Iroquois assault were forced west of the Mississippi River.

Increased warfare among indigenous peoples also resulted from epidemics. As in the Caribbean, Mexico, and Latin America, indigenous peoples in North America fell victim to European-transmitted diseases derived from the domesecration of other animals. And as did those in Latin America, northern indigenous peoples who began to experience the devastation and trauma of smallpox and other diseases frequently blamed the calamity on their long-time rivals. For example, smallpox epidemics first struck the Iroquois in 1634 and killed roughly 60 percent of the populations of the villages affected.[16] "The epidemics . . . triggered a paroxysm of grief and revenge. The Iroquois lashed out at their traditional enemies, inflicting hideous deaths on some and using others to repopulate their decimated villages."[17]

Violence against indigenous peoples and animals by colonists increased in the 1640s, when the English Civil War hindered British merchants' control of the "meat" trade to West Indies sugar plantations. Elite colonists took over the trade by selling plantation administrators "barreled *beef* and *pork*, *bacon* and *hams*."[18] Domesecrated animals were also shipped alive to the islands, including horses that were put to work in sugar mills. The North American colonizers, now more like their Latin America counterparts in their violence against human populations, encroached continuously onto Native American land for commercial purposes. The "need for more and better land for pasturage was a primary reason for founding many, if not most, of the new settlements."[19] In 1666, a member of the Nanticoke society complained to colonial officials in Maryland about free-ranging cows and pigs entering their villages and eating their corn. Pressing for more land, some colonists even had resorted to burning the fences Native Americans had erected around their cornfields.[20] One Nanticoke leader appealed to the officials: "Your *hogs* and *cattle* injure us, you come near us to live and drive us from place to place. We can fly no further, let us know where to live and how to be secured for the future from the *hogs* and *cattle*."[21]

The initial value that indigenous peoples had for the Europeans as suppliers of animal skin and hair diminished as the populations of beavers, deer, and other animals were decimated. Some Native American communities sought to adapt to the invasion by raising and selling cows and pigs themselves, especially given the invasion-linked decline of other free-living animals the indigenous people used as food. In New England, Native Americans angered many colonists by selling "meat" in Boston at lower rates than colonial ranchers. Colonists responded to such attempts at acculturation with charges of "livestock" theft and the massacre of pigs under Native American control. Native Americans learned the colonial justice system was quick to punish them for alleged misdeeds but "failed to provide the same swift justice when . . . [they] accused colonists of misdeeds."[22]

Native Americans came to understand that colonists viewed cows and pigs as personal property and took great offense at their theft or destruction. Therefore, they sometimes tortured the colonists' domesecrated animals to underscore their opposition to ceaseless land expropriation. Many animals suffered horrendous deaths in the process. One contemporary reported "what *cattle* they took they seldom killed outright: or if they did, would eat but little of the flesh, but rather cut their bellies, and letting them go several days, trailing their guts behind them, putting out their eyes, or cutting off one leg."[23] Other animals had their tongues cut out or were burned alive. Full-scale war erupted in New England in 1675, in part because two members of the Wampanoag Nation killed several cows. King Philip's War, as it was called, resulted in the deaths of approximately eight thousand cows, seven thousand Native Americans, and three thousand English.[24]

Naturally, not all British colonists shared in the profits produced by nascent North American ranching, as ranching was a land-intensive and thus essentially elite pursuit. Wealthy colonial landholders monopolized ownership of expropriated Native American pastures and fields; they levied high taxes against the less affluent and strove to keep poorer and newly arrived colonists marginalized and thus available as a source of cheap labor. On the heels of King Philip's War in 1676, propertyless colonists in Virginia who had expropriated land occupied by Native Americans entered into a violent conflict with the natives over the "ownership" of two pigs. When the governor of Virginia refused to provide the protection requested by the land-seeking groups who pushed farther west—in part because some Native Americans still were providing the skins of other animals to affluent colonial merchants—a rebellion was organized by Nathaniel Bacon, an aggressive proponent of westward expansionism. "It was Bacon who implied that recurrent *Indian* depredations against *livestock* and other property justified English aggression."[25] After Bacon became ill and died, the colonial elite subdued the rebellion; the governor made a public display of mass hangings, to teach "the poor of Virginia that rebellion did not pay."[26]

## COMMERCIAL RANCHING AND VIOLENCE

In 1670, a number of British colonizers migrated from the West Indies to South Carolina to begin ranching there. Ranching in South Carolina and the deep South was very profitable, as the mild weather permitted year-round grazing and made the use of winter feed unnecessary. As in Virginia and New England, Native Americans in the Carolinas became a source for the animal skins coveted by British traders, especially the skins of deer, or "buckskin." "By the end of the 17th century this trade included most of the southern tribes east of the Mississippi and between 1699 and 1714 South Carolina exported to England a yearly average of 54,000 skins."[27] British colonizers encouraged conflict between indigenous communities for the purpose of securing captives who were sold as enslaved laborers in the West Indies and in New England.

However, most profits in the region came from ranching. As in the north, colonists continually took more land, and by 1682 the export of products from the bodies of pigs and cows dominated the burgeoning market economy of South Carolina.[28] "Between 1700 and 1715 [South Carolina] colonial records include numerous Indian complaints against planters for settling on *Indian* land and for permitting their *livestock* to invade *Indian* cornfields and against traders for beating *Indians* and stealing their goods."[29] One contemporary asserted he had both heard colonial traders brag about and witnessed the "forceful debauching" of Native American women.[30]

As was the case with Native Americans further north, their usefulness to the colonial business elites declined with the falling number of animal skins they were able to supply. Overhunting and the increasing numbers of cows and pigs had a devastating effect on the population of deer, whose bodies served as the primary source of Native American currency in the region. When Native Americans began defaulting on their debts to the colonizers, efforts were made to enslave the debtors, sparking warfare. In 1715, the Yamassee Nation led a coalition of other Native American groups in an uprising against the British in the region. The colonizers were able, with the assistance of indigenous auxiliaries, to repel this offensive, but sporadic fighting went on for the next thirty years. The violence spread south with British Carolinian raids on Spanish ranching operations in Florida. By the mid-1700s, there were one hundred thousand cows in South Carolina, and much of the Carolinian "beef" was exported to provision enslaved humans on sugar plantations in the West Indies.[31]

Cows in the Carolinas, like countless domesecrated animals before them, resisted human control and exploitation. And, like the controllers of captive cows in Mexico and Latin America, Carolinians used whips to drive them. With the pastures losing their nutritional quality, the cows suffered from sodium chloride deficiencies and developed cravings; ranchers used salt to lure them in the desired direction. South Carolina ranchers also initiated the practice of "calf capture," a callous and opportunistic technique based on the deep bond between a cow and her calf.

> Each spring the newborn calves were gathered during roundups and confined in special padlocks at the cowpen, thereby controlling the milch cows [cows exploited for their milk], who gathered faithfully each evening at the cowpen after grazing all day, in order to suckle their calves. Let into an enclosure by themselves, the cows were milked in the evening and again the next morning before being allowed to tend the calves. Daily milk gathering reflected . . . highland British dietary preferences. . . . All through the summer and up to the first killing frost, the calves remained penned.[32]

Profits from the exploitation of domesecrated animals represented much of the capital necessary for the development of large Southern plantations. As Terry Jordan notes, ranching "offered a means of accumulating wealth with a minimal expenditure of labor or capital and attended by minimal risk. The profits, invested in land and slaves, assisted the rise of a Carolina plantation system in the 1690s."[33]

The French similarly relied on the bodies of cows to facilitate their incursions into the Caribbean and North America. Beginning with ranching operations in the eastern portion of Haiti, which they wrested away from the Spanish, French colonizers took cows and pigs to Louisiana and Alabama to sustain their northward invasion. However, in 1754 disputes over claims to the Mississippi River Valley and portions of the Gulf Coast resulted in war between the French and the British. Many Native Americans sided with the French, as French colonizers were far fewer in number than the land-grabbing British and because the French seemed largely content to engage in the trade in animal skins. When the

French withdrew in 1763 and ceded to the British lands they controlled between the Appalachian Mountains and the Mississippi River, English colonists pushed in with domesecrated cows and pigs.

Many South Carolinian ranchers, seeing their pastures deteriorate and crop-based plantations expand, migrated into Florida, Georgia, Alabama, Louisiana, and eastern Texas—the latter territory then part of the nation of Mexico. These incessant incursions undermined Native American ways of life, as large numbers of Anglo-controlled cows and pigs again depleted the resources needed by the indigenous animals of the woodlands. The numbers of free-living animals plummeted, and the artificially large population of cows and pigs continued to encroach on Native American croplands. Native Americans again complained to British authorities about the incursions of ranchers.

> A 1771 congress between British authorities in West Florida and representatives of the Creek nation reflected the difficulties that arose from the arrival of *cattle herders* from the east. . . . After naming eight *cattlemen* who had settled within Creek territory, . . . [Creek delegates accused the British] of breaking a 1765 agreement when . . . the [British delegate] had his *cattle* driven through Creek lands on the way to his plantation east of Mobile Bay. Furthermore, the chief complained of a herder whom the Cherokees had allowed to settle along the upper forks of the Coosa River, from which location he drove *cattle* into Creek territory.
>
> When Creek agent Benjamin Hawkins came to Alabama in the 1790s, he found native-white struggles over *livestock* continuing.[34]

Other ranchers pushed northwest. Their move into western North Carolina wreaked so much environmental damage and so harmed small farmers in the area that in 1766 colonial officials there passed a law preventing ranchers from driving cows into their region. Carolinian ranchers flooded into northern Cherokee and Creek homelands, crossing the mountains and moving northward into areas that are now Tennessee, Kentucky, West Virginia, western Pennsylvania, and Ohio. Many immigrants from the British Isles—including some who had colonized and then been displaced to make room for ranching—now pursued opportunities for this oppressive livelihood themselves in North America.

These people entered America . . . at Philadelphia and headed to the Appalachian backcountry, more than half the population was from Scotland, Ireland, and northern England. Here they resumed their farming and herding, relying on family and clan support and protection. They battled the *Indian* residents and each other in a world of anarchy like the one they had left behind in Britain.[35]

Native Americans resisted the incursion and formed an alliance to repel the intruders. In the face of this resistance, the British government in 1763 forbade migration west of the Appalachians, declaring the region reserved for Native Americans. However, some factions of the British elite who purportedly agreed to set aside land for indigenous people in fact simply wanted to slow a westward migration that might undermine coastal markets for British goods—and to undercut speculative land grabs for territory they wanted for themselves. Nonetheless, colonists with cows and pigs continued their incursions to the west.

With the outbreak of the Revolutionary War, colonial ranchers seized the opportunity to raid British ranching operations in Florida. Usually attacking at night, raiding colonists forced large groups of cows into Georgia. British loyalists retaliated by attacking colonial forts and "in one foray, they returned from Georgia with 2,000 *cattle*, which they sold at public auction for twenty-five shillings a head."[36] When the British withdrew from Florida in 1782, scores of opportunists rushed in to take control of the domesecrated animals, and violence ruled much of Florida for years as gangs fought over control of the cows.

Although the Northwest Ordinance, an early act of the U.S. Congress in 1787, established the rights of Native Americans to their land and security, the pressure for land expropriation soon eclipsed government promises. When Native Americans in Ohio refused to accept the new government's demand that they cede a significant mass of territory, violence erupted. The first military action of the newly founded United States was to send U.S. "cavalry" and artillery to smash Native American resistance there. After the U.S. army suffered several defeats at the hands of Native Americans, in 1793 President George Washington put General "Mad" Anthony Wayne in charge of the Ohio campaign. Ranchers in the Ohio Valley and Kentucky, benefitting from U.S. suppression of Native American resistance, also prospered by selling the government horses and cows, who were then exploited as instruments of war, laborers, and provisions. "Tall, sturdy Kentucky horses formed the core of Wayne's *cavalry* while more diminutive equines and *oxen* pulled supply wagons."[37] After Wayne's force of three thousand soldiers defeated roughly eight hundred Native Americans at the Battle of Fallen Timbers, "Wayne initiated a scorch-and-burn policy that forced *Indians* north and west, exiled remaining *Indians* from their homelands, and reduced most refugees to starvation. Wayne leveled and torched Native dwellings, hauled away the winter stores of *Indian* grain to American markets and burned agricultural fields."[38] The government claimed much of Ohio as undisputed U.S. territory in 1795. One twentieth-century writer who both chronicled and celebrated the oppression of Native Americans and domesecrated animals in Ohio, provides a glimpse of the economic forces and prejudicial attitudes that promoted and supported the oppression:

> Two events greatly stimulated *settlement* in Ohio and also encouraged *cattle* and *hog* raising. The first was the elimination of the *Indian menace* after the fall of Fallen Timbers. The second was the Whiskey Rebellion, the establishment of an internal revenue system and the placing of an excise on whiskey. When the farmer lost the right to convert corn into whiskey he turned his attention to the raising of *cattle* and *hogs*.[39]

Ranchers pressed into the expropriated lands accompanied by farmers, who coveted the rich soil of the Ohio valley. While some sought to grow corn, it was soon established that corn "was a somewhat unsalable surplus crop that could be marketed more profitably in the form of *beef* and *pork*."[40] Paul Henlein observes, "A corn-and-*livestock* economy soon gained dominance. Many of the *livestock* were *hogs*, but *cattle* offered a chance for bigger profits. The *beef-cattle* business spread gradually to span the valley by 1830."[41]

As cows were moved into expropriated lands in Illinois, a division of labor ultimately developed, with cows being bred and raised on the Illinois plains and then driven east to be fattened on corn in Ohio or to graze the vast areas of Kentucky bluegrass. From there, many cows were driven to Philadelphia, New York, or Baltimore to be killed for their flesh, skin, and body fat. Cows driven long distances suffered exhaustion and weight loss, which reduced their "market value." These cows were held over at special "fattening farms"—early feedlots—"where they could be *upgraded* for market."[42]

Drovers used weapons to drive domesecrated animals such long distances. "The Centreville whip was a famous weapon for these drovers. It was originally manufactured by a harness-maker there and attained great fame. These whips had line or silk 'crackers' and the report of them was like a rifle shot."[43] The experience of violence by cows driven to "market" can be gleaned from this report in a mid-nineteenth-century periodical:

> All morning the butchers and the drovers are busily engaged in their traffic. The fattest and best of the *cattle* in the pens find a ready sale, and long before all the drovers are in, select lots begin to be driven from the grounds. Men and boys hurry up and down the lanes and through the pens, each armed with a stick which is a sort of a shillalah, shouting to the half-crazed *cattle*, and with screams and blows directing them where they should go. Occasionally a drove of cows and calves come along, the latter muzzled, and the former looking and bellowing in chorus to the shouts of their drivers. Farmers from the neighboring towns are selecting "stores" from the large number of that class in the pens, and dairymen carefully examining the "milky-mothers" that are so anxiously seeking their young from the midst of their companions. . . . In the midst of these, dogs and goats and mules are offered for sale, and nearby, are the *hog* pens.[44]

The actual killing of those countless individuals, relegated to the status of commodity, was a terrible and frequently gruesome process, and many domesecrated animals struggled against their murder. For example, one period observer recounted:

> We stood by while one animal was dispatched, which happened to be a fractious *steer*, with no notion of being killed any faster than he could help it. He utterly refused to hold his head still for the axe, being apparently possessed of the idea that the iron might be too hard for his skull. Consequently the axeman, though apparently skilled in his business, failed to strike correctly and it was several minutes before the poor *beast* could be got down, filling the room in the meantime with his roars of terror and pain.[45]

The ranching of sheep, whose hair was demanded by eastern textile mills, also expanded during this period, causing much suffering and death.

In spite of the fact that sheep could not be kept upon the prairies without considerable attention, especially during the winter months, the *industry* rapidly gained favor among the farmers. Heavy losses were at first experienced due chiefly to mismanagement, for the animals usually purchased in western New York or Philadelphia were driven the entire distance during the hot summer months or the colder ones of autumn to a new home where scarcely any provision had been made for their sheltering. As a consequence, many died.[46]

## RANCHING EXPANSION AND INDIGENOUS DISPLACEMENT

The push to expand ranching and "livestock" farming to the farthest limits of the continent continued. In 1817, the U.S. government sent three thousand soldiers, led by Andrew Jackson (who drove cows to commercial areas as a young man), into Spanish-controlled Florida in response to several charges, including allegations that people of the Seminole Nation were stealing cows. Although the Seminoles had resorted to raising cows years earlier, making it unlikely that the cows they held were stolen, Jackson's campaign against them (the First Seminole War) captured an estimated 1,600 cows. During the invasion, Jackson's Khan-like "bloody campaign . . . left Indian villages and Spanish forts smoldering."[47] Claiming the Spanish were conspiring with the Seminoles in the theft of cows, the United States pressured Spain to negotiate the transfer of control of Florida.

While some pastoralists moved deeper into Florida, others pressed further west. One historian, romanticizing the early "settlement" of Illinois, stated, "The hunter and backwoodsman with his rifle and hunting knife slowly moved onward before the increasing tide of *civilization* combating the *savages* and *wild beasts*."[48] The expropriation of Native American lands in Indiana, Illinois, Michigan, and Wisconsin was executed to a large degree by William Henry Harrison, a member of the Virginia aristocracy, veteran Ohio "Indian fighter," and future president. It was Harrison's "coercive methods in dispossessing the tribes of the Northwest Territory [that] set a pattern for future relations between the two races."[49]

Playing off one tribe against another, and using whatever tactics suited the occasion—threats, bribes, trickery—Harrison made treaty after treaty with the separate tribes of the [then] Northwest. By 1807 the United States claimed treaty rights to eastern Michigan, southern Indiana, and most of Illinois. Meanwhile, in the [then] Southwest, millions of acres were taken from other tribes in the states of Georgia and Tennessee and in Mississippi territory. Having been forced off their traditional . . . [lands], the *Indians* throughout the Mississippi Valley seethed with discontent.[50]

All the while, the South was being invaded by ranchers and planters who pressured the federal government for the removal of Native Americans. In 1830, the Indian Removal Act, promoted by President Andrew Jackson, called for the eventual relocation of Native Americans to lands west of the Mississippi. While proponents of the legislation claimed the relocation was for the benefit of indigenous people whose lives were deteriorating in the face of Anglo incursion, "directly behind these lofty motives were the baser ones of hunger for land."[51] Although the government made numerous agreements with Native American nations for their relocation, the claimed negotiators for the people of the various nations often either were not empowered to negotiate on their behalf or had been bribed by interested parties. Native Americans who resisted relocation were harassed by Anglos, and many lost possessions in criminal raids on their homes—including the theft of many domesecrated cows under their control. One of the worst episodes of the official removal process was the forcible dislodgment of people of the Creek, Choctaw, Chickasaw, and Cherokee Nations from several southern states. On marches to the Oklahoma territory forced by the U.S. army, known as the Trail of Tears, thousands of Native Americans died from exhaustion and exposure. One period observer described the ordeal of the Cherokee people in 1838:

The Cherokees are nearly all prisoners. They have been dragged from their houses, and are encamped at the forts and military posts, all over the nation. In Georgia, especially, multitudes were allowed no time to take anything with them except the clothes they had on. Well-furnished houses were left a prey to plunderers, who, like hungry wolves, follow in the train of the captors. These wretches rifle the houses, and strip the helpless, unoffending owners of all they have on earth. Females, who have been habituated to comforts and comparative affluence, are driven on foot before the bayonets of brutal men. Their feelings are mortified by vulgar and profane vociferations. It is a painful sight. The property of many has been taken, and sold before their eyes for almost nothing—the sellers and buyers, in many cases, being combined to cheat the poor *Indians.* These things are done at the instant of arrest and consternation; the soldiers standing by, with their arms in hand, impatient to go on with their work, could give little time to transact business. The poor captive, in a state of distressing agitation, his weeping wife almost frantic with terror, surrounded by a group of crying, terrified children, without a friend to speak a consoling word, is in a poor condition to make a good disposition of his property and is in most cases stripped of the whole, at one blow. Many of the Cherokee, who, a few days ago were in comfortable circumstances, are now victims of abject poverty. Some, who have been allowed to return home, under passport, to inquire after their property, have found their *cattle,* horses, *swine,* farming-tools, and house furniture all gone. And this is not a description of extreme cases. It is altogether a faint representation of the work which has been perpetrated on the unoffending, unarmed and unresisting Cherokees.[52]

Ranchers, planters, and land speculators poured in to grab the most desirable lands and grazing areas—much of the land used to create pastures to raise other animals for profit—and personal empires were established on the rubble of Native American lives. Between 1840 and 1860, the number of cows in the southern states increased from almost three and a half million to more than eight million.[53] In 1860, the economic value of mules, cows, and pigs in the South "was twice that of the same year's cotton crop and roughly equal to the combined value of all Southern crops."[54] "Grazing . . . was of greater importance to the antebellum South than in any other part of the United States,"[55] and the most lucrative market was the "slave"-labor plantations of the West Indies. Much of this industry was controlled by absentee owners, and the operations frequently were staffed by enslaved humans. For planters who operated cotton and tobacco plantations in the South, cows and pigs "not only contributed to the self-sufficiency of the plantations, but sales of the animals also provided badly needed cash."[56]

While ranchers in the South could pasture animals throughout the year, the northern winters were such that domesecrated animals generally could not survive by grazing alone, and ranchers there increasingly had to provide food for cows and other animals during the colder months. Although some hay and grains were used to feed cows, corn soon came to be favored, as it yielded more per acre and also was more economically functional because it increased desirable body fat on cows.

Native Americans were pushed even farther westward by the encroachment of the ranchers and their endless appetite for land. By the 1840s, the eastern part of Kansas already contained a number of small reservations occupied by tribes that had been moved there from the Northeast. "These tribes were among the first to feel the new pressures, being forced to make new concessions"[57] as the ranching industry and related invasive ventures moved west; when they resisted, the U.S. military was set upon them. In many instances, the government promised Native Americans protected areas if they would agree to leave newly colonized regions. However, even when the government did not outright refuse to honor such agreements, swindles and fraud were used to acquire Native American lands.

> *Indian* lands were *fair game* for speculators who used both legal and illegal means to secure them. Traders and speculators devised a method by which treaties of cession would include 640-acre allotments of the choicer land to chiefs and *half-breeds*. . . . By this means most of the desirable land along the upper Wabash Valley in Indiana and other valuable tracts in Illinois, Mississippi, Alabama and Wisconsin passed into the hands of speculators including the great trading firm of W. G. & G. W. Ewing of Fort Wayne, Senator John Tipton of Indiana, and Simon Cameron of Pennsylvania.
>
> In Kansas speculator influence carried this method of land acquisition even farther. Here *Indian* tribes such as the Potawatomi (whose members had already been victimized by the Wabash traders), the Kickapoo, the Delawares, the Cherokees, and the Osage were induced to cede over 9,000,000 acres of land in trust, to be sold for their benefit. . . . Tracts were being rapidly conveyed to groups and individuals close to the Indian Office for distinctly less than their actual market value at the time.[58]

"The [Kansas] tallgrass prairie was the [base for] ranching systems of the Euro-American settlers who displaced the *Indians*."[59]

## REIGN OF THE "CATTLE" KINGS

In the Midwest, the historically elite-dominated practice of ranching continued with the "*cattle* kings." Two types of "cattle" kings presided over Indiana and Illinois in the mid-1800s. The first were large ranchers who concentrated on raising cows and pigs, which they fed local corn. As they accumulated large profits, they bought increasing amounts of land as a buffer against growing numbers of people moving into the area. The others profited, more or less directly, from the exploitation of cows and pigs and the theft of Native American land through interests in "railroads, grain elevators, or slaughterhouses or from land transactions or a law practice."[60] Many affluent families from the East were among the speculators and investors in the development of the Midwestern "cattle" culture, including alumni of Yale, whom locals referred to as the "Yale Crowd."[61]

Though newcomers came west searching for a better life, their lack of capital rendered them vulnerable to the machinations of the "cattle" kings. Large-scale ranchers and investors used tenants to cultivate their lands and to tend the cows and pigs under their control. A system of tenant farming emerged that was not unlike the feudal manorial systems of the Middle Ages, as elites erected "baronies tenanted by scores of farm operatives."[62] Tenants were used to drain wetlands and to build structures and fences, all of which increased the market value of the land. In return, they were permitted to keep a portion of the corn they raised on the ranchers' land. Typically, rancher landlords permitted tenants to keep half the corn they produced, but tenants usually sold their portion back to the ranchers. Often, "the tenant houses . . . were little more than shacks";[63] the large ranchers, by contrast, lived opulently. Paul Gates writes:

> The wealth that came to them from the *cattle* industry, rents, and sales of their holdings permitted them to live in regal grandeur on their estates, in Lafayette or in one of the smaller towns of the region. . . .
>
> They built huge mansions with Brussels carpet on the floors and decanters of port on the walnut sideboards. . . .

With these mansions and the lavish decorations, oil paintings, European and oriental bric-a-brac, and furniture that fill them from floor to garret, went a social life that was scarcely harmonious with frontier existence. High society, an aristocracy, had come to the prairies. . . .

The gulf between these aristocratic landlords and the *cow hands*, the hired laborers, and the tenants living in crude shacks was as great as that which existed between the eastern industrialists and the low-paid workers who operated their factories.[64]

As is generally true under the capitalist system, economic control was intertwined with political control.

Wealth amassed locally won for these *cattle* kings prestige and a respectful following among rural neighbors who measured success in terms of accumulation of land and *livestock*. This permitted the *cattle* kings and other large landlords to exercise political power out of all proportion to their numbers. They were found in the inner circles of the Republican and Democratic parties in which they exerted a conservative and not altogether enlightened influence. Some, affected by the respectful attention paid them by the small farmer element, wrapped themselves in the mantle of statesmanship and were elected to the state legislature, to Congress, and to the governor's chair, not always, however, to the advantage of their state or section.[65]

The control the "cattle" kings held over much of the Midwest, Indiana and Illinois in particular, "had not established democratic farm ownership but had produced a system at variance with American democratic ideals."[66]

The exploitation of tenants went hand in hand with the oppression of domesecrated animals. The practice of raising pigs to be consumed as food expanded because they could be raised cheaply, roaming woodlands searching for nuts and acorns. After this taste of freedom, however, the pigs were rounded up, fed corn to increase their size, and then driven considerable distances, in groups as large as five thousand, to be killed and dismembered. Pigs resisted this treatment. "Whenever animals were wilder than usual they were enticed into a pen, and after being caught their

eyelids were stitched. Although thus blinded, the *hogs* were able instinc-
tively to keep to the road."[67]

Cincinnati became an end destination for pigs, where they were
killed and their flesh salted, packed, and shipped east on the Ohio River
and south on the Mississippi. The enormous number of pigs killed
in Cincinnati earned it the name "Porkopolis." One contemporary
observer described the horrific violence suffered by pigs at the
slaughterhouse:

> It is a large, clean, new brick building, with extensive yards adjoin-
> ing it, filled with *hogs* from the forests and farms of Ohio, Indiana,
> and Kentucky. From these yards to the third floor of the house
> there is an inclined plane, up which a procession of the animals
> march slowly to their doom from morning until evening. . . . They
> walk to the scene of the massacre at the top of the building. . . .
> Arrived at the summit, the fifteen foremost find themselves in
> "a tight place," squeezed into a pen, in which they must remain
> standing from lack of room to lie down. There are two of these
> pens, and two "pen men"; so that the moment one pen is empty,
> there is another ready filled, and the work thus goes on without
> interruption. The fifteen animals which stand compressed, with
> their heads thrust upward, awaiting the stroke of fate, express their
> emotions in the language natural to them and the noise is great.
> The executioner, armed with a long-handled slender hammer, and
> sitting astride of the fence, gives to each of these yelling creatures
> his quietus by a blow upon the head. The pig does not fall when he
> is struck; he cannot; he only stares and becomes silent. The
> stranger who is unable to witness the execution has an awful sense
> of the progress of the fell work by the gradual cessation of the
> noise. When silence within the pen announces the surrender of its
> occupants, a door is opened, and the senseless *hogs* are laid in a row
> up an inclined plane, at the bottom of which is a long trough of
> hot water.
>
> The long room in which the *creatures* are put to death, scalded,
> and japanned presents, as may be imagined, a most horrid scene of
> massacre and blood, of steaming water and flabby, naked, quivering
> *hogs*, of men in oil-skin suits all shining with wet and grease.[68]

As commercial-ranching operations expanded on lands taken from Native Americans in the Midwest, rancher incursions in Florida contributed to another war with the Seminole people.

> As *cowmen* settled among Seminoles in northern Florida, there were the inevitable conflicts over grazing rights. In 1823, the federal government removed most Seminoles to a reservation south of what is now Ocala, and the Seminoles were forced to give up many of their *cattle*. Even this drastic move failed to reduce tensions, for Florida *cowmen* accused Seminoles of stealing *cattle* from the open range. Responding to complaints of *cowmen*, the federal government attempted to remove the Seminoles to a reservation in what is now Oklahoma, but the Seminoles resisted, touching off the Second Seminole War (1835–42). At the war's end, the federal government removed most of the surviving Seminoles and opened southern Florida to white settlement. Scrub *cattle* which had once been *property* of the Seminole Indians were incorporated into the *herds* of the Anglo-American *cowmen* who settled southern Florida after 1842.[69]

The Seminoles who remained in Florida resolved that "since the question of *cattle* and range rights had been one of the principle causes of the wars, [they] . . . vowed not to raise *cattle* again."[70]

The general historical pattern revealed so far is one in which the exploitation of large numbers of domesecrated animals—a practice largely concentrated in the hands of elites—both enabled and promoted large-scale violence and epidemic zoonotic diseases. Domesecration-related violence in North America took a somewhat different form than was seen in Eurasia, where elites cultivated vast numbers of other animals before launching aggressive incursions. The situation also differed from Mexico and Central and South America; many of the Spanish and Portuguese conquistadors there had come from Iberian ranching families, and their early quest for gold and silver prompted the rapid creation of ranching operations for military and commercial purposes.

In North America, however, in the absence of large gold and silver deposits, and because of the necessity for winter feed production and storage, the colonizers were able to build a sizable population of domesecrated animals only over time. Cows, horses, pigs, and other animals initially were exploited for the most basic provisions, permitting the invaders to establish a stable presence. European entrepreneurs and investors found more immediate sources of wealth in the export of skins taken from free-living animals, with Native Americans becoming valuable suppliers.

The earliest form of conflict between colonizers and indigenous people that domesecration produced in North America was simply a reprise of the age-old dispute between pastoralists and soil cultivators: the damage that domesecrated animals caused to croplands. Violence erupted as Native Americans resisted the destruction of their fields and increased as subsistence pastoralism led to commercial ranching operations.

Through the use of state-chartered company militias and government forces, the British and Dutch colonizers sought to protect their "stock" of domesecrated animals from attack by angry indigenous peoples, who were acting mainly in reprisal for the destruction of their crops. State support for the displacement and repression of Native Americans in the new U.S. republic was enabled by the use of horses as instruments of war, as seen in the violent repression of resistance in the Ohio territory. And, as occurred with the European invasion of Central and South America, Native American resistance in the North was weakened by epidemics of smallpox and other diseases carried by the colonizers and their domesecrated animals.

The control of large numbers of cows, pigs, sheep, horses, and other animals in North America, as in other regions and earlier times, remained in the hands of elites, who profited from supplying "meat" to developing urban centers and exporting salt-"meat" as rations for enslaved people on Caribbean plantations. As ranching operations expanded into the Midwest, regional "cattle" kings and affluent Eastern investors cultivated control and "ownership" of domesecrated animals. Much as Spanish ranchers used the capital obtained from exporting animal skins to develop mining and sugar operations run with enslaved people, some ranchers in the southern United States parlayed their profits into tobacco and cotton plantations also staffed by enslaved humans who were fed salted "meat."

As in Latin America, the vast expansion of ranching operations and the reliance on domesecrated animals as food, resources, and instruments of war promoted the development and expansion of capitalism in the United States. Enormous wealth—for an elite minority—also came through the work of nearly four million enslaved people in the United States by the mid-nineteenth century. The use of other animals on Southern plantations—as laborers, as a source for the production of salt-"meat," and as salable commodities during lean years—unquestionably made the plantation system more practical and profitable. As commercial ranching expanded, entire industries emerged to specialize in one aspect of production or another. Feed production and storage facilities, animal transport companies, fattening farms, "packinghouses," textile mills, "tanneries," and retail establishments grew in number and size. All of these businesses developed a vested interest in the maintenance and expansion of ranching. Increasingly, profits from such enterprises, especially in the production of textiles, were invested in more efficient and, frequently, mechanical methods of production, leading the way for the development of industrial capitalism. Domesecration facilitated the growth of capitalism, which in turn advanced the even greater expansion of domesecration.

The contention that domesecration made possible the "advancement of the human race" is belied by the reality of the enormous loss of life and culture of oppression that the exploitation of domesecrated animals actually facilitated in the Western Hemisphere. The historian Alfred Crosby called the population collapse of indigenous people in the Americas after the European invasion the "greatest tragedy in the history of the human species."[71] The tragedy in the Americas was in fact simply a continuation of the entangled violence, warfare, and disease that had plagued much of Eurasia (and Africa, as will be seen) for many centuries—a colossal catastrophe for humans and other animals that was enabled and promoted by domesecration.

CHAPTER FOUR

# DOMESECRATION IN THE WESTERN PLAINS

In so short a time . . . [we have] replaced the *wild* buffaloes by more numerous *herds* of *tame cattle*, and by substituting for the useless *Indian* the intelligent owners of productive farms and *cattle* ranches.
—U.S. Army General William Tecumseh Sherman

In many sections of the country, notably throughout regions dominated
by *cattle* raising interest, entries [in federal public land records] were chiefly
fictitious and fraudulent and made in bulk through concerted methods
adopted by organizations that had parceled out the country among themselves and enclosures defended by armed riders and protected against immigration and settlement by systems of espionage and intimidation.
—William A. Sparks, *Annual Report of the Commissioners of the General
Land Office*

Somebody is doing a satanic wrong.
—Reverend Adolph Berle

In 1821, James Taylor White and his family migrated from Louisiana to
the Mexican province of Texas with a small group of domesecrated cows.
Ten years later, he had three thousand cows under his control, and by
1836 he was the wealthiest person in the province. Many ranchers, like
James Taylor White, "utilized *slave cowboys* to run *cattle* and *hogs* on the
coastal prairie."[1] Near the end of his life in 1850, he controlled more than
fifty thousand acres of land and had deposits of more than $150,000 in
New Orleans banks from the sale of cows.[2] White was the first Anglo
"cattle" king in Texas, one of hundreds of U.S. migrants who expanded
ranching operations into Mexico.

Growing numbers of Anglo-American ranchers from the Midwest—in
part because of pressure from the growing numbers of agriculturalists and
in part to obtain fresh grazing areas—moved westward into Missouri. In
the South, ranchers pushed through the pine barrens of the Gulf Coast

toward Mexico, which became independent from Spain in 1821. Arriving in Mexican territory, southern ranchers set up large-scale operations in three areas, "the southeastern coastal prairies, the pine forests south of the Nacogdoches, and the prairies of northeastern Texas."[3] Mexican officials encouraged this immigration into the Texas province, as long as the foreigners pledged to become loyal Mexican citizens and pay taxes. The Mexican government gave 177 acres of land to families intending to engage in planting; those who wanted to pursue ranching, like James Taylor White, were given 4,428 acres.[4] In the early 1820s, Stephen Austin established a large colony in the Texas territory of Mexico; after six years, the colony controlled roughly 3,500 cows, and just four years later the number of cows it controlled had grown to twenty thousand.[5]

Ranchers, planters, and other expansionists in the United States coveted Mexican lands. Twice in the early nineteenth century, the U.S. government sought to purchase some of its neighbor's territory, including Texas, but Mexico was not interested. Ranchers and planters who relocated from the United States chafed at Mexican taxes and antislavery laws and openly expressed their resentment. Resolving to end Mexican control, U.S. immigrants in Texas crafted their own declaration of independence in a meeting at White's ranch, and armed resistance began in 1835.

Considerable racism helped justify and legitimate the expropriation of Mexican land. People in Mexico "were viewed largely as a despicable, inferior and subhuman race."[6] Stephen Austin stated: "A war of extermination is raging in Texas . . . a war of barbarism and of despotic principles, waged by the *mongrel* Spanish-*Indian* and *Negro* race against civilization and the Anglo-American race. . . . *Indians*, Mexicans, and renegados, all mixed together, and all the natural enemies of white *men* and civilization."[7]

Texans from the United States wrested the province from Mexico and declared the territory an independent republic in 1836. In 1845, President Polk sent U.S. officials to Mexico in a quest to purchase what is now California and New Mexico, and, not surprisingly, the Mexican government declined the offer. In the spring of 1846, the U.S. government declared Texas a state and provoked a border skirmish, resulting in the deaths of sixteen U.S. soldiers and prompting a congressional vote for war.[8] A fierce invasion of Mexico followed, and "shameful atrocities" were committed by U.S. infantry and "cavalry" forces, who robbed, raped, and killed many Mexican civilians.[9] The war's supporters pronounced the move the God-given destiny of the United States, and others bolstered existing racism by proclaiming the inferior genetic nature of people in Mexico—and, thus, the necessity for the United States to "civilize" the nation. Many in the United States, however, expressed outrage and called the invasion criminal. One period critic of the invasion noted: "The allegation that the subjugation of Mexico would be the means of enlightening the Mexicans, of improving their social state, and of increasing their happiness is but the shallow attempt to disguise unbounded greed and cupidity."[10]

Predictably, as U.S. military forces advanced on the Mexican capital, Polk ordered the occupation of California and New Mexico. Mexican ranches were confiscated, and many cows and other animals were forcibly taken. By early 1848, the U.S. government had defeated the Mexican army, and that nation was forced to give up an enormous amount of its territory—529,000 square miles, including California—for an "agreed upon" payment of $15 million. The war the United States provoked with Mexico cost 26,000 Mexican lives, and 13,000 from the United States perished. The number of domesecrated animals who died after being exploited to support the invasion is unknown. Many Mexican citizens who remained in the expropriated territory—ostensibly now U.S. citizens—were robbed and cheated of their land holdings and displaced.[11]

> As a minority in his [or her] own homeland, the Mexican American became *fair game*—an appropriate scapegoat to take the blame for lawlessness and an appropriate target for further violence. As we have seen, the Anglos drove the *Indians* out of Texas, or exterminated them. They tried to drive Mexicans out of Arizona and Texan towns. They also found means of running Mexican ranchers off their lands in Texas, New Mexico, and California and there harassed the Spanish-speaking miners.
>
> These tactics were not enough to satisfy people bent on completely subduing the Mexican Americans. After mid-century, lynching became a common outlet for anti-Mexican sentiment, justified, according to its adherents, as the only means of dealing with Mexican *banditry* [read: resistance]. The vigilance committees of California and the Texas Rangers gave lynching a semiofficial status—an aura of official support for this most lawless act. The

tragedy was that many victims were labeled as bandits and they were lynched for minor crimes they had not committed at all.[12]

During the early days of the Anglo takeover of Texas, many Spanish ranchers were forced to flee, allowing many cows to escape captivity. These domesecrated but now free-living cows became nocturnal and traveled in relatively small social groups, hiding in thickets by day and grazing and drinking from streams and rivers at night. Their highly developed sense of smell alerted them to potential dangers. When threatened, several cows would form a circle around young calves, with their heads lowered. However, like the cows who struggled for freedom in Europe and Latin America, they were hunted continuously. Free-living cows were declared by Texan authorities to be public "property," "booty" derived from the war. However, capturing the free-living cows was difficult, and those who were retaken became "sullen and died."[13] Their skin was sent to New York and Pennsylvania to be turned into "leather."

Like their European counterparts, "leather" workers in the eastern United States also suffered from the capitalists' effort to obtain wealth from the skins of other animals and the labor of exploited humans. Paid extremely low wages and forced to work long hours, "leather" workers tried to organize. However, "tannery" owners and their allies responded aggressively to defend their privilege.

Employers' associations were quick to crush unions and keep wages down. The courts rushed to the aid of the employers and prosecuted unions for "conspiracy." The press, too, denounced trade unionists as "foreign agitators" who should be "deported instantly."

In the Spring of 1836, when the *leather* workers of New York and Newark demanded higher wages, they encountered furious opposition. In April, the *leather* bosses in both cities locked out their workers. They declared they would not employ any man who was known to belong to an organization which attempted to "dictate" wages or conditions for employment. Union members, cried the employers, were infected with the "moral gangrene" of trade union principles.[14]

By the 1850s, "leather" manufacturing was the fifth largest industry in the country, and it was becoming an increasingly concentrated form of business.[15]

Some relatively affluent migrants to Texas sold or traded enslaved people in order to obtain cows. Many other migrants who came West to escape poverty faced new exploitation as ranchhands.[16] "Cowboys," who were not enslaved, primarily were low-paid, seasonal hands who worked about five months a year and were laid off after the cows were rounded up for drives. The unemployed hands rode the grub line much of the time, "drifting from ranch to ranch in hope of a free meal."[17] A few hands would be retained and given jobs around the ranch, performing the violent acts of branding and castrating calves.

> When a calf was roped *it* was dragged towards the branding irons, which were heated in a long pit. . . . At the fire, one "flanker" grabbed the calf by the head, another by *its* tail, and the calf was thrown down. The brander then stamped the animal's flank with the sizzling iron. . . .
>
> If the calf the flankers were holding down for branding was a male, the *cowboy* took the opportunity of castrating *it* with a knife. Castration or "steering," added weight to the animal and made *it* more docile. The wound caused, however, often became infected by blowfly, the worms of which would eventually cause the animal to die. . . . Another job most conveniently done at round-up time was dehorning, whereby *cattle* whose horns had become so sharp or long that they were a danger to man and cow were reduced to a stump.[18]

Such painful and traumatic treatment boosted profits, returns that could be increased further with the acquisition of more land and water.

## Expropriation of Western Lands

For ranchers in Texas, ecological damage from overgrazing was already beginning to threaten their enterprises. Like Midwestern ranchers and Eastern speculators and syndicates, Texans saw the expansion of ranching onto the Great Plains as a potential bonanza. There were, however, obstacles to this lucrative move.

> The large numbers of buffalo living on the Great Plains were "an awe-inspiring sight for all who witnessed it," indisputable proof that

the grasslands were an extraordinarily productive environment for grazers. . . .

But if *livestock* was to become the new foundation for agriculture on the High Plains, would-be settlers and ranchers had to alter the earlier landscape of the region. In particular, they had to confine or eliminate its original human and animal inhabitants.[19]

Before European incursion, the economies of Native Americans in the West were a combination of agriculture, gathering, and hunting—with limited killing of buffalo.[20] Contact with Europeans—Spanish from the south and European trappers from the east—exposed Native Americans in the West to infectious diseases, "and the prairie tribes are said to have lost more than half their population."[21]

Outside of their encounters with violent Spanish adventurers, the indigenous groups for the most part were peaceful, and "warfare among these societies was almost unknown."[22] The Apache, living closest to the Spanish colonizers, likely were the first to adapt to a culture based on the exploitation of horses, and the practice quickly spread. And, like the mounted Eurasians thousands of years before them, the Native Americans' use of horses enabled and promoted extensive violence.

The speed of diffusion was due in part to the tremendous military advantage that mounted warriors had over pedestrian peoples. The Apache began raiding neighboring tribes to drive them out of coveted areas and to acquire captives which they then sold as *slaves* to Spanish settlements in exchange for more horses. Thus a kind of chain reaction took place that led to almost universal utilization of the horse on the Great Plains by about 1750.[23]

The Spanish rate of exchange for captive Native American women twelve to twenty years of age was two horses. They were exploited sexually and forced to perform hard labor, including being made to prepare cow and buffalo skins for sale. The standard price of young boys, who were frequently used to control groups of domesecrated animals, was a horse or mule and a bridle.[24] The fates of the indigenous peoples and domesecrated animals remained closely intertwined.

With the expansion of capitalism into the Southwest in the early nineteenth century, raiding was transformed from a subsistence practice into a commercial enterprise. U.S. traders began buying cows and horses that southwestern Native Americans raided from Mexican ranches in the Texas region. Traders from Louisiana, Texas, and New Mexico were the primary buyers of domesecrated animals and their skins in this growing, market-oriented raiding system.

A portent of the treatment of Native Americans in the Western territory occurred in January 1840, when representatives of the Texas Republic met with a number of Comanche leaders to talk peace and to arrange for the release of captives taken in raids on Anglo ranches. When the Comanche leaders attending the talks indicated they did not speak for all Comanches and could not authorize the release of all captives, Texas troops attempted to take them hostage. When the Comanches tried to escape, they were fired upon, and twelve chiefs were slain. The killing of the Comanche chiefs and many in their entourage, including women and children, outraged the Comanche people. They continued to raid Anglo ranches, and to sell the animals acquired in raids at New Mexico markets, for another forty years.[25]

The raiding, warfare, and violence that accompanied the exploitation of horses and other animals in the West intensified as displaced Eastern indigenous peoples were forced westward. Competition for land and resources among growing numbers of Native Americans created inevitable conflict, and "group after group in the central plains converted from a pedestrian and agricultural to a horse-based buffalo-hunting economy and to mounted warfare."[26] Horse raiding and competition for buffalo hunting territory were primary causes of warfare among the indigenous peoples on the plains.

In the early nineteenth century, an estimated twenty-five to thirty million buffalo lived in the Western states. Increasingly, they were being used for food and resources by Native Americans. Commercial traders conveyed manufactured goods, especially guns and ammunition, in exchange for sheep, cows, horses, and buffalo skins, and Native Americans were important suppliers. The buffalos' numbers also were affected by the invasion of commercial caravans traveling the Santa Fe Trail between New Mexico and Missouri, each relying on hundreds of mules, horses, sheep, and cows for transport and as resources. The increasing presence of other animals was "destroying vegetation, polluting springs, accelerating erosion," and displacing buffalo.[27] "It is also possible that traders' *livestock* introduced anthrax, brucellosis, and other bovine diseases to the bison *herds*."[28]

Growing numbers of cows and sheep on the Great Plains led to the same types of conflicts between Native Americans and Anglos that occurred in the East in the early colonial era. And the "cavalries" of the U.S. military—which were provided rations consisting primarily of "poor quality salt or fresh *beef* or *pork*"[29]—continued the violence against Native Americans that "Mad" Anthony Wayne demonstrated in Ohio. For instance, in 1854 a cow being marched along the Oregon Trail escaped and wandered close to a Sioux village, where he was killed and eaten. A complaint was made to the army unit stationed at Fort Laramie that Native Americans had stolen the cow, and an army lieutenant "launched an impulsive punitive attack" on the Sioux village.[30] A number of U.S. soldiers were killed in the battle, and the Sioux fled the area. In retaliation a year later, General W. S. Harvey made a surprise attack on a Sioux encampment at Blue Water Creek in eastern Wyoming. Harvey's forces fired blindly into caves where numerous children and women sought refuge, and many were killed.

Increasingly, the ranchers' expropriation of land and water sources led to violent conflict. For instance, ranchers largely were responsible for the displacement of the Nez Percé peoples. In 1855, as miners and ranchers poured into their territory, the U.S. territorial governor pressured the Nez Percé to give up fifteen million acres of their Idaho homeland. In 1863, gold was discovered in the land afforded to the Native Americans by the 1855 treaty, and they were compelled to give up nearly 80 percent of their remaining territory. Ranchers flooded into the area to serve the mining centers. By the 1870s, ranchers coveted the lush Wallowa Valley in Oregon, lands inhabited by the Nez Percé led by Chief Joseph, and pressured the federal government for their removal to a reservation. Angered by their impending displacement, four young Nez Percé men killed four Anglos believed to have slain several tribe elders, forcing the entire group to flee the wrath of the U.S. military. After a valiant effort to reach Canada, the group was caught forty miles short of the border. The Nez Percé surrendered on the condition that they be returned to the designated reservation in Idaho. Instead, they were imprisoned at Fort Leavenworth, Kansas.

Shifted from place to place over the next several years, the Wallowa Nez Percés sickened and died. In 1885 the government allowed remnants of Joseph's band to return home. During the intervening years the 418 people who had surrendered with Joseph had dwindled to 268. As was typical of many tribes, more Nez Percés had died after surrendering to the Americans than had died fighting them.[31]

By the early 1860s, the Cheyenne also were being pushed from the plains. Suffering from hunger and malnutrition, they were sequestered on a barren reservation in Sand Creek, Colorado. "It was country in which they found it nearly impossible to support themselves, and they fumed as they watched American ranches and taverns spring up at every one of their traditional water holes."[32] After they attempted several raids to acquire cows and horses from government contractors and began stopping trains and demanding food, Cheyenne leaders initiated peace talks and withdrew to an encampment at a reserve established for them at Sand Creek in Colorado. However, Colonel John Chivington of the First Colorado Volunteer "Cavalry" "ordered that the Cheyennes be 'chastised severely.'"[33] "In a public speech in Denver not long before his assault on the Cheyenne, Chivington advocated the killing and scalping of all *Indians*, even infants. 'Nits make lice!' he declared."[34] At daybreak on November 29, 1864, Chivington's "cavalry" launched a surprise attack on the encampment at Sand Creek. A civilian observer's horrifying description of the murder of children, women, and men at Sand Creek in Colorado is cited by Dee Brown:

> I saw the American flag waving and saw Black Kettle tell the *Indians* to stand around the flag, and there they were huddled—men women and children. This was when we were within fifty yards of the *Indians*. I saw a white flag raised. These flags were in so conspicuous a position that they must have been seen. When the troops fired, the *Indians* ran, some of the men into their lodges, probably to get their arms . . . I think there were six hundred *Indians* in all. I think there were thirty-five braves and some old men, about sixty in all . . . the rest of the men were away from the camp, hunting . . . After the firing the braves put the *squaws* and children together, and surrounded them to protect them. I saw five *squaws* under a bank for shelter. When the troops came up to them they ran over and showed their persons to let the soldiers know they were *squaws* and begged for mercy but the soldiers shot them all. I saw one *squaw* lying on the bank whose leg had been broken by a shell; a soldier came up to her with a drawn saber; she raised her arm to protect

herself, when he struck breaking her arm; she rolled over raising her other arm, when he struck, breaking it, and then left her without killing her. There seemed to be indiscriminate slaughter of men, women and children. There were some thirty or forty *squaws* collected in a hole for protection; they sent out a little girl about six years old with a white flag on a stick; she had not proceeded but a few steps when she was shot and killed. All the *squaws* in that hole were afterwards killed, and four or five *bucks* outside. The *squaws* offered no resistance. Everyone I saw was scalped. . . . I saw one *squaw* cut open with an unborn child, as I thought, lying by her side. Captain Soule afterwards told me that such was the fact. I saw the body of White Antelope with the privates cut off, and I heard a soldier say he was going to make a tobacco pouch out of them. I saw one *squaw* whose privates had been cut out. . . . I saw a little girl about five years of age who had been hid in the sand; two soldiers discovered her, drew their pistols and shot her, and then pulled her out by the arm. I saw quite a number of infants in arms killed with their mothers.[35]

A dispute over stolen horses was the impetus for another massacre of Native Americans in Montana. In 1869, a rancher accused a young Pikuni Blackfeet warrior, Owl Child, of stealing horses. The rancher showed up at Owl Child's encampment, insulted and whipped the young warrior, and took horses that Owl Child maintained belonged to him. Afterward, Owl Child and several young friends went to the ranch, killed the rancher, and recovered the horses. On New Year's Day, 1870, U.S. General Alfred Scully met with a number of Blackfeet chiefs and demanded they hand over Owl Child and his accomplices. None of the chiefs was from the Pikuni group, and they pledged peace. Shortly thereafter, General Sheridan dispatched four "cavalry" companies under the command of Colonel E. M. Baker to find the Pikuni and "strike them hard."[36] Baker drove his companies through subzero January Montana weather and came on an encampment of Blackfeet just before dawn on January 23. As the soldiers were preparing for the attack, a scout realized the people at the encampment were not Pekuni but one of the groups of Blackfeet that had pledged peace. Upon hearing from the scout, Baker replied, "That makes no difference, one band or another of them; they are all Piegans [Pikunis] and we will attack them."[37] When the attack began, the chief of the group, running from his tent with a letter of safe passage signed by General Scully, was shot down. The rest of the group was massacred, many still in their lodges. As most of the men were out on a hunting expedition, the vast majority of those killed by Baker's "cavalry" were women, children, and the elderly.

The fates of Native Americans and the buffalo were deeply intertwined. With the coming of railroads to the Great Plains, thousands of buffalo killers poured into the region. Initially, they were killed by contractors, such as William F. Cody (Buffalo Bill), to feed exploited railroad construction crews who labored under demanding and dangerous conditions. As railroads penetrated the plains, an all-out massacre of the buffalo began.

Suddenly it became possible for market and sport hunters alike to reach the *herds* with little effort, shipping back black robes and tongues and occasionally trophy heads as the only valuable parts of the animals they killed. Sport hunters in particular enjoyed the practice of firing into the animals without ever leaving their trains. As they neared a *herd*, passengers flung open the windows of their cars, pointed their breechloaders, and fired at random into the frightened *beasts*. Dozens might die in a few minutes, and rot where they fell after the train disappeared without stopping.

Then, disastrously, in 1870 Philadelphia *tanners* perfected techniques for turning bison *hides* into a supple and attractive *leather*. The next year, all hell broke loose. Commercial hunting outfits . . . descended upon the plains in greater numbers than ever before. So great was their enthusiasm and so little their skill that three to five animals died for every robe that eventually made the rail journey back east.[38]

The commander of U.S. forces in the West, General Philip Sheridan, boasted that the hunters would eliminate "the *Indians'* commissary" and declared: "For the sake of a lasting peace, let them kill, skin, and sell until the buffalo is exterminated. Then your prairies can be covered with speckled *cattle* and the festive *cowboy*."[39] Ernest Staples Osgood writes that ranchers in Montana were awaiting the extermination of buffalo in Wyoming.

*Stockmen* were riding down from the Musselshell to look over this new empire of grass. Buffalo hunters were clearing the way for them.

"The bottoms," wrote one observer, "are literally sprinkled with the *carcasses* of dead buffalo. In many places they lie thick on the ground, fat and *meat* not yet spoiled, all murdered for their *hides* which are piled up like cordwood all along the way. . . . Probably ten thousand have been killed in this vicinity this winter (1879–1880). Slaughtering buffalo is a Government measure to subjugate the *Indians*."[40]

## THE BLOODY WESTERN BONANZA

By 1880, the annihilation of the buffalo marked the end of the substantial resistance by Native Americans living on the plains. They were forced onto reservations where "beef" rations from the government provided them enough sustenance to prevent uprisings. Thus, after tremendous violence and suffering, the Great Plains had been prepared for the expansion of ranching.

> Now the *livestock* industry was free to expand. And expand it did. As wealthy investors from the East and Europe joined the mounting *cattle* boom, the expansion became a craze—a frenzied quest for easy money that spread like wildfire through the West. Huge *herds* of Longhorns were driven from Texas to other states and even Canada. . . . In haste to get all the western ranges fully stocked, buyers began to bring large *herds* from the East to the West.[41]

Lewis Atherton noted that "virtually every Easterner with a few thousand dollars . . . wanted to enter ranching."[42] "Capitalists were crowding each other to buy the golden cow."[43] Writing in 1888 of his experiences as a rancher in western territory, Theodore Roosevelt wrote:

> The great grazing lands of the West lie in what is known as the arid belt, which stretched from British Columbia [Canada] on the north to Mexico on the south, through the middle of the United States. . . . In this arid belt . . . *stock*-raising is almost the sole industry, except in the mountain districts where there is mining. The whole region is one vast stretch of grazing country . . . . The ranching industry itself was copied from the Mexicans, of whose land and *herds* the Southwestern frontiersmen took forcible possession.[44]

U.S. Army General William Tecumseh Sherman saw the expansion of the ranching complex into the Great Plains as pivotal in the "conquest of the far West." "In so short a time," Sherman noted, "[we have] replaced the *wild* buffaloes by more numerous *herds* of *tame cattle*, and by substituting for the useless *Indian* the intelligent owners of productive farms and *cattle* ranches."[45] Western ranching offered opportunities for profit, with almost unlimited access to public lands and low labor costs, and the plains were flooded with cows and sheep. The number of cows in the Western states grew from an estimated four to five million in 1870 to 26.5 million in 1890.[46] And between 1865 and 1900, fifteen million sheep were loaded on trains bound for the East.[47] "Thus . . . the great empty rangelands, once thought to be inexhaustible, have been filled with *cattle* and other *livestock*."[48]

Like the Ohio "cattle kings," those in the business of raising and selling cows on the plains were shrewd in the use of their wealth and power, and they exerted profound influence over territorial and state government policy while extending their economic control by investing in banks and railroads. And like their predecessors from the Eurasian steppes, "*cattlemen* considered themselves superior to farmers, settlers, public employees, and other persons who labored for a regular salary."[49]

Some ranchers acquired enormous areas of land. For example, Richard King amassed for his ranching operation a total land area in Texas that was larger than the entire state of Rhode Island. Another rancher, Henry Miller, became one of the largest land owners in the United States through his control of 1.4 million acres in California, Nevada, and Oregon. Typical of the determined capitalists of the period, Miller acquired land and wealth through legal—and extralegal—machinations.

> One of the numerous tricks used by Miller in acquiring his initial holdings was to buy out one or more of the Spanish heirs to whom ownership of a grant had descended by inheritance. Ownership of this interest gave Miller a right, as a tenant in common, to range his *cattle* over the entire grant. For all practical purposes, he would soon be in complete possession of the grant and the heirs would be forced to sell out to him at his own price. The canniest of traders and a shrewd practical politician, he usually kept the local officials, particularly the county assessors, in his debt. He followed this

method of indirect bribery for years, so that his vast holdings might escape taxation.[50]

By 1860, in California alone Miller controlled three million cows and one million sheep.[51]

Ranchers formed associations to deter competitors and eastern migrants. Lawlessness prevailed, and range wars between ranchers were frequent. Like the leaders of the Eurasian nomadic pastoralist societies and the affluent ranchers in Roman history, the Western "cattle" barons and corporate ranching outfits took over desirable lands and water sources. Many ranchers were ruthless in their treatment of those who challenged their use of the land and water, and the entire profit-driven system encouraged lawless and brutal practices. Large ranching operations dominated water sources by "pretending to settle next to streams, then fencing off thousands of square miles along their length."[52] In some areas, violence erupted between former "cowhands" who were attempting to start their own operations and the more established ranching companies. "The *cattle* 'barons' refused to allow *cowboys* to purchase *cattle* of their own, . . . and no small landowners were allowed into their domain," and "areas of the west were embroiled in class warfare."[53] One particularly violent episode occurred in Johnson County, Wyoming:

> Large operators there ran thousands of head of *cattle* onto small landowners' places, tearing out fences and trampling gardens and small fields. Lynching of the small operators followed at the hands of hired assassins. When small ranchers who had been "blackballed" by the wealthy interests sold *cattle* in the rail yards at Omaha, their payments were seized by the Wyoming *Stock* Commission, the *cattle* deemed to be stolen, and the money kept by the large corporate interests.[54]

When the small ranchers created a protective association, the Eastern investors recruited mercenaries from throughout the West and transported them by railcar to the Johnson County area. After the hired gunmen killed some of the small operators and burned their homes, locals organized a siege of a ranch that was sheltering a number of the mercenaries. A U.S. military force was needed to intervene and quell the violence.

Illegal takeover of public land by ranchers was so widespread in 1883 that the commissioner of the U.S. General Land Office reported:

> At the onset of my administration I was confronted with overwhelming evidence that the public domain was being made the prey of unscrupulous speculation and the worst form of land monopoly through systematic frauds carried on and consummated under the public lands laws. In many sections of the country, notably throughout regions dominated by *cattle* raising interest, entries were chiefly fictitious and fraudulent and made in bulk through concerted methods adopted by organizations that had parceled out the country among themselves and enclosures defended by armed riders and protected against immigration and settlement by systems of espionage and intimidation.[55]

Many sheep and sheep ranchers faced violent death at the hands of "cattlemen."

> In some areas, [ranching] associations declared large tracts of rangeland to be for *cattle* only. . . . Sheep were poisoned, clubbed, and denied access to watering holes, *sheepherders* were beaten or murdered, and groups of men were hired to shoot sheep. In Oregon, the Crook County Sheep Shooters brazenly published their annual tallies in newspapers.[56]

However, the Western ranchers associations did not entirely control the press, especially in larger cities. For example, in 1892 the Denver-based *Rocky Mountain News* printed the following editorial: "When the true history of the range *cattle* business, since the first days of its conflict with the vanguard of the Western Pioneer *husbandmen*, is written, it will disclose a record of intimidation, oppression, pillage and outrage perpetuated by big *cattle* companies that will arouse the just indignation of all fair minded readers."[57]

Reflecting on the practices of nineteenth-century U.S. "cattle" barons, the historian John Upton Terrell writes, "Their historical significance is not to be found in beneficial contributions to the national welfare, for they made none. Quite to the contrary, they are worthy of note for the political corruption they engendered, for the illegal conquests they executed and for the cold-blooded murders committed."[58]

Meanwhile, as the rush to accrue oppression-based wealth proceeded, grazing lands became seriously overpopulated with cows. The widespread belief that cows could be grazed year-round in areas north of Texas and the refusal of ranchers to provide food to sustain cows in colder areas had terrible consequences. Enormous numbers of cows crowded onto insufficient rangeland were subjected to harsh winters and died from starvation or exposure. The suffering and death, made visible by the bodies of cows littering the plains, caused many observers to protest the ongoing calamities.

> Newspaper editors fretted about the rotting *carcasses* littering the countryside, wondered about who was responsible for their disposal, and openly feared for the health of the citizenry. Editors also chided *cattlemen* for their inhumane refusal to provide winter feed and shelter for the *cattle*. . . .
>
> Other bad years followed, but not often enough to force drastic changes. The winter of 1880–81 was particularly severe, both in the Far West and Great Plains. . . .
>
> Public revulsion against the inhumanity of the *cattlemen* continued to grow, and even *livestock* journals published complaints about the barbarous cruelty on public lands and asked the government to intervene and stop the practice of allowing *cattlemen* to starve hundreds of thousands of *cattle* each year. . . . [59]

In 1886, after ranchers scurried to "restock" Montana pastures, a blizzard with temperatures of 46 degrees below zero saw 70 percent of the cows in the area freeze to death. Meanwhile, in the southwest, periodic droughts led to the deaths of huge numbers of cows there, with as many as 75 percent of southwestern cows dying in the drought on 1893.

The exploitation and brutal killing of growing numbers of cows continued to be entangled with the oppression of Native Americans even after their armed resistance ended. Overcrowding and rangeland depletion caused ranchers to encroach yet again on lands promised by law as reservations.

> *Cattlemen* saved their most dastardly bag of tricks for the *Indians*. Early *cattlemen* tolerated *Indians* as long as they didn't get in the way, but the accepted belief was that "the only good *Indian* is a dead

*Indian*." . . . But as the public rangelands became crowded, *cattlemen* began to covet the unused forage on reservations—forage that was being wasted on *savages*. Soon ranchers were demanding that western congressmen reduce the size of reservations to make more land available for *cattle* grazing. In 1880, four reservations in Oregon contained 3,567,360 acres, but by 1890, these reservations were reduced to only 1,788,800 acres; similar reductions in the size of reservations took place in other western states.[60]

Still, even this expropriation of land promised to Native Americans by the U.S. government did not satisfy the insatiable drive for rangeland.

But stealing a portion of the *Indian* land failed to satisfy greedy *cattlemen*—they wanted more. As encroachment by sheep and homesteaders crowded them, the *cowboys* began to run *cattle* on reservations. *Indian* agents reported swarms of *cattle* and counted as many as 10,000 trespassing *cattle* on a single reservation, but they were helpless to stop it. On some reservations, trespassing thrived for 20 years, after which *Indian* agents reported that the native bunchgrasses had been eaten out and destroyed. Even when agents reported names of offending ranchers and numbers of trespassing *cattle* to the superiors, little was done. . . .

Because of the prevailing belief that the only good "Indians" were underground, law officers, courts, and juries refused to punish trespassers.[61]

## Growing Levels of Animal Oppression

The daily treatment of ranched animals was every bit as violent as what ranchers, hunters, and the military meted out to Native Americans, buffalo, sheep "herders," and homesteaders. "Indeed, violence towards animals . . . [was] a widespread feature of ranch economies."[62] Indifference to the experiences of other animals was a common thread that linked both farmers and ranchers.

Farmers and ranchers differ in their attitudes and values directed at some animals, but with respect to *cattle*, members of both occupations regard them as economic objects, without sentimentality or affection. The cow is there to produce calves to sell; bulls are there to service cows. *Cattle* are a saleable item, and also a form of property that can be borrowed against. Since the end of most *cattle* is the slaughterhouse, little affection comes their way; they are *herded*, not petted; they are manipulated en masse, not treated as individual animals. . . .

These utilitarian attitudes toward *livestock* are accompanied by a good deal of indifference to pain, illness, and decrepitude.[63]

The profitable exploitation of domesecrated animals not only necessitated wars on Mexico, Native Americans, and buffalo but also led to the killing, in large numbers, of any free-living animals perceived as having the potential to decrease ranchers' profits. Among these animals, the wolf was seen as the greatest threat. Those calling for the destruction of wolves included U.S. Senator John R. Kendrick of Wyoming, "a rancher himself (like many western politicians)," and Theodore Roosevelt, who claimed wolves had killed cows on his own ranch in the Dakota Territory.[64] Roosevelt referred to the wolves as "*beasts* of waste and desolation."[65]

The "perennial crusade" to exterminate wolves and other "troublesome" free-living animals of the plains, which began with guns, traps, and snares, also came to include the use of strychnine, which began as early as 1849. "One poisoned buffalo *carcass* (*bait station*) could yield thirteen wolves, fifteen coyotes, and forty skunks (and numerous other nontarget species)."[66] The violence against wolves extended to pouring kerosene into wolf dens and burning pups alive. Rancher associations and the regional governments they controlled offered bounties for wolves; those captured alive frequently were publicly tortured and sometimes set on fire. The violence done to wolves and other free-living animals on the plains reflected both a desire to stem perceived economic losses as well as more general anxieties related to the vagaries of the ranching business. Peter Coates observes:

Why did emotions run so high over wolves and other predators? Victims of hatred in the human world are often scapegoats—those blamed for taking jobs, threatening morality and spreading crime. In like-style, *stockmen* blamed *cattle* losses—which might be attributed to drought, severe weather, rustling, disease, drowning and other *natural* causes—exclusively on a wolf that might simply have been scavenging. . . . The wolf was a tangible target.[67]

Barry Lopez notes, "You couldn't control storms or *beef* prices or prevent hoof and mouth disease, but you could kill wolves."[68] By the end of the nineteenth century, wolves—like Native Americans and buffalo—largely had been removed as an obstruction to profitable ranching on the Western plains.

The oppression and violence against free-living animals and Native Americans on the plains was deeply entangled with the violence endured by the hundreds of thousands of cows and sheep who were marched to destinations in Kansas, Missouri, and even as far as New Orleans, where they were brutally killed and dismembered for profit. By the 1870s, cows and other animals were forced into railroad "*cattle* cars" and steamers for transport from the plains or the Southern ranches to the Midwestern and Eastern slaughterhouses. An 1871 report by the Massachusetts Railroad Commissioners found:

> *Cattle* trains yield the road to most others and pass hours on the sidings; the animals are without food or water and often with insufficient ventilation in summer or shelter in the winter; they are jolted off their legs and then goaded till they struggle up, for they can not be permitted to lie down. They thus arrive at their destination trampled upon, torn by each other's horns, bruised, bleeding, having in fact suffered all that animals can and live. Under the most favorable circumstances they leave the train panting, fevered and unfit to kill; under the least favorable a regular percentage of dead animals is hauled out of the car.[69]

In 1875, George T. Angell, the founder of the Massachusetts Society for the Prevention of Cruelty to Animals, documented the "reckless barbarity" toward the domesecrated animals transported from Indianola, Texas, to Eastern slaughterhouses:

> All authorities agree that the transportation of these animals is attended with great suffering to the animals from want of food, water and rest; also from overcrowding, and the crowding of smaller animals with the larger in the same cars; so many of them die in tran-

sit, many more become diseased, and on all there is a large percentage of loss of weight.

Between Indianola, Texas and New Orleans they are carried on steamers, under deck, in crowded conditions, with poor ventilation, four and five days, and sometimes more without food or water, about 40 die on the passage. . . .

Another gentleman, familiar with the Chicago *stockyards*, says that, "many animals die on the cars before reaching that point." That he had seen "about forty lying there in one pile. Cars are terribly overcrowded, and animals are carried great distances without food or water. The result is that they are taken out of Chicago with bruises and sores, and legs and horns broken; many of them dead, and more almost dead; and sometimes *cattle* and *hogs*, and sometimes *cattle* and sheep are packed in the same car, which results in the smaller animals being trampled upon by the larger."

At Chicago animals are driven, or if unable to walk taken, from the cars and fed, watered and rested for a few hours. They are then reloaded for the East in the following manner: "The men employed to drive them into the cars are armed with saplings weighing often from eight to ten pounds, with sharp spikes, or goads, at the end. They rush upon the *cattle*, yelling, swearing and punching them with these spikes often 20, 30 or forty times, taking little care to avoid the eyes. Eighteen to twenty *cattle* are thus forced into 30-feet cars, giving less then two feet space to the animals, and not unfrequently smaller animals—calves, sheep and *swine*—are crowded under them. In this way they are carried for days without food, water or possibility of lying down." And it appears, from various authorities, that this system of loading and transportation prevails over the United States, as a rule.[70]

The efforts of domesecrated animals to resist such treatment are seen in accounts of sheep jumping from the upper decks of these railway cars, forcing shippers to construct roofs to prevent their escape.[71]

By the mid-nineteenth century, Chicago had become the final destination for millions of domesecrated animals. It was able to surpass Cincinnati as the largest "packing" city during the Civil War, when government contracts for Chicago's "packing" industry led to the killing of countless cows and pigs. The slaughterhouses increased production to meet the demand for supplies to sustain the war that itself cost hundreds of thousands of human lives and thousands of horses and mules—both men and other animals thrust onto the battlefield with little or no choice. Many period writers celebrated the marvels of the Chicago slaughterhouses of the late nineteenth century, extolling their efficiency and the sheer quantity of "production." Some observers, however, considered the experiences and treatment of the cows, pigs, and horses whose lives ended in Chicago. William Cronon wrote that some who witnessed the activities of the slaughterhouse felt "appalled that the taking of animal life could have become so indifferent, so efficient, so calculating and cold blooded. The *stockyards* might be 'of vast importance and of astounding dimensions,' one such visitor admitted, but 'the whole business [is] a most unpleasant one, destitute of all semblance of picturesqueness, and tainted with cruelty and brutality.'"[72]

Rudyard Kipling was horrorstruck by what he saw at a slaughterhouse in Chicago in the late 1880s and worried "about the effect of so mechanical a killing house on the human soul."[73] But for those who built their wealth on such oppression and suffering, the plush accommodations of their hotels and trading houses distanced them from the terror and suffering of the slaughterhouse. Cronon described the contrast between the horrors of the killing floor and the luxury of the Chicago Exchange Building:

> Here, then, was the whole point of the [Chicago] *stockyard*, the ultimate meeting place of country and city, West and East, producer and consumer—of animals and their killers. Its polished wood surfaces and plush upholstery offered an odd contrast to the wet muck and noisy, fecund air in the pens just outside its doors. The Exchange Building seemed somehow at a distance from the animals in whose flesh it dealt, as if to deny the bloody consequences of the transactions that went on within it. For some, this was a sign of civilization, whereby "a repulsive and barbarizing business is lifted out of the mire, and rendered clean, easy, respectable, and pleasant." Those who handled the animals in their pens had little to do with those who bought and sold them, and vice versa. "The controlling minds"—the large traders and *meat*-packers—were thereby "let free to work the arithmetic and book-keeping of the business," undisturbed by manure or blood or the screams of the dying animals.[74]

Still, Cronon wondered if those who heard the squeals and bellows of the terrified animals "or who saw the vast industrial landscape devoted to its exploitation, could avoid wondering what it might signify about animals, death, and the proper human relationship to both."[75] Every day, thousands of other animals "mooed, squealed, bleated, or whinnied their discomfort, displeasure and sheer frustration at being *herded* and crowded into strange, noisy pens, either in the hot sun or freezing cold wind."[76] The numbers of cows whose lives ended in violent death at Chicago slaughterhouses was 1.16 million a year by 1885. By 1890, the numbers of individual sheep whose lives ended in Chicago was nearly 1.5 million.[77]

The primary leaders of the industry during this period, Philip Armour, Gustavus Swift, and Nelson Morris, "were Chicago's most formidable capitalists."[78] Like the large corporate ranching complexes in the West, huge slaughterhouse firms learned the value of eliminating smaller companies, combining to set prices and controlling all aspects of "meat" production and distribution.

> The big *packers* were joined not only through their marketing agreements, but also through joint ownership or control of hundreds of subsidiary and affiliated *packing* companies, *stockyards*, financial institutions, and other businesses. Among them they owned 91 percent of all refrigeration cars in the country and held controlling interest in most of the major *stockyards*, making it extremely difficult for the independents to compete effectively.[79]

The big Chicago slaughterhouses employed about one-eighth of the city's blue-collar laborers.[80] The treatment of employees also was designed to maximize profit, and the working conditions were hellish.

> Within the plants the atmosphere was dominated by the sight, sound, and smell of death on a monumental scale. On the *hog* killing floor, the ear was constantly assaulted by the lamentations of dying pigs. "The uproar was appalling, perilous to the ear drums; one feared there was too much sound for the room to hold—that the walls might give way or the ceiling crack. There were high squeals and low squeals, grunts and wails of agony; there would be a momentary lull, and then a fresh outburst, louder than ever, surging up to a deafening climax." In the midst of all this squealing, gears ground;

*carcasses* slammed into one another; cleavers and axes split flesh and bone; and foremen and straw bosses shouted orders in half a dozen languages.[81]

Workers were given low-skilled (*dis*)assembly-line jobs, and foremen were under pressure constantly to increase the speed of the work. High levels of unemployment in Chicago meant that on any given day anywhere from two hundred to one thousand prospective workers would line up outside the largest slaughterhouses vying to fill many fewer available jobs, resulting in depressed wages. "The packing firms exploited the divisions of sex, race, and ethnicity among the *packinghouse* workforce to inhibit formation of labor organizations."[82] People of color were given the most undesirable jobs, and women the lowest paying. The workers lived in tenements close to the plants and suffered from poverty, overcrowding, and disease, often related to the slaughterhouse "waste" that was dumped in city waterways. The tenements

typically lacked indoor plumbing and often housed several families in a few tiny rooms. During the 1880s, growing numbers of immigrant wage laborers crowded into the 2- and 3-story wood frame or brick buildings that lined dusty, unpaved streets within walking distance of the factories west of the Chicago River and surrounding the slaughterhouses just south of the city limits. Living conditions in many of the city's tenements did endanger the health of residents. Diphtheria, typhoid, cholera, smallpox, and yellow fever regularly appeared in working-class neighborhoods.[83]

Meanwhile, fortunes also were being made from the hair of sheep and the workers whose labor converted the hair into textiles. One of the most notable was William Madison Wood, the owner and president of the American "Woolen" Company. Wood's textile mills were located in Lawrence, Massachusetts, where his poorly paid employees, mostly recent immigrants to the United States, were housed in squalid housing a short walk from the factories. The tenements Wood rented to his workers were "vile beyond description."[84] As many as seventeen people lived in five rooms, and one in six children died before their first birthday; those who survived often suffered from malnourishment and rickets.[85] After visiting the area, the Reverend Adolph Berle of Tufts College declared, "Somebody is doing a satanic wrong."[86] Meanwhile, Wood—a multimillion-aire—spared no expense for his own comfort and prestige. The headquarters of the American "Woolen" Company was an architectural marvel:

> The interior was opulent: marble wainscot, oak-paneled walls, and cork floors in public corridors. There was a grand staircase inside the main entrance with inlaid marble flooring. On the lower level was an auditorium that seated 300 persons. The executive suites were almost baronial. They had baroque designs carved on the ceilings and over the doorways, the fireplaces were built with marble facings, and the chandeliers were made of hand-wrought pewter. Wood's presidential suite occupied rooms 310–312.[87]

The employees of the American "Woolen" Company and other textile and "leather" workers lived like most of the industrial workers in the United States and Europe under nineteenth-century capitalism. They suffered from malnutrition, diseases related to poor sanitation, polluted water and air, and grim housing conditions. The journalist H. L. Mencken, reflecting on the quality of life for the masses in Pittsburgh, for instance, commented:

> Here was the very heart of industrial America, the center of its most lucrative and characteristic activity, the boast and pride of the richest and grandest nation ever seen on earth—and here was a scene so dreadfully hideous, so intolerably bleak and forlorn that it reduced the whole aspiration of man to a macabre and depressing joke.[88]

While domesecrated and free-living animals, Native Americans, Mexicans and Mexican Americans, "cowboys," and slaughterhouse, "leather," and textile workers suffered interlinking oppressions, the "meat" they produced disproportionately was consumed by the affluent.[89] Well-to-do people in England, for example, had a long history of "beef"-eating, and in the eighteenth century "England was already the *beef*-eating capital of the world."[90] Aware of the opportunity to profit by purchasing land and raising cows in the western United States, British companies in the 1870s started buying vast areas of the plains; British bankers assisted in financing the development of Western railroad lines to facilitate cow transport. The historians Frink, Jackson, and Spring observed:

Ten major British-American carrel companies had been incorpo-
rated during 1882. Capitalization of the smallest, Western Land and
*Cattle*, was $575,000; that of the largest, the Matador in Texas,
$2,000,000. Total subscribed capital of these *cattle* companies was
almost $11,000,000. Approximately seventy-five percent of the sub-
scribed capital had been called-up to purchase land and *cattle* in
western America, amounting to nearly eight million dollars. When
the investments of the early English companies, the Prairie Company
and the Texas Land and *Cattle* Company by 1882 are included, the
staggering total reached $15,500,000 subscribed and ten and a quar-
ter million dollars expended within a three year period.[91]

Jeremy Rifkin writes,

> The British set up giant *cattle* companies across the plains, securing
> millions of acres of the best grasslands for the British market. While
> the West was made safe for commerce by American frontiersmen
> and the U.S. military, the region was bankrolled in part by English
> lords and lawyers, financiers, and businessmen who effectively ex-
> tended the reach of the British *beef* empire deep into the short grass
> of the Western plains.[92]

The British corporate ranchers were every bit as ruthless as their U.S.
counterparts. For example, one British-owned company operating in Nebraska and Wyoming, the Swan Land and "Cattle" Company, Ltd., "illegally ran *cattle* on *Indian* land, fenced public lands, and controlled with
force nearly every aspect of business and government in the area."[93] In
1886, an annual report of the commissioner of the U.S. General Land
Office listed ten large companies in Wyoming that had illegally enclosed
land, "among which was the Swan Land and *Cattle* Company with one
hundred and thirty miles of illegal fence."[94] To defend "their" cows, rangelands, and water supplies, companies like Swan employed hired guns, including the notorious Tom Horn, who was reported to have said, "Killing
men is my specialty. I look upon it as a business proposition, and I think I
have a corner on the market."[95] Horn eventually was hanged after he attempted to shoot a sheep rancher but killed the man's fourteen-year-old
son by mistake.

By 1886, approximately twenty million acres of land in the United States were controlled by foreign interests, mostly British "cattle" companies.[96] So much plains land was purchased by British firms that in 1887 Congress adopted a law to restrict future foreign ownership of land in U.S.-controlled territory. The act was prompted in large part by the growing sentiment in Illinois, Nebraska, Kansas, and other plains states that "the great volume of land being acquired by British *cattle* interests was dangerous for America."[97]

British financiers arranged for cows to be transported to the Midwest (where they would be fattened on grains to produce the fatty taste that privileged members of British society enjoyed) before being shipped first by rail and then by steamer to England. Cow flesh was shipped to England with the advent of refrigerated steamers beginning in the late 1870s, but many cows continued to be shipped alive to Britain during the period. In the mere four years from 1888 through 1891, more than two million cows were forced onto ships bound for across the Atlantic.[98]

A rare glimpse of the torturous existence of cows mistreated and cruelly transported on this journey was provided by Samuel Plimsoll's harrowing 1890 book *Cattle Ships*. Although Plimsoll's primary concern was for the men who staffed the ships—and who also suffered—he did address the conditions experienced by the cows. Plimsoll reported that most ships were so overloaded with cows that they were unstable and susceptible to rolling and even capsizing. The experiences of the cows, packed head to rump in order to get six cows in a space designed for three, were horrible. He writes:

> One of the men told the reporter that the sufferings of the *brutes* during a voyage were horrible to behold. A sea-sick man, he said, is one of the most pitiful things one can see, but his sufferings are nothing to those of a dumb *brute*. They will look at one so pleadingly and helplessly that you almost feel like crying for them. You have no idea how they are knocked about when a wave strikes the ship. Between overcrowding, the storms, and our sticks, the poor *beasts* have a hard enough time.[99]

The reference the witness makes to "sticks" refers to the implements used to prevent the cows from lying down at all during the journey, as they would be trampled and killed while underfoot of their cagemates. Plimsoll quotes an observer who was aboard a ship transporting both cows and human passengers:

> The signs that were witnessed on that first Sunday at sea, and the sounds of the moaning of the poor *beasts*, were so shocking as to sicken the majority of the passengers. All Sunday the *cattle*-men were busy keeping the *cattle* awake, and guarding them against lying down or going to sleep. Those that showed any indications of weakness or exhaustion were cruelly goaded with sharp-pointed bludgeons. They were beaten on the sides and heads, cold water was dashed in their faces; this failing, they were mercilessly thumped on the head with heavy, iron-bound buckets. The cords by which they were made fast to the stalls were drawn tighter, so that it was impossible for them to kneel, as *cattle* do when lying down, without inflicting upon themselves such excruciating torture that they were forced to their feet. . . .
>
> Some of the men in charge, who are paid a percentage on the number of *cattle* they bring alive into Deptford, tortured the animals most fiendishly into a semblance of animation. Their cruelty called forth a cry of horror from many of the passengers who witnessed it, and they subsequently held an indignation meeting.
>
> On several occasions I saw the men pour paraffin oil into their ears, which, as soon as it reached the brain, caused the poor *brutes* to fairly shriek with pain. Occasionally the ears were stuffed with hay, which was then fired; while in many instances the tails were snapped in the endeavors of the *cattle*-men to force animals that had laid down from sheer exhaustion to regain their feet. The commander of the vessel was appealed to, in hope that he would order a cessation of these cruel practices.
>
> "I am aware," he said, "of the cruelties practiced on *cattle* in transport from New York to London, and I will say at once that you see less of it on this line of steamers than on many of the other ships, for a very simple reason, that our steamers are better adapted for the business. I am, however, powerless to interfere in the matter. My duties are simply to carry out the instructions of my employers, the *cattle* being regarded by me as but *freight*, nothing else. The reason that these animals, no matter how horribly mutilated, sick,

or suffering, are not put out of their misery, is to be found in the imperative rules of the insurance companies, both in New York and London."[100]

Cows were forced to endure the harrowing transatlantic journey aboard the steamers because it was more profitable for them to be killed in Britain. Affluent British consumers believed cows raised and killed in Britain provided superior "beef." British butchers cut cow flesh differently than their counterparts in the United States, and refrigerated flesh (46,778 tons shipped from North America in 1889)[101] brought a lower price than that of cows killed and dismembered in Great Britain. Plimsoll wrote:

> The *beef* that is brought over alive . . . is killed and dressed by English butchers who are the best in the world, and so it fetches a higher price, as the importer and *carcass*-butchers in Deptford, Birkenhead, Glasgow, &c, all send this *meat* to market as "best Scotch," or "town killed," which means here "English."
> There is a great difference between English killing and butchering and American. The English kill the animals in a moment by a blow from a pole axe; the American puts a chain round the hind legs, just above the hocks, and then hoists the animal by machinery clear off the ground, the head, of course, being downwards.
> They then cut *its* throat and so kill *it*.[102]

Many cows perished during the terrible trip, and exporters sought to reduce their financial losses by insuring the lives of the cows. Like the ranchers and exporters, the insurance companies were interested only in profits. Plimsoll noted:

> To show how inexorable are the insurance laws on the subject, last winter the captain of a *cattle*-ship was caught in a hurricane. All the *cattle*-pens were blown overboard at once, and the animals, let loose on the deck, were thrown violently from side to side, until they lay writhing from side to side, with broken legs, backs, or horns. The ship was in immediate danger of sinking, so the captain ordered the animals to be thrown overboard. Many were dead, but neither the captain nor the head *cattle*-man could swear they were

dead. The companies, therefore, refused to pay the insurance. The exporters sued the company, and, the court deciding against the latter, they were mulcted out of six thousand pounds.[103]

Plimsoll reported that, during a seven-year period in the 1880s, an average of 434 sailors were lost at sea each year from overloaded ships.[104] The widows of the missing sailors were given only the wages the shipping companies owed their spouses up to the day the ship was last seen, and the companies that "had drowned their husbands, never dreamed of giving them the least assistance."[105] Plimsoll sadly noted that most of the wives and children of the missing sailors faced a future of grief, poverty, and destitution.

Notably, during the period when all this domesecration-generated torture and deprivation was occurring, scholars such as Blackmar and Shaler—quoted in the introduction to this book—were extolling the "social advancements" made possible through the "service rendered" by other animals.

## RANCHING IN CANADA

The expansion of ranching in North America was not limited to the United States but also moved north into Canada. When ranching arrived there, the profit-driven exploitation of domesecrated animals again promoted violence and the entangled oppression of domesecrated animals and indigenous humans—a conflict of the same type but on a smaller scale than in the United States. While the exploitation of cows, pigs, and other animals also facilitated the French and British colonization of Canada, the climate of eastern Canada was not conducive to the development of an extensive ranching industry. The colder environment would have provided less pastureland and required much more corn to feed cows and pigs, and the region was better suited to producing wheat than corn.

The smaller number of domesecrated animals meant that the displacement of Native Americans in Canada was not as extensive nor as violent as in the United States. In the Canadian east, "conflicts between *settlers* and *Indians* over land were practically nonexistent,"[106] and indigenous groups played a major role as suppliers of skin and hair of free-living animals to British and French trading companies. Similar to "warrified" Native American societies in the United States, groups such as the Blackfeet and Atsinas in Canada, supplied with horses and guns by their European trading partners, attacked their neighbors and drove them westward across the Rocky Mountains.

Racism and violence against Native Americans in Canada were most pronounced when the ranching industry from the western plains of the United States moved north into Alberta and British Columbia.[107] Initially, many of the cows exploited in these regions were used to supply western Canadian gold-mining areas. It was not until after eastern markets became available to western Canadian ranchers by railroad that they sought more territory and seized Native American land. "Not the presence of the Indians but the absence of a railroad delayed the *cattlemen's* occupation. As long as local markets remained the only outlet, the Indians were unmolested. Once railroads opened the profitable markets of the East, an obliging government reduced the reservations."[108]

As ranchers encroached on lands reserved for Native Americans and commercial hunting diminished the buffalo population, some Native Americans raided ranches to feed themselves, and violence erupted on the Canadian prairies. "Almost all losses of *cattle* were routinely attributed to 'the red men.'"[109] In 1883, an editorial in a southern Alberta newspaper stated: "These *Indians* must be kept on their reservations else the indignant *stockmen* will someday catch the red rascals and make . . . an example of them. . . . That a lot of dirty, thieving, lazy ruffians should be allowed to go where they will, carrying the latest improved weapons, when there is no *game* in the county, seems absurd."[110]

Native Americans in the northern plains of the United States and southern plains of western Canada frequently did not distinguish between the two countries' territory. The situation created anger among ranchers on both sides of the border, especially as indigenous peoples—hungry and distressed—struggled to survive:

Desperate *Indians* moved from Canada to follow the buffalo, as they traditionally had, into land now controlled by the United States. In 1880 the Weekly Record-Herald of Helena, Montana complained that Canadian Crees were selling everything they owned of value for food and that "women were prostituting themselves to save their children from starvation."[111]

Ranchers and their employees tormented and harassed Native Americans at their encampments on the Canadian plains, and vigilantes lynched indigenous people suspected of rustling. When many Native Americans, especially the Crees and Métis, fled to Montana, they were denied food or supplies by the government because they were not "U.S. Indians." Many died in the subzero temperatures and heavy snows of the winter of 1886–1887. Their ethnicity and their poverty brought vicious attacks from whites in Montana. The *Fort Benton River Press* called for the deportation of "these lazy, dirty, lousy, breech-clouted, thieving *savages*" who were "a constant source of trouble, in that they secretly kill *cattle*, fire the ranges and commit innumerable petty crimes and offenses too numerous to mention."[112]

Although Canadian ranchers blamed rustling primarily on Native Americans, white men conducted extensive raiding, including many cross-border incursions. Some rustling of horses and cows was conducted by professional gangs who "instigated a reign of terror" on the southern Canadian plains.[113]

Like their counterparts in the United States and others throughout history who profited from the control of large numbers of domesecrated animals, the ranchers on the southern plains of western Canada became both politically powerful and wealthy. "Ranch owners and professional ranch managers visited each other at the Grande Ball, the fox hunt, and meetings of the polo league, served brilliant dinners catered by their Chinese cooks, and, when financially possible, sent their children to Victoria, Montreal, or England for schooling."[114]

As ranching in North America expanded westward in the nineteenth century, large-scale violence was the inevitable result. Zoonotic diseases that killed many indigenous people, the invaders' exploitation of horses as instruments of warfare, and other animals' use as provisions of fresh and salted "meat" all helped the United States wrest by military power vast amounts of Mexican territory and force Native Americans onto reservations. And, predictably, the European introduction of horses also increased violence among Native American societies, who fought one another in raids for horses and battles for coveted buffalo-hunting regions.

The violence was promoted in most instances—as it had been for thousands of years—by the quest for land and water necessary for ranching large numbers of domesecrated animals. While profits were made from supplying "beef" to the U.S. military, Native American reservations, and mining regions, an expanding capitalist system increasingly demanded the hair, skin, and fat of other animals for the production of commodities. And, with the extension of the railroads, there were opportunities to sell more flesh from ranched animals as food. During the nineteenth century, elites protected their investments in ranching and animal-exploiting industries through the use of both political influence and hired mercenaries. Ranchers fought one another for control of land and water and, like the ancient Roman ranchers, often used both legal and extralegal measures to obtain sought-after land from others. Following the timeless pattern, ranchers in the West also battled growing numbers of people who wanted to use the land to cultivate crops. Small freeholders were targets because they not only occupied valuable grazing lands and water sources but also created obstacles for the movement of large groups of domesecrated animals.

The violent expansion of cow and sheep ranching in the West both drove and was driven by financial investments by British and American capitalists as well as by the demands of the "leather" and textile industries and Eastern slaughterhouses. The profits built on worker exploitation and cheap sources of the flesh, skin, and hair of growing numbers of domesecrated animals in the nineteenth century not only funded opulent lifestyles for elite business owners but were also reinvested to create even larger and ultimately more destructive enterprises. Companies involved in the profitable raising, fattening, transportation, and killing of domesecrated animals were growing in size and number, and their increased economic, political, and cultural influence supported and promoted enormous levels of oppression, violence, and suffering among humans and other animals alike. The wealth garnered from this domination helped to fuel the expansion of a society in which elites continued to keep control of the wealth and power of the nation.

The expansion of ranching systems in the West greatly increased the numbers of both free-living and domesecrated animals who experienced violence and death. Tens of thousands of cows and sheep forced onto the Western plains suffered and died from drought and winter storms, and many more experienced the terrible conditions of rail or ship transport before they were brutally killed. After the buffalo were almost completely exterminated, ranchers began a war against any other free-living animals they believed could reduce their profits.

The power of the state was enlisted to clear the land for this form of economic development, and racist ideologies justified the violence done to and oppression of indigenous people, Mexicans, and Mexican-Americans. Speciesist ideology was used to rationalize the killing of "*beasts* of waste and desolation" and other animals, and these deaths became increasingly profitable with the expansion of U.S. capitalism.

The exploitation of domesecrated animals obviously was not the source of all of the violence and suffering in the nineteenth-century United States. However, many of the worst practices and the most horrific conflicts and abuses were the result of capitalists seeking to maximize profits in one way or another. Women, children, and men were exploited terribly in a range of industries, from coal mining to tobacco harvesting, and the escalation of capitalism led to vast inequality; by the 1860s "the top five percent of American families owned more than half the nation's wealth, and the top ten percent owned almost three-quarters."[115] However, the exploitation of domesecrated animals was a primary factor in the most extensive violence in the United States during the period, including the terrible Civil War that devastated the nation. For example, without the availability of large numbers of mules and horses to be used as laborers and instruments of war, the conflict would have been much smaller in scale. Similarly, the exploitation of large groups of domesecrated animals as rations, whether in groups of live animals forced to follow soldiers or in the form of salted "meat" from those killed elsewhere, permitted a much longer and more extensive war. And, tragically, after the Civil War tens of thousands of freed women and men whose enslavement had depended in part on the availability of cheap rations of salted "meat" perished from an epidemic of smallpox—a disease resulting from animal oppression.[116]

Certainly, the violence against Native Americans would have been greatly reduced if there were fewer domesecrated animals, since there would have been little need to struggle for land for pasture. This observation is supported by comparing the experience of indigenous peoples in Canada and in the United States. While certainly there was prejudice and discrimination against Native Americans in Canada, the violent treatment of indigenous people there increased dramatically only with the development of ranching in the southwestern plains.

And as the violent but profitable expansion of the ranching of domesecrated animals in North America proceeded, equally deadly invasions—also promoted by capitalism and related expansions of ranching operations—were taking place in other parts of the world.

# CHAPTER FIVE

# CAPITALIST COLONIALISM
# AND RANCHING VIOLENCE

Sweet is the din of war to the *pork*-curer or *meat*-salter. It is a charmed sound to him, breathing of brisk trade and large profits. When fleets and armies are being fitted out, barrels of pickled *beef* and *pork* are required in tens of thousands.
—George Dodd, *The Food of War*

Exploration was the Empire's scout: settlement and pastoralist expansion were its bulldozers.
—Donald Denoon, Philippa Mein-Smith, and Marivic Wyndham, *A History of Australia, New Zealand, and the Pacific*

These *cattle*-farmers were seeking good lands and rivers in abundance. What made them kill each other was not so much the difference in their colour as the similarity of their ambitions.
—Robert Lacour-Gayet, *A History of South Africa*

Before the British elite began their violent and destructive colonization of distant parts of the globe, they first began closer to home. The growth of capitalism in Britain and that nation's emergence as a major world power were rooted in the expropriation of land for ranching operations and the exploitation of labor in Ireland and Scotland. The oppression of Ireland began when British "cavalry" forces, including mounted archers, led an invasion there in the twelfth century; soon after, the monarch began giving British aristocrats vast areas of expropriated lands. Although the new landlords rented out small tracts of land back to the Irish, over time they saw that greater profits were to be gained by using the land to raise cows and sheep for emerging British markets.

Ranchers in Britain, concerned by the price-lowering effects of these imports from Ireland, successfully pressed for the enactment of the seventeenth-century "Cattle" Acts that "totally prohibited the import into Britain of Irish *cattle*, sheep, *beef, butter* and *pork*."[1] Because of the "Cattle"

Acts' restrictions on access to British markets, the price of Irish salt-"beef" dropped dramatically. As a cheap and plentiful commodity, salt-"beef" became a critical factor in profitable sugar production in the Caribbean because it was an important source of food for enslaved laborers on Britain's plantations.[2] This export also became very important to the French, who used it to feed enslaved people on sugar plantations on the Caribbean islands that France had wrested away from Spain. The importance of salt-"beef"—"cheap, high protein, durable *slave* food"[3]—to the profitable use of enslaved labor is illustrated by the response to a French temporary ban on imports from Ireland in 1672. The French governor on the islands appealed to the French naval secretary: "I am daily tormented with trying to explain to you that if the prohibition on Irish *beef* continues, it is certain that the Islands couldn't be struck by a worse catastrophe, because if the *slaves* are lacking in *beef*, colonists will be lacking in *slaves*."[4] Anglo-Irish ranchers also profited by exporting salt-"beef" to sustain the crews of the navy ships necessary for Britain to establish itself as the dominant global power.

As did indigenous peoples in North America, some in Ireland who were displaced by the extension of ranching operations resisted by killing and maiming cows and sheep, a practice the British called "houghing." "Sheep and *cattle* were either killed outright or else disabled by the cutting of their hamstrings, a quick and reliable method of inflicting irreparable damage which was already well known in both Ireland and Scotland."[5] "The Archbishop of Dublin attributed these assaults to rent raises, evictions and the conversion of tillage land to grazing."[6]

By the mid-eighteenth century, Irish families already had been forced to rely heavily on potatoes as a dietary staple, as potato seeds were inexpensive and yielded relatively large amounts of food on small plots of land. However, the forced reliance on a single crop made the people vulnerable to famine.

> By all accounts, the famine of 1740–1 was the most devastating of the century, when a series of bad harvests was followed by a frost that lasted for seven weeks in late 1739 and early 1740. The frost destroyed the potato crop, leaving large sections of the Irish population without food. By the Spring of 1741 the weakened population was racked by epidemics of typhus and dysentery, which probably resulted in more deaths than starvation.[7]

An anonymous observer described the catastrophe in a 1741 pamphlet:

> Having been absent from this country some years, on my return to it
> last summer, I found it the most miserable scene of distress that I ever
> read of in history. Want and misery on every face, the rich unable to
> relieve the poor, the roads spread with dead and dying bodies; man-
> kind the color of the docks and nettles which they fed on; two or
> three, sometimes more, on a cart, going to the grave for want of bear-
> ers to carry them, and many buried only in the fields and ditches
> where they perished. The universal scarcity was followed by fluxes
> and malignant fevers, which swept on multitudes of all sorts, so that
> whole villages were laid waste. If one for every house in the kingdom
> died—and that is very probable—the loss must be upward of four
> hundred thousand souls. If only half, a loss too great for this ill-
> peopled country to bear, as they are mostly working people. When a
> stranger travels through this country, and beholds its wide, extended,
> and fertile plains, its great *flocks* of sheep and black *cattle*, and all its
> natural wealth and conveniences for tillage, manufacture, and trade,
> *he* must be astonished that such misery and want should be felt by its
> inhabitants.[8]

The people of Ireland had not yet recovered from the disaster when
they were struck by more domesecration-related adversity. Cows in Britain began to die in large numbers from an infectious disease, and elites
there were fearful the masses of people displaced by disclosure and exploited by nascent industrialists would agitate for higher wages so they
could pay for food, including the dregs of the domesecrated animal products the elites were consuming.

> There were . . . shortages and rising prices, which industrialists were
> eager to moderate for several reasons. First, they were becoming
> a major focus for working-class discontent and protest by the end of
> the 18th century and thus threatened social and economic stability.
> Second, increasing rivalry with other developing industrial nations
> in Europe compelled English factory owners to sell at competitive
> prices, which required holding down wages—a process that, in
> turn, was seen to depend to some degree on the cost of basic foods.
> It was these economic imperatives, as much as anything else, that

lay behind England's impulse to procure Scottish and Irish *meat* and, in the end, to base her own industrial growth on the relegation of these peripheral regions to an ancillary role as pastoralist food reserve.[9]

In 1758, Parliament repealed the "Cattle" Acts, removing "the embargo off Irish *cattle, meat, butter* and *cheese* at the English ports, thus partly establishing free trade in those articles between the two countries."[10]

The immediate result was that all such provisions brought such a price in England that tillage farming in Ireland became unprofitable by comparison, and every effort was accordingly made to transform arable lands into sheep-walks or grazing lands. The landlord class commenced evicting their tenants; breaking up small farms, and even seizing upon village common lands and pasture grounds all over the country with the most disastrous results to the labouring people and cottiers generally. Where a hundred families had reaped a sustenance from their small farms, or by hiring out their labour to the owners of large farms, a dozen *shepherds* now occupied their places.[11]

People in Ireland resisted British control, but land expropriation continued for decades. Between just 1820 and 1840, the number of cows exported from Ireland quadrupled, and "90 percent of the laborers previously needed for planting and harvesting had become superfluous."[12] In 1845, the potato crop on which so many exploited people in Ireland depended was struck by disease. The suffering of the native Irish turned calamitous; "most historians placed the number of those who died at over one million and those who emigrated at about two million."[13]

Without the nutritious potato, the Irish people suffered from malnutrition which reduced their body's resistance to viruses and bacteria. It is estimated that ten times as many people died from disease than from hunger during the famine years. The exact number will never be known, since whole families disappeared and thousands lie buried in unmarked graves. . . .

While the people were starving, ships filled with Irish grain and *livestock* headed to England and other markets.[14]

This tragedy for millions in fact led to more profits for ranchers and their associates, as abandoned land was converted into pasture. "Between 1846 and 1874 the number of *cattle* exported from Ireland to England more than doubled, from 202,000 to 558,000," and more than 50 percent of the land was used to raise cows.[15]

To the north, similarly, the English monarchs during the fourteenth century—again with the use of soldiers on the backs of horses—asserted control over Scotland. In the seventeenth century, British elites began replacing the subsistence agricultural economy there, first by promoting the ranching of cows. By the late eighteenth century, the capitalist industrialization of the British textile industry created demand for the hair of sheep, and English landholders in Scotland began a new round of evictions. The displacement was horrific for both humans and other animals. An eyewitness account of some of the ruthless expulsions was provided by Donald Macleod in 1841:

In former removals the tenants had been allowed to carry away . . . [house] timber to erect houses on their new allotments, but now a more summary mode was adopted: by setting fire to the houses!

The lands were now in the hands of the factor [landowner's agent] himself and were to be occupied by sheep farms—and as the people made no resistance, they expected at least some indulgence, in the way of permission to occupy their houses and other buildings till they could gradually remove and look after their growing crops.

Their consternation was therefore the greater when, immediately after the May term day, and about two months after they had received summonses of removal, a commencement was made to pull down and set fire to the houses over their heads! . . .

These proceedings were carried on with the greatest rapidity as well as with most reckless cruelty. The cries of the victims, the confusion, the despair and horror painted on the countenances of the one party, and the exulting ferocity of the other, beggar all description. . . .

Many deaths ensued from alarm, from fatigue, and cold—the people being instantly deprived of shelter and left to the mercy of the elements. Some old men took to the woods and precipices, wandering about in a state approaching to, or of, absolute insanity. Several of them in this situation lived only a few days. Pregnant women were taken with premature labor, and several children did not long survive their sufferings.[16]

Macleod gave numerous examples of atrocities and the suffering that resulted. In the follow passage, he describes the treatment of one elderly woman:

> I was present at the pulling down and burning of the house of William Chisholm . . . in which was lying his wife's mother, Margaret McKay, an old bedridden woman of near one hundred years of age— none of the family being present. I informed the persons about to set fire to the house of this circumstance, and prevailed them to wait till Mr. Sellar [the landholder] came. On his arrival I told him of the poor old woman being in a condition unfit for removal. He replied: "Damn her, the old witch; she has lived too long; let her burn." Fire was immediately set to the house, and the blankets in which she was carried were in flames before she could get out. I got my hands burnt taking out the poor old woman from amidst the flames of her once comfortable though humble dwelling. . . .
>
> When she came into the pure air, her bosom heaved to a most extraordinary degree, accompanied by a deep hollow sound from her lungs, comparable to the sound of thunder at a distance. . . . She died within five days.[17]

Macleod also described the treatment of domesecrated animals held by the displaced Highlanders when the evictions occurred:

> The poor animals, in a starving state, were continually running to and fro, and frequently could not be prevented from straying toward their former pasture grounds, especially in the night, notwithstanding the care taken to prevent it. When this occurred, they were immediately seized by the *shepherds* and impounded without food or water till trespass was paid. . . . It was nothing strange to see pinfolds of twenty or thirty yards square, filled to the entrance with horses, cows, sheep and goats, promiscuously for nights and days together, in that starving state, trampling on and goring each other. The lamentable neighing, lowing and bleating of these creatures, and the pitiful looks they cast on their *owners* when they

could recognize them, were distressing to witness—and formed an addition to the mass of suffering then prevailing.

But this was not all that beset the poor *beasts*. In some instances when they had been trespassing, they were hurried back by the pursuing *shepherds* or by their *owners*, and in running near the precipices many of them had their bones broken or dislocated, and a great number fell over the rocks into the sea, and were never seen after.

Vast numbers of sheep and many horses and other *cattle*, which escaped their keepers and strayed to their former pastures, were baited by men and dogs till they were either partially or totally destroyed, or became *meat* for their hunters. I have myself seen instances of the kind, where the animals were lying partly consumed by the dogs, though still alive, and their eyes picked out by birds of prey.[18]

Once the existing population of humans and their own domesecrated animals were cleared, growing numbers of exploited sheep were raised on the land; their hair "went to the mills of Yorkshire and Scottish *mutton* ended up in the butcher shops and markets of London."[19] While many people in Scotland and Ireland were forced to migrate to the Americas because of the appropriation of their land for ranching operations, hundreds of thousands of immigrants from other areas of Europe also were pushed out for the same reason.

The main factors pushing these people out of Europe were the spread of industrial capitalism and the commercialization of agriculture. . . . Transformation in agriculture burdened Irish and southwestern German cultivators with increased rents, mortgages, and indebtedness, and drove Scottish, English, and Scandinavian cultivators off the land to make room for sheep or *cattle*.[20]

The British pursuit of ranching in Ireland resulted in the entangled oppression of humans and other animals; their fates then were linked to those of the enslaved workers in the Caribbean who lived largely on salt-"beef," a commodity that also would become important in the control of exploited workers in Britain when rising food prices brought the threat of social unrest. The growing number of marginalized people in Britain, labeled as vagrants and criminals, was a factor in the British colonization of Australia—a continent that also held profitable ranching potential.

# British Invasion of Australia
## and New Zealand

Australia initially was valuable to the British elite as a place to send large numbers of "convicts," who were generally poor and marginalized people whose numbers were growing along with British capitalist industrialization. However, prospects for new commercial gains there soon became apparent. Australia "also had potential as a source of raw materials, as a focus for fresh avenues of investment and as a growing market for British goods. The temperate climate and the abundance of land were ideal for large-scale farming, enabling Australian-grown *wool* in particular to reduce British dependence on foreign supplies."[21]

Stuart Macintyre notes the rapid expansion of ranching operations:

> The pastoral occupation proceeded apace. During the 1820s *stockholders* moved out of the Cumberland Plain (which was now surrounded by nineteen new counties of New South Wales that extended more than 250 kilometers from Sydney), over the Blue Mountains and along the inland creeks and rivers. In the 1830s they breached the boundaries of the nineteen counties, and rapidly occupied the grasslands south of Murray, which became known as the Port Phillip District. . . . Sheep numbers on the mainland increased from 100,000 in 1820 to one million in 1830, and from 180,000 to one million on the island colony. Production of other *livestock*, especially *cattle*, and cultivation of cereals also increased rapidly but in the next two decades sheep surpassed all instruments of the European economy. They were the shocktroops of land seizure. New South Wales *flocks* numbered four million in 1840 and thirteen million in 1850. By then there were some two thousand *graziers* operating on a crescent that stretched more than 2000 kilometers from Brisbane down to Melbourne and across to Adelaide.[22]

There were problems, however, because the desired territory—as has been true of other colonial lands—already was occupied by humans and other animals. British colonizers frequently sought to expropriate grazing lands that were of importance to indigenous peoples, especially areas with fresh water. Aboriginal groups sought to defend their homelands and, increasingly deprived of food, began killing the invaders' cows and sheep. "In the selection of pastoral runs [ranches], squatters were particularly vulnerable to attacks from Aboriginal groups. From an Aboriginal point of view, if the mix of factors, such as drought and sporadic attack on sheep and *cattle*, was right, a run might be abandoned or the home station relocated."[23]

Conflict over scarce resources and attacks on domesecrated animals quickly escalated into violence, and as early as 1795 military expeditions were sent from Sydney to kill "troublesome" Aborigines—from atop the backs of horses. "Australian Aborigines' first contact with European animals was one of bewilderment and terror. . . . Aboriginal people had good cause to fear the horse. Violent massacres and vicious unprovoked attacks were conducted from *horseback*."[24]

"But, as violence escalated and European competition for land and water intensified, many Aboriginal groups moved decisively . . . to warfare, engaging in concerted guerrilla attacks on the settlers, their crops and *flocks*, huts and *herds*."[25] Just as in the Americas, many Aborigines were tortured and murdered for their attempts to defend their lands, and many others died from zoonotic diseases brought by the Europeans. Military expeditions frequently were dispatched to deal with the indigenous people, but in many cases colonizers simply took matters into their own hands. If there was resistance, if a sheep was stolen, or if indigenous people simply were "in the way," a gang would form and go hunting. Such attacks by colonizers or by government police forces usually were not publicized or recorded. How many incidents occurred and how many people were killed will never be known, but the number of victims certainly was in the tens of thousands.[26] In his work *Scars in the Landscape: A Register of Massacre Sites in Western Victoria, 1803–1859*, Ian D. Clark cites the diary of an early nineteenth-century squatter who candidly discussed "the need to massacre local Aboriginal populations when occupying their lands" for sheep runs:

> The best way [to procure a run] is to go outside and take up a new run, provided the conscience of the party is sufficiently seared to enable him without remorse to slaughter natives right and left. It is universally and distinctly understood that the chances are very small indeed of a person taking up a new run being able to maintain possession of his place and property without having recourse to such means—sometimes by wholesale . . . . (9 December 1839)[27]

A minority of the colonizers were troubled by the treatment of the indigenous peoples. In 1846, one wrote:

> The *blacks* are very quiet now, poor wretches, no wild *beast* of the forest was ever hunted down with such unsparing perseverance as they are; men, women and children are shot wherever they can be met with. Some excuse might be found for shooting the men by those who are daily getting their *cattle* speared, but what they can urge in their excuse who shoot the women and children I cannot conceive.[28]

One of the only such massacres for which British colonizers were punished occurred in 1838. Believing that indigenous people had stolen "cattle," a group of eleven Britons murdered twenty-eight Aboriginals in what was called the Myall Creek Massacre. In this rare instance, seven of the eleven British colonizers were hanged.[29] As a consequence of the Myall Creek trial, "murders of Aborigines did not so much decline as become more secret."[30] As land expropriation continued, the number of sheep alone in Australia increased to seventy million by 1900.[31] Eric Wolf notes:

> In the last quarter of the century, Australian *cattle* keeping also expanded inland. Sheep and *cattle* came to compete increasingly for vegetation and water with the kin-ordered aboriginal population. This drew aborigines and Europeans into inevitable conflicts. Some groups, like the Ngadidji and Aranda, were simply overrun by the pastoralists.[32]

The entangled nature of oppression, especially the linked violence against women and other animals, emerged in Australia as it had elsewhere. "As soon as the colonizer's eye turned to Aboriginal women, it perceived them as *chattels*."[33] The historians Denoon, Mein-Smith, and Wyndham note:

> The *black* "gin" [an European-Australian term for an Aboriginal woman], like the convict woman, was almost invariably cast as a sexual object . . . used, discarded and despised. In the predominantly male workforce of the northern maritime industries, and in pastoral areas, Europeans were known to abduct women and keep

them by force. . . . Unlike convict women, they [Aboriginal women] had no path, personal or professional, out of their plight.[34]

As with the indigenous peoples in the Americas, the effects of zoonotic diseases brought to Australia by the Europeans were disastrous for the Aborigines. The combined effect of violence and disease epidemics reduced their population, which was between half to three-quarters of a million people before colonization, to roughly fifty thousand by 1930.[35] Many who survived were relocated to missions and government settlements and reserves, where efforts were made to acculturate them to European ways—and thus to neutralize their resistance and prepare them for the exploitation of their labor.

While the experiences of the Aborigines were very similar to those of the indigenous peoples experiencing colonization and extermination in the Americas, the experiences of kangaroos, wallabies, and dingoes also paralleled in many ways those of the buffalo, wolves, prairie dogs, and other animals of the U.S. plains. Kangaroos are grazers and live in organized family groups; they have long been viewed as "pests" by ranchers, as they compete with cows and sheep for vegetation. A. J. Marshall writes of the practices of European colonizers:

The thing to do was to kill all the bigger animals on "the place." . . . And so it was understandable that the early settlers would want to kill off kangaroos. What was inexplicable was that these people savagely butchered every kangaroo on the property; and every koala, paddymellon [a small, kangaroo-like species], bilby [a rabbitlike marsupial] and bustard [large birds related to cranes] too.[36]

Kangaroos were hunted and killed so extensively that they became endangered, and several subspecies were completely lost. Dingoes were baited and poisoned in large numbers. These destructive patterns continued throughout the nineteenth century as the ranching industry, based on oppressing captive sheep and cows, exterminating and displacing indigenous people, and killing other "pest" animals, continued to profit from providing animal skin, hair, and flesh to the British market.

As ranchers penetrated deeper into the Australian interior, camels and camel "drivers" were imported from Afghanistan to transport supplies to "cattle" and sheep stations in the outback. The oppression of cows and sheep thus was profoundly entangled with the oppression of the Aborigines, of kangaroos and other animals indigenous to the area, and even of camels from thousands of miles away whose labor power was expropriated to support the enterprise.

The British invasion extended to Tasmania, an island 150 miles southeast of Australia. Colonization intensified "after 1817 when Tasmania's potential for pastoralism became apparent. A secondary invasion of colonists, sheep and *cattle* followed, quickly occupying Aboriginal hunting grounds in the central corridor between Launceston and Hobart and later river valleys and plains country adjacent to the central corridor."[37]

The Tasmanian Aborigines' defense of their homelands and their communities prompted genocidal responses from the British. The violence, combined with the effects of infectious diseases spread by the invaders, reduced the indigenous population drastically. One estimate put the population of indigenous people on the island between six and eight thousand in 1803, the time of the arrival of the British; another contemporary estimate was twenty thousand.[38] Although the exact number is unclear, it is undisputed that within a few decades the population was almost entirely annihilated. By 1830, just a few hundred remained, and arguably the last full-blooded Tasmanian Aborigine died in 1876.[39] Many other animals in the Tasmanian region also were widely hunted and killed by ranchers, including the thylacine, or Tasmanian Tiger Wolf, which is now believed to be extinct.

Surviving Aborigines, displaced from land expropriated for profitable capitalist expansion, now faced exploitation of their labor by ranchers— labor that frequently was forced and that rarely resulted in wages.

> Dispossession shaped four unofficial rules of labour relations: violence was necessary to establish who was boss; insubordination was intolerable; training for pastoralism was to be by pastoralists; and Aborigines were not free agents. They were "run down" and "broken in", as if animals, and then excluded from institutions devised by and for "free" labour. . . . "I don't know what we pioneers should have done without the *blacks*," wrote a *cattleman* in 1864, "for they can't be beat at looking after horses and *cattle*."[40]

The success of the Australian ranching industry "depended almost entirely upon the work of indigenous *cattle* workers," who were given only meager provisions of food and clothing.[41] Of the companies that took advantage of the expropriated land in Australia and the dispossessed indigenous population, Vestey Brothers was one of the most notable.

In the late nineteenth century, two brothers, William and Edmund Vestey, traveled to the United States from Britain to facilitate the sale and transport of "beef" and "dairy" products to their family's wholesale distribution business in Liverpool. The brothers founded the Union Cold Storage Company in 1897 and began building a worldwide "meat" empire. They became masters of the system of vertical integration, developing a shipping line to deliver their products to their chain of retail butcher shops in Britain, and in a short time they became one of the wealthiest families in Britain. Between 1914 and 1916, the Vesteys acquired 36,000 acres of land in Australia at pennies an acre from a business-friendly Australian administration.[42] The company built a "packing" plant in Darwin and by the 1930s had developed a highly profitable chilled "beef" export operation. On its way to becoming the largest "meat" company in the world by the mid-twentieth century, the company's exploitation of Aboriginal people's labor became notorious. For example, the Vesteys were criticized in a 1929 report by John William Bleakley on the welfare of Aborigines in the Northern Territory.

> Bleakley, a man not easily shocked by the pastoralists' treatment of aboriginal workmen—he was Protector of Aborigines in the state of Queensland, not the most enlightened state in Australia—was scathing about the Vesteys and other pastoralists. He said the accommodation provided on some stations (ranches) consisted of iron huts that were little better than dog kennels. Aged dependents of the workmen were often starving and no station manager thought it necessary to make even the most rudimentary provision for educating the *stockmen's* children, arguing that education would only make them "cunning and cheeky."[43]

Bleakley reported that "80 per cent of [Aboriginal] labour is absorbed by *cattle* stations" and that "the pastoral industry in the Territories is absolutely dependent on the *blacks* for labour, domestic and field, necessary to successfully carry on."[44] He also noted:

> One deplorable result of the semi-starvation that often exists is that the women find the temptation to supplement their meager re-

sources by trading in prostitution too strong to withstand. As practically all public roads lead through the stations, and the camps are of necessity in the vicinity, these simple women are an easy prey to passing travellers, who, at times, are low enough to cheat them by paying them with bogus money, in the way of painted coins, advertisement coupons, and worthless cheque forms.[45]

A 1946 report by researchers from Sydney University noted that conditions for indigenous peoples on Vestey ranches had not improved:

The aborigines lived in crudely-built shacks of old bagging and iron. They were rarely waterproof and would disintegrate in a strong wind. Sanitation and rubbish disposal were virtually nonexistent. There was scarcely any access to potable water. . . . The working day had no limits and depended on the inclination of the employer. Children were allocated various functions from an early age even though the government *Aboriginals Ordinance* prohibited the employment of those under twelve. The Vestey management attitude was "catch them young and train them." . . .

[The researchers] found that on some Vestey stations, the aboriginal women supplemented their rations by prostitution. . . . At one Vestey station girls as young as seven had been taken into traffic ostensibly to assist Europeans to avoid venereal disease.[46]

The researchers reported that in some areas indigenous people who tried to escape the ranch were labeled runaways and forcibly returned by the police. In 1966, an investigation by an Australian newspaper found the living conditions for indigenous people on Vestey ranches unchanged, almost forty years after Bleakley's original report.[47]

The people and other animals of New Zealand suffered a similar fate at the hands of European ranchers. The indigenous human population of New Zealand, the Maori, had shared the land and practiced communal agriculture. The first Europeans to intrude upon New Zealand sought profits from killing seals and whales—and then saw opportunities for ranching on the island. As Anglican missionaries first led the incursion onto Maori territory, the indigenous peoples believed that the agreements reached were for temporary borrowing of land, not purchases. Moreover, these sales "were made for next to nothing: seeds, a gun, a little gunpowder, a few blankets, or some musket balls sufficed to buy tracts of land measured in miles by missionaries."[48] For the European colonists who took control of the land in New Zealand, the only profitable venture was raising sheep for export to Britain. Keith Sinclair writes:

"Agriculture," as the writer of many a handbook for immigrants advised, "did not pay." Until later in the nineteenth century the only form of farming which was really profitable was to run sheep. Consequently the New Zealand frontier, like the Australian, was in most Provinces a "big man's frontier." The sheep farmer needed considerable initial capital, not to buy land, which he leased illegally from the Maoris or legally from the provincial governments, but to buy sheep, and, if he were not the original run-holder, to purchase the "goodwill" of a sheep run.[49]

In 1840, some Maori leaders agreed that New Zealand would become part of the British Empire, with the promise that their people would become British citizens and would retain all rights to their land. However, other Maori leaders resisted, as evidenced by the following statement by the Maori leader Te Kemara in 1840:

This is mine to thee, O Governor! I am not pleased towards thee. . . . I will not consent to thy remaining here in this country. If thou stayest as Governor, then perhaps, Te Kemara will be judged and condemned. Yes, indeed, and more than that—even hung by the neck. No, no, no; I shall never say yes to your staying. Were all to be on an equality, then, perhaps, Te Kemara would say, "Yes;" but for the Governor to be up and Te Kemara down—Governor high up, up, up, and Te Kemara down low, small, a worm, a crawler—No, no, no. O Governor! This is mine to thee. O Governor! My land is gone, gone, all gone. The inheritances of my ancestors, fathers, relatives, all gone, stolen, gone with the missionaries. . . . I say, go back, Governor, we do not want thee here in this country.[50]

Dom Felice Vaggioli, a Benedictine priest in New Zealand, wrote in 1896:

When it became known that New Zealand would eventually become a British colony, theft of Maori land became endemic. . . .

Statistics show that, from 1830 until the end of 1839, people acquired 12,360,000 acres. If the New Zealand Company's purchase claim of 20 million acres in 1839 were added to this figure, the combined total acquired in about ten years would be 32,360,000 acres (13,266,000 hectares). In 1840 alone it was boasted that a further 20,000,000 acres, or 9,500,000 hectares of Maori land were bought. Land grabbing by Europeans reached such a fever pitch that by the time Captain Hobson, the first Governor, arrived in 1840, purchase claims had risen to 45,976,000 acres, or 21,838,000 hectares, not including Stewart Island at the bottom of New Zealand, which was 1800 square miles, and other smaller islands. So already, half the country or nearly 72 thousand square miles had been bought. There is no other record in history of such an outrageous theft of other peoples' lands by Europeans.[51]

In the mid-1840s, the Maori rebelled against this European expropriation of their land, and battles continued until the British military finally defeated the indigenous people in the 1870s. The Maori population decreased from roughly sixty thousand to an estimated 48,000 in 1874.[52] Like displaced Aborigines, dispossessed Maori were drawn into the ranching economy; in New Zealand, they were used primarily as "shearers" and hired hands. "Pastoralists depended on Maori labour and their custom of working in kin groups which included women and children."[53] The number of sheep in New Zealand increased from 1.5 million in 1858 to thirteen million by 1881, the number of cows rose from 137,000 to seven hundred thousand,[54] and "wool" and "hides" increasingly were exported to Great Britain. Losses from declining prices for "wool" in the late nineteenth century were offset by the advent of refrigeration, which permitted the export of lamb flesh to be consumed as food, keeping sheep ranching profitable. Refrigeration equipment transformed the raising of cows from a subsistence practice in New Zealand to a profitable enterprise, with increased exports of "butter" destined for Britain. Between 1882 and 1902, the revenues from "dairy" products exported from New Zealand climbed from £7,000 to £1.4 million.[55] By 1913, twenty-four million sheep occupied New Zealand, the income acquired from their hair and flesh was £12.5 million,[56] and "half the world's *wool* supply was drawn from Australia and New Zealand."[57]

## RANCHER DOMINANCE IN LATIN AMERICA

In Latin America, the Spanish and Portuguese invasion and quest for wealth and power had led to a system in which devalued humans and other animals were oppressed on large estates to produce profitable exports. As warfare engulfed Europe in the early nineteenth century, Napoleon's takeover of Spain created a political vacuum in Latin America that sparked independence movements. Independence, however, did not bring peace, equality, or land redistribution in Latin America. "The large estate, generally operated with primitive methods and *slave* or *peon* labor, continued to dominate economic life."[58] *Caudillos*, or military strong men, (disproportionately from among the ranks of large ranchers, with their natural armies of *gauchos*, *llaneros*, *or charros*, generally counterparts to the North American "cowboy") took political and economic control in many areas. Periodic efforts at reform in many areas of Latin America, seeking changes that would benefit the majority of the population, were undermined by the political power of the large estate owners, whose "only economic concern was the export of *hides* and salted-*meat* and the import of foreign goods."[59] Masses of landless people, ill served by the first decades of independence, were a potential threat to ranching operations.

> *Cattle* raising undoubtedly contributed to the widespread vagrancy. . . . The rural *lower* classes were blocked from achieving the landholding status that defined an individual as a member of the political community. Denied ownership and social honor, the *lower* classes— many of them *mestizos*, but also *Indians*, *mulattos*, free or runaway blacks and even a few whites—were left with two alternatives: life as a settled *peon* on one of the great ranches, or vagrancy. Many chose the latter. Once a *vagrant*, an individual was a threat to landowners. He might easily become an independent rustler or bandit. . . .
>
> In a word, the *lower* classes apparently shared a mentality of resistance to oppression that gave banditry a character of social rebellion.[60]

In Central and South America, Spain's control was replaced by that of ranchers and other large landowners and middle-class merchants, who quickly shrugged off the authority of the Spanish-friendly Catholic

Church and the minimal protections for indigenous peoples the church promoted.[61] Ranching operations "exhibited broadly similar political, economic, and social patterns across a diverse geography of areas ranging from northern Mexico to portions of Argentina."[62] Ranchers from Mexico to Venezuela to Argentina in the early nineteenth century framed the problem posed by large masses of landless people as one of vagrancy and sought to control this population through their control of federal and local governments. For example, in Venezuela landed elites created antivagrancy laws that included the use of identity cards and forced military service. In northern Mexico, "workers were attached to property mainly through debt peonage, and deserters were fiercely pursued."[63]

Similarly self-serving policies were pursued in what is now Argentina by a powerful postindependence *caudillo*, Juan Manuel de Rosas of Buenos Aires, a wealthy rancher and owner of a *saladeros* who exported salt-"beef" to Brazil, Cuba and the United States, where it was used to feed *slave* populations.[64] Rosas's business success also was attributable to increasing demands for skins and tallow by the British. The killing of cows in Buenos Aires increased from seven thousand in the 1790s to 350,000 annually by 1827.[65] When Rosas became governor of the region in 1829, 538 ranchers controlled 8.6 million hectares of land—an average of 15,000 hectares each.[66]

In his policies as governor, Rosas neglected artisans and nascent manufacturers and instead favored ranchers and *saladeros* owners, providing inexpensive laborers for large ranches by procuring larger numbers of enslaved people and introducing indentured servants from Spain. Rosas also rigorously enforced laws similar to Venezuela's that required men labeled as vagrants to work on ranches or serve in the military.

Continuous violence and warfare were byproducts of the profitable ranching industry. Ranchers fought each other over land, water, and domesecrated animals, and in some areas they battled Native American groups that continued to retain control of vast areas of land. "In 1820, most of central Chile and the Argentine pampas were occupied by thousands of autonomous Araucanian and Tehuelche *Indians* who had successfully held back the frontiers of European settlement during nearly 300 years of continuous fighting."[67] As ranchers pushed farther into the vast Argentine pampas, or plains, the indigenous peoples there resisted. In the 1830s (the same decade of the deadly forced trek of the Cherokee in North America and of the massacre of Aborigines at Myall Creek in Australia),

Rosas waged a military campaign against the indigenous peoples in Argentina and sold expropriated lands to other ranchers for low prices.

Like other ranchers in Latin America, Rosas used violence against any animals he believed posed a threat to his profits. "Rosas directed his overseers to kill, while rounding up *cattle*, as many *wild* dogs and other *bichos* (lions, tigers, and skunks) as they could without disregarding their main task."[68] Other Latin American ranchers killed horses and spiked their bodies with arsenic to poison free-living animals.[69] Cougars, jaguars, wolves, and foxes all were hunted and poisoned.

While violence was directed at indigenous people and domesecrated and free-living animals, the ranching industry in Latin America also was deeply linked to the large-scale violence associated with postindependence civil, economic, and boundary wars in the region. For example, after Uruguay's independence from Spain, there was a fierce struggle over control of the land "as older estancieros [ranchers] sought to secure their possessions and newcomers contended for a share."[70] The civil war that ensued, the Guerra Grande (Big War), began in 1838 and lasted thirteen years, ending without a clear victor. With Uruguay weak and impoverished after years of war, Brazilian ranchers took the opportunity to appropriate territory there and wrested a treaty permitting the untaxed movement of cows from Uruguay to Brazilian *saladeros*.

In postindependence Brazil, the ranching of domesecrated animals remained a dominant part of the economy. "In northeastern Brazil, huge *cattle* ranches effectively colonized the frontier and concentrated immense tracts of lands into the hands of a few."[71] Such practices also dominated the southern state of Rio Grande do Sul, which colonists carved up into massive ranching estates. The plains that once were used to raise cows, mules, and horses for mines and plantations, fought over by the Spanish and Portuguese, now were even more valuable because of the growth of the trade in *charque* (dried, salted "beef"), skin, and fat. Ranching easily eclipsed agricultural exports, and "by the year of Brazilian independence [1822] the ranching complex had triumphed over agriculture."[72]

Large ranchers and their armies of *gauchos* exerted considerable political and economic influence; when the administrators of the Brazilian Empire promoted policies that were inconsistent with the interests of the ranchers, warfare ensued. For instance, between 1835 and 1845 civil war raged over the government-sanctioned importation of Argentine *charque*. The government finally conceded and resolved the conflict by imposing a

25 percent import duty on *charque* from Argentina. The decision of the Brazilian Empire to pacify the ranching interests paid off when armies of *gauchos* later defended the empire in border wars and battles with Paraguay and Argentina over land, water, and ports.

Charles Darwin provided a glimpse into the lives of domesecrated animals in Latin America during this period, in his accounts of his travels in the 1830s. Darwin writes of a drought that plagued the region from 1827 to 1830:

> While traveling through the country, I received several vivid descriptions of the effects of a late great drought; and the account of this may throw some light on the cases where vast numbers of animals of all kinds have been embedded together. . . . During this time so little rain fell that the vegetation, even to the thistles, failed; the brooks dried up, and the whole country assumed the appearance of a dusty high-road. . . . I was informed by an eyewitness that the *cattle* in *herds* of thousands rushed into the Paraná, and being exhausted by hunger they were unable to crawl up the muddy banks, and thus were drowned. . . . Without doubt several hundred thousand animals thus perished in the river.[73]

Another view of the effects of "embedding together" large numbers of domesecrated animals and the violence perpetrated against them by the dominant ranching and *saladeros* interests in Latin America was provided by the South American traveler C. B. Mansfield in the 1850s:

> I need not tell you that all the land almost, between the Andes and the Paraná-Paraguay, is one of vast plain; all the southern part of which, almost, is now sacrificed to that lowest and most degraded form of occupation, that sham of industry, the feeding and butchering of *cattle*,—a vile occupation, delighted in by master capitalists, because it yields them a return on their money with the employment of the smallest possible number of workmen,—delighted in by workmen, because their employment is a lazy one, which excites none of their faculties, except those necessary to enable them to sit on *horseback*, and to rip the *hides* off half-killed *oxen*. I should like some of your lovers of flesh to see the reeking horrors of these *saladeros* of the River Plate. Do not fancy these *Gauchos* are fine fellows

because they can ride . . . ; they care not one straw for their horses, except to use them, spur them to death, and then buy another for a song. . . .

We passed . . . the most horrible sights in the road—dead horses and *oxen* everywhere, pools of stagnant water in holes, and sometimes over the road also, where it lay rather low; these holes generally contained a *carcass* or bones, and one that was positively full of the intestines of slaughtered animals. . . . I have seen one or two *corrals* [italics in original] (as they call the enclosures into which they drive horses and *cattle* when they want to catch them) surrounded by fences made entirely of the bones which form the cores of the horns of *oxen*, and so close and thick that you cannot see light through them. Besides the waste of land (which might grow corn), the cruelty and the disgusting scenes . . . , I am annoyed at the consideration of enormous waste. . . .

A little further on we came upon a horrible scene, one of the slaughterhouses (mataderos). Fancy a square enclosure, sixty or seventy yards across, slightly sloping down to the beach; the three upper sides forming the boundaries of enclosures confining *bullocks* [castrated cows], the lower side occupied by two slaughterhouses. In the enclosure were several men on foot and *horseback*, with lassos; *beasts* were continually being driven out of the pens through doors in the sides. As fast as each came out a *horseman* threw or tried to throw a lasso over *its* horns, and then, with the assistance of the foot-lasso-men, dragged the animal to the sheds at the bottom, where in a minute or two he was deprived of his *hide*. Previously to taking off the skin, a man plunges a knife into the neck of the *creature*, so as to injure the spinal marrow and make it fall like a shot, deprived of all power of motion,—whether of feeling or not I cannot tell, neither do I think do the butchers much care. . . . I hope never to see anything so horrible again as this.[74]

Descriptions of the nineteenth-century *saladeros* and of the experiences of cows and workers are scarce. Unlike C. B. Mansfield, "most travelers kept away from the plants, concentrating on the repugnance they felt for both the operations and for the treatment of their labor force of *slaves*."[75] In the mid-nineteenth century, enslaved workers remained "important as ranch hands and as workers in the *charqueadas*."[76]

As they had in the United States and Australia, Britain's elites invested heavily in ranching and packing operations in Brazil, Argentina, Chile, and Uruguay and in the infrastructure necessary for efficient export. "In the River Plate region [of Argentina] *livestock* improved by the continued heavy import of British blooded animals, moved on British-owned railroads to British-equipped and financed plants, from which the finished product was shipped on British steamships to England, for a long time the only important market."[77]

Uruguay, after thirteen years of civil war, by 1860 had forged an economic recovery thanks in part to "strong European demand and good process for pastoral products during the Crimean War."[78] In 1861, as Brazilian ranchers occupied increasing amounts of land in Uruguay, the Uruguayan president required Brazilian ranchers to pay their share of taxes as well as duties for driving cows from Uruguay to rival *saladeros* in Brazil. Angry Brazilian ranchers in Uruguay appealed to their own government to overthrow the Uruguayan government and install a regime friendlier to their interests. In 1863, an invasion supported by Argentine and Brazilian forces (including ranchers from southern Brazil) put a new government in power in Uruguay.

In Paraguay, which had developed a system of state-operated ranches after independence, President Francisco Solano López had used the nation's revenues to build a strong military force to deter the expansionism from Brazil and Argentina. In 1864, feeling threatened after the overthrow of the government of Uruguay and seeking to stop Brazilian ranchers from occupying disputed territory between the two nations, López invaded parts of southern Brazil. He believed he had the support of a powerful Argentine rancher, general, and political leader, Justo José de Urquiza, as well as ranching elites in Uruguay. However, the Brazilian-backed government in Uruguay joined forces with Brazil against Lopez; Paraguay's potential ally in the hinterlands of Argentina, Urquiza, instead joined the war against it and became a primary supplier of provisions. The conflict, called the War of the Triple Alliance (Paraguay against the triple alliance of Brazil, Argentina, and Uruguay), lasted from 1864 to 1870. The conflict "spiraled out of control to become a total war, and one of the bloodiest international confrontations in the Western Hemisphere. Expanding beyond the ability of the combatants to manage it, the war nearly devastated all the actors, particularly Paraguay, whose people suffered horrendous casualties and privations."[79]

In Paraguay alone, roughly three quarters of the population of half a million was lost from fighting, famine, and infectious disease, and the number of adult males fell to an estimated thirty thousand.[80] "Among the greatest beneficiaries of the war with Paraguay was Urquiza: by 1869 he had amassed a personal fortune said to include 600,000 *cattle*, 500,000 sheep, 20,000 horses, and more than two million acres of land."[81]

During this period, the largest markets for South American salt-"beef" still were found "in the Caribbean area, especially Cuba, where it was chiefly used for feeding the *slave* population."[82] Meanwhile, Britain, which now dominated the economies of numerous Latin American nations, also continued to demand exports derived from ranching, in part because the "world's principal economic power could no longer feed itself and came to depend increasingly on imported food."[83] South American ranching exports were needed to supplement products from Ireland, Australia, New Zealand, and the United States and to stave off worker resistance to high food prices. One entrepreneur from Brazil, who made soap and candles by boiling the skins of cows for their oils, observed the poverty in Britain firsthand—and saw an opportunity to profit from it. Upon returning to Brazil, he began to salvage the foul residue from the candle and soap operation, sealed it in cans, and shipped it to Britain to become workers' lunches. "Such was the hunger in England . . . that even this product was used as food."[84]

In Argentina in the latter half of the nineteenth century, profits from exporting the hair of sheep to Europe surpassed those from the sale of cow skins. Sheep raising grew dramatically from 1850 to 1870, with increased demand for hair coming from the mills of Britain, France, Germany, and the United States; the number of sheep on the pampas increased from four to forty million.[85] While cows and horses were driven to slaughter areas to be killed, in many instances "*flocks* of sheep valued for their *pelts* were *herded* to the coast and driven over the cliffs to kill them before skinning."[86] Throughout this period, indigenous peoples in remote regions of the pampas and in Patagonia in southern Argentina faced deeper incursions of ranchers of sheep and cows.

Settlement by Europeans and people of European descent began in Patagonia in the mid-1860s when Welsh settlers established a colony based on sheep raising. . . . The increasingly important role of *cattle* in the economy of the Pampa in the 1860s and 1870s caused the displacement of sheep from the Pampa and provided the main reason for the settlement of Patagonia.[87]

Indigenous peoples entered into agreements with the Europeans about the land they would relinquish and the land they would retain; however, the newcomers took some of the most fertile land for grazing. Treaties provided that the Argentine government would supplement the subsistence requirements of the Native Americans by providing rations. However, the responsibility for providing the rations was given over to contractors, whose motivation was to "make as much profit out of it as possible."[88]

Lean and worthless *cattle* were furnished in quantity less than stipulated and notes were given for balance due. These notes were then discounted by the contractors or paid in other merchandise at exorbitant prices. Sometimes a contractor would weigh out 300 pounds of *yerba mate* [a traditional drink similar to tea] and charge it as a ration of 700 pounds. When the poor, bewildered *Indians* were so impoverished as to be forced to sell the *cattle* back to the contractors at much less than their original value, the contractors would reissue these same *cattle* as part of the next periodical consignment. Thus the contractors won and the *Indians* lost in every deal. Agents were appointed by the government to protect the interest of the *Indians*, but instead of giving justice, these agents frequently contrived at and even aided the contractors in extorting their illicit profits.[89]

As in North America during this same period, Native Americans in Argentina, provoked by hunger and frustration, resorted to stealing cows. The response was a genocidal campaign carried out by the Argentine army against the Native Americans from 1879–1880, a war known as the "Conquest of the Desert." The assault was led by General Julio Roca, who later would become president of Argentina. Roca commanded thousands of "cavalry" soldiers; his strategy was to terrorize and demoralize the indigenous people so they would flee the plains with no thought of returning. Thousands of indigenous people were killed, and captured women and girls were sexually assaulted and humiliated.[90] In his report on the campaign, Roca wrote, "Not a single place is left in the desert where *Indians* can now gather to threaten colonists on the Pampa. . . . It is everywhere covered with good pasturage."[91]

Reflecting on the "Conquest of the Desert" in 1972, Glyn Williams and Julia Garlant wrote:

> The native population had survived for more than twelve thousand years until the genocidal policies of the Argentine government during the last quarter of the nineteenth century all but eradicated portions of the indigenous population in Patagonia. The few native peoples that survived either were incorporated into the large haciendas as a *peasantry*, isolated on reservations and/or obliged to support their families by taking menial jobs in a variety of locations. . . .
>
> Although the end of the *Indian* wars was officially announced on February 9th, 1885 it was not the end of the hounding of the indigenous. The cruel campaign continued for many years not only through depriving the indigenous of their homeland and their dignity but also of their lives. As recently as 1910 a prize of one pound sterling was offered for each *Indian* "head or genitals" surrendered to the authorities. . . .
>
> The subsequent fifty years have been disastrous for the native population.[92]

Once the Native Americans were vanquished, land values on the plains soared. Argentine officials concluded, "On the whole the conquest of the desert, from a financial and business point of view, was an excellent investment."[93] The region was soon swimming in colonists, domesecrated animals, and investment capital.

> Argentines, as well as immigrants, including Welsh, British, Spanish, and Chilean flows, established vast sheep estancias during the last two decades of the 19th century, effectively *settling* the region. However, because sheep raising requires little labor, inhabitants were few. British landowners and investors played a critical role in providing the investment capital necessary to stock the *flocks* with improved *breeds* as well as to develop an infrastructure to ensure effective export of their products.[94]

The numbers of cows and sheep soared in Argentina and, as in the United States, the British elite invested heavily in railroads to get animal-derived products to port, especially after the development of refrigeration processes. When the ability to refrigerate railway cars was transferred to oceangoing vessels, exports of Latin American "beef" to Britain soared. By 1889, the flesh from one million cows from the pampas was sent to Britain each year.[95] The sheep population and *wool* exports also grew progressively, from 2.5 million sheep and 1,812 metric tons of *wool* in 1830 to 41 million and 65,704 tons in 1870, to 61 million sheep and 92,112 tons in 1880, and to 75 million sheep and 228,358 tons in 1901.[96]

As indigenous peoples were being killed and displaced in Argentina to make room for expanding cow and sheep ranching, with Brazil's change from a monarchy to a republic violence erupted there as ranchers and other large estate owners chafed at the new power of reformers. Civil war erupted in several states between 1893 and 1895; the worst violence occurred in rancher-controlled Rio Grande do Sul, resulting in what has been called "the single bloodiest episode in Brazilian political history."[97] Ghastly mutilations were common, and mass executions occurred.

> The degola, the *gaúcho*'s preferred form of execution . . . became commonplace. Though the degola can be performed in a variety of ways, typically the *gaucho* slaughtered his victim in much the same way he slaughtered sheep. The victim was forced to kneel with his hands tied behind him and to place his head between the legs of the executioner, who ruptured the carotid arteries in a single stroke of his knife.[98]

"By and large . . . estandieiros [Latin American estate owners] would continue to rule Rio Grande do Sul under the Republic as they had ruled it under the empire."[99] A prominent Brazilian essayist and philosopher of the period, Sílvio Romero, asserted that Rio Grande do Sul, an area larger than both Ecuador and Uruguay combined, was controlled by "semi-barbarous souls created by a pastoral system."[100]

Now that profits from cow ranching could include frozen and chilled "beef," ranching expanded further into many parts of Latin America in the late nineteenth century. In some areas, primal forests were destroyed to create pasture, including parts of southern Mexico, Guatemala, Nicaragua, Costa Rica, and Colombia.[101] In Colombia, for example, lowland forests were burned, cleared, and seeded with African grasses, which suppressed the regrowth of forest vegetation.

As "beef" production became more profitable in Latin America in the early twentieth century, the big U.S. "meatpacking" firms began investing heavily in subsidiary plants there. "From 1910 to World War I the four largest American packers controlled more than half and at times as much as two-thirds of the *beef* export trade from Argentina and Uruguay, and a partial list of foreign companies operated by the Big Five [the U.S. 'beef' trust] in 1916 totaled thirty-eight in twelve countries."[102]

British companies also continued to extract large profits from raising domesecrated animals in Latin America and processing their bodies into food and materials. The Vesteys, the brothers who already had vast holdings in Australia, acquired large ranching and processing operations in Brazil, Venezuela, Uruguay, and New Zealand, as well as in Argentina, where they were in strong competition with the U.S. firms. The Vesteys invested heavily in refrigerated storage and conducted business with rancher-controlled governments in Latin America and in Venezuela— with its rancher president, Juan Vicente Gómez.

> Gómez had become Venezuela's most successful *cattleman* by the time the Vesteys established their enterprise in Venezuela, and many of Gómez's state governors . . . became his partners in an ever-expanding *cattle* empire. Indeed, the web of business partnerships between Gómez and his political collaborators suggests that Gómez may have viewed political power primarily as a means toward a larger end, the defense and advancement of his *cattle* business (which, by all accounts, he loved much more than politics).[103]

Revolts against Gómez were unsuccessful, and he exerted enormous power over Venezuelan policy until his death in 1935, when many expected his land would be turned over to the people. Instead, however, the large ranches remained mostly in the hands of elites. A Catholic priest in Venezuela observed:

> The former critics of Gómez are the most greedy in grabbing the estates of the deceased Dictator. A very few people have been favored in the dividing up of the estates. . . . We have talked at length with hundreds of *peons* and visited their huts. It would take but few words to put in motion the great mass of discontented people. When there is hunger in the stomach there is revolt in the heart.[104]

By the early twentieth century, the legacy of the conquistadors remained strong throughout most of Latin America, where powerful, self-interested, landed elites enriched themselves at the expense of devalued humans and other animals. The capitalist-driven growth in the numbers of domesecrated animals sometimes led to a terrible and widespread loss of lives, as in 1902, when fourteen million sheep in Argentina were killed by extensive flooding.[105] In 1913, C. Reginald Enock, a British mining engineer, made the following observation regarding the treatment of domesecrated animals in the region:

> The *cattle* are not housed as in cold climates, and they bear the full brunt of the scorching sun or piercing wind. Three great scourges afflict the land at times; droughts, locusts and storms. If the rain fails death is the only escape from thirst for myriads of *beasts*; the consequence of the bringing to being great multitudes of *cattle* upon a territory where nature herself has not provided either food or water for them. The castigation of drought falls with terrible suddenness on the great pampas, and at such seasons harvests, grass, and forage fail, and if with the spring the rain does not fall, the plains are strewn with dying or rotting *cattle*—a lamentable spectacle. It is impossible to feed artificially *herds* so vast, and equally impossible to bury them when dead. The inhabitants of the *cattle* farms do not bother themselves to bury dead *cattle*, and the *carcasses* are left, to mummify under the action of the wind and sun, or to putrefy amid flies and dust. . . . Thousands of animals perish upon single estates in times of drought, and it is difficult to excuse a system which is so prodigal of animal life. . . . As regards horses, the breaking in of these is often primitively brutal in its methods, as indeed is the management of all kinds of animals in the hands of the Latin American, who is far from being a merciful man to his *beast*. The horse and the *ox* have a heavy reckoning to settle with the Spanish people. . . .
>
> At present the contrast between the luxury of the home of the wealthy *estanciero* and the primitive condition of his land, *cattle* and dependents is probably more marked than in any other land. Agricultural feudalism in the new world, from Mexico to Argentina, dies slowly.[106]

## DOMESECRATION IN AFRICA AND THE
## EUROPEAN INVASION

The practice of exploiting domesecrated animals also has had a long and violent history in Africa. The predictable competition for land and water—between nomadic pastoralist societies and between pastoralists and cultivators—led to warfare, invasions, displacement, and countless fatalities.[107] Over the centuries, nomadic pastoralists displaced and enslaved members of farming villages while warring with each other over control of territory. As in other parts of the world, pastoralists dominated and frequently enslaved communities of cultivators, and caste systems developed. From the Maasai in East Africa to the Fulani in the west to the Zulu in the south, the exploitation of cows, goats, camels, sheep, and other animals has been deeply intertwined with warfare and oppressive social systems.

While widespread invasion and considerable loss of life occurred, in some areas of Africa violence largely was more limited to raids and ambushes, as was typical of Turkana pastoralists in what is now Kenya.

> The attackers . . . would descend suddenly on their victims, capturing *livestock* and young boys and girls as quickly as possible. Men, adult women and very small children all might be speared in the confused mêlée. The raiding party would then break up into small groups, each driving away part of the captured *herds* in different directions to frustrate pursuit. Goading the animals along with spears, the individual parties might keep going for a full day and night without a pause. . . . Having covered perhaps 50 miles, the individual parties would come together at a predetermined location where the *booty* would be divided. Captive children and young women were retained by the men who seized them to be incorporated into their respective families. Some animals would be reserved for the war leader and others for a diviner if his or her advice had been solicited. The remainder were up for grabs, and the men of the raiding party would engage in an all-out brawl to lay claim to as many as possible. As soon as a man cut his clan's brand on an animal, it was considered rightfully his. Clubs, whips, and wrist-knives could be used in the fighting; only the use of spears was prohibited. . . .

In common with other East African pastoral communities, then, an outward and visual emphasis on martial affairs and trappings masked what was essentially a rudimentary military system.[108]

The exploitation and violence toward humans that stemmed from animal exploitation was compounded with invasions by Middle Eastern nomadic pastoralists. For instance, in the eleventh century a massive invasion into Africa resulted in widespread devastation. George Murdock wrote:

North Africa was plunged suddenly into an era even darker than that which engulfed Europe. The cause was a mass invasion of Bedouin nomads from central Arabia, beginning about 1045 and continuing at a decreasing rate for several centuries. These . . . invaders—who numbered, according to various estimates, anywhere from several hundred thousand to several million—poured into Egypt and spread like a swarm of locusts throughout the former Berber regions of North Africa. Illiterate nomads, intolerant alike of agriculture and urban civilization, they preempted all land suitable for grazing. . . . They converted fertile fields to pasture by destroying or neglecting the waterworks constructed by the labor of centuries. Their *flocks* devoured the natural cover of vegetation, ultimately ruining the forests . . . and by overgrazing induced erosion which converted even pasture lands to barren semi-desert. Populations, of course, withered. The vast Roman amphitheater of Thysdrus in central Tunisia, which seated 60,000 spectators, overlooks today a scene of utter desolation, and, on the coast, hamlets of a few score fishermen now occupy the sites of once flourishing cities of 100,000. . . .

Fighting indiscriminately with one another and with the settled Berbers, they infiltrated everywhere, depriving the vanquished of their independent livelihood and reducing them to the status of tributary *serfs*.[109]

There is evidence that invaders from Eurasia used horses to facilitate their African conquests, and some mounted pastoralists became settled rulers in invaded parts of West Africa. However, most indigenous pastoralist societies did not use horses, as subtropical and tropical climates and the animals' susceptibility to regional diseases made their use impractical. Many pastoralists controlled sheep, goats, and cows on foot, although in parts of northern Africa camels also were exploited as instruments of war or labor or killed for food. Like their Eurasian counterparts, wide disparities in the distribution of wealth within African nomadic pastoralist societies were the rule, and hereditary slavery was common.[110] As the demand for enslaved laborers grew, especially in the Western Hemisphere, nomadic pastoralists—such as the Fulani of the Sahel in West Africa—became an important sources of "slaves" for the transatlantic trade.[111]

As in the stratified social systems of other nomadic pastoral peoples, the role of women in Africa was undermined by the practice of exploiting large numbers of domesecrated animals. In African nomadic pastoralist societies—which, like other pastoral societies, were patriarchal, hierarchical, and stratified—a man's status was determined by the number of captive animals he controlled. Male responsibility for and control of domesecrated animals developed in part out of a need to defend against their abduction by other pastoralists; furthermore, other animals—especially cows—increasingly came to represent bridewealth.[112] Bridewealth is a payment from the groom's family (or, more rarely, the groom himself) to a girl or woman's family for the right to marry her. In exchange for the payment, the male obtained various rights over the "bride," and children resulting from the arrangement became his "property."

A glimpse of the intertwined relationship among sexism, speciesism, and human enslavement is provided by John Lewis Burckhardt's observations of nineteenth-century Sudan marketplaces where horses, camels, goats, sheep, cows, and humans all were sold, much as the Spanish traded in domesecrated animals and enslaved humans in the Americas. Burckhardt estimated that one marketplace alone annually sold five thousand enslaved humans, most being fifteen years and younger. Many of the older enslaved men were used to control domesecrated animals.[113] Some enslaved boys were castrated to make them more compliant and easier to control (as is done with male cows).[114] Burckhardt noted:

In fact [human] *slaves* are considered on the same level with any other kind of merchandise, and as such are continually passing from one merchant to another. The word Ras (*head*) is applied to them as to the *brute* species; and a man is said to possess ten Ras Raghig, or ten *head of slaves*, in the same manner as he would be said to possess fifty Ras Ghanam, or *head* of sheep. When the buyer is desired to take the *slave* away, it is usual to say, Soughe, drive him out, an expression which is applied only to *cattle*. . . .

It is falsely asserted by the caravan traders in Egypt, that it is a custom among them to respect the chastity of the handsomest female *slaves*; on the contrary, the traders do not observe the slightest decorum in their intercourse with the *slavegirls*. During our journey to Souakin, where the caravan often encamped . . . I frequently witnessed scenes of the most shameless indecency, which the traders, who were the principal actors, only laughed at. . . . When a favorite little *slave girl* died during our stay at Shendy, [her *master*] with the utmost indifference ordered the body, after stripping it of every rag . . . , to be laid on an *ass* and carried to the Nile to be thrown in. It is true, indeed, that *slaves* are very seldom buried, the corpse being usually thrown into the river.[115]

As in other parts of the world where the domesecration of animals enabled and promoted European invasions, so it was with South Africa. For example, when the Dutch East India Company colonized South Africa in the seventeenth century, they turned to pastoralism.

These crop growers became *stock-breeders*, changing their sedentary existence for a nomadic life. Why, at the cost of such great effort, should they cultivate the soil and grow produce for which they would find no market? *Cattle* now became their primary concern and since pasture-land was soon exhausted, they were constantly having to move on.[116]

Subsistence pastoralist practices pushed the Dutch colonizers, or Boers, into competition with indigenous Khoikhoi pastoralists for prime land and water. Using horses as instruments of war, the Dutch waged several wars against the Khoikhoi and their neighbors in the seventeenth century, expropriating thousands of cows and sheep and seizing for grazing lands an area roughly the size of Great Britain.[117] Many of the cows and sheep used by the Dutch "stockmen," or "*trekboeren*," were taken from the Khoikhoi. As in other regions, the Dutch invasion was facilitated by the epidemic of smallpox they had introduced, which "ravaged the Khoikhoi."[118] Some Khoikhoi people were enslaved as servants and controllers

of domesecrated animals for Dutch colonists; others, after the expropriation of their land, had to sell their labor to colonizers at low wages.

As with colonizers in other parts of the world, for the Dutch "the
major component of the frontier diet was *meat*."[119] Their practice, again
much the same as with all pastoralists, was to maintain the largest group
of domesecrated animals possible, against the possibility of drought,
disease, or attack. Increasingly, the colonists drove cows to port areas to
trade them for guns, gunpowder, and luxury items. As the numbers of
domesecrated animals controlled by the Boers increased, they began to
encroach on grazing lands long occupied by the amaXhosa pastoralists,
resulting in a series of wars beginning in 1779. Writing of both the amaX-
hosa and the Boers, the historian Robert Lacour-Gayet notes:

> These *cattle*-farmers were seeking good lands and rivers in abun-
> dance. What made them kill each other was not so much the differ-
> ence in their colour as the similarity of their ambitions. . . .
>
> Obviously, neither the Boers nor the Blacks sent trumpeters out
> to sound a declaration of war. Hostilities commenced, halted,
> resumed, slackened and accelerated without its ever being possible
> to determine whether they were spontaneous or planned. In any
> case, the cause was always the same—*cattle*.[120]

At first, the driving force behind the Europeans' acquisition of large
numbers of domesecrated animals was the need to sustain their colony.
By the late eighteenth century, however, large commercial operations
developed: "Capetown's demand for fresh *meat* was insatiable."[121] Much of
the demand came from European ships stopping in Cape Town or Simon's
Town for provisions necessary for their exploitation of India, China,
Southeast Asia, and Oceania.

The Boers' displacement of the amaXhosa from their land was reinforced by the presence of British colonizers in the region. Conflict over
land and allegations of stolen cows led to a series of wars between the
amaXhosa and the growing numbers of British colonizers, wars that
continued until the mid-nineteenth century. Perhaps upset by both the
continued British incursions and the inability of her people's elite leaders
to transform these events, a young amaXhosa woman reported in 1856
that spirits had told her that, if the amaXhosa killed all of their own cows
and destroyed their grain supplies, the amaXhosas' ancestors would re-

turn from the dead to drive out the British and restore their wealth. The amaXhosa carried out the deed, purportedly by order of the spirits—but it generally is believed that their actions were a rebellion against the wealthy leaders of their society, who controlled the vast majority of cows and thus the political power of amaXhosa society. Some four hundred thousand cows were killed, and grain supplies were destroyed, eventually causing the deaths of many amaXhosa from starvation and permitting the British to expropriate even more territory.

As the British came to gain increasing control over South Africa, many Boers migrated with their domesecrated animals into grazing lands in the Natal region of South Africa, lands controlled by a powerful group of seminomadic pastoralists, the Zulu. Before the Dutch entered the region, the Zulu had waged an expansionist war against other indigenous peoples in the region that was known as the Mfecane, a Zulu word meaning the "crushing." Thousands were killed, displaced, or forced into a Zulu confederacy, all to satisfy increasing Zulu needs for land and water for domesecrated animals.

> The agricultural system by which *cattle* had access to both sour pastures in the spring and sweet grasses in the late summer could not contain the pressures on the land. This led to intensive competition for power over land and *cattle*, and the adaption of Sotho-Tswana centralized initiation ceremonies for the recruitment of military regiments. This was the Shaka revolution that triggered off the Mfecane.[122]

A brief peace between the Zulu and the in-migrating Dutch was undercut in 1838 when a dispute over stolen cows led to war. Ultimately, with the use of horses, guns, and cannons, the colonizers defeated the Zulu in 1838, at the cost of thousands of lives, and took control of prime grazing territory.

Commercial opportunities for ranchers in the region grew in the early nineteenth century as the development of sugar plantations on the island of Mauritius in the Indian Ocean created a demand for salt-"meat" for the enslaved laborers there, and a salted-"beef" plant was constructed on Algoa Bay. By the 1860s, the discovery of gold and diamonds in South Africa created an additional commercial market for domesecrated animals, which were used both as laborers and as food.

Violence continued in the late nineteenth century, with British colonizers and Boers fighting one another over control of the region—and its gold. During this three-year conflict, known as the Second Boer War, the British confined tens of thousands of captured Afrikaner (Boer) women, children, and men in concentration camps, along with indigenous Africans they feared were sympathetic to the Afrikaners. The deprivation and suffering in the camps were appalling; by the end of the war, 28,000 Afrikaner women and children and 14,000 indigenous Africans in the camps had perished.[123] Approximately 29,000 soldiers died in the field or from disease. Of half a million horses forced into the conflict as instruments of war, 335,000 were killed; the number of mules and donkeys killed is unknown.[124] Moreover, during the war the British expropriated or killed several million cows, sheep, and horses controlled by Afrikaners and indigenous Africans so they could not be used as resources by the Afrikaners.[125]

This conflict is a prime example of how large-scale violence during the period, including warfare not driven directly by the expansion of ranching, was enabled by domesecration. British forces were supported by the importation of tens of thousands of horses from ranches in the United States—ranches established on lands expropriated from Native Americans and free-living animals. (Two notable suppliers of horses to the British were William and Malcolm Moncrieffe, the sons of a Scottish baronet who ran a large ranching operation in Wyoming, from which they shipped twenty thousand horses to South Africa beginning in 1880.)[126] In addition to using other animals as instruments of warfare, the British military relied on the use of domesecrated animals as rations. The British policy was for contractors to follow the soldiers with large groups of cows, who were killed in the field for consumption. However, this practice was hindered after rinderpest struck the South African region beginning in 1896 and the number of domesecrated cows available to the British plummeted. Moreover, British officers sought

> freedom from the filth that large *herds* following the troops involved; no disease breeding offal from slaughtering near camps; no need for forage, water, guards, butchers; and the probability that the *meat* would be better tasting than that of worn-out trek *oxen* or animals driven hard and pastured on whatever grasses were available in the day-to-day pursuit of the troops.[127]

The British solution to the shortage of domesecrated animals and the logistical difficulties in feeding soldiers in South Africa was to use refrigerated "meat" from Australia, New Zealand, and Argentina.[128] The vast oppression and death that underlay the expansion of ranching operations in other parts of the world also enabled violent conflicts such as the one in South Africa, which included the deaths of 28,000 women and children in British concentration camps.

By the late nineteenth century, elites in Europe's expanding capitalist economies widely recognized Africa as the "prize": it was where cheap resources and labor—and new markets—could be cultivated. However, powerful European nations were not anxious for disputes over African territory to result in more intra-European warfare, so a conference was convened in Berlin in 1884 to decide how to handle claims to seized African lands. While the conference did not result in an explicit partitioning of Africa, a general agreement was reached that claims to territory would be recognized internationally only if the claimed areas were effectively occupied. The incentive this created for invasion and occupation launched a capitalist "Scramble for Africa."

Germany invaded the southwest region of Africa that is now Namibia, where lands were occupied by a semipastoral society, the Herero. The invaders intended to replace the Herero pastoralists with German ranchers and turn the indigenous peoples into an exploitable workforce. The goal was stated explicitly by the head of the German Settlement Commission.

The decision to colonize in Southern Africa means nothing else than that the native tribes must withdraw from the lands on which they have pastured their *cattle* and so let the white man pasture his *cattle* on these self-same lands. If the moral rights of this standpoint are questioned, the answer is that for people of the cultural standard of the South African natives, the loss of their free natural *barbarism* and the development of a class of workers in the service of and dependent on whites is above all a law of survival of the highest order.[129]

In a 1904 rebellion, the Herero resisted domination and expropriation of their land; Germany responded by killing some 63,000 Herero, roughly three-quarters of the population. The German colonizers' killing of the Herero is regarded by many as the first act of human genocide in the twentieth century. The Herero's cows and other animals were seized, their land was divided into large ranches, and a brutal system of forced labor was imposed on the human survivors. Germany made it unlawful for indigenous peoples in the territory to own land or animals, and they were compelled "to labour at whatever job their colonial *masters* allotted to them."[130]

When the French invaded West Africa, they also encountered resistance, especially from the Tuareg society of nomadic pastoralists. The French killed thousands of Taureg people and cemented their domination by imposing an animal tax. "These taxes had to be paid in cash, and one of their express purposes was to oblige subsistence producers to produce more for market."[131] Because of the need to pay the taxes, pastoralists worked to increase the numbers of domesecrated animals they controlled and then sold the animals to large, European-owned ranching operations based in northern Nigeria. The area came to be a "vital source" of the skin and flesh of domesecrated animals.[132] There were hopes that the French control of Algeria, a colonization and domination based on genocidal practices that took hundreds of thousands of lives, would provide the source for almost all of France's frozen "meat." Writing in 1918, the journalist William Harper Dean lamented the economic problems associated with transporting domesecrated animals alive from the region:

> For more than forty years Algerian *cattle* and sheep have been crowded alive on vessels, losing weight and dying on their way to Marseilles. . . . Of course this system, or lack of one, has been expensive. Live animals take up more room than dressed *carcasses* under refrigeration. And this runs up freight charges. The French are trying to set up in the most promising *livestock* producing colonies enough slaughterhouses and refrigerating plants to encourage increased production. . . . Algeria alone could take care of all France's demand for frozen *beef, mutton* and *pork*.[133]

The market-driven production and sale of cows resulted in increased conflict over land and water between pastoralists and subsistence farmers. Environmental damage increased as many pastoralists overgrazed animals around base wells; others expanded into the Sahel, including areas that had not recovered from earlier periods of grazing. With their growing dependence on the market for cash and necessities, pastoralists were badly affected by market fluctuations. The market surplus of domese-crated anmals during droughts reduced the cash available to purchase grain, which rose in cost during times of reduced rainfall. During such periods, many domesecrated animals suffered and died from a lack of food and water, and pastoralists faced famine. Over time, the Tuareg were re-placed by "highly capitalized ranches, where jobs were only offered to a few of the former nomadic pastoralists."[134]

In the late nineteenth century, the British, already firmly entrenched in South Africa, invaded the eastern African region that is now Kenya and waged war with the Maasai, the Turkana, and other seminomadic pastoralist societies. For centuries, the Maasai had been a united people whose own militant expansionist practices had wreaked havoc on all the peoples in their path. By the time of the British incursions, however, the Maasai were weak from the effects of drought and civil war.

> The Maasai wars of the mid-nineteenth century affected the his-tory of a wide area of the north-eastern interior of East Africa throughout the second half of the century. This was because the long series of civil wars ultimately weakened the Maasai whose con-trol of the Uasin Gishu plateau had been a major factor in the dis-tribution of power in the region.
>
> The wars were caused basically by conflicts arising from the competition to control *cattle* and pasture land, both of which were considered important to the Maasai *cattle* culture or pastoral way of life.[135]

In 1904 and again in 1911, the British found questionable Maasai lead-ers who signed treaties giving away the rights to much of the Maasai's lands, consigning the Maasai to reserves in southern Kenya. As Britain expanded its control in the region, conflict developed between the Tur-kana and the colonizers, especially ranchers. Turkana losses were terrible; between 1897 and the early 1920s, hundreds of thousands of captive ani-mals were expropriated and about five thousand humans, 14 percent of the Turkana population, lost their lives.[136]

Much of the expropriated land became the basis for vast British ranch-ing operations, whose exports of "beef" and "dairy" products went to both Europe and Asia. One of the ranchers who acquired land in Kenya was Hugh Cholmondeley, who bore the aristocratic title Lord Delamere. He was given a ninety-nine-year lease on one hundred thousand acres, which he named Equator Ranch, and he later acquired another two-hundred-thousand-acre ranch. Delamere was instrumental in creating the Kenya Cooperative Creameries, an organization of European colonizers that prevented Africans from selling cows' milk without the approval of the cooperative.

Maasai peoples further south in the Tanganyika region, which is now Tanzania, were beset in the 1880s by German colonizers, who forced the southern Maasai onto reserves. The German East African Company established extensive ranching operations in the region, and animal skins and flesh were a principal export by the turn of the century. The brothers Adolph and Friedrich Siedentopf started a large ranch with two thousand domesecrated animals acquired from the Maasai through four years of "hunting wildebeests and trading their tails (for use as fly whisks) with the Maasai in exchange for *cattle*."[137] The brothers financed the construction of their ranch by killing elephants and selling their ivory tusks. Adolph Siedentopf built a canning factory and began exporting "delicacies" such as buffalo and wildebeest tongues to Germany.

Predictably, the development of European ranching operations in Africa had disastrous consequences for the free-living animals there. Incalculable numbers were ruthlessly killed because they were viewed as a threat to the maximization of profits for ranchers. Antelope were killed in large numbers because they were grazers and thus "competed" with cows and sheep. Other grazers, such as the bluebuck (a subspecies of the antelope) and the quagga (a subspecies of zebra), were hunted into extinction. Animals regarded as predators of ranched animals were hunted, trapped, and poisoned in large numbers. Lions usually were the first to be cleared out, because of their inclination to hunt in the daytime near fresh sources of water. Hyenas, jackals, leopards, baboons, caracals, wild cats, and free-living dogs also were killed in large numbers, either by being shot or by being caught in baited spring traps.

In the Western Cape region of South Africa, hunt clubs and poison clubs proliferated, and for years there were "Wild Animal Poisoning Congresses." Local governments put bounties on the lives of these free-living animals and paid out rewards when their skins were presented. In the early twentieth century, organized hunting groups were authorized to "enter private property without consent of the owner if they had reasonable grounds to believe that *vermin* may be breeding."[138] Landowners were required to kill targeted animals on their property and could be fined if hunting groups found any designated animals there. In Kenya, the British rancher Lord Delamere, an ardent recreational hunter before he embarked on his ranching career, "would use his old safari skills to cut down on the toll of *predators*. Often his guests, anxious to bag a lion, would do the job for him."[139] The Siedentopf brothers also sought to exterminate any free-living animals in the region they believed threatened their enterprise and "hunted the lion population unmercifully in defense of their *livestock*."[140] The recreational killing of free-living animals, which became widespread across Africa, also generated profits for ranchers.

> When Delamere and other Kenya *pioneers* needed recreation or cash, they either went on safari or went to Nairobi. Ivory, lion skins and clients were profitable, and a safari was merely an extension of their normal life on farm or ranch. They would no more be without a gun than without their boots, and it was a natural step from shooting lion to protect one's *cattle* to hunting lion with well-paying clients.[141]

Many ranchers cashed in on the interest of tourists from Europe and the United States in recreational hunting. Friedrich Siedentopf established the East African Hunting Bureau to promote safari hunting of lions, buffalo, rhinoceros, and elephant. While countless animals died at the hands of recreational hunters, others were the victims of European and U.S. "specimen" hunters. One of these hunters wrote a book in 1850 detailing his exploits—totaling nearly five hundred pages. He recounts, for example, how he killed a lion at a watering hole.

> I had not an instant to lose; he stood with his right side exposed to me in a very slanting position, and, taking him rather low, I fired; the ball took effect, and the lion sank to the shot. All was still as death for many seconds, when he uttered a deep growl, and slowly gaining his feet, limped toward the cover, where he halted, roaring mournfully, as if dying. . . . [I] rode to the spot where I had last heard him roar, when I had the immense satisfaction of beholding the magnificent old lion stretched out before me.

The ball had entered his belly a little in front of his flank, and traversed the length and breath of the body, crippling him in the opposite shoulder. No description could give a correct idea of the surpassing beauty of this most magnificent animal, as he lay still and warm before me. I lighted a fire and gazed with delight upon his lovely black mane, his massive arms, his sharp yellow nails, his hard and terrible head, his immense and powerful teeth, his perfect beauty and symmetry throughout; and I felt that I had won the noblest prize that this wide world could yield to a sportsman. . . . We bore the lion to camp. On my way from the water I shot with a single ball an extremely old black bull rhinoceros.[142]

Other such enthusiasts captured free-living animals alive for the purpose of exhibition, as "exotic" animals brought considerable prestige to the zoos of London, Paris, and Berlin. That prestige emanated from the power amassed through conquest. John Berger notes:

The prestige was not so different from that which had accrued to the private royal menageries. These menageries, along with gold plate, architecture, orchestras, players, furnishings, *dwarfs*, acrobats, uniforms, horses, art and food, had been demonstrations of an emperor's or king's power and wealth. Likewise, in the nineteenth century, public zoos were an endorsement of modern colonial power. The capturing of animals was a symbolic representation of the conquest of all distant and exotic lands.[143]

The pursuit of elephants was the most profitable of the African hunting enterprises, because of the value placed on their ivory tusks. Between the savage scramble for ivory and the loss of habitat as European ranching operations expanded throughout the savannas, the population of elephants in Africa plummeted.

The violence and loss of life of indigenous animals and peoples in Africa, which was facilitated by the expansion of European ranching operations, was both built on and deeply entangled with the suffering and violence experienced by the ranched cows and sheep. As in the Americas, while many individuals experienced death directly at the hands of their oppressors or after being dispatched to slaughterhouses, millions died more slowly and torturously from diseases resulting from their highly concentrated living conditions, such as rinderpest and diseases transmitted by tsetse flies. Countless others died from lack of food and water brought on by droughts and warfare.

Many surviving indigenous pastoralists, squeezed by colonial ranchers, competed even more intensely with one another for grazing lands and water. For instance, the Nuer, a pastoral society in the Upper Nile Basin, forcibly expanded its territory largely at the expense of the agro-pastoral Dinkas. Nuer warriors inflicted a high level of human causalities, took young women and children captive, and raided populations of cows and sheep controlled by the Dinkas. Such raids by the Nuer and other pastoral societies continued into the twentieth century.

The development of industrialized society under nineteenth-century capitalism, a process controlled by elite groups and driven by avarice, brought violence and oppression throughout the world—and much of the aggression was *enabled* by domesecration. Britain's ascendency as the major world power in the nineteenth century was advanced by its earlier colonization and deadly plundering of Ireland and Scotland, incursions made possible in no small part by the use of horses as instruments of war. The nineteenth-century invasions of Australia and New Zealand also relied on the exploitation of horses as well as on the availability of salt-"meat" (much of which came from Ireland)—and took advantage of the infectious zoonotic diseases the British brought to the region.

Latin America, which had been plagued with domesecration-related violence and death since the fifteenth century, saw this conflict continue after independence, as landed elites, especially ranchers, asserted control over much of the region. Violence against indigenous peoples, the suppression of landless "vagrants" and widespread civil and international wars all made use of horses as instruments of warfare. Countless domesecrated animals were killed to produce the salt-"meat" that formed soldiers' rations and made possible the profitable enslavement of people in *saladeros*, on plantations, and in mines.

Africa also long had been afflicted by the violence and stratification that accompanied the exploitation of large numbers of domesecrated animals. For centuries, nomadic pastoralists fought one another and invaded sedentary societies, creating stratified, patriarchal, militaristic social systems. The role of domesecrated animals in the large-scale violence in the region is seen not only in the case of indigenous warfare, such as the Zulu Mfecane, but also in the European invasion of South Africa. As did other invaders around the world, the Dutch relied heavily on domesecrated animals as provisions; their invasion also was enabled by the exploitation of horses as instruments of warfare and by the importation of deadly zoonotic diseases. Britain's similar use of domesecrated animals in its wars against both indigenous peoples and the Afrikaners and its importation of animals and "meat" from other subjugated parts of the world were central to its success in the region.

Much of the use of domesecrated animals as instruments of warfare, as laborers, and as rations during the nineteenth century was similar to the ways they had been used for thousands of years. While the dominance of nomadic pastoralists in Eurasia had waned by the nineteenth century, and guns and related weaponry had come into widespread use, the use of horses and other animals remained key to both European global domination and the suppression of indigenous peoples in the United States. It was in the later part of the nineteenth century that the long-used method of salting animals' flesh to slow decomposition began to be replaced by refrigeration, making it much easier to provision armies.

Just as in centuries past, the use of domesecrated animals not only enabled violence but promoted it, as their exploitation produced resources necessary for the growth of industrial capitalism. Elite British landowners in Ireland and Scotland prospered as displaced people were exploited and starved, and the profitable trade in salt-"beef" was made possible in part by the need to victual armies and seamen as well as enslaved people in the Caribbean. As the textile industry mechanized in Europe, the aggressive expansion of ranching operations increasingly included sheep, prompting the violent invasions of Australia, New Zealand, and Tasmania. While the European "Scramble for Africa" certainly pursued various resources and markets, as in other parts of the world, the expansion of ranching operations resulted in enormous levels of violence and displacement.

The ill treatment of so many people during the nineteenth century because of the aggressive expansion of ranching enterprises also was little different from what occurred at the hands of nomadic pastoralists and militaristic agrarian states centuries before. They suffered from violence, infectious disease, displacement, hunger, trauma, and various other forms of victimization. Also in the nineteenth century, as in the past, the displacement of large numbers of people by the expansion of ranching and domesecration-enabled warfare created highly exploitable and at times enslaved workforces, another resource necessary for profits and the expansion of an elite-dominated capitalist system.

The awful, profit-motivated oppression of so many people throughout the world was thoroughly entangled with the fate of other animals, both domesecrated and free living. Hundreds of millions of domesecrated animals experienced brutal violence or suffered from disease, drought, floods, and freezing weather and from their forced concentration in such large numbers. Increasingly, free-living animals were killed or displaced by ranching incursions, hunted and poisoned by ranchers, or—in the case of Africa—hunted for profit as a supplement to ranching income.

In a truly vicious circle, the violence against free-living animals and devalued people permitted ranching expansion, and the increasing populations of domesecrated animals then required the continued expropriation of even more land. The death and dismemberment of animals to create salt-"meat" furthered the exploitation of human enslavement, and such enslavement in turn drove the demand for the salt-"meat." Such entanglements, increasingly intricate and global in scope, grew in the nineteenth century. European capitalists could profit from expanding ranching enterprises largely because they were supported militarily by state power and supported ideologically by racism—especially in the late nineteenth century, by a distorted version of Darwin's concept of the "survival of the fittest," which rationalized U.S. and European policies and practices.[144]

Certainly, not all of the imperialist practices of the nineteenth century were driven solely by the desire to expropriate land for ranching. For example, Europe colonized Southeast Asia, which did not offer the same ranching opportunities as the Americas, Oceania, and Africa. However, at a minimum, the successful colonization and control of parts of Asia and other regions were enabled by the use of domesecrated animals as instruments of war, victuals, and other resources. It is difficult to imagine how nineteenth-century imperialism—with all the death and destruction it entailed—could have been attempted, much less have succeeded, without the extensive use and oppression of domesecrated animals.

While the oppressive use of domesecrated animals expanded under nineteenth-century capitalism, social elites—from British bankers to

powerful ranchers to families like the Vesteys—continued their disproportionate control of large numbers of ranched animals. This concentrated control of growing numbers of domesecrated animals and their
lucrative exploitation increased dramatically in the twentieth century as
the widespread, daily use of other animals as food grew—especially in the
United States.

# SOCIAL CONSTRUCTION OF THE "HAMBURGER" CULTURE

A great deal of study had gone into creating the appearance and personality of Ronald McDonald, right down to the color and texture of his wig. I loved Ronald. So did the kids.
—Ray Kroc, in *Grinding It Out: The Making of McDonald's*

A food scientist signed a report that a normal healthy child could eat nothing but our *hamburgers* and water, and fully develop all its physical and mental faculties.
—Billy Ingram, in *Selling 'Em by the Sack: White Castle and the Creation of American Food*

*Meat* from our farms and *packinghouses* is playing a part almost on par with tanks, planes, and bullets.
—1943 U.S. Office of Price Administration pamphlet

If one person is unkind to an animal it is considered to be cruelty, but where a lot of people are unkind to animals, especially in the name of commerce, the cruelty is condoned and, once large sums of money are at stake, will be defended to the last by otherwise intelligent people.
—Ruth Harrison, *Animal Machines*

The state-supported expropriation of nearly half of Mexico, the "virtual extermination of the buffalo and the destruction or control of the remaining *Indian* population"[1] were critical to the profitable expansion of U.S. capitalism in the nineteenth century. Racism legitimated the war with Mexico, the repression of Native Americans, and much of the oppressive treatment of workers whose labor was essential for capital accumulation; speciesism rationalized the ruthless exploitation of other animals and the horrors of the slaughterhouse. The wealth generated from expropriating vast areas of land, exploiting workers, and killing millions upon millions of animals created growing numbers and types of enterprises that in turn both capitalized on and drove the expansion of the oppressive practices. Ranchers, land speculators, railroad companies, railroad holding-yard operations, corn and other grain producers, commission agents who managed the sale of other animals, packinghouse buyers, market news services, railroads and trans-Atlantic shipping firms, commercial retail operations, marketing and advertising firms, legal and banking services—with increasing support from government agencies such as the U.S. Department of Agriculture—all were profiting from the consumption of domesecrated animals. By 1907, more than 88.7 million mammals alone—cows, pigs, sheep, and goats—were being killed annually in slaughterhouses in the United States.[2]

Ranching and the emergent "meat" industry not only caused deprivation and violence for growing numbers of domesecrated animals but also began to exact a heavy toll on the environment as well. As early as 1879, a U.S. government report warned of "improvident pasturage" and the rapid depletion of freshwater supplies in the Western states.[3] As their privately owned grazing lands in the United States deteriorated, ranchers increasingly sought rights to use public lands. In 1905, with prompting from the largest western "cattle"-ranching organizations, Congress created the United States Forest Service. With ranchers' input, the Forest Service was placed under the jurisdiction of the "meat"-industry-friendly Department of Agriculture—instead of the Department of the Interior—and the grazing regulations it established served the interests of the powerful ranchers.

> Old aristocrats of the western rangelands were given preference rights without competitive bidding. Public-land leases essentially became property rights, bought and sold by ranchers as part of a ranch. No Forest Service administrator would dare substantially reduce or transfer a grazing lease from a large and influential *cattle* rancher, no matter how abused the public's land might be.[4]

And as ranchers increased the population of cows and sheep on both private and public lands, the numbers of exploited slaughterhouse workers grew, too. By the early twentieth century, two hundred thousand people struggled at subsistence wages in slaughterhouses around the nation, sixty thousand of them in Chicago alone. Slaughterhouse workers in Chicago went on strike for higher wages in 1904 but were "shot, clubbed, and arrested by the score for their efforts. After the second week, violent clashes between police and strikers were daily occurrences."[5] The strike brought little redress for the workers because the industry was growing rapidly, especially with the start of World War I—a conflict that arose largely because "the advanced capitalist countries of Europe were fighting over boundaries, colonies, spheres of influence; they were competing for Alsace-Lorraine, the Balkans, Africa, the Middle East."[6]

As usual, war was good for the "meat" industry, and U.S. exports to Europe nearly tripled. Although Phillip Armour's "meat"-packing company was suspected of selling spoiled "meat" to the government during the Spanish-American War, leading to the deaths of thousands of U.S. soldiers,[7] after the United States entered the war in 1917, "Armour alone was netting profits of $40 million."[8]

Ranchers benefited from their political power and ties to government power in other ways, including by lobbying Washington for programs and funds to exterminate free-living animals that "competed" with cows and sheep for pasture or were considered profit-reducing predators. The Forest Service began advising ranchers on the use of techniques to kill the "troublesome" animals, and by 1914 the federal government was funding their extermination. In 1920, the United States was pursuing chemical warfare against free-living plains animals and created the Eradication Methods Laboratory in New Mexico to experiment with toxins. In 1921, the project was moved to Denver and renamed the Control Methods Research Laboratory.

As the "meat" industry stepped up the level of violence against free-living animals in ranching areas, ranched animals continued to experience the same torturous transport and slaughterhouse treatment that critics had decried decades earlier. In 1921, a writer for an industry publication, *The Breeders' Gazette*, offered a by now familiar account of the transportation of animals bound for the slaughterhouse.

> The high arbitrary carload rates then charged for the transportation of *stock* induced overloading as a measure of economy. The result was that the weaker animals were knocked down by the bumping and rolling of the train, and trampled on by others until helpless or dead; or, if they were able to rise, were frequently so injured that they afterwards died. In hot weather the suffering was intense. All this added to the death toll and loss to the shipper. . . .

Railroad pens at places where the *stock* was loaded or unloaded were as a rule not sheltered, and much of the time knee-deep in mud and filth, making it impossible for animals to lie down to rest. . . .

It was the invariable custom for shippers and attendants in charge of *cattle* shipments to carry lanterns and an instrument known as a "prod pole." It consisted of a heavy handle, nearly six feet long, with a sharp iron or steel spike extending from one end a half-inch or more. This was used to prod the other animals in the car aside, while a "down *steer*" could be encouraged by the sharp point to take his place in the ranks. The prod pole was also equipped with a flat-headed screw, driven into it near the "business" end, and extending out a short distance at right angles from the pole. When the "down *steer*" refused to respond to the numerous jabs and such language as was employed on those occasions, the end of the pole with the attached screw was engaged with the matted end of his tail, and by sundry twists, turns or pulls on the pole a severe strain was applied to that sensitive appendage. If the prostrate *steer* had life or strength enough left in him to rise, this treatment would bring about the desired results.[9]

Public consumption of commodities derived from such oppression, especially "hamburgers," got a fateful boost in 1916, when J. Walter Anderson, a short-order cook in Wichita, Kansas, began selling "hamburger" sandwiches for five cents apiece from a former shoe repair shop that he fashioned into a sandwich stand. By 1920, Anderson had established four "hamburger" stands that catered to men with factory jobs. Consumers in the United States remained wary of mass-produced "meat," in part because of Upton Sinclair's novel *The Jungle*, which detailed the horrific and unsanitary slaughterhouses of Chicago. Although many potential customers were suspicious of the quality and fitness for consumption of ground "beef," Anderson turned a profit. Hoping to expand further, he sought potential investors, but most were hesitant, as "the nature of his business was still suspect."[10] Anderson eventually found a willing partner in Edgar Waldo "Billy" Ingram, an insurance and real estate broker who sold his company to join Anderson in the "hamburger" business. Ingram brought his business savvy to the venture and realized that success was linked to improving the public's perception of ground "beef." Shabby sandwich stands needed to be replaced with respectable buildings, and the company needed a name that would engender confidence. Ingram suggested the growing business be named White Castle.

> Ingram later explained that the rationale for this new name was to convey a more positive image of their business, with "White" signifying purity and "Castle" signifying strength, stability and permanence. He also wanted to demonstrate this positive change in the buildings themselves. Rather than just another shabby *hamburger* "stand," Ingram decided to create a unique structure that would represent the company's ideals and help change the public perception of the *hamburger* business.[11]

Ingram set out to convince the public that "hamburgers" were not only safe to consume but healthy and nutritious as well. In doing so, he joined the growing number of capitalists in the United States who were beginning to realize the potential of both mass communication and their own increasing power to manage the citizenry and promote consumption. In the early twentieth century, ambitious big-business owners saw mechanization, automation, and increasing consumerism as the keys to maximizing profits.

## CORPORATE ENGINEERING OF PUBLIC CONSCIOUSNESS

One of the greatest factors in building the power and influence of capitalism was the development in the late nineteenth century of limited-liability corporations. Under this new form of business organization, if a corporation fails, the shareholders may lose their investments, but they are not *personally* liable for the corporation's debts. Furthermore, in 1896 the Supreme Court ruled that corporations were legal *persons*, a decision that granted these increasingly powerful, profit-driven organizations the same rights ostensibly afforded to individual citizens, including the rights to own property, to sue, and to exercise free speech. What was missing, however, was personal accountability for harms resulting from a corporation's pursuit of profit.

Faced with an increasingly rebellious society, one in which farmers, workers, and other exploited humans railed against the priorities of the elites, business leaders utilized their growing political power to co-opt reform measures and repress dissidents, including labor leaders and socialists. For instance, it was illegal to speak out against the First World War in the United States, and notable citizens such as Emma Goldman and Eugene V. Debs were imprisoned for speaking publicly against U.S. militarism. Between 1919 and 1921, the federal government undertook a series of illegal raids against labor leaders, socialist leaders, and others organizing for democratic social change. Activists were beaten, imprisoned, and deported, profoundly undercutting the democratic resistance to the capitalist control of the economy, political system, and culture.[12] The growing influence that elites were exercising over the state to promote capitalist development was supplemented ideologically with Social Darwinism, a "scientific" theory that suggested that the poverty, crime, and deprivation that resulted from capitalist exploitation and maldistributed wealth and income instead was attributable to "unfit humans with biological deficiencies," especially people of color.[13]

Increasing corporate control of the state expanded beyond controlling dissidents to creating a government and cultural infrastructure that further promoted the capitalist agenda. Colleges and universities began developing business programs that helped the expansion of sophisticated banking, accounting, retailing, and consumer credit systems—consumer credit being crucial in the continuous expansion of capitalism—and courses of study in marketing, advertising, and sales. Both the federal and state governments supported the creation of land-grant universities, whose primary purposes included the continued development and expansion of "livestock" agriculture, and the United States was prompted in the 1920s to create the Department of Commerce, which encouraged the consumption of commodities.

It detailed where the consumers were and what quantities of goods they would consume; it pointed out areas where goods were "overdeveloped" and which goods were best carried by which stores. The commerce department endorsed retail and cooperative advertising and advised merchants on service devices, fashion, style, and display methods of all kinds. The agency advised retail establishments on the best way to deliver goods to consumers, redevelop streets, build parking lots and underground transportation systems to attract customers, use colored lights, and display merchandise in "tempting ways."[14]

Corporate leaders realized that, for capitalism to expand and thus for profits to increase, the public had to be transformed from citizens into consumers. Capitalists had to promote "a spiritual framework and an intellectual justification that glorified the continued consumption of commodities as personally fulfilling and economically desirable."[15] Stuart Ewen writes that the business elite of the early twentieth century viewed advertising as a tool to control the social order. "They looked to move beyond their nineteenth-century characterization as captains of industry toward a position in which they could control the entire social realm. They aspired to become captains of consciousness."[16]

An early example of this developing power is the campaign to persuade people to eat "bacon" and "eggs" for breakfast. In the 1920s, the Beechnut Packing Company, producers of "ham" and "bacon," contracted with the "father of public relations" Edward L. Bernays—a nephew and student of Sigmund Freud—to increase sales. The typical breakfast at the time was juice, toast, and coffee. Bernays's tactic was to boost overall sales—that is, not merely to increase Beechnut's share of the existing market but to increase public consumption of pigs. One of Bernays's means of manipulating the public was to represent the stance of "experts" in a way that promoted his clients' aspirations. Bernays wrote in his 1928 book *Propaganda*, "If you can influence the leaders, either with or without their conscious cooperation, you automatically influence the group which they sway."[17] Bernays surveyed physicians, asking what they believed was better, a hearty breakfast or a lighter meal. When the physicians responded that a hearty breakfast was better, Bernays instituted a public education campaign and successfully pitched "bacon and eggs" as a hearty breakfast recommended by physicians. "Thus, the artery-clogging combination became forever linked in the American lexicon as well as on the American breakfast table."[18]

Growing capitalist control of major newspapers, magazines, and film and newsreel makers helped business interests shape public opinion. This power was boosted dramatically by the advent of radio, which entrepreneurs wrested away from educators in the late 1920s and early 1930s. They used the new medium to inundate listeners with entertainment programming while turning homes into salesrooms.[19] For instance, among the early "products" to be hawked on radio was *Spam*, a new commodity made from the flesh of the shoulders of pigs and championed by the "meat" industry mogul Jay Hormel. Spam sponsored *The George Burns and*

*Gracie Allen Show,* a popular 1930s radio broadcast. Much of the on-air hyping of *Spam* was done by the show's announcer, who would introduce the chorus to sing its jingle: "Slice it, dice it, fry it, bake it. Cold or hot, *Spam* hits the spot." Outside the program, Burns and Allen promoted *Spam* in various ways, including posing for photographs with a baby pig named *Spammy.* Such promotion was quite effective at increasing public consumption of pigs; urban residents who had eaten *Spam* climbed from 18 percent in 1937 to 70 percent by 1940.[20]

It was in this context of increasingly capitalist-controlled government and culture that in 1932 White Castle's co-owner Billy Ingram hired a well-spoken, charismatic woman, Ella Louise Agniel, to help sell "hamburger" to the people of the United States. Until then, the primary consumers of "hamburgers" were working-class men; Agniel's objective was to sell the "hamburger" to women, especially middle-class women. Under the pseudonym of Julia Joyce, Agniel became the "White Castle hostess." As the company grew, she traveled the country, insinuating her way into any organization of middle-class women. She pitched the corporate line on the merits of White Castle "hamburgers," highlighting their purported nutritional value and encouraging her audiences to make them a regular part of the family diet. Agniel suggested the women buy "hamburgers" "to go" to serve at home, and she always brought bags of "hamburgers" for her audience to sample. Agniel was also the face of White Castle's charitable promotions, presiding over the distribution of "hamburgers" at children's picnics, at settlement houses in low-income districts, and at holiday meal events. These well-publicized events served to boost "the company's image in its market cities."[21]

Ingram also built the business by constructing White Castles near college campuses, where the relatively inexpensive "hamburgers" were popular with students. "Most college students in the 1930s were exposed to fast-food *hamburgers,* whether from White Castle or a competitor, and unconsciously accepted *hamburgers* as part of their regular diet. By developing this '*hamburger* habit' during their college years, these college students continued to crave the familiar sandwiches after graduation"[22]—and they would pass this socially constructed preference on to future generations. Ingram also began newspaper and radio advertising "to hawk *hamburgers*"[23] and used discount coupons to entice new customers.

Early critiques of "hamburgers" continued, including one written in 1933 by the consumer advocates Arthur Kallet and F. J. Schlink.

One of our modern national institutions is *hamburger*. . . . The *hamburger* habit is just about as safe as walking in an orchard while arsenic spray is being applied, and about as safe as getting your *meat* out of a garbage can standing in the hot sun. . . . The fresh red color you see on chopped *meat* may be no more natural than the green color of St. Patrick's Day carnations; it may be there only by grace of a generous dosing of stale, partially decomposed *meat* with sodium sulphite. This preservation not only restores the color and appearance of fresh *meat*, but also destroys the odor of putrefaction. Eating putrid *meat* is not the only risk you run when you order *hamburger*; the sulphite itself is one of the most severe of all digestive and kidney hazards. . . . In one state 71 out of 76 samples of *hamburgers* picked up by inspectors were illegally preserved. But so easy and profitable is the fraud, and so slight the punishment, that it goes on with little abatement anywhere.[24]

Ingram countered these critiques by accentuating the hygienic nature of White Castle restaurants and the cleanliness of his restaurant workers. One advertisement touted the "Energy-Building Vitamins in White Castle *Hamburgers*."[25] White Castle in 1930 also commissioned a "scientific study" on the nutritional value of its "hamburgers." Billy Ingram cited this "study," involving only a single research subject, as proof that White Castle produced the perfect food.

We arranged for a medical student to live for thirteen weeks on nothing but White Castle *hamburgers* and water. The student maintained good health throughout the three month period, and was eating twenty to twenty-four *hamburgers* a day during the last few weeks. A food scientist signed a report that a normal healthy child could eat nothing but our *hamburgers* and water, and fully develop all *its* physical and mental faculties.[26]

Such pseudoscientific reports, the ceaseless public relations campaigns, and the gleaming "pure" appearance of the ubiquitous White Castle establishments all sanitized the reality of the suffering and violent death experienced by domesecrated animals, the awful experiences and conditions of the slaughterhouse workers, the environmental destruction, and the long-term health consequences for "meat" consumers. J. Walter Anderson,

Billy Ingram, and their many imitators across the nation succeeded in increasing the consumption of the flesh of cows as food—particularly among many whose incomes precluded regular consumption of more expensive cuts of "beef." The cultivated consumption of other animals as food, especially as "hamburger," was so successful that the practice was presented as a natural part of Americana.

> By the 1930s, in addition to being eaten on a daily basis across America, the *hamburger* was already entrenched in American popular culture, regularly appearing in the mainstream press, literature and entertainment. Pictures of *hamburgers* and the word *"hamburger"* were commonplace, adorning billboards and restaurant facades. . . . The fast-food *hamburger* was fast becoming more of a universal "American food," devoid of class stigma or prejudice. The *hamburger's* legitimation was corroborated in 1937 by R. D. Clark, then president of the National Restaurant Association, who proclaimed that it was truly a national food, joining only apple pie and coffee on that very short list.[27]

## FEDERAL POLICY AND "MEAT" PRODUCTION

The growth of this iconic "food" continued to have disastrous consequences for free-living animals. The federal government stepped up the effort to assist ranchers and the growing "meat" industry with the 1931 National Animal Damage Control Act, which authorized the creation of a ten-year plan for the extermination of free-living plains animals and included the purchase of a factory to make poisonous bait. Soon the government would replace strychnine as its poison of choice with sodium monoflouroacetate, known as compound 1080, a tasteless, odorless, water-soluble poison that results in terrible deaths for unsuspecting animals. Many who did not fall victim to chemical poisoning suffered and died as a result of desertification of the land produced by overgrazing.

Overgrazing was also a factor in the disastrous Dust Bowl era of the 1930s, when drought in several western states led to the terrible dust storms that destroyed tens of millions of acres of arable land and killed many humans and countless other animals. More than two million people were forced from their homes, and many migrated to California looking for work as agricultural laborers, creating an enormous labor force that drove wages well below subsistence levels. The tremendous suffering associated with the Dust Bowl tragedy compounded the misery caused by the economic calamity of the Great Depression—the collapse of the capitalist system that was the result of greed and Wall Street machinations and a growing number of capitalist powers competing for limited markets.[28] Even before the Wall Street crash of 1929, mechanization and concentration of U.S. agricultural production created grain surpluses, causing farming families' incomes to plunge.

Seeking to resurrect a failed economic system and stabilize U.S. agriculture, President Franklin Roosevelt initiated a program of federal government spending. One component of his "New Deal" policies was to remedy the problem of agricultural overproduction, especially surpluses of corn. Bill Winders explains:

> This legislation was composed of two key policies: price supports and production controls. Price supports were essentially guaranteed minimum prices for certain commodities, but farmers were required to agree to programs to limit their production in order to receive the guaranteed prices. These policies had two goals: (1) to reduce the supply of agricultural commodities, such as grains; and (2) to raise farm incomes. While New Deal agricultural policy was successful at the second goal, it failed miserably at the first. In fact, the combination of price supports and production controls actually encouraged greater productivity, leading to growing surpluses.[29]

Facing federal limits on the land they could cultivate, farmers sought to maximize the harvests from their limited acreage. More efficient mechanization, chemical fertilizers, and hybrid corn seeds led to increased production per acre. Agricultural concentration intensified as large farming operations, with the resources to purchase these new and costly innovations, profited and expanded, while smaller farms disappeared, and hundreds of thousands of sharecroppers were forced from the land they worked. The surpluses of corn that were developing in the United States "contrasted sharply with the state of corn in the rest of the world and very especially with the availability of corn in those countries where it served as the primary staple food."[30] However, the excess U.S. corn was not sent to nations where it was needed, because the hungry could not pay. Instead, as surpluses grew, depressing prices and reducing profits, U.S. agribusiness proposed a solution: increase the U.S. demand and consumption of "meat." Noting that much more grain is consumed if it is used to grow and fatten domesecrated animals destined for slaughterhouses than if it is eaten by humans directly, agribusiness, with its supporters in the federal government, sought to promote greater "meat" consumption.

While grain producers were prompting the government to champion greater "meat" production and consumption, powerful ranchers got behind the U.S. representative and Colorado rancher Edward Taylor, who in 1934 pushed through an act of Congress that abolished methods of pasturing commonly used by smaller cow and sheep ranchers. Under the new law, only "established" ranchers with substantial properties were eligible for federal land leases. The Taylor Grazing Act, obviously unpopular with small ranchers, further secured the dominance of elite ranching operations.

While Roosevelt's New Deal policies forestalled the collapse of capitalism, World War II played a more significant role in salvaging the system, especially in the United States. As the Great Depression of the 1930s reverberated throughout the world, global industrial production and global trade plummeted. The leading capitalist nations desperately sought cheap resources, highly exploitable labor, and new markets for corporate products. Germany's leaders aggressively sought control over much of Europe, while scapegoating people who were Jewish and other devalued groups for the country's economic crisis—with catastrophic consequences. The United States finally was drawn directly into the conflict when Germany's ally, Japan, bombed Pearl Harbor, a strike that was prompted in part by U.S.-enforced naval embargoes against Japan intended to limit that nation's growing control of Asian resources and markets.

As in most military invasions and warfare, domesecrated animals played a key role in World War II, especially as rations. Consumption of the flesh of other animals, long viewed as symbolic of male strength and virility from the time of the ancient nomadic pastoralists, was strongly endorsed by the military establishment. A 1943 U.S. government pamphlet stated, "American *meat* is fighting food. It's an important part of a military man's diet, giving him the energy to outfight the enemy. . . . *Meat* from our farms and *packinghouses* is playing a part almost on par with tanks, planes, and bullets."[31]

Again profiting handsomely from war, the Armour "Meat"-Packing Company stated proudly in a World War II–era advertisement that the

U.S. soldier was the "greatest *meat* eater in the world."[32] U.S. ranchers rushed to profit from the provision of "meat" to the soldiers, leading to even greater destructive overgrazing and imprudent water use.

The war revitalized the U.S. economy. Due largely to government spending for guns, ships, airplanes, rations and other implements of war, the nation experienced dramatic economic growth during the 1940s; the primary beneficiaries were large corporations, as the country's 100 largest firms received 70 percent of the government contracts during the period.[33]

It is a common belief that the United States entered the war to help the Jews and others being killed in concentration camps, but saving those lives was not a priority for the government, despite considerable pressure from the Jewish community for the government to assist directly those in the camps.[34] The U.S. government's lack of consideration for life was also demonstrated near the end of the war, when the military firebombed sixty-seven Japanese cities, killing tens of thousands of civilians, and dropped atomic bombs on two major cities, despite the fact that Japan was on the verge of surrender.[35]

After the war, in which the other powerful capitalist nations had suffered profound damage to their infrastructures and systems of production, the United States became the leading global commodity producer. Filling the worldwide demand for manufactured and agricultural commodities and convincing the government to maintain a huge military, U.S. capitalism was revitalized. However, growing corporations continued to eclipse small business enterprises, and four-fifths of the population were now working as salaried employees for the 3 percent of the population that had assumed control of much of the national wealth.[36] Although wealth was profoundly maldistributed, the distribution of income was somewhat more equal during the middle of the twentieth century than in previous decades—but the poorest one-fifth of the U.S. population still received only about 5 percent of the total national income.[37]

With the resurgence of capitalism provided by World War II and its aftermath, automobile use increased across the U.S. landscape. People in the United States were cool to automobiles in the early twentieth century, and mass transit was popular in most cities. To overcome this disinterest, early automakers promoted their products as aggressively as Ingram promoted "hamburgers" and Hormel pushed "Spam." The car makers even went so far as to create demand for their products in several cities by purchasing, sabotaging, or otherwise undermining efficient mass transit systems.[38] The automobile-based society was furthered substantially in the 1950s when the highway lobby, led by General Motors, convinced the federal government to construct 46,000 miles of interstate highways (a decision that would lead to apparently endless public expenditures for road expansion and repair). Subsequently, automobile sales soared. The North American "love affair" with the car, as with the "hamburger," was not so much a natural romance as an arranged marriage.

The public had little insight into the machinations of the automobile, steel, and rubber industries that promoted the ascent of this new cultural icon. Certainly, there was little thought of the disastrous consequences that lay in the future, including vast suburbanization and sprawl, urban decline, air pollution, oil depletion, millions of motor vehicle accidents and deaths or injuries, and the deaths of countless animals on the nation's roads. Like the college students who unquestioningly accepted fast-food "hamburgers," the general public came to accept the rapid proliferation of automobiles without any public discussion, debate, or conscious, collective deliberation.

The ability of car makers, fast-food companies, and myriad other businesses to reach the public grew substantially in the late 1940s and early 1950s with the advent of corporate-controlled television.

Television has been embraced with hungry eagerness by advertisers who recognize how nearly they've come to reaching the saturation point in sales through older mediums. Obviously the comparatively fresh selling power of television contributes to this warm welcome. Experiments with the new medium are backing up early predictions that television's selling power would be approximately ten times that of radio.[39]

Another early commentator on television, and a cheerleader for the capitalist system, cautioned:

In order that television can grow to give the public the best with a variety of program service the competitive urge of free enterprise should prevail. . . . Advertisers and their agencies will supply money and program ideas for better and varied entertainment. The increase in television homes will then be automatic, a benefit to all.[40]

Television advertising further cultivated consumer desires, and the news and entertainment programming presented political and social views that supported the status quo.[41] Not surprisingly, "meat" consumption in the U.S. increased dramatically, especially the consumption of "hamburgers."

## THE RISE OF FAST FOOD

With family incomes bolstered by the increasing entry of women into the paid workforce, greater numbers of people in the United States were able to afford homes, automobiles, televisions, and "meat." Increasingly, the U.S. economy was driven by consumer spending, and people were exhorted to buy, buy, buy. It was in this context that the fast-food "hamburger" business, with its drive-in convenience, grew to enormous proportions.

Contributing to the profit-motivated promotion of "meat" consumption were two brothers who opened a "barbeque" and "hot dog" restaurant in Pasadena, California, in 1937. Several years later, the brothers, Maurice "Mac" and Richard McDonald, moved to San Bernardino and opened a drive-in "hamburger" business near a high school, and the profits rolled in. They were content with this achievement until 1948, when a changing society prompted them to adjust.

Realizing that people increasingly wanted fast-service food to take out or eat on the move, the McDonald brothers converted their business to a streamlined restaurant that served only a limited menu of "hamburgers," fries, and "milkshakes" at low prices. The new restaurant, "McDonald's Speedy *Shakes* and *Burgers*," was organized by the assembly-line principles of manufacturing to provide faster service. Speedy service increased sales volume, and the simple assembly-line tasks allowed the company to hire inexpensive and inexperienced workers. This new system of counter service for finger food in disposable packaging allowed the restaurants to dispense with carhops, dishwashers, and even utensils, all of which led to increased profits. The McDonalds' building was designed with a giant M that could be seen by motorists on the much-traveled Route 66.

Then, in 1954, a "milkshake"-mixer salesman named Ray Kroc discovered the McDonald brothers' business. Realizing the potential for McDonald's to compete successfully against White Castle and newcomers like "InstaBurger," "Burger" King, and Big Boy Restaurants, Kroc persuaded the McDonald brothers to make him their franchising agent. After working with them for several years, he bought the business in 1961 for $2.7 million—but the McDonald brothers angered Kroc by insisting on retaining their original restaurant. In 1962, Kroc forced them to remove the McDonald's name from their establishment, since he now held rights to the business name. Then, in Kroc's words, "Eventually I opened a McDonald's across the street from that store, which they had renamed the Big M, and ran them out of business."[42] Kroc continued the assembly-line approach to "hamburger" production, emphasizing standardization and uniformity and relying on low-paid, easily replaceable workers.

Just as Billy Ingram of White Castle targeted middle-class homemakers to change the public's image of ground "beef" in the 1920s, the rising "hamburger" giants of the 1950s began aggressively to market to children using clever programs, advertisements, and gimmicks, all designed to generate lifelong customers. White Castle again emerged as a leader in this particular form of consumer propaganda.

> Almost without exception, . . . [White Castle] managers used their advertising money to reach the children in the 1950s, who accounted for 36 percent of the total population of the United States in 1955, with fifty-four million youngsters eating 40 percent of the nation's food. Marketing studies of the era indicated that 81 percent of American mothers consented to buying at least one item each week asked for by their child. With these statistics in mind, White Castle managers resolutely went after the children's market. White Castle advertising was almost exclusively focused on kids. . . . Some areas offered *hamburger* boxes that could be folded into the shape of a castle. Other cartons had trading cards printed on them, with prizes such as footballs and flash cameras given to children who collected the entire set. Other areas featured displays with railroads or space travel themes. New York experimented with small kiddie rides at their Castles.[43]

Ray Kroc also saw the benefits of targeting children.

> Children would be the new restaurant chain's target customers. The McDonald brothers had aimed for a family crowd, and now Kroc improved and refined their marketing strategy. He'd picked the

right moment. America was in the middle of a baby boom; the number of children soared after World War II. . . . Promoting McDonald's to children was a clever, pragmatic decision.[44]

McDonald's shrewdly decided to create a clown character to reach more enticingly into the world of children. Ray Kroc wrote: "A great deal of study had gone into creating the appearance and personality of Ronald McDonald, right down to the color and texture of his wig. I loved Ronald. So did the kids."[45] Ronald McDonald was thrust upon the children of the United States when he made his national television debut during the 1966 Macy's Thanksgiving Day Parade—accompanied by the "McDonald's All-American High School Band." By 1966, "the McDonald's 'You deserve a break today' theme song placed second only to the national anthem in terms of public awareness."[46]

Jim McLamore, one of the founders of "Burger" King and its CEO for years, writes of his company's early efforts to market to children with television programs in southern Florida:

By late 1958 we had reached a size sufficient to launch our first television advertising campaign. Our strategy was to take the *Burger* King story directly to the kids. . . . In 1958 we agreed to sponsor a . . . children's television show, called the Jim Dooley Show. Mr. Dooley also had a live audience of children. His show featured a chimpanzee named Mr. Moke, whose antics delighted the viewers. We met with Mr. Dooley, liked him and agreed to become a sponsor. The only condition I laid down was that we would be permitted to deliver a bag full of freshly made Whoppers during every live broadcast. That was OK with Jim, so at a certain hour every weekday our delivery man would carry a paper bag full of Whoppers into the studio. . . .

I think this daily event with the Whoppers was the high point of the show in many ways. It certainly was for us at headquarters. We received at least three minutes of advertising for every minute we paid for. . . .

This important marketing experience and our experiment with children's advertising served us well during the years of our national expansion. It also taught us the value of supporting quality programming when directing the *Burger* King message to young kids.[47]

Fast-food advertisements and messages disproportionately were directed at children, who increasingly were inundated with images of happy clowns, fantasy characters, amusing toys, and good times. The happy-meal image covered up the suffering, privations, and brutal deaths of domesecrated animals.

Another factor in the social construction of a fast-food culture as a way to increase "meat" consumption and make profits was the enormous expansion of the practice of using chickens as "food." This trend was driven by a man who was quick to anger in private but presented himself publicly as a soft-spoken and courtly Kentucky colonel in a white suit and string tie to promote fried chicken flesh as fast food. The entrepreneurial "Colonel" Harlan Sanders (an honorary commission eventually bestowed by a Kentucky governor) started selling parts of chickens he cooked in oil in a pressure cooker. In the 1950s, he began franchising the recipe to restaurant owners. In 1964, Sanders sold the business but retained control of Canadian and British franchises and remained involved as the public face of the company. The new owners franchised carryout stores in the United States, and cooked chicken parts began to be packaged and promoted as fast food. With sales of $15 million in 1966, the company started selling stock to the public. Kentucky Fried Chicken was one of the first fast-food firms to expand globally, and Colonel Sanders became an international celebrity. (Indeed, his image, in a slightly more cartoonish form, is still used today by the company known as KFC, a change apparently made in response to health-conscious consumers who wish to avoid fried foods, if not animal flesh.)

## THE "HAMBURGER" CULTURE AND ENTANGLED VIOLENCE

One of the many ways in which government was enlisted in the expansion of domesecrated animal products was to fund and support research and development. State-funded land-grant colleges and other public institutions used taxpayer funds to develop ways to manipulate biologically and raise other animals economically and to force them to grow more rapidly. Moreover, to meet the spatial requirements for vastly increasing numbers of domesecrated animals—and to reduce labor costs—the U.S. Department of Agriculture promoted the use of mechanically operated, intensive confinement ranching systems. Factory farming was born.[48] The development of confined animal feeding operations (CAFOs) led to a tremendous increase in the level of suffering experienced by domese-crated animals. An early critique of the "monstrous" effects of such intensive confinement on other animals appeared in Britain in 1964, in the book *Animal Machines: The New Factory Farming Industry*, by Ruth Harrison. Detailing the miserable confinement and violent treatment of chickens, cows, pigs, and rabbits, Harrison noted, "if one person is unkind to an animal it is considered to be cruelty, but where a lot of people are unkind to animals, especially in the name of commerce, the cruelty is condoned and, once large sums of money are at stake, will be defended to the last by otherwise intelligent people."[49] While Harrison's book evoked some calls for reform, given agribusiness's great influence over the state, only modest reforms for animals on factory farms resulted in Britain. In the United States, other than a weak and largely unenforced "humane" slaughter law, reformist pieces of legislation specifically excluded "animals raised for food" from any legal protection.

The factory model of production of enormous numbers of domesecrated animals, a culmination of decades of oppressive and exploitative—but profitable—policies and practices, ultimately evolved into what Barbara Noske aptly called the "animal-industrial complex."[50] Growing numbers of enterprises—not only ranchers, grain producers, factory farms, slaughter-houses, and others directly involved with domesecrated animals but also fast-food, retail, and advertising companies—coalesced with financial institutions, lobbyists, politicians, and government agencies to form an immense, powerful network promoting the increased consumption of other animals as food.

Sentient beings with preferences and desires, who are capable of profound social relationships, and who have inherent value apart from their exploitation by the animal-industrial complex now were essentially regarded as inanimate objects, as "biomachines." Experiencing torturous confinement and with no opportunity for normal activity or stimuli, many animals in the rising factory farms were kept in darkness for long periods. Their bodies were crudely and painfully mutilated to facilitate growth or to mitigate the pathological behavior produced by overcrowding. Some animals were so genetically manipulated that they developed difficulty even in standing. And, as in the past, these domesecrated others were roughly handled and cruelly prodded when transported to slaughterhouses.

Once there, they continued to be beaten and forced with electric prods onto the slaughterhouse floor, where many were still conscious when the "disassembly" began and where the goals of speed and efficiency overtook any pretense of humane handling. Barbara Noske writes:

> Under capitalism animals have come to be totally incorporated into production technology. . . . Particularly since the Second World War animal industries have become increasingly mechanized, automated and "rationalized." In many industrial countries small farm units were bought up by agricultural companies operating on a large-scale basis. . . .
>
> Animals nowadays are increasingly made to produce in huge buildings, in systems ranging from moderate to total confinement. The surrounding physical environment is completely human-made and human-controlled; no open air, no feel of earth, artificial temperatures, artificial daylight or darkness, wire mesh, concrete or metal-slat floors and so forth. Confinement systems serve a twofold purpose: to crowd as many animals together as possible in one spot and to manipulate them toward ever greater productivity.[51]

By the early 1960s, there were more than 106 million cows, fifty-one million pigs, twenty-six million sheep, one hundred million turkeys, and 2,703 million chickens in the United States alone.[52] The increased oppression of "farm animals" was accompanied by the escalated killing of free-living animals. By the 1960s, the murder of free-living animals deemed to interfere with maximal profits from ranching or feed production was under the control of the Bureau of Land Management.

> In the western states the Bureau employs a field force that in peak season reaches a thousand men, who annually poison more than a million acres to destroy . . . [small animals] and shoot, trap, and poison possibly several hundred thousand larger *wild* animals. . . .
>
> [Between 1960 and 1970, the Bureau] distributed 6,400,000 strychnine baits, staked out 140,000 chunks of poisoned *meat*, each large enough to last a season, and logged 410,000 "getter years." (A "getter," designed primarily to kill coyotes, is a cyanide device with a scented wick. It is stuck in the ground, and it injects cyanide into the mouth of any animal that tugs at its wick. ) . . .

The purpose of this vast destruction is, of course, to aid *husbandry*. It is a form of subsidy for farmers, *cattlemen*, and *sheepmen*. . . . Advocates of the system say that land yields a larger crop when it is free of competing *wildlife*, and that removing the *wildlife* is no more than a sound "management practice."[53]

Denzel and Nancy Ferguson note:

With such an arsenal of toxic chemicals, federal predator control quickly turned into an absurd and senseless orgy of killing with minimal regard for life in general and scant relationship to the original goal of reducing predation on *livestock*. It was predator genocide—not predator control.[54]

Wild mustangs, described by one rancher as "small, ugly animals,"[55] also were killed because they competed with ranched cows and sheep for grass. Moreover, countless other animals were killed or harmed by government-subsidized "range improvements," such as killing sagebrush with herbicides and reseeding these areas with grasses preferable for grazing. The population of birds who normally nest in sagebrush, such as sage sparrows, Brewer's sparrows, sage thrashers, and the sage grouse, declined dramatically after sprayings. On a daily basis, ranchers and farmers who grew hay to feed cows killed countless other animals while mowing, particularly birds attempting to hide themselves and their young from the approaching mowers.

With their political leverage, large ranching operations also gained permits in the late twentieth century to graze in national "wildlife" refuges. By 1975, grazing was occurring on 103 refuges in thirty-six states. After several decades in which captive cows were grouped together in the Malheur "Wildlife" Refuge in Oregon, the destruction was shocking.

In the spring of 1976, refuge visitors, many of whom had driven hundreds of miles to reach the refuge, were greeted with scenes of total devastation—cow manure as far as the eye could see, emergent vegetation trampled and reduced to filthy mats, dead *cattle* and *cattle* skeletons littering refuge waterways and canals, cattle wading and urinating in streams soon to be opened to public fishing, trenches worn several feet deep into ditch banks and levees, willow thickets broken and scattered, and vegetation eaten to bare ground. All this for the benefit of about 60 ranchers, many of whom owned airplanes and Cadillacs. In contrast, refuge visitors numbered about 25,000 per year—most of them bird-watchers.[56]

Countless other animals not killed directly by ranchers and government employees at taxpayer expense were unable to survive on the approximately 30 percent of the land of the United States affected by desertification, largely a result of overgrazing. Many animals perished—and continue to perish—from lack of food, water, and ground cover.

The growing levels of violence and destruction that the animal-industrial complex was perpetrating against both domesecrated and free-living animals were intertwined with the devastating effects of its practices on the health and well-being of consumers—harm generally of the form referred to as structural violence.[57] One striking example is the effects on human health of a diet increasingly comprising food from domesecrated animals and less from fruit, vegetables, grains, and other plants. Arturo Warman observes:

> Meat made up the difference [from the reduced consumption of fruits and vegetables], especially beef, whose annual per capita consumption rose from 50 to 120 pounds between 1929 and 1975. Poultry consumption also rose from 14 to 40 pounds over the same period. . . . If the consumption of milk, eggs, butter, and lard were added to these categories of meat, then in 1975 the average annual consumption of products of animal origin was 450 pounds, a little more than a pound a day. This implied that U.S. inhabitants not only received all their protein from animal products, but also the largest part of their calories.[58]

The United States witnessed a "heart disease epidemic"[59] in the twentieth century, and increased "meat," "dairy," and "egg" consumption unquestionably was a major cause, since such fare contributed "all of the cholesterol and the great majority of the saturated fat to the diet typical in the USA."[60] Between 1900 and 1960, the number of people in the United States who died prematurely from cardiovascular disease increased from 149 per 100,000 annually to 522 per 100,000.[61]

The consumption of food derived from other animals also contributed to increased risk for certain types of cancer.[62] Between 1900 and 1960, the number of people in the United States who died from cancer grew from 64 per 100,000 each year to 345 per 100,000.[63] (Today, researchers have strong evidence that protein derived from other animals causes cancer cell growth.)[64] While increasing numbers of people developed chronic diseases and died prematurely from eating animal "products," as they were encouraged to do by the animal-industrial complex, other public health hazards from the increased oppression of domesecrated animals were growing rapidly. Following the advice of government-backed researchers, agribusiness began giving large doses of antibiotics to factory-farmed animals to try to stave off the widespread infections that result from the overcrowding and stress experienced by animals in intensive confinement. The rampant use of high doses of antibiotics led to the growth of antibiotic-resistant organisms in both humans and other animals. Further, the growing numbers of domesecrated animals confined in factory farms and in overcrowded, filthy feedlots were starting to generate enormous amounts of manure and urine, which seeped into groundwater, streams, and the air and that made the environment increasingly dangerous for workers and neighboring communities. Chickens and other forms of "poultry" also now joined the ranks of the long-oppressed large mammals whose exploitation promotes great social harms. As enormous factory farms stuffed with tens of thousands of intensively confined birds—exploited for their flesh and their eggs—spread around the country, the eating of chickens grew faster than any other form of "meat" consumption in the latter half of the twentieth century.[65]

The historical pattern of the elites' use of domesecration, enabling and promoting large-scale violence against both humans and other animals, was altered in the United States under twentieth-century capitalism. The use of domesecrated animals as instruments of warfare diminished in nations like the United States, as new technologies produced far more efficient tools of war and transport. And, after the enormous amount of violent land expropriation that occurred in the nineteenth century, the infectious zoonotic diseases that had helped imperialist invasion were no longer important elements in the continued development of domesecration and capitalism. Major landmasses had been brought under capitalist control and exploitation, and resistance by the devalued people living there largely had been subdued. Large-scale warfare still raged over the course of the twentieth century, as capitalist nations fought one another for resources and markets and forcibly suppressed efforts to create alternative economic systems. However, the use of the bodies of domesecrated animals as rations and resources by military forces remained a highly profitable enterprise.

In nations like the United States during the century, growing numbers of both domesecrated and free-living animals suffered violent treatment. And increasingly, domesecration-related harm included chronic disease and premature death—structural violence against a citizenry encouraged to consume large amounts of products derived from animals. Coronary artery disease and cancer claimed many human lives as the twentieth century progressed. Human death linked to domesecration in the twentieth-century United States was brought not by bow-wielding nomadic pastoralists invading atop the backs of horses but by "Burger" Kings and friendly clowns named "Ronald," whose seductive pitches would have more long-term but equally deadly effects.

This twentieth-century domesecration-related violence was driven by capitalism, as multiple industries coalesced into the animal-industrial complex and pushed for increased consumption of other animals as food. The state began to play an increasingly important role in the growth of products derived from animals, with activities ranging from the extermination of free-living animals to research and development projects in land-grant colleges to the implementation of production controls and subsidies for agricultural commodities, especially corn. Expanding corn surpluses were consumed by the ever-greater number of domesecrated animals used for food; daily consumption of "meat"—historically a diet of elite groups—became more commonplace in the United States as taxpayers subsidized profitable production.

The enormous increase in the numbers of domesecrated animals in the United States exceeded the limitations of existing grazing lands, leading to the creation of a new, intensive ranching method: the use of concentrated animal feeding operations (CAFOs). The transition from pasture-based operations to intensive ranching systems—factory farms— led to colossal increases in the number of domesecrated animals and required enormous levels of fresh water and feed. The profit-driven and federally subsidized production of vast amounts of corn and other grains used as feed discouraged responsible soil conservation, and larger quantities of synthetic fertilizers, pesticides, and herbicides were required to sustain production—all requiring the greater use of fossil fuels.

The profit-minded push for increased consumption of domesecrated animal products by producers of feed grains was compounded by the growth of the retail "meat," "dairy," and "egg" industries and the rise of fast-food companies. Achieving large increases in the sale of their products required considerable ideological manipulation of the populace by armies of social-engineering experts who generated, with state support, ubiquitous advertisements and educational programs designed to increase human consumption of domesecrated animals—campaigns disproportionately directed at children.

As people in the United States and other capitalist nations in the mid-twentieth century were being exhorted to consume more products from domesecrated animals—largely raised on land taken forcibly from Native Americans—the American Indian Movement (AIM) emerged in the early 1970s and called upon the government to address the injustices they had experienced. In response, they were subjected to a public relations smear campaign and violently repressive tactics from the FBI.[66] At the same time, Cesar Chavez helped launch a movement for better conditions for exploited farm workers, who were disproportionately Mexican and Mexican American. But while these groups sought redress for the past expropriation of land, which had usually been taken for the expansion of ranching operations, other devalued groups of people were about to experience a new round of rancher-promoted violence, as the ever more entangled oppression of humans and other animals began to spread into Latin America. In a show of state power that would have consequences the likes of which had not been seen since the terrible invasion by the conquistadors or the ranchers' battles for economic and political control after the fall of Spain, the corporate-driven U.S. "hamburger" culture turned to Latin America for "beef."

# THE "HAMBURGER" CULTURE AND LATIN AMERICA

> While the struggle for land in Central America has drawn worldwide attention, not many have associated it with *cattle* ranching.
> —Patricia Howard-Borjas, *Cattle and Crisis*

> The roads and bridges built for strategic purposes could support *cattle* trucks as well as tanks, and the guard units could be relied on to remove the intransigent "rebel sympathizers" from the areas that had been cleared for corn.
> —Robert G. Williams, *Export Agriculture and the Crisis in Central America*

In the late 1950s, the U.S. restaurant industry, especially companies selling large numbers of "hamburgers," began to search for stable and cheap supplies of "ground beef." "Beef" imports "began in earnest in the 1960s, when the emphasis placed by U.S. *cattlemen* on higher-profit grain-fed *beef*" created "a shortage of the cheap *cuts* used in *hamburgers* and processed *beef* products."[1] It was only natural for eyes to turn to Latin America.

Over the course of the twentieth century in much of Latin America, close bonds remained between powerful ranchers and business and political elites, and participation in commercial ranching continued to confer social prestige. For example, in Uruguay,

> many of the early banking and commercial enterprises were financed by major *estancieros*, while at the same time the urban commercial elite invested in land for purposes of social status. . . . Both ranching and commercial interests have generally favored laissez-faire economic policies, strong guarantees on private property, and relatively free trade and export subsidies (or, at least, low export taxes).[2]

In Chile, where ranchers controlled vast estates and exerted enormous political influence, just 3 percent of the ranchers controlled 80 percent of the agricultural land of the central valley.[3] In Central America, "cattle" production "provided the material basis for the social, economic and political structures of the colonial and post-colonial period."[4]

U.S. corporations were the primary beneficiaries of inexpensive imports of natural resources from Latin America during the first half of the twentieth century, and the U.S. government forcibly supported these companies' profitable expansion in the region. For example, in the 1920s, it helped crush an anti-U.S. "peasant" rebellion in Nicaragua led by Augusto Nicolás Calderón Sandino and supported the rise to power of the Somoza family. With U.S. assistance, the Somozas came to own one-quarter of Nicaragua's agricultural land and became one of the largest "beef" providers in Central America.

By way of another example, in 1944 a democratically elected government began the process of agrarian land reform in Guatemala. Land reform posed a threat to the enormous holdings of the North American conglomerate United Fruit, which grazed cows on company-held land not being used for fruit production. Tom Barry writes:

> Only a small percentage of the banana enclaves . . . were used to grow bananas, because the world market wasn't big enough to absorb all the fruit the land could produce. During the 1950s, just 5 percent of United Fruit's holdings in Central America were in banana production. The rest lay idle or provided pasture for *cattle*.[5]

The Central Intelligence Agency and a U.S.-sponsored paramilitary  launched a coup in Guatemala and turned back the land-reform policies; thousands were arrested on suspicion of "communist activity," and many were tortured or killed.[6]

These and many other attempts at democratizing Latin American countries and creating moral egalitarian systems of land distribution were stymied with the support of the U.S. government. A successful revolution did occur in Cuba, where large U.S. ranching interests—including the King Ranch of Texas—and big sugar companies had expropriated seventeen million acres previously occupied by small farmers and had dominated agriculture until the 1959 revolution.[7] In response to the success of the revolutionaries in Cuba, the United States sought to suppress revolutionary impulses using "low intensity" warfare. Michael Parenti explains:

It was with domestic opinion in mind that the U.S. imperialists developed the method of "low intensity conflict" to wreak death and destruction upon countries or guerrilla movements that pursued an alternative course of development. This approach recognizes that Third World guerrilla forces have seldom, if ever, been able to achieve all-out military victory over the occupying army of an industrial power or its comprador army. The best the guerrillas can hope to do is wage a war of attrition, depriving the imperialist country of a final victory, until the latter's own population grows weary of the costs and begins to challenge the overseas commitment. The war then becomes politically too costly for the imperialists to prosecute. . . .

To avoid stirring up such political opposition at home, Washington policymakers have developed the technique of low intensity conflict, a mode of warfare that avoids all-out, high-visibility, military engagements and thereby minimizes the use and loss of U.S. military personnel. A low intensity war is a proxy war, using the mercenary troops of the U.S.-backed Third World government. With Washington providing military trainers and advisers, superior firepower, surveillance and communications assistance, and generous funds, these forces are able to persist indefinitely, destroying a little at a time, with quick sorties into the countryside and death-squad assassinations in the cities and villages. They forgo an all-out sweep against guerrilla forces that is likely to fall short of victory and invite criticism of its futility and savagery.[8]

In 1961, the Kennedy administration supplemented this tactic with a foreign "aid" program for Latin America euphemistically called the "Alliance for Progress." This program largely promoted Latin American compliance with U.S.-endorsed economic and political structures, both of which facilitated the export of inexpensive resources to the United States—especially exports of "beef."[9] The Alliance for Progress provided aid in the form of U.S. loans controlled by the newly created U.S. Agency for International Development (U.S. AID), the U.S. Export-Import Bank, the Inter-American Development Bank, and the Social Progress Trust Fund. However, the alliance's goals of fully integrating Latin America into the U.S.-dominated, global capitalist system were promoted most effectively by loans issued by the International Bank for Reconstruction and Development (now known as the World Bank) and its affiliates, the

International Finance Corporation and the International Development Association—all based in Washington and all subject to considerable control by the U.S. government.

U.S. officials encouraged Latin American governments and entrepreneurs to cultivate for export the "commodity" that was linked historically to so much death and destruction in the region—"beef." U.S.-controlled "aid" for Latin America largely was directed at "financing and requiring the establishment of a *cattle* infrastructure."[10]

During the 1960s, U.S. AID provided large amounts of financial and technical support to "cattle"-related activities throughout the region, ranging from "livestock" purchase to slaughterhouse construction.[11] Alliance for Progress funds funneled through U.S. AID financed the construction of roads and bridges that facilitated the expansion of ranching into tropical forests in Latin America and other infrastructure necessary for "beef" export. Through the 1970s, most agricultural loans to Latin America by the World Bank Group were for large commercial "livestock" projects.[12] Between just the years of 1974 and 1978, the World Bank alone made loans of more than $3.6 billion for "cattle" projects in tropical areas of Latin America.[13] Between 1961 and 1978, the Inter-American Development Bank directed loans of more than $363 million to Latin American "livestock" projects.[14]

It is estimated that more than half of all of the loans made to Central America in the 1960s and 1970s by the World Bank and Inter-American Development Bank for agriculture and rural development "promoted the production of *beef* for export."[15] Not surprisingly, "beef" exports from Central America grew enormously, from $9 million in 1961 to $290 million in 1979.[16] "By the end of the period, the region had 28 modern *meat*-packing plants authorized to export to the United States."[17] Most of this "beef" went into the corporate fast-food machine;[18] "Burger" King alone purchased 70 percent of the "beef" exports from Costa Rica.[19]

In South America between 1970 and 1987, the World Bank Group issued loans for the development of "cattle" projects in Bolivia, Ecuador, Uruguay, Paraguay, Colombia, Chile, and Brazil totaling more than $283 million. Another $180 million in loans went to agricultural projects with substantial "cattle" elements.[20] Between 1978 and 1988, in Brazil alone some $5 billion in various international loans promoted the expansion of "cattle" production.[21] The goal of this activity was "to make Brazil a major supplier of *beef* to Europe and the United States."[22]

The increasing monopolization of land by ranchers in Latin America beginning in the mid-twentieth century was compounded by the growing use of arable land to produce feed grains for domesecrated animals destined to become high-quality "prime" and "choice meat." This practice, which increasingly replaced the production of crops for direct human consumption, was initially promoted in 1971 when the UN Food and Agricultural Organization suggested that Third World nations begin cultivating "feed" grains for export and when the United States tied food aid to coarse-grain export production. U.S. corporations such as Cargill and Ralston Purina received low-interest government loans to develop feed-grain operations in Third World countries. In Mexico, a shift to feed-grain production was promoted by U.S. agribusiness and facilitated by price supports from the Mexican government.[23]

> Between 1950 and 1980, *livestock* production grew at a faster rate than did overall crop production in Brazil, Mexico, Peru and Venezuela. In Brazil and Mexico, for example, *livestock* increased its share of total agricultural output from 24% to 38% and from 28% to 42% respectively.[24]

## Hunger and Environmental Degradation

Despite the USDA's assertion that increased Latin America ranching would encourage self-sufficiency in food production, almost all of the "beef" produced there was shipped to the United States and other more affluent areas for consumption. The USDA reported as early as 1973 that "the principal reason that these exports occurred was that the demand [read: purchasing power] for *meat* was stronger in the United States than in Central America. . . . Prospects are that the Central American consumer will continue to lose ground to the U.S. consumer."[25] E. Bradford Burns noted the association between exports, particularly exports of "cattle" and grains used for "cattle" and other "farm animal" feed, and the obvious deterioration in the quality of life for humans in Latin America in the late 1970s.

> In effect, over the 1970–1976 period, agriculture grew at an average rate of 2.9%, while the population went up at a 2.8% rate. Agricul-

tural production per inhabitant thus remained virtually static. All this would suggest the standard of living suffered no significant change, but there are features which make it possible to claim that, in reality, deterioration occurred, particularly the fact that a growing proportion of the cereal crop went to producing *cattle*-feed. Thus, in the 1972–1974 period, Latin America utilized an average of 26.1 million tons of cereals to feed *cattle* (40% of the grain availability, as opposed to the 32% utilized in the 1961–1963 period). The amount of grain available for foods accessible to the masses is thus reduced. Meanwhile, *cattle* products are mainly consumed by those in high-income brackets and undernourishment among the poor is augmented by both factors. . . . Throughout Latin America malnutrition is a problem that cannot be hidden.[26]

By 1975, more than ten million cows were grazing on twenty million acres of land in Central America, an area exceeding that of all other agricultural land combined,[27] while fully half of Central Americans did not "receive minimal nutritional needs."[28] The production of "beef" for export to the affluent in the region was crowding out food production for the poor in Brazil, Colombia, Mexico, Peru, Venezuela, and other periphery countries[29] as well as destroying forest land. James Nations observed:

The tropical forests of Mexico and Central America are not being sacrificed to grow food for the regions' expanding populations. They are being destroyed, largely by *cattle* ranching, to produce profits and land titles for a small percentage of the region's citizens and to produce *hamburgers* and *steak* dinners for the urban elite in Mexico and Central America and the United States.[30]

U.S. capital also promoted the cultivation of coffee, cotton, and sugar, but the expansion of the ranching industry was particularly destructive. Writing of the expansion in Central America, Daniel Faber notes:

*Cattle* ranching was less restricted geographically than production of cotton or coffee. *Beef* could be raised wherever pasture grass would grow, particularly in the lush lower montane and lowland Caribbean rain forests of the interior. Funded by grants and/or loans from U.S. government agencies and international financial institutions, large-scale *cattle* ranches quickly expanded towards the rolling mountains and valleys in the interior, displacing *peasant* farmers from their traditional agricultural lands. . . .

During the 1980s, Central America's rainforests, one of the richest reserves of biological and genetic diversity in the world, disappeared at a rate of almost 3,500 to 4,000 square kilometers annually. In fact, over two-thirds of Central America's (broad-leafed) lowland and lower montane rain forests, the largest expanse north of the Amazon Basin, have been destroyed . . . [between 1960 and 1986. By 1987,] 22 percent of the region's landmass, more land than used for all other agricultural commodities combined, is in permanent pasture.[31]

Between 1950 and 1990, the most significant change in land use in Central America was the destruction of forests for the purpose of creating pasture. The amount of tropical forest in the area fell from twenty-nine million hectares to seventeen million.[32] Throughout virtually all of Latin America, the conversion of tropical forests into pastures and ranches for raising cows for food was "responsible for more deforestation than all other production systems combined. . . . The main exceptions to this rule may be Guyana, Suriname and French Guiana where *cattle* ranching has not emerged as a major land use."[33] Writing in 1986, the biologists Christopher Uhl and Geoffrey Parker discussed a problem that has only worsened in the last quarter century:

> Much of Central America has been deforested over the past 25 years to form *cattle* pastures. A portion of the *beef* produced on these pastures is imported into the United States and transformed into luncheon *meats, hamburgers,* baby foods and *pet* foods. The *beef* is lean and less expensive than anything we produce domestically. And for consumers, the notion that the *meat* on our lunch plate might have come from a *steer* that grazed on land that was previously tropical rain forest remains abstract.[34]

The burning of tropical forests—a common method of clearing the land for pasture—contributes to global warming, as does the loss of carbon-dioxide-absorbing trees and plants. Moreover, the steady increase in the number of cows on the planet contributed substantially to the release of methane gas into the atmosphere, and methane is one of the three gases creating the greenhouse effect.

## REPRESSION AND POVERTY

Seeking to capitalize on the global demand for "beef" in the late twentieth century, Latin American elites—in the tradition of the nineteenth-century *caudillo* Juan Manuel de Rosas and other powerful *estancieros* and with the assistance of international loans and pressure from such corporate investors as International Foods, R. J. Reynolds, and United Brands—redistributed land holdings and open-range woodlands from subsistence farmers, rubber tappers, and Native Americans to the ranchers who supplied the export *packers*. The World Bank projects during the period did "little or nothing" for the landless.[35] This and other U.S.-based financial institutions strongly supported the neoliberal economic ideology[36] and free-trade practices—while opposing public ownership of natural resources and any meaningful land reform. World Bank loans went to mid-sized and large ranchers (many of whom were urban investors) and were used to expand already highly concentrated land holdings.[37] All the while, the World Bank pressured countries to liberalize their trade policies to boost "beef" and cash crops for export.[38] "The *cattle* fattened on the plains while the people often . . . [had] to struggle for a bare existence in the hills,"[39] and the World Bank "became identified with forces of rural inequality in the countryside."[40] While other cash crops, including cotton, coffee, sugar, and bananas, led to the displacement of subsistence farmers, "cattle" production was disproportionately responsible for land expropriation and placed much greater pressure on the rural populace—and small farmers resisted having their homes and livelihoods taken away. Robert G. Williams observes:

> Ranchers who were having difficulties evicting *peasants* were able to convince the national security forces that there were communist threats in these areas. The national security forces were able to convince Washington of the same, so the areas of strongest *peasant* resistance were declared counterinsurgency zones. Local *cattle* ranchers in this way got free eviction forces, armed and trained at U.S. taxpayer expense. The strategic roads that were built into the

trouble areas further enhanced their viability as *cattle* zones. When *peasants* fled the gunfire and napalm, the lands they left were turned into *cattle* ranches. And officers in the national security forces became *cattle* barons as they shared the booty of war with local ranchers, local officials, and *peasant* collaborators.[41]

Ranchers and other landowners in Latin America—with the help of the police and paramilitary groups—forced or frightened many into leaving the land. Many facing displacement in Latin America "did not accept slow death through starvation as inevitable but struggled against the ranchers at every step of the way."[42] For example, the journalists Sue Branford and Oriel Glock note that, while some people faced with displacement in Brazil succumbed to violence and intimidation, others contested such treatment.

Many of the families, brought up in the isolated and perhaps surprisingly peaceful *serta* (hinterland), have been traumatized by the repression they have received from the landowners and the police and have been frightened into leaving. Other families . . . have decided to stand up to the landowners and fight for their plots, even if this means facing up to repression on a daily basis.[43]

In addition to such violent conflict, the overall effects of U.S. and Latin American government support of expanding "beef" production have been devastating. In the 1960s, exports of "beef," or "red gold,"[44] became a leading source of foreign exchange, and ranchers continued to seek to expand land holdings. Ownership of land became increasingly concentrated among wealthy ranching families. Much of the new land taken for ranching was expropriated from small farming families, including indigenous communities, who eventually tried to organize to resist violence by ranchers and the military that supported them. The forced evictions of subsistence cultivators created growing levels of rural landlessness and large populations of unemployed. While many migrated to urban areas, others moved into rainforests to try to develop land for their crops. The growing problem of displacement of farm families was compounded by the practice of ranchers of buying up land once used to produce cotton, coffee, and other labor-intensive cash crops. Labor requirements for ranching were small compared to other productive activities, and the increasing numbers of unemployed served to suppress wages for the remaining jobs in both rural and urban areas. Thus, the effect of U.S.-promoted ranching operations in Central America beginning in the early 1960s "was to provoke a rural tidal wave," and ranching and "beef" production "became the basis for the region's wholly unsustainable form of development."[45]

As hunger, deprivation, and resentment increased, the rural landless and growing urban proletariat tried to organize, but they faced oppression on a shocking scale. To facilitate capitalist expansion, extract cheap "beef" and other commodities, and tie the Latin American nations more securely into the global economy, the United States helped install and protect repressive governments. It backed covert operations, provided weapons and military advisors, and trained select Latin American soldiers in "counterinsurgency warfare" at U.S. military schools, including the notorious School of the Americas at Fort Benning, Georgia.[46] The tactics taught were effective and shameful.

## "Low-Intensity" Terrorism

In the 1950s, with the rapid growth of the U.S. "fast-food" industry, Nicaraguan "beef" exports grew rapidly. *Campesinos* (subsistence cultivators) resisted as farms and forests were converted to pasture, but protest movements were repressed brutally by the U.S.-backed Nicaraguan National Guard. "As a result, landlessness soared in rural Nicaragua, and Managua began to swell with immigrants from the countryside."[47] Many rural residents were forcibly relocated to areas in the rainforest where, after land they had cleared for cultivation was taken by ranchers, they had to press deeper into the forest. In the Nicaraguan region of Matagalpa, after subsistence cultivators organized to resist land expropriation, President Somoza declared the area a "counterinsurgency zone."

The ranchers of eastern Matagalpa must have been pleased with the designation of the area as a counterinsurgency zone. The roads and bridges built for strategic purposes could support *cattle* trucks as well as tanks, and the guard units could be relied on to remove the intransigent "rebel sympathizers" from the areas that had been cleared for corn. Furthermore, the local ranchers did not have to pay for the services rendered. Both the roads and the expense of the eviction force were financed by the Nicaraguan government, with a portion of the tab paid for by U.S. taxpayers.

Local magistrates, guard officers, and *peasant* informants for the guard also appreciated the designation of the area as a counterinsurgency zone, for at last they had an opportunity to become landowners and ranchers themselves. The land was quickly vacated of corn producers as the "Communist guerrilla sympathizers" were rounded up, tortured and shot. Many voluntarily fled the area to avoid reprisals at the hands of the guard.[48]

Between 1960 and 1979, the production of cows for food in Nicaragua increased by 300 percent, and cow flesh for export by 550 percent; Nicaragua became the region's leading "beef" supplier to the United States.[49] By the time of the Sandinista Revolution (named after the 1920s-era revolutionary Augusto Cesar Sandino) in 1979, the ruling Somoza family owned six "beef"-importing facilities in Miami and slaughterhouses in Nicaragua. One of the Sandinista government's first actions was to initiate land reform; ten thousand square kilometers were redistributed to landless, subsistence-farming families in the form of cooperatives. Meanwhile, the Reagan administration began illegally funding a military force to destabilize and undermine the new government. The CIA hired mercenaries (the *contras*) to wage a campaign of murder and mayhem on the people of Nicaragua and embarked on a program of national destabilization to undermine the Sandinistas—a program that left 45,000 people dead or wounded.[50] A U.S.-friendly leader resumed control in 1990.

In Honduras, subsistence-farming families who resisted evictions were subjected to terrorism and violence. Murders by ranchers were common in the 1960s and early 1970s, and several massacres became public. For instance, in 1975, on a large ranch called Los Horcones, five people were shot by men in military uniforms, five people were burned to death in a bread oven, two priests were castrated and mutilated, and two women were thrown into a well that was then dynamited. All the victims were connected to a movement organized by subsistence farmers.[51] The regional "cattlemen's" association even raised funds to pay for the assassination of a Catholic bishop who supported the farmers.

In El Salvador, the post–World War II expansion of cotton and sugar production for export displaced subsistence cultivators, many of whom in turn sought employment in export production, only to lose their jobs to increased mechanization. Landless families from El Salvador crossed into Honduras in search of land to farm. When the rural migrants from El Salvador joined Honduran farmers in resisting rancher encroachments, the ranchers looked for an opportunity to expel the Salvadorans. The chance came in 1969, when a brawl broke out at a World Cup soccer match played by the national teams of the two countries, leaving many Honduran spectators hurt. The Honduran ranching association represented the conflict as a scene of nationalist fervor in opposition to the immigrants and convinced the government to forcibly expel one hundred thousand Salvadoran migrants from the country.[52] The government of El Salvador retaliated by invading Honduras, precipitating three months of warfare and leaving thousands dead on both sides. Tens of thousands became refugees in both countries; the initial tragedy in El Salvador was compounded by a decision of Honduras to refuse to accept any Salvadoran migrants. Honduras, Nicaragua, and Costa Rica all closed their borders to products from El Salvador—creating more forced layoffs there and exacerbating unemployment and deprivation.

Then, in the early 1970s, the U.S. Department of Agriculture approved the development of several "packinghouses" in El Salvador for the export of "meat" to the United States, and ranching operations there began to expand. "Estimates of landlessness rose from 29 percent of rural households in 1971, before El Salvador entered the *beef* trade, to 41 percent of rural households by 1975."[53] By 1978, "beef" exports were as important as coffee and cotton, and rural landlessness climbed to 65 percent by 1980.[54]

Subsistence cultivators, the urban poor, low-wage workers, and teachers' unions in El Salvador all organized for land reform, higher wages, and better living conditions and pressed for change through political elections. But, "as the poor were organizing for social change, the Salvadoran oligarchy was organizing for repression."[55] Attacks on leaders of the reform movement occurred in the early 1970s; in 1972, Salvadorian elites stole a national election, and the military government purged university professors and staff believed to be supporters of the reform movement. When mass demonstrations were organized, the military opened fire on them. However, protests continued to occur, and increasing numbers of rural families were evicted to make room for expanding cotton plantations and ranches.

Grassroots militias rose up against the El Salvadoran military and the landed oligarchy, leading to a bloody civil war beginning in 1980. The

Catholic Church was supportive of the peoples' resistance, and Archbishop Óscar Romero publicly called on the U.S. government to stop military aid to the government and urged rank-and-file El Salvadoran soldiers not to follow orders to kill subsistence farmers and other civilians. One month later, on March 24, 1980, soldiers assassinated Archbishop Romero while he performed mass. In a classified memo, the U.S. ambassador to El Salvador under the Carter administration, Robert White, observed:

> The major, immediate threat to the existence of this government is the right-wing violence. In the city of San Salvador, the hired thugs of the extreme right, some of them well-trained Cuban and Nicaraguan terrorists, kill moderate-left leaders and blow up government buildings. In the countryside, elements of the security forces torture and kill the *campesinos*, shoot up their houses and burn their crops. At least two hundred refugees, from the countryside, arrive daily in the capital city. This campaign of terror is radicalizing the rural areas, just as surely as Somoza's National Guard did in Nicaragua. Unfortunately, the command structure of the army and the security forces either tolerates or encourages this activity. These senior officers believe, or pretend to believe, that they are eliminating the guerillas.[56]

When Ronald Reagan took office in 1981, White was replaced by a new U.S. ambassador to El Salvador. With U.S. support of the landed oligarchy and military, the civil war raged in El Salvador for twelve years, resulting in some 75,000 deaths.[57]

In Guatemala, armed resistance to the expansion of ranching and the expropriation of land also emerged in the 1960s. When ranchers had difficulty evicting subsistence cultivators in the northeast of the country, officials in Washington approved the designation of the region as a counterinsurgency zone. Death squads terrorized the rural populace, and U.S. Special Forces teams provided support for attacks on villages believed to be sympathetic to the resistance. The U.S. Air Force trained Guatemalan soldiers to use U.S.-supplied helicopter gunships, fighter jets, and bombers for dropping napalm. Between 1966 and 1968, some six to eight thousand people were killed, subsistence farmers were evicted, and ranchers expanded their pastures.[58] One notable figure involved in crushing the resistance movement in Guatemala was rewarded in much the same way as Hernando Cortés was more than four hundred years earlier for similarly brutal tactics: "Aided by U.S. counterinsurgency advisers, Colonel Carlos Arana Osorio crushed the rebellion, in the process earning the epithet 'Butcher of Zacapa.' Arana was given a large *cattle* ranch by the government as a reward for his brutal counterinsurgency campaign and went on to become president of Guatemala."[59]

Indigenous peoples in Guatemala, who initially shunned armed resistance to land expropriation, took up arms when six hundred women, children, and men from a region seeking to legally establish a land claim were massacred in Panzós in 1978.

> By the end of the 70s, the entire country was engulfed in a reign of state terrorism that continued into the present decade [the 1990s]. According to the British Parliamentary Group on Human Rights, the death toll after military rule has climbed to over 100,000 killed and 38 thousand disappeared; another million were internal refugees. . . . Although all sectors of the society have suffered from the terror, the majority of the victims have been *peasants*.[60]

It eventually was estimated that Guatemalan security forces largely were responsible for the killing of 160,000 people and the disappearance of another forty thousand.[61] Meanwhile, net "beef" exports from Guatemala increased nearly twentyfold in twenty years, from 1,420 tons in 1960 to 24,950 tons in 1980.[62]

In South America, powerful ranchers and repressive governments continued to be allied in the second half of the twentieth century. Ranching practices were particularly oppressive in Brazil, where the U.S. government used both economic and military power to bring about policies and leadership that were amenable to U.S. transnationals. Jack Nelson writes: "American foreign aid to Brazil was drastically cut between 1962 and 1964 during the liberal presidency of Joao Goulart. Goulart was committed to policies unfavorable to powerful domestic and foreign groups, including agrarian reform."[63] In response, the Brazilian military—working closely with the U.S. embassy—overthrew President Goulart and then "proceeded to install and maintain for two decades one of the most brutal dictators in all of South America,"[64] Castello Branco. Branco, born into a wealthy ranching family, bankrolled his government in part by loans from the World Bank, the International Monetary Fund, and numerous transnational corporations.

Under Branco's government, ranching expanded in Brazil and moved deeper into areas of the Amazon rainforest. Hungry for more pasture, ranchers encroached on lands inhabited by indigenous peoples and thousands of rubber tappers and their families. Chico Mendes, an internationally recognized leader of the rubber tappers union and a champion for conservation of the rainforests, wrote:

> The landowners say we are holding back progress and harming the country's economy. They say rubber is not important to the economy and the future lies with *cattle* raising. . . . It is the deforestation carried out by the big landowners to open up pasture for their *cattle* that is threatening the forest. . . . The landowners use all the land at their disposal. They bribe the authorities. . . . The other tactic landowners use, and it's a very effective one, is to use hired guns to intimidate us. Our movement's leaders, not just myself, but quite a few others as well, have been put on the death list of the UDR's assassination squads.[65]

As he foresaw, Chico Mendes was assassinated in 1988 by a member of a Brazilian "cattle" ranchers association. "An Amnesty International report revealed that there were more than a thousand land-related murders in rural Brazil in the 1980s, and fewer than ten convictions."[66]

In Mexico, violence associated with the ranching of domesecrated animals, initiated by the conquistadors, plagued the country well before the Alliance for Progress in the 1960s. In the state of Veracruz, for example, subsistence farmers organized a union in 1915 after land expropriations by large ranches. Ranchers responded with an organization of their own, and "bloody battles took place."[67] Subsistence farmers became the targets of assassins throughout Veracruz. With government approval, ranchers and other large landowners started hiring gunmen, referred to as "White Guards," to repress resistance. In some areas, subsistence farm families were pushed by ranchers to forested areas, which were less than ideal for crop cultivation and required considerable effort to clear.

*Cattle* ranchers rarely paid for the transformation of forest to pasture because the immigrant subsistence farmer conducted the first phase of the expansion. . . . Powerful ranchers were the landowners, and authorized subsistence farmers to cut areas of their forests to plant corn, as long as farmers agreed to plant grass among the maize, a plant also in the grass family. After the first year, this area was then used as pasture and was never left fallow again.[68]

With increasing demand for "beef" in the United States, investment in ranching in Mexico nearly quadrupled between 1950 and 1960, and by 1970 "almost 70 percent of all agricultural land in the nation was dedicated to *livestock*."[69] In the late 1950s, U.S. agribusiness companies promoted the use of hybrid sorghum seeds for the production of feed in Mexico, and in the 1960s the Mexican government established price supports for sorghum, encouraging its production over maize and wheat for human consumption.

In southern Mexico, "ranching in the tropics was explicitly linked to the need to dominate, populate and conquer territory" and to the effort to integrate the region into the world economy. Loans from the World Bank and related institutions, coupled with enormous tax breaks for ranching, substantially increased the numbers of domesecrated cows. In the state of Chiapas alone, the number of cows grew by 260 percent between 1950 and 1970.[70] As resistance emerged and people made concerted efforts to retake the land in organized resettlements, ranchers countered with violence and oppression. Opposition leaders frequently were assassinated by private security forces, and scores of resisters were murdered. When the numbers of those in revolt were too large for ranchers' private security forces to control, the Mexican army was called in.[71]

The January 1, 1994, Zapatista uprising in Chiapas largely was motivated by such land disputes. Many of the participants were residents of the Lacandón rain forest. By 1981, one-third of the Lacandón forest had been razed, and "80 percent of the cleared area was dedicated to *cattle* pasture."[72] The Zapatista movement arose "as a self defense group to defend against the ranchers' hired gunmen, who try to take their land and maltreat them."[73] In a prepared statement, the Zapatistas asserted, "Land is for the *Indians* and *peasants* who work it, not for large landlords. We demand that the copious lands in the hands of ranchers, foreign and national landlords, and other non-*peasants* be turned over to our communities, which totally lack land."[74] Hundreds died in battles with the Mexican army before the resisters could position themselves in the Lacandón forest and began a nonviolent campaign for justice and a democratic global economy.

## DOMESECRATION AND THE DEVALUED

Many of the people adversely affected by ranching violence, especially in Guatemala and Chiapas, were ethnic Mayans, and native peoples in Central and South America in the twentieth century continued to suffer disproportionately from growing levels of "beef" production. Ranchers continuously expropriated Native American lands, and the government-sponsored construction of roads facilitated the sale and export of "beef" and feed crops to affluent countries. In Brazil, many ranchers and "cattle" companies resented indigenous people and their claims on the land, and some "sprayed with grass seed the patches of ground that the *Indians* had planted with food crops."[75] At an assembly of the leaders of indigenous societies in 1975, one representative stated, "We are all suffering from the same massacre. The *civilized* people invade, kill our children. We have no support. . . . People let *cattle* loose all over the land of the *Indians*."[76]

Seeing the destruction of their homelands and faced with violence and privation, many indigenous women refused to have children.[77] Journalists Sue Branford and Oriel Glock described the stark condition of one indigenous society in Brazil:

> By the early 1970s, the Nambikwara in this region [of Brazil] seemed to be heading towards rapid extinction. They were left with just a few strips of untouched forest and even became dependent on the *cattle* ranches for their food. Their number fell rapidly as they succumbed to measles, flu, tuberculosis, pneumonia and malaria, which spread to the area after the forest clearances. They suffered from chronic dysentery because the water they drank was polluted with *cattle* dung. Their lands were occasionally sprayed with the defoliant Tordon 155, a form of Agent Orange. After visiting the area in 1973, Bo Akerren, a Swedish doctor attached to the international commission of the Red Cross, said: "The condition of these *Indians* is a disgrace not only for Brazil, but for *mankind* as a whole."[78]

In 1980, another group of indigenous people in Brazil, the Gorotire, launched an attack in response to an invasion of their land. But, as a local rancher told a U.S. journalist: "The USA solved the problem with its army. They killed a lot of *Indians*. Today everything is quiet there and the country is respected throughout the world."[79]

The violent displacement of rural people not only freed up land for use by the global animal-industrial complex but also benefitted manufacturers and transnational corporations seeking cheap labor. Patricia Ballard writes:

> The term which Latin Americans use to characterize the process of *livestock* expansion—*ganaderización*—connotes a process of taking over, of total domination. It succinctly expresses the massive changes in land use that occur as *livestock* and pasture encroach upon areas settled by farmers who till the soil and upon "virgin" forested land. . . . The spread of *cattle* ranching not only effectuated major changes in land use: it affected the process of capital accumulation as a whole, especially as a principal force in the creation of a relative overabundance of labor, a "relative surplus population." . . . The impoverishment of the rural masses became the impoverishment of the urban masses, which translated into below-subsistence wage rates for the proletariat.[80]

As in other areas of the world, displacement caused by land expropriation and the violent and often ruthless repression of reformers and resistance movements have been particularly hard on the women of Latin America. They disproportionately experience deprivation, brutality, and exploitation and have long faced terrible victimization at the hands of the military and paramilitary groups, including torture and sexual assault.[81] For example, in 1976 women in rural areas of Brazil were tortured in efforts to obtain information on the whereabouts of men resisting displacement.

> Sixty-five-year-old Dona Margarid Saa had had needles inserted under her nails and into her arms, breasts and legs. For good measure the fugitive man's wife, Santana, had also been tortured, though it must have been clear to the policemen, as it was to us when we talked to her a few days later, that she did not know where her husband

was. As a gratuitous act of violence, perhaps giving vent to their frustration, the police had burnt down Santana's house while she was detained.[82]

Women who must seek employment because of displacement from the land often continue to be victimized, especially in Central American and Caribbean "free-trade zones"—manifestations of the neoliberal-directed global economy. Viewed by multinational corporations and their contractors as docile and possessing manual dexterity, young, childless women are used for unskilled work that pays low wages. The international women's organization MADRE reports:

> For thousands of women, the workplace itself is a site of abuse. In fact, the sector most emblematic of Latin America's role in the global economy is also the most notorious for the abuse of women. Export manufacturing sweatshops, or maquilas, hire mainly women who are paid less, work longer and are subjected to worse conditions than men. Many of these women are migrants who have left behind social networks that could provide protection from violence. Documented examples of violence against women in maquilas include humiliation, sexual harassment and intimidation, sexual assaults and beatings, strip searches, forced pregnancy tests, termination of pregnant workers and violence against union organizers.[83]

*Campesinas* in rural areas also struggle to provide for their impoverished families by working for agribusinesses in the production of fruits and vegetables. Large fruit companies often prefer women employees because "they are submissive when reproached; they will accept any salary and type of work under whatever conditions."[84] Philip McMichael observes that supervisors "intimidate women workers through displays of anger or physical force, accompanied by threats of firing."[85] Tom Barry also notes: "Women help keep down the cost of labor and food through their unpaid work. From an early age they work tirelessly—helping with the farming, tending the dwelling, going to the market, gathering firewood, rearing children, and preparing food. By their thirties, *peasant* women are often old and worn."[86]

In their struggle to support their families, some Latin American women eventually turn to prostitution,[87] while others are forced into it more directly. Many young women and girls are lured by traffickers into sexual bondage, brought to Latin American cities with promises of jobs and then forced into the sex trade. Noting that this problem is greatly exacerbated by rural displacement and migration, the International Human Rights Law Institute observes that deception with false promises of employment to women and adolescents is the most common tactic used by traffickers.[88] The possibility of recovery from this form of oppression is significantly reduced by the probability that these oppressed women will contract HIV/AIDS.

Latin American cities expanded greatly from rural migrations, increasing the numbers of people experiencing deprivation and exploitation there. In 1950, only 25 percent of the population of Latin America lived in urban areas. By the 1980s, that number grew to 40 percent; the number of landless *campesinos* more than tripled over the period.[89] And by 2007, 77 percent of the residents of Latin America and the Caribbean were living in urban areas.[90] Funding for social services was sparse in part because of, ironically, downturns in the ranching economy. After so much effort to create ranching and slaughterhouse enterprises in the region, with so much attendant suffering and destruction, U.S. ranchers successfully lobbied to limit competition through "voluntary quotas" on imports of Latin American "beef." The quotas, coupled with wide fluctuations in the global "beef" market, made the enterprises in Latin America only marginally profitable and contributed to the accumulation of enormous debt in the region. In 1998, the combined long-term debt of Latin America and Caribbean nations was $537.6 billion.[91] The International Monetary Fund presented Latin American countries with debt restructuring programs requiring the implementation of structural adjustment programs that cut government expenditures for health care, education, and other public services while pushing privatization and other neoliberal-friendly policies. Already limited social, education, and medical services became even more difficult to obtain.

The U.S.-led global economic policies of promoting "meat" production and consumption not only have spelled disaster for millions of humans in Latin America but also have meant that enormous and growing numbers of cows and other domesecrated animals face increasingly intensified violence and oppression. The greater use of land for the production of cows and other domesecrated animals has led to the death or displacement of countless free-living animals, especially in the tropical forests where their homelands rapidly are being destroyed in favor of pastures and feed-crop estates. The fate of free-living animals in the forest rarely is considered, except perhaps when the threat of actual extinction of an entire species causes alarm, at least in some quarters. Countless numbers of animals, such as tapirs, red uakari monkeys, marmosets, sloths, anacondas, toucans, and parrots, have been displaced or killed. Other animals, including howler monkeys, anteaters, white-lipped peccaries, nine-banded armadillos, the aguti, the coyote, the grey fox, the tepescuintle, the puma, and the white-tailed deer, as well as large birds such as the ornate hawk-eagle, the scarlet macaw, the yellow-headed parrot, and the great curassow, largely have been eliminated.[92] Jaguars, long hunted and killed for recreation, for their skins, and by ranchers who see them as threats to profits, are now endangered.

Moreover, with greater human incursions into tropical regions many free-living animals are captured for the lucrative trade in exotic "pets" and "zoo" animals; thousands of captives do not survive the trauma of capture or the torturous process of confinement and transport. The widespread killing of free-living beings in the forests because of the priorities of the capitalist export economy in the twentieth century—like the other resultant harms—have been only distant "externalities" for the global animal-industrial complex.

## Global Ranching and Oppression in Oceania and Africa

Despite all the death and destruction resulting from the press for increased ranching operations and "beef" production in Latin America—which has helped increase the region's dependence on the United States and made it subject to the dictates of the international capitalist establishment—the relative importance in the global economy of "beef" exports from the region actually has been fairly slight. Imports of "beef" to the United States and Europe from Latin America were relatively small compared to the amount imported from Australia and New Zealand. And as in Latin America, indigenous peoples in these regions—and in Africa—suffer from landlessness and discrimination.

During the growth of the fast-food industry in the United States and the increase in consumption of "hamburgers" in the 1960s, Australian Aborigines were striking Vesteys ranching operations for decent wages and treatment while pressing, unsuccessfully, for land rights. In New Zealand, Maori attempts for legal recognition of their land claims were largely futile. In Africa, European powers continually moved indigenous pastoralists into the international "beef" trade. U.S. AID funded the drilling of deep water wells in various parts of the continent in the 1960s so pastoralists would settle and raise cows to sell for cash. With seemingly stable supplies of fresh water, the numbers of domesecrated cows increased—leading to overgrazed, denuded lands, and vulnerable human populations.

> The overgrazing of *cattle* and periodic droughts have created an ever-widening human crisis. Millions of rural refugees attempting to flee the path of spreading desertification have migrated into crowded urban areas. . . . In the major droughts from 1968 to 1973 and 1982 to 1984 more than 250,000 people died of famine in the African countryside.[93]

With funds from the World Bank and other sources of international finance, African nations began a transition to a "modern ranching economy, adopting western technologies and *husbandry* practices in an attempt to gain an even larger share of the European and international *beef* market."[94] Increasingly large ranching operations installed hundreds of miles of fence to keep indigenous animals away from coveted grass and water. "Tens of thousands of *wild* animals have died of dehydration and starvation, some bleeding to death entangled in wire mesh, in a frantic effort to reach water and forage on the other side."[95]

In the 1970s, the United Nations Food and Agricultural Organization (FAO) instituted a program to eradicate the tsetse fly, which infects cows with disease. "The object of the exercise as declared by the FAO was to clear this land in order to introduce 120 million additional head of *cattle* for the production of some 1.5 million tons of low-grade *beef* a year."[96] Over the course of ten years, between 150,000 and 175,000 tons of toxic chemicals, including DDT, rained down on affected regions of Africa— with little success against the tsetse flies.[97] How much illness and death the pesticide caused to humans and other animals is unknown.

The historical violence and conflict between pastoralists and farmers, combined with the force of European imperialism and World Bank policies, contributed to one of the worst episodes of genocide in the twentieth century. Nomadic Tutsi pastoralists migrated in the sixteenth century into the area that is now Rwanda and dominated the Hutu people, a society of soil cultivators. When Germany invaded the region during the late nineteenth-century "Scramble for Africa," the colonizers lent their support to the numerically smaller but socially dominant Tutsi, who collected taxes and enforced German rule. Belgium took control of Rwanda after Germany's defeat in the First World War, and the new colonizers gave the Tutsi even greater economic and political control over the Hutu, whose landholdings were reduced greatly. Disproportionately conscripted as forced laborers on Belgian coffee plantations, Hutus were required to carry identity cards that noted their ethnicity.

When struggles for independence swept across Africa in the midtwentieth century, Hutus began to rise up against Tutsi domination. Widespread violence followed, leading to the deaths of tens of thousands. Large numbers of Tutsi fled to neighboring countries, where they staged periodic raids on Rwanda; those Tutsi who remained in Rwanda faced limitations on their political power and landholdings. In the context of this history of conflict, the World Bank promoted the expansion of ranching operations in Rwanda.

In 1974, the World Bank financed a project to establish *cattle* ranches over an area of 51,000 hectares. The bank hired a Belgian anthropologist, René Lemarchand, to appraise the project; he warned that the Hutu were using the project to establish a system of patronage and spoils that served to reduce the size of Tutsi *herds* and grazing areas and to increase Tutsi economic and political dependence on the Hutu, and that the project was aggravating Hutu-Tutsi conflicts. Lemarchand's warnings were ignored.[98]

When the global price for coffee, a key export product for Rwanda, fell in the early 1990s, the nation was plunged into economic crisis, with the deprivation compounded by the austerity budget required in the structural adjustment programs stipulated by the IMF. Tutsi militias took advantage of the economic disaster and launched an effort to unseat the Hutu-led government. The French government, looking for opportunities to strengthen its influence in Africa, supported the buildup of the Hutu government's military, and death squads were created. Approximately eight hundred thousand Tutsi were massacred, and thousands of Hutu who favored peace were murdered by French-backed government forces.[99]

Amid all this violence and deprivation, profitable industrial systems of "meat" production in Africa expanded. As violence against domesecrated and free-living animals in Africa increased, conflict and violence between pastoralists and cultivators continued, as did the practice of "livestock" raids. Driven by the demand from growing global levels of "meat" consumption—and the increasing availability of automatic weapons—"cattle" raiding in Africa intensified in the late twentieth century. Murder rates soared as the practice of "cattle" raiding for the market was taken to a new level, and captured animals were sold for hard currency—sometimes delivered by raiders directly to the slaughterhouses.[100]

The treatment of the growing numbers of domesecrated animals in African slaughterhouses is not unlike that of domesecrated animals in the United States. Writing of conditions in South Africa, Michelé Pickover observes:

> At the slaughterhouse, despite codes which state that animals should be free from discomfort, pain and fear, their welfare is, for the most part, not monitored or enforced. These codes also state that no animal is supposed to watch another animal die and that they are supposed to be unconscious before they are suspended. But all investigations into the industry have shown that they are "not worth the paper they are written on." Industrialised animal production means that animals in slaughterhouses are being forced through the disassembly line at such great speed that they have to endure enormous stress, injury and pain and are increasingly left conscious as they are yanked up by one leg and their throats are slit. An animal could therefore be either fully conscious during the brutal slaughtering process or regain consciousness while having *its* skin removed. The pace at which the *meat* and *poultry* industries slaughter animals means that even if they are not properly stunned nothing is done, because every minute of "down time" hurts profits.[101]

As in the past, widespread violence emerged from the desire for the land and water sources needed to expand the numbers of wealth-producing domesecrated animals. The U.S. animal-industrial complex had orchestrated large increases in the use of domesecrated animals as food, and this general consumption was made affordable in part by public subsidies for grain fed to the growing numbers of animals living in appallingly intensive, crowded conditions. However, as profits from grain-fed cows were greater than those from grass-fed cows used for the popular "hamburger," and as cheap supplies of this ground "beef" from the United States were not keeping pace with the socially engineered demand, suppliers and "hamburger" retailers turned to Latin America.

In contrast to earlier invasions that supported ranching operations in the Western Hemisphere, in the twentieth century the violence did not involve conquering entire societies but, rather, hundreds of rural villages and countless subsistence farming families—aggression that contributed to civil war in several nations. Similarly, the twentieth-century ranching invasion did not rely on disease to diminish the local populations nor on the use of animals as instruments of war or as laborers to accomplish land expropriation, although the flesh of other animals most certainly was used as rations, especially for U.S.-backed military units.

The terrible violence that the growth of ranching operations brought to the region was deeply fused with the general capitalist imperative for expansion. Troubled by the precedent set by the Cuban revolution and concerned about growing agitation for land reform, economic democracy and social equality in the region—and desiring to further integrate Latin America into the global economy—the United States promoted "beef" production and export. Through an "aid" program designed to increase cash-crop exports—especially land-intensive "beef" production—the land occupied by countless subsistence producers could be expropriated for profitable use. Moreover, the people in rural areas displaced by expanding ranching operations, like many before them, could be transformed into highly exploitable workers, now to be employed by transnational corporations. What is more, Latin American countries became increasingly dependent on revenues from U.S.-cultivated exports of "beef" and other cash crops, further tethering the region to the capitalist global economy.

As an added benefit for U.S. elites, Latin America's contribution to the availability of affordable "hamburgers" and other fare no doubt helped to blunt the societal response to the loss of jobs and increasing income disparities in the United States resulting from deindustrialization during the same period. (This move to keep the price of "meat" affordable is similar to efforts elites made to make "meat" and "dairy" commodities more affordable to exploited workers in Britain, to lessen resistance there to the deprivations resulting from the growth of industrialization during the nineteenth century).

The extensive violence resulting from the expansion of ranching operations in Latin America was both promoted and facilitated by the United
States and by U.S.-friendly governments there. The use of state power to
support the expansion of ranching was supplemented with the exercise of
ideological control, as the violence in the region largely was portrayed as
the work of troublesome "communists." Elites in the United States promoting the expansion of U.S. capitalism—including those with substantial
investments in the animal-industrial complex—and elites in Latin American nations who were beneficiaries of increased "beef" production profited
from the violent expropriation of land and the expansion of ranching
enterprises. Tens of thousands of people in rural areas were terrorized and
murdered and many more displaced, frequently by forces receiving military
and technical assistance from the U.S. government. Increasing numbers of
domesecrated animals were objectified and subjected to barbaric treatment,
and countless free-living animals were killed as the destructiveness associated with ranching claimed enormous areas of rainforests.

The displacement, destruction, and, increasingly, human hunger produced by decerealization were compounded by the rapid growth of the
feed-grain industry. New sections of rainforests were destroyed and fields
for food production were transferred to more profitable feed production.
The direct violence against the rural human populace, the free-living
animals, and the growing numbers of domesecrated animals was deeply
entangled—and also was intertwined with the structural violence against
people in the United States and other nations who were exhorted to consume domesecrated animal products that contributed to chronic disease
and premature death.

At the same time that the ranching-promoted violence engulfed areas
of Latin America, the World Bank and European elites' promotion and
expansion of commercial ranching operations in Africa led to violence,
displacement, and environmental destruction there as well. These factors
increased peoples' vulnerability to drought and famine. As it became profitable for traditional pastoralist societies to supply cows and other animals
to the European and international "meat" market, murderous raids for
domesecrated animals continued to be a serious problem in many parts of
Africa. As increasing numbers of subsistence pastoralists were being
brought into the global economy as producers of domesecrated animals,
more people were displaced from lands, which were often made barren by
overgrazing and drought, to become a source of exploitable labor. Clashes

between pastoralists and soil cultivators continued, and capitalist intervention exacerbated longstanding rivalries and conflicts, as in Rwanda.

While the promotion of ranching and feed-grain production in the twentieth century was not responsible for all the violence and problems in Latin America and Africa, the level of entangled violence produced by these practices was enormous. And in those situations where capitalist-promoted ranching was not directly linked to violence, struggles among capitalists or between capitalists and dissenters frequently were the underlying cause. However, pervasive violence, deprivation, and environmental devastation were associated with the oppression of domesecrated animals in the twentieth century, and the highly destructive, increasingly global animal-industrial complex poses grave dangers to the world at the start of the twenty-first century.

# CHAPTER EIGHT

# DOMESECRATION AND
# IMPENDING CATASTROPHE

The accelerated growth of *livestock* production and processing will require far-reaching changes in the roles of the public and private sectors in *livestock* development. . . . The *developing world* [read: oppressed Third World] is projected to be the most important supplier to this growing market.
—World Bank, *Livestock Development*

How we relate to animals as voiceless beings suffering under the forces of capital becomes an ethical question, much as the question of how we relate to any other group that suffers under the exploitative forces of capital.
—Bob Torres, *Making a Killing*

The Darfur crisis is a poignant reminder of the violence that can erupt between pastoral nomads and sedentary agriculturalists.
—Lawrence Kuznar and Robert Sedlmeyer, "Collective Violence in Darfur."

McDonald's cannot flourish without McDonnell Douglas.
—Thomas Friedman, *The Lexus and the Olive Tree*

How is one to begin to think about futures in genocide? One way to use the sociological imagination is to construct scenarios based on ideal-types and typical processes abstracted from the past, assuming not that the future repeats the past mechanically but that social facts, structures, systems of belief and conflicts which have led to deadly endings before still have the potential of doing so again if neither reversed nor deterred.
—Helen Fein, "Scenarios of Genocide."

The much-touted notion that a "natural partnership" between humans and "domesticated" animals promoted the advancement and well-being of human society is an ideological construct that supports the status quo—and it largely masks the reality of a history deeply steeped in violence and deprivation. While specific circumstances varied from case to case, the exploitation of large groups of domesecrated animals through-out the centuries has resulted in deadly violence; displacement; enslave-ment or exploitation of the labor of the displaced; deaths from diseases brought on by domesecration, hunger, and malnutrition; impoverish-ment; marginalization; and, frequently, sexual exploitation. While the oppression of domesecrated animals certainly is not directly connected to all human conflict and violence, the death and destruction enabled and promoted by this practice has been monumental; such oppression cer-tainly played a major, if not a pivotal, role in the emergence and expan-sion of capitalism and the predatory quests for profits that fueled domese-cration-related violence over the past four hundred years.

With this history in mind, one may ponder whether the enormous level of bloodshed and suffering experienced by humans and other animals over the centuries—violence enabled and promoted by domesecration—was an acceptable price to pay for "modern society," such as it is. However, such a reckoning is premature. The violence and damage produced by domese-cration are not merely the historical underpinnings of the contemporary global order but remain among the most serious problems confronting the world today.

## Contemporary Ranching and the Oppressed

In the twenty-first century, hundreds of millions of humans around the world do not have access to land to produce plant-based food for them-selves or their communities. Their situation has deep roots in the colo-nial and imperialist policies of powerful capitalist nations that relied on expropriated land, water, and labor to fuel profitable expansion. Profit-driven food production has resulted in widespread global hunger; today, nearly one billion people are malnourished and at increased risk for dis-ease, and their numbers are growing.[1]

Indigenous people in the Americas, Africa, Oceania, and other parts of the world continue disproportionately to experience material depriva-tion, as much of the land they once occupied and used for subsistence food cultivation has been expropriated and used to create commodities derived from domesecrated animals. Added to this structural violence against indigenous people and the millions of other dispossessed people

in the Third World is the continuation—and, in some cases, the intensi-
fication—of racism and even physical violence.

In Brazil, now the world's biggest exporter of "beef" and a leading supplier of "meat" and feed grain to Europe, Russia, and China, ranchers
continue to terrorize people who resist displacement or organize for land
reform. For example, indigenous Guarani people there have struggled for
their rights since ranchers appropriated their ancestral lands in the 1960s.
Sequestered on impoverished and overcrowded reservations, some five
hundred Guarani have taken their own lives in the last two decades.
Many of these deaths surely were the result of the deprivation and despair
they experience. However, many Guarani—and some journalists and
scholars—believe a large number of the purported suicides actually have
been acts of murder by area ranchers, staged to look like suicides.[2] Most
recently, prompted by the deaths of children from malnutrition, Guarani
families in early 2012 began occupying ancestral lands seized by ranchers
and soy producers, only to face murder at the hands of hired "security"
forces.[3]

As soy-based feed production in Brazil grows, ranchers are pushed
deeper into the Amazon rainforest, and logging in the region increases.
Powerful transnational corporations, including Monsanto, Cargill, ADM,
Bayer, and Nestlé, are among those firms that further the violent expropriation of land in order to acquire the resources necessary for growing
levels of global "meat" consumption.[4] Ranchers, soy producers, and loggers are believed to be responsible for the deaths of many indigenous
people and subsistence farmers in Brazil—including 1,150 rural activists
since the early 1990s.[5] However, there is seldom any serious investigation,
and the murders get almost no international attention—unless the victims have some form of organizational support and have achieved a level
of international recognition, as in the case of Dorothy Stang. Sister Dorothy, a seventy-three-year-old Catholic nun of the Sisters of Notre Dame
de Namur order from Dayton, Ohio, was shot and killed by gunmen hired
by ranchers in 2005. She had worked in Brazil for thirty years as an advocate for subsistence farming families, helping them to organize against
the expropriation of their land by ranchers and loggers. In May 2011, the
internationally known Brazilian environmental activists José Cláudio Ribeiro da Silva and Maria do Espírito Santo, working to resist rancher and
logger incursions into the Amazon rainforests, were murdered. Four months

later, two ranchers were arrested for the murders.[6] In October 2011, the environmental activist and farmer João Chupel Primo was murdered outside his home after continued denouncements of illegal logging and ranching forays into the rainforest.[7] While a few of these murders have made international news, they seldom are placed in the larger context of the ongoing violence that ranchers, soy producers, and other large landowners perpetrate against devalued people in many areas of Latin America.

Many displaced subsistence farmers in Brazil who manage to escape being murdered in the wake of expanding ranching and feed-crop operations often seek employment on large ranches simply to feed themselves and their families. These laborers end up in debt bondage, a situation not much different from enslavement.[8] In their search for easily exploitable, low-cost laborers, ranchers and their operatives also deceive and exploit the urban poor.

> Thousands of impoverished people are lured away from squalid city slums or small villages of Maranhão State, east of Pará, and other poor states of the northeast of Brazil, by hopes of making their fortunes. However, they end up in very isolated areas of Pará, generally at gunpoint, clearing areas of forest to make way for enormous *cattle* ranches producing *beef*. Between 1995 and 2001, 49% of the cases of slavery in Brazil occurred in *cattle* ranches and 25% were related to deforestation. The expansion of the soya frontier is drawing on *slave* labor—already six percent of all known cases.[9]

An estimated 25,000 people are living as enslaved workers for ranchers in the Amazon. As rainforests continue to be destroyed, "*cattle* pasture accounts for six times more cleared land in the Amazon than crop land; even the notorious soya [feed] farmers who have plowed some 5m hectares of former rainforest cover just one-tenth of the ground taken by the *beef* producers."[10]

Efforts to fight rancher violence have begun in Venezuela, a nation where in 2002 "an estimated 5 percent of the population owned 80 percent of the country's private land" and "vast *cattle* ranches take up large areas of arable land," exacerbating poverty and hunger there.[11] After the socialist president Hugo Chávez initiated land reform in the country in 2001, hundreds of subsistence farmers were killed; wealthy opponents tried to oust Chávez in an unsuccessful 2002 coup, allegedly with U.S. complicity.[12] In 2010, Chávez instructed the Venezuelan military to assist small farmers trying to defend themselves against armed groups financed by ranchers and other wealthy landowners. The Venezuelan president justified the use of the army in this way: "Faced with the onslaught against *peasants* through an escalation of aggressions, sabotage and hired killings by the most reactionary forces of our society, the duty of the state . . . is to protect the poor farmers."[13]

In Paraguay, President Fernando Lugo, a former priest and supporter of land reform and *campesino* rights, was forced out of office in 2012 after conflict erupted when landless *campesinos* attempted to squat on land held by ranchers and large soy producers. Lugo was ousted by a congress that long has been friendly to the large landowners who dominate the nation's economy. One of the poorest nations in South America, Paraguay is a leading exporter of soy and "beef."

In Guatemala, powerful drug organizations have razed rainforests and invaded national reserves to establish ranches used to launder drug profits and conceal trafficking centers. "*Cattle* ranching in the Petén [rainforest in northern Guatemala] has quadrupled since 1995, with *herds* totaling 2.5 million . . . according to the region's governor. Organized crime and drug traffickers have usurped large swaths of protected land . . . and are creating de facto ranching areas."[14] With forces more powerful than the government can muster, drug barons have taken lands reserved for cougars, monkeys, and other animals, as well as a sanctuary for endangered scarlet macaws.

Central American residents, pushed to marginal, hillside areas by vast ranching estates and other export businesses, often are killed by flooding and mudslides, which have been exacerbated by the vast deforestation in the region. For example, rainstorms, floods, and mudslides ravaged much of Central America in October 2005 and killed hundreds, many of whom were buried alive. The deaths were represented in the U.S. media as the result of a tragic but unpredictable act of nature. Few were aware that, as stated by Carlos Fernandez of the Latin American Faculty of Social Sciences, "part of the reason the mountains melted into mud was the generations of deforestation."[15] The *Independent* reported, "The immediate cause of the flooding was the torrential rainfall that has lashed the region for the past few days. But the disaster that has killed 39 [in the town of Colón, El Salvador] was, to all intents and purposes, man made."[16] In

June 2010, another tropical storm in the region led to mudslides that took the lives of several hundred in rural hillside villages and left tens of thousands homeless.[17] The primary cause of the deforestation in Central America has been the expansion of ranching operations.

Many people from Mexico and Central America have migrated from U.S.-dominated economies of despair in their home countries for jobs and better wages in the United States. Ironically, many of those pushed to a marginalized existence in their home countries because of commercial ranching operations there are highly sought after as workers in corporate slaughterhouses in the United States. Their often undocumented status, their usually desperate need for jobs, and their lack of English skills and access to community support make them highly exploitable—and thus ideal employees for the "meat" industry. Slaughterhouse workers are paid low wages and forced to work in dangerous, horrific conditions, as terrified and struggling other animals are murdered at a staggering pace.[18] Undocumented workers are unlikely to make official complaints against their employers or organize to join a union. The presence of new Latin American immigrants among white, African American, and recent Asian immigrant workers contributes to an atmosphere of competition, distrust, and racism that employers exploit to dampen prospects for labor organizing or solidarity.

In the United States, where the rich are increasing their wealth while growing numbers struggle economically and cannot manage housing and health care costs, Mexican and Central American immigrants are easy targets for their frustration and anger. In addition to facing racism at work and in the community, immigrants often are used as scapegoats, being portrayed as the source of various social ills by opportunistic politicians or government officials who react to the public's misguided frustration and prejudice. For example, the Department of Homeland Security staged highly publicized raids to arrest "illegal aliens" at "meat"-processing plants throughout the Midwest. In one such raid in 2008, nearly four hundred employees from Mexico and Guatemala were arrested at an Agriprocessor "packinghouse" in Postville, Iowa. (In a stunning irony, they were taken to a local "cattle" exhibition hall for processing.) Before deportation, many were sentenced to five months in prison for illegal use of a social security card. At the same time, agribusiness corporations that commit immigration violations seldom are charged.[19]

In 2010, the Arizona legislature both pandered to and encouraged blame and persecution of Latin American immigrants by enacting a law requiring the aggressive identification, arrest, and deportation of undocumented workers; similar laws have spread to Georgia, Alabama, and South Carolina and are under debate in other states. A statement by the Mexican American Legal Defense and Educational Fund predicted such laws would create "a spiral of pervasive fear, community distrust, increased crime and costly litigation, with nationwide repercussions."[20] Few anti-immigrationists in the United States connect their economic problems to the disparities inherent in the capitalist system, nor do they see any links between the desperate migration from Mexico and Central America and their own socially constructed appetite for "hamburgers" and other forms of "meat."

While devalued people in Latin America continue to suffer deprivation and exploitation as vast areas of land are used to raise cows destined to become "hamburgers," their fates are entangled with that of the free-living animals who are being killed and displaced at such a rate that entire species in the region are endangered. For example, more than 90 percent of the population of the golden lion tamarin, a catlike monkey whose home has been the rainforests of Brazil, has vanished as forests continue to be destroyed, mainly for ranching and feed production.[21] Seventy species of mammals alone are endangered in just the Brazilian rainforest.

In Indonesia, a primary contributor to the rainforest destruction is Asia Pulp and Paper (APP), a firm that provides packaging and paper products for fast-food companies. One of its largest clients is KFC, which relies on the Indonesian rainforest fiber for its "cups, food boxes, French fry holders, napkins and the famous *chicken* buckets."[22] Preserving rainforests is critical in the struggle against climate change, and Indonesian forests also are home to many endangered species, including the Sumatran Tiger.

In Australia, New Zealand, and the Americas, the indigenous populations—already reduced by hostile invasions and the incursions of ranching—today are plagued by alcoholism, high rates of poverty, and disparities in educational attainment, employment, income, health care, and infant mortality. For instance, James Anaya, the UN special rapporteur on the rights of indigenous peoples, reported in May 2012 that Native Americans in the United States "suffered a history of dispossession of their lands and resources, the breakdown of their societies," and from continued practices of racial discrimination. "Anaya visited an Oglala Sioux reservation where the per capita income is around $7,000 a year, less than one-sixth of the national average, and life expectancy is about 50 years."[23] Anaya called on the U.S. government to return a portion of the stolen land back to Native Americans to help alleviate systemic discrimination and continuing injustice. In Australia, similarly, the life expectancy for indigenous people is twenty years less than that of the overall population.[24] The Aboriginal people there continue to struggle for rights and self-determination. At the same time, Australia is on the list of the top twenty countries with the largest number of threatened mammal species.[25]

In Africa, the demand for "meat" among the continent's urban affluent and the European and international "beef" trade has escalated violence. According to a 2007 UN report titled *Between a Rock and a Hard Place: Armed Violence in African Pastoralist Communities*, many communities in twenty-one nations there are seeing increasing levels of armed violence and lawlessness as successful "livestock" raids yield cash.[26] The increasing availability of "modern automatic weapons is well documented as having had a negative effect on the scale and impact of armed violence in pastoral communities."[27]

As the oppression of domesecrated animals grows in Africa, the condition of free-living animals there becomes increasingly precarious. For example, as competition for land and water intensifies and the number of domesecrated animals increases, many elephants—increasingly confined to small parks and reserves—have been killed to reduce their populations. In South Africa alone, thousands of elephants have been killed over the past several decades to control their numbers—in a nation with 47.1 *million* domesecrated cows, pigs, sheep, and goats.[28] Like countless other free-living animals throughout the world, many elephants also are dying from drought and starvation; others continue to be killed for their tusks. The government of Zimbabwe, a "beef"-exporting nation, maintains that a "culling" of the elephant population is needed there. However, "critics respond that Zimbabwe simply wants to kill elephants for their ivory, and indeed government officials have been accused of illegally exporting tusks to China in an ivory-for-arms deal."[29]

In Kenya, the population of lions plummeted by 85 percent in under twenty years, from two hundred thousand in 1990 to fewer than thirty thousand in 2009.[30] The leading cause of the lions' death is poisoning, primarily by Maasai pastoralists-turned-ranchers who see the lions as a threat to the cows they sell for cash. The poisoning of lions also occurs in Tanzania, a nation that has attracted U.S. investment dollars because of its potential to be a leader in the international "beef" trade. One speculator, a Georgia businessman, shared his vision in an interview with *Bloomberg Business Week*:

> We've founded a joint venture called Triple S *Beef* in Shinyanga, Tanzania. That's in the northern part of the country, just south of Lake Victoria. We'll begin by selling local *beef* on the national market and once we get the packing house [to fully meet] European and American standards, we'll begin to export into the Middle East. Of course, everyone's goal is to export to the European and U.S. markets eventually.[31]

As climate change and desertification reduce grazing areas and as arable land becomes an increasingly scarce resource for growing populations, the traditional conflict between pastoralists and settled communities has become more violent. Pastoralist and ranching practices played a significant, if not widely known, role in the first case of genocide in the twenty-first century, in the Darfur region of Sudan. Over the decades, there had been conflict over land and water in Darfur between farmers and a society of Arabic-speaking nomadic pastoralists known as the Janjaweed. (Janjaweed translates as "devils on *horseback*.") When farmers and other sedentary communities charged that Sudanese officials strongly favored the interests of the Arabic-speaking groups, the government responded by arming Janjaweed combatants. The Janjaweed were responsible for much of the barbarism, displacement, and death that occurred in Darfur—atrocities that also permitted the expropriation of land and the theft of domesecrated animals. The raiding of cows and other animals in Darfur has been

> organized almost on an industrial scale. Dozens of displaced villagers told Human Rights Watch that stolen cows are gathered in

Janjaweed *cattle* camps or "collection points—the largest of these reportedly at Um Shalaya—from where they are driven to government slaughterhouses in Nyala for export from Nyala, by air, to Arab countries like Lybia, Syria and Jordan."

"It's a very big business—and brings the government lots of money," one witness said. 'That's why the government likes the Arabs. They don't get much return from the poor farmers."[32]

Violent Janjaweed raids on farming villages were responsible for many of the estimated three hundred thousand human deaths in Darfur between 2003 and 2008; some people were murdered directly, but many became refugees and died later from hunger and disease.[33] Although a peace agreement was signed in 2005, violence continues for the 2.7 million refugees who live in unprotected villages and are still terrorized; the sexual victimization of women and girls in particular remains a serious problem.[34]

Foreshadowing the violence and genocide in Darfur, a 1999 report sponsored by the UN Development Program stated that "the scarcity of water, over the next 25 years, will possibly be the leading reason for major conflicts in Africa, not oil."[35] Similarly, a later report by the National Council on Foreign Relations noted:

> While water stress occurs throughout the world, no region has been more afflicted than sub-Saharan Africa. The crisis in Darfur stems in part from disputes over water: The conflict that led to the crisis arose from tensions between nomadic farming groups who were competing for water and grazing land—both increasingly scarce due to the expanding Sahara Desert.[36]

This conclusion is supported by a 2005 anthropological study that concluded,

> While the complicity of the Sudanese government is evident, a closer analysis of the sequence of events suggests that the crisis is rooted in local conflicts over material resources brought about by an eco-logical crisis. . . . The Darfur crisis is a poignant reminder of the violence that can erupt between pastoral nomads and sedentary agriculturalists.[37]

While it was hoped that the creation of two separate nations, Sudan and Southern Sudan (the Republic of South Sudan), in the summer of 2011 would ease the violence in the region, border disputes and conflict over the control of domesecrated cows continues. For instance, armed with weapons pouring into the area as a result of recent border disputes, violent "cattle" raids have intensified among pastoralist communities in the region. In June 2011, Dinka and Nuer fighters attacked the Murle, killing more than four hundred people and stealing thousands of cows. Two months later, Murle fighters raided the Nuer, taking thirty thousand cows, killing six hundred people, and abducting two hundred women and children.[38]

Moreover, the genocidal violence grounded in long-term conflicts between the Hutu and Tutsi in Rwanda spilled over into Zaire, now the Democratic Republic of the Congo, and millions there died from violence, starvation, and disease between 1997 and 2004; rape was widespread as a tactic to terrorize and demoralize rival civilian populations. As the conflict continues, tens of thousands continue to perish from hunger and disease. And mountain gorillas have been among the victims of the violence and conflict that plagues the region.[39]

## Growing Global Consumption of Domesecrated Animal Products

In 2010, an estimated 2.25 billion people lived primarily on a "meat"-based diet, while 4.5 billion lived primarily on a plant-based diet—and almost one billion had little access to any food and were malnourished.[40] In the United States, home of the "hamburger culture," it was estimated in 2002 that people consumed an average of 275 pounds of "meat" a year—twice the world average per capita consumption.[41] The annual U.S. consumption of cheese derived from cow's milk is more than thirty-one pounds per person—more than eight times the consumption rate in the early twentieth century—and U.S. residents consumed an average of 250 chicken eggs each year.[42]

Until the 1980s, the vast majority of regular "meat," "dairy," and "egg" consumption was in the United States, Canada, Western Europe, and Japan. However, international consumption of such products has grown enormously over the past several decades; the global supply of "meat" alone increased fourfold, from seventy-one million tons in 1961 to 286 million tons by 2010.[43]

As in the United States, where a surplus of corn prompted the expansion of domestic "meat" consumption, the increased global consumption of "meat" and related fare also has been promoted by U.S. feed-grain producers. "Throughout the 1960s, the USDA worked closely with Cargill and other grain companies to establish Asian *poultry* industries, baking industries, *cattle*-fattening yards, and fast food chains—all of which absorbed U.S. grains."[44] By the early 1990s, U.S. corn exporters were anxious to profit from China's growing economy.

> U.S. producers were in a position to control this potentially tremendous market since they dominated world corn markets. Consequently, U.S. agriculture was an important advocate of China receiving most favored nation status with the United States as well as admission to the World Trade Organization.[45]

The global dominance of U.S. corn producers was furthered by the passage of the 1996 Farm Bill, an act that ended most agricultural supply management measures and price supports created during the New Deal. (Price supports largely were restored by the Farm Security and Rural Reinvestment Act of 2002[46] and are likely to be replaced by guaranteed minimum revenues in 2012.)[47] The 1996 legislation—successfully promoted by feed-grain producers and other key players in the animal-industrial complex—led to the overproduction of feed grains, after which prices dropped, often below production costs. While feed-grain producers used the surplus to promote increased global "meat," "dairy," and "egg" production, the reduced prices for feed saved factory farms an average of $3.9 billion dollars a year beginning in 1997, before recent ethanol production increased the price of corn.[48] Sales of U.S. corn to China got another boost in 1999 when "the World Bank signed off on a $93.5 million loan to build 130 feedlots and five processing centers for China's nascent *beef* industry."[49] Not surprisingly, the largest increase in consumption has been in China, which accounted for 57 percent of the increase in "meat" consumption in what is euphemistically referred to as the "developing world."[50]

What is considered food, and what food is considered desirable, is largely dictated by one's culture. As U.S.-based corporations cultivate global cultural hegemony, "hamburgers" and related fare have become a major symbol of progress and modernity. As transnational companies compete for global market share, advertising by fast-food and other restaurant companies has intensified. In the words of the chairperson of the International "Meat" Secretariat, the world has "never seen global competition for *meat* protein markets this intense. And we haven't seen anything yet."[51]

At the forefront of the global expansion of "meat" consumption is the world's largest retail food corporation, McDonald's—whose ubiquitous advertisements in the United States now include sponsorship of the public television children's program *Sesame Street*. A glimpse of the company's aggressive plan for expansion was provided in an interview with Jeff Schwartz, CEO of McDonald's China, in a 2007 CNBC news program titled *Big Mac: Inside the McDonald's Empire*.

> REPORTER: When you look at the map can you imagine how many stores might be in China one day?
> SCHWARTZ: I don't need to look at the map to imagine that, I just look at the 1.3 billion population. Easily, we're talking 10,000 restaurants, 15,000 restaurants, as it continues to develop, so the opportunity is endless.[52]

Seeing the potential for drive-through service in China increase as more people there purchase automobiles, in 2006 McDonald's signed an agreement with the Chinese state oil company, Sinopec, giving it the right to open a restaurant at any of Sinopec's thirty thousand gas stations.[53] According to Wall Street watchers, McDonald's aggressive promotion in Asia and Africa has created "a fundamental long-term opportunity for investors."[54] With such intensive promotion of "meat," "dairy," and "egg" consumption by McDonald's and other participants in the global animal-industrial complex, it is estimated that global consumption of such commodities could double from its 2010 level by 2050.[55] Fast-food giants in the United States, including McDonald's, *Burger* King, and Wendy's, in 2005 formed the U.S. Food Trade Alliance to work through the World Trade Organization to "lower barriers to trade in processed foods and commodities" that preclude easy access to less affluent nations throughout the world.[56]

## CAFO Explosion

Even though enormous amounts of land in the United States and around the world have been expropriated for grazing, for some years now that land has been inadequate to allow large increases in domesecrated animal products. For production and consumption to expand profitably, it was necessary to increase dramatically the factory farming of domesecrated animals through the greater use of confined animal feeding operations (CAFOs).

In the United States alone, in 2010 there were more than twenty thousand CAFOs, enormous buildings where billions of pigs, cows, chickens, turkeys, and "dairy cows" are confined in horrific conditions. In more than 21,000 feedlots, "beef" cows "spend their last 100–120 days crammed together by the thousands standing in their own excrement, with little or no shelter from the elements."[57] More than ten billion domesecrated animals in the United States, amounting to 15 percent of those killed each year worldwide, experience what can only be characterized as a hellish existence to produce "meat," "dairy," and "eggs."[58] The use of CAFOs has allowed enormous increases in the oppression of domesecrated animals without requiring vast new expropriations of land for grazing (although enormous areas still are being taken for increasing production of feed crops). This new and more intensive form of commercial ranching has promoted a modern version of the historical pastoralist/rancher conflict with sedentary communities.

The evolution of commercial ranching of domesecrated animals into geographically fixed, intensive-confinement operations has harmed growing numbers of nearby human communities. Local residents' quality of life suffers from the noxious odors generated by the keeping of tens of thousands of other animals in close quarters and from accompanying respiratory illnesses. "A single large CAFO can produce more than 300 tons of manure in a year, more than the entire city of Philadelphia."[59] People living near CAFOs experience frequent fly infestations and contaminated groundwater and usually see their property values decline.

The minimalist regulations that exist to limit the environmental effects of CAFOs are violated routinely. In 2002, the Sierra Club compiled a "rap sheet" on factory farms to document CAFO and feedlot violations in forty-four states, creating a document longer than Tolstoy's *War and*

*Peace*—and the authors believe the publicly documented cases were just the tip of the iceberg.[60] In 2003, when roughly 54 percent of domese-crated animals in the United States were confined on just 5 percent of the nation's factory farms—and with industrial-scale "meat," "dairy," and "egg" operations growing rapidly[61]—the American Association for Public Health urged

> federal, state and local governments and public health agencies to impose a moratorium on new Concentrated Animal Feed Opera-tions until additional scientific data on the attendant risks to public health have been collected and uncertainties resolved. . . . [The APHA urged] federal and state governments to initiate and support research to quantify more precisely the exposures to pol-lutants in air, water and soil emissions of CAFOs experienced by communities surrounding CAFOs, as well as to investigate the greater vulnerability of infants and children to harm from such pollutants, deriving from either greater exposure or increased toxicity.[62]

A 2008 report from the Johns Hopkins Bloomberg School of Public Health, commissioned by the Pew Charitable Trusts, condemned the continued expansion of CAFOs. The report documented mounting pub-lic health threats, including the growing risk of antimicrobial-resistant organisms and the harm to workers, neighbors, "and even those living far from the facilities" because of air and water pollution. It also cited the growing contamination of groundwater, streams, and rivers with harmful levels of nutrients, toxins, bacteria, fungi, and viruses.[63] The report cited the wide variations in the regulation of CAFOS from one state to an-other and noted that in many cases there were no legal protections for public health or the environment. The report also acknowledged the treatment of other animals in these intensive settings.

> Confinement animals are generally raised indoors and, in some cases . . . the group size when raised indoors is larger than outdoors. In other cases (e.g., *veal* crates or gestation crates) animals are separated and confined to spaces that provide for only minimal movement. . . . [The animals have little] ability to express natural behaviors, for example—having natural materials to walk or lie on,

having enough floor space to move around with some freedom, and rooting. Crates, battery cages, and other such systems fail to allow for even these minimal natural behaviors. . . .

Most animals are physically altered without pain relief when raised in concentrated, confined production systems (as well as in some more open systems), even though it is widely accepted that such alteration causes pain. For example, *hogs* have their tails docked to avoid tail biting by other *hogs* in close proximity. *Laying hens* and *broilers* have their toenails, spurs, and beaks clipped. *Dairy cows* may have their horns removed or their tails docked.[64]

A separate report in 2008 by the Union of Concerned Scientists titled *CAFOs Uncovered: The Untold Costs of Confined Animal Feeding Operations* also was highly critical of factory farming—and of the transfer of billions of dollars in environmental and health care costs from agribusiness to U.S. taxpayers and rural communities.

The costs we pay as a society to support CAFOs—in the form of taxpayer subsidies, pollution, harm to rural communities, and poorer public health—is much too high. For example, conservative estimates of grain subsidies and manure distribution alone suggest that CAFOs would have incurred at least $5 billion in extra production costs per year if these expenses were not shifted onto the public. The figure would undoubtedly be much higher if truly adequate manure distribution was required.[65]

Increasingly, throughout the country "turf wars" have erupted as citizen groups press for relief in the face of local government laws and regulations that have been shaped by powerful agribusiness interests. Frustration, anger, and resentment toward industrial ranching operations are growing in many communities. According to Don Stull, an anthropologist at the University of Kansas, "I've seen serious rifts. There have been shootings over CAFOs . . . . This shows the level of anger that's present in these communities."[66]

Because of the enormous influence the animal-industrial complex exerts over the state, citizens' efforts toward substantive regulation meet with strong resistance. For example, in 2003 the Wisconsin state legislature enacted a law that limited the ability of local communities to oppose factory farms. The legislation was promoted by the Wisconsin "Dairy" Business Association, the Wisconsin Farm Bureau Federation, the Wisconsin "Cattlemen's" Association, the Wisconsin Corn Growers Association, the Wisconsin "Pork" Association, and the Professional "Dairy" Producers of Wisconsin.[67]

Where the law has not been co-opted in such ways, people sometimes have achieved some success in the courts. For example, in 2006 in Missouri a state court jury heard evidence that corporate owners of pig CAFOs there had subjected area residents to "massive quantities of liquid *hog* manure" and awarded the plaintiffs $4.5 million in punitive damages.[68]

Predictably, in the face of growing criticism in the United States about the environmental and public health impacts of more and ever-larger CAFOs, agribusiness giants have expanded into the Third World, where potentially burdensome regulations are not a hindrance—and where, conveniently, the industry is cultivating growing numbers of consumers of domesecrated-animal products. CAFOs now are the fastest growing form of "meat," "dairy," and "egg" production in the world and constitute 80 percent of the global growth in such commodities.[69]

> These intensive and environmentally destructive production methods are spreading all over the globe, to Mexico, India, the former Soviet Union, and most rapidly throughout Asia. Wherever they crop up, they create a web of related food safety, animal welfare, and environmental problems. Philip Lymbery, the campaign director of the World Society for the Protection of Animals, describes the growth of industrial animal production this way: Imagine traditional *livestock* production as a beach and factory farms as a tide. In the United States, the tide has completely covered the beach, swallowing up small farms and concentrating production in the hands of a few large companies. In Taiwan, it is almost as high. In the Philippines, however, the tide is just hitting the beach.[70]

Nations like the Philippines and Thailand, with little history of land expropriation and violence linked to traditional ranching practices, are rapidly becoming centers of intensive CAFO ranching operations.[71] As in the United States, the CAFOs there each year produce tens of millions of tons of manure, which is stored in lagoons and uncovered containment pits and which seeps into underground water supplies and contaminates the air. When storms or hurricanes occur, neighboring lands and miles of waterways become contaminated with manure and bacteria.

> According to the FAO [United Nations Food and Agricultural Organization], the trend toward increased commercialization and intensification of *livestock* production is leading to a variety of food safety problems. Crowded, unsanitary conditions and poor waste treatment in factory farms exacerbate the rapid movement of animal diseases and food-borne infections. *E. coli* 0157:H7, for instance, is spread from animals to humans when people eat food contaminated by manure. Animals raised in intensive conditions often arrive at slaughterhouses covered in feces, thus increasing the chance of contamination during slaughtering and processing.[72]

In addition to the growing environmental and public health problems caused by CAFOs in the United States and throughout the world, a tremendous amount of grain is required for the rapid growth of tens of billions of other animals. As the world increasingly pursues the same "meat"-based diet as the United States, more than a billion humans are malnourished while growing amounts of grain are used to feed domesecrated animals. "Mexico now feeds 45 percent of its grain to *livestock*, up from 5 percent in 1960. Egypt went from 3 percent to 31 percent in the same period, and China, with a sixth of the world's population, has gone from 8 percent to 26 percent. All of these places have poor people who could use the grain, but they can't afford it."[73]

## MISUSE OF FINITE RESOURCES

"Loss of topsoil has been a major factor in the fall of civilizations over the ages."[74] Healthy, fertile soil is the foundation of life on the planet, and the rapid erosion of this resource has been called "the silent global crisis";[75] raising other animals for food "is one of the main activities responsible for soil erosion around the world."[76] An estimated two-thirds of all corn produced in the world—a grain associated with high rates of soil erosion—is used as feed for domesecrated animals.[77]

The first major study of global soil misuse in 1991 revealed that human practices have "degraded more than 7.5 million square miles of land" (an area the size of Canada and the United Stated combined).[78] According to the 2009 UN Intergovernmental Panel on Climate Change, as a result of such misuse of precious topsoil for "livestock" and feed-grain production, "one third of the earth's surface is affected by desertification and land degradation and nearly 75 percent of all pastureland is in the process of turning into desert."[79] As a crisis in global food security grows, Rajendra Pachauri, the director of Yale's Climate and Energy Institute and chair of the UNIPCC panel, states flatly, "We should eat less *meat*."[80]

An enormous amount of fossil fuel also is necessary to sustain the growing levels of animal exploitation for food consumption in the world. In the United States, as soil is leached of nutrients from years of intensive production of grains—80 percent of which becomes feed—nearly six gallons of oil are needed to create the fertilizer necessary for production on a single acre.[81] Taking into account these petroleum-based fertilizers and the energy used in all the processes of production and distribution— including mechanization and hydrocarbon-based herbicides and pesticides—it is estimated that it takes roughly 25 kilocalories (25,000 calories of heat energy) of fossil fuel to create one kilocalorie (1,000 calories) of "meat."[82] So much oil is needed for the "meat," "egg," and "dairy"-based diet of the United States that it has been estimated that, if everyone on the planet ate in the same way as U.S. consumers, the world's remaining oil resources would be depleted in seven years.[83]

The use of domesecrated animals for food is also a significant drain on the world's diminishing supply of fresh water. Half of the water consumed in the United States is used to produce feed grains.[84] On average, almost 26,000 liters of water (one liter = 1.06 quart) is necessary to produce one kilogram (2.2 pounds) of "meat," while only 900 liters of water is required for the production of one kilogram of wheat.[85] Put another way, according to a special report in *Newsweek*, "the water that goes into a 1,000 pound *steer* would float a destroyer."[86]

As the production of "animal products" expands, the global supply of fresh water is disappearing, and millions are affected by water scarcity. "More than 2.3 billion people in 21 countries live in water-stressed basins . . . and some 1.7 billion people live in basins under scarcity conditions. More than one billion people do not have sufficient access to clean water."[87] The physicist and environmental activist Vandana Shiva notes that "the water crisis is the most pervasive, most severe and most invisible dimension of the ecological devastation of the earth."[88] In 1995, a vice president of the World Bank noted, "if the wars of this century were fought over oil, the wars of the next century will be fought over water."[89] However, rather than advocate for changes in the way water is used, especially by the animal-industrial complex, the World Bank—while continuing to press for expanded production of "meat"—has promoted water privatization. This policy has resulted in sharp increases in the cost of water for people in the Third World, as powerful global corporations seek to dominate the emerging "water industry."[90]

Meanwhile, treating domesecrated animals as food and resources is also the world's largest source of water pollution, from enormous levels of animal wastes, pesticides and herbicides, antibiotics and hormones, and toxic chemical residue from "tanneries." The pollution is not limited to local or regional waterways but is the cause of coastal "dead zones" and coral reef destruction.[91]

In addition to the role of oppression of domesecrated animals in world hunger, environmental destruction, and soil, water, and oil depletion, the practice is also a *leading contributor* to global warming. This is the result of such factors as the burning of fossil fuels for production and transport, methane gases emitted from domesecrated animals, methane and nitrous oxide produced from enormous amounts of manure, and the deforestation of land for pasture and feed production. According to a 2006 UN FAO report:

> The *livestock* sector is a major player, responsible for 18 percent of greenhouse gas emissions in CO2 equivalents. This is a higher share than transport. . . .
>
> *Livestock's* contribution to environmental problems is on a massive scale and its potential contribution to their solution is equally large. The impact is so significant that it needs to be addressed with urgency.[92]

## LOOMING REGIONAL AND INTERNATIONAL CONFLICT

According to the United Nations, 70 percent of all of the world's agricultural land—30 percent of all the land surface of the planet—is used in some form of "livestock" production, including vast areas of the Americas, Africa, and Oceania.[93] In 2001, a report by a team of scientists cautioned that, if the emphasis on animal-based diets does not change, by 2050 an area the size of the United States would need to be found for additional pasture and cropland. They predicted that the expansion would come in Latin America and Africa, areas already plagued with large populations of landless, impoverished, and hungry people struggling over land and water.[94] As early as 1993 a report published in *Scientific American* warned, "scarcity of renewable resources is already contributing to violent conflicts in many parts of the *developing world*. These conflicts may foreshadow a surge of similar violence in coming decades, particularly in poor countries where shortages of water, forests and, especially, fertile land, coupled with rapidly expanding populations, already cause great hardship."[95]

This anticipated expansion of conflict over land—fueled further by global concerns over global warming, food insecurity, and growing profits from biofuels—already is occurring in the form of "land grabs" by corporations and investors. In a 2011 report, the World Bank noted:

Interest in farmland is rising. And, given commodity price volatility, growing human and environmental pressures, and worries about food security, this interest will increase, especially in the *developing world*. . . .

The demand for land has been enormous. Compared to an average annual expansion of global agricultural land of less than 4 million hectares before 2008, approximately 56 million hectares worth of large-scale farmland deals were announced even before the end of 2009. More than 70 percent of such demand has been in Africa; countries such as Ethiopia, Mozambique, and Sudan have transferred millions of hectares to investors in recent years.[96]

An Oxfam report issued in late 2011 estimated that, as of that time, a total of 227 million hectares of land, mostly in poorer nations, have been acquired by corporations or other outside interests such as larger and wealthier countries.[97] Such land grabs are viewed as a good investment by banks and hedge fund managers, and affluent nations view the acquisition of land as a means to buttress food security, especially for "meat." China, for example, is acquiring land for the production of feed crops in Brazil and launching "livestock" projects in Tanzania. Oil-rich Middle Eastern nations are "extra nervous about the vulnerability of their *meat* supplies. *Meat* imports have skyrocketed, as have imports of feed."[98] As the affluent work to secure their access to products derived from domesecrated animals, growing numbers of people in the Third World face food shortages and hunger.

The anticipation of imminent resource and food shortages is compounded by climate change—a problem brought about in no small part by the practice of raising other animals as food—which is linked to volatile weather patterns and an increasing incidence of severe storms, tornados, hurricanes, floods, droughts, and heat waves around the world.[99] For instance, floods in the United States, Australia, Pakistan, and India—and severe droughts in Russia, Eastern Europe, China, Argentina, and the southwestern United States—have driven up the cost of food. Since 2008, as tens of millions have been pushed into poverty and joined the ranks of the malnourished, food riots have occurred in countries ranging from Haiti to Egypt to Bangladesh.[100]

And as climate change continues to unfold and global temperatures increase, the problem of food security will grow even worse. "When crops are subjected to temperatures above a certain threshold—about 84 degrees for corn and 86 degrees for soybeans—yields fall sharply . . . making it likely the challenges to food production will grow in an era when demand is expected to rise sharply."[101] The 2011 famine in Somalia—a tragedy that took the lives of tens of thousands of people (disproportionately pastoralists) and innumerable numbers of domesecrated animals—has been linked by UN officials and climate researchers to global warming.[102]

The depletion of finite resources historically has produced conflict,[103] and a primary factor in such historical conflicts has been food scarcity.[104] As global warming unfolds, the nations most at risk are those in the Third World that lack adequate water supplies and have few resources to handle severe weather patterns and food shortages.[105] Regional conflict and violence over resources, compounded by mass migrations caused by severe weather events and water and food shortages, are possible in several areas of the world, including Africa—especially sub-Saharan Africa—and parts of Latin America, the Middle East, and Southeast Asia.[106]

How has the U.S. government—an institution that has used military power and economic coercion to secure resources, exploitable labor, and markets for more than two centuries—responded to climate change, the looming scarcity in vital natural resources, and its implications for such crucial activities as food production? As early as 1974, a report by the U.S. Central Intelligence Agency stated that climate change was a "long-term reality" requiring new alignments "among nations to insure a secure supply of food resources."[107] Indeed, the CIA, which has been instrumental in promoting the interests of powerful capitalists and corporations, for years has been analyzing the level and sustainability of global food supplies. Writing in 1985, Marcus Linear observed that the CIA "works intimately with the National Aeronautics and Space Administration (NASA) in evaluating 'spy-in-the-sky' photographs of the world's croplands, and keeps a running check on world harvests and crop potentials. The agency is thus fascinated by food and agriculture, and the organizations which influence its production."[108]

The government's awareness of the increasing scarcity of key resources, now compounded by global warming, can be seen in recent, unclassified reports by U.S. intelligence organizations. A 2003 report, for example, by military officials in the United States cautioned that rapid climate change could produce megadroughts, famine, widespread rioting, and a threat to global security surpassing that of terrorism.[109] Similarly, a 2007 report by a panel of eleven retired U.S. generals and admirals concluded that climate change poses a "serious threat to America's national security and energy dependence" and will exacerbate global instability and tensions. The report recommended that "the national security consequences of climate change should be fully integrated into national security and national defense strategies."[110]

The growing scarcity of vital, finite resources—a problem compounded by global warming—also is being watched by the U.S. intelligence agencies. For instance, discussing the crisis of diminishing global water supplies in a 2001 television interview, a spokesperson for the National Intelligence Council, a think tank for the U.S. intelligence organizations, stated, "Life of all kinds depends upon it [water], there is no substitute for it. It is replenished, but at a finite rate. And it is very unevenly distributed. . . . It could lead to wars."[111]

Congress also has prompted U.S. intelligence agencies to analyze the possible effect of climate change on national security, including the potential for scarcity and conflict; study of the growing global adoption of the U.S.-model diet is central to their work. A 2008 report by the National Intelligence Council noted the links among global warming, water shortages, declining oil reserves, and the spread of Western food models:

Food and water also are intertwined with climate change, energy, and demography. . . . The World Bank estimates that demand for food will rise by 50 percent by 2030, as a result of a growing world population, rising affluence, and shifts to Western dietary preferences by a larger middle class. . . .

Between now and 2025, the world will have to juggle competing and conflicting energy security and food security concerns, yielding a tangle of difficult-to-manage consequences.[112]

The report noted that twenty-one nations with a combined population of six hundred million humans currently are "either cropland or freshwater scarce." By 2025, it is projected that thirty-six nations—with a combined population of 1.4 billion—will be similarly affected. "Lack of access to stable supplies of water is reaching unprecedented proportions in many areas of the world and is likely to grow worse owing to rapid urbanization and population growth," and "demand for water for agricultural purposes and hydroelectric power generation also will expand."[113] The report cited the decline in global crude oil and natural gas resources, and noted that two-thirds of the world's reserves are in the Middle East.[114]

Perceptions of energy scarcity will drive countries to take actions to assure their future access to energy supplies. In the worst case this could lead to interstate conflicts if government leaders deem assured access to energy resources to be essential to maintaining domestic stability and the survival of their regime. . . .

Perceptions of a rapidly changing environment may cause nations to take unilateral actions to secure resources, territory, and other interests.[115]

In the words of one former military commander, "It will initially be people fighting for food and shelter. When the migration starts, every state would want to stop the migrations from happening. Eventually, it would have to become a military conflict. Which other means do you have to resolve your border issues?"[116]

Also in 2009, the CIA created a Center on Climate Change to monitor the national security impact of global warming,[117] and the Pentagon officially recognized global warming as a threat to U.S. national security and began including an analysis of climate change in its reports to Congress.[118] In its 2010 *Quadrennial Defense Review Report*, the U.S. Department of Defense observed: "Rising demand for resources, rapid urbanization of littoral regions, the effects of climate change, the emergence of new strains of disease, and profound cultural and demographic tensions in several regions are just some of the trends whose complex interplay may spark or exacerbate future conflicts."[119]

In like fashion, a 2008 report by two senior European Union officials stated that increased competition for water, grain, and energy had the potential to create significant conflicts in Africa and the Middle East and between Russia and the European Union.[120] In 2009, a report by the Australian Defence Force warned that global warming could create failed states across the Pacific as sea levels rise and conflict over resources develops.[121]

It is unlikely that the U.S. military and intelligence organizations and those of its global allies are planning for and developing more sustainable uses of oil, land, and water or for the transformation to a world where all are fed. The history of the capitalist system is one in which the lives of humans and other animals are expendable—indeed, are fodder for the acquisition of wealth. History demonstrates the violent and chauvinistic ways the U.S. government in particular has promoted the interests of the nation's affluent—from the extermination of Native Americans and buffalo to the "low-intensity" wars in Central America to the recent deaths of tens of thousands of civilians after the U.S. military intervention in the Middle East (the location of two-thirds of the remaining global oil resources). This historical pattern does not bode well for those living in less-powerful nations, as climate change occurs and scarce resources are squandered by the corporate-promoted expansion of "meat," "dairy," and "egg" consumption. In all likelihood, the elites in the most powerful countries in the world will support the use of military power to expropriate dwindling global resources and to suppress resistance and calls for justice; they will seek to keep global capitalism functioning as long as possible.

## THE POTENTIAL GLOBAL INFLUENZA PANDEMIC

As the escalating oppression of domesecrated animals in turn increases the likelihood of violence and wars, the possibility of even greater death and social upheaval looms. The world faces the growing potential for a deadly influenza pandemic, which is being made increasingly possible by the spread of industrial ranching operations.

Infectious disease resulting from animal domesecration, responsible for hundreds of millions of deaths of humans and other animals over the past several thousand years, remains a serious threat to the world today. Indeed, in the early twentieth century, as the exploitation of domesecrated animals was rapidly accelerating, disaster struck. In 1918–1919, an influenza pandemic took the lives of an estimated fifty million humans around the world.[122] "Approximately 550,000 died in the United States, more than the number of Americans killed in World War I, World War II, the Korean War, and the war in Vietnam combined."[123] Considered the deadliest disease event in human history, the source of the deadly influenza is debated. Some contend that the close proximity of chickens and humans in China was the origin; others point to the use of pigs as food on a military base in Kansas. However, it is widely believed that domesecrated chickens contracted a virus infecting free-living birds, and it then may have passed through pigs and been transmitted to humans.[124] Following the 1918–1919 catastrophe, the immune systems of humans and pigs eventually adapted to the virus, which then became a reoccurring but usually nonfatal influenza. In 1957, genetic input from a different bird flu virus triggered another pandemic (the Asian Flu), and two million died. A similar event in 1968 (the Hong Kong Flu) took an estimated one million human lives. Those pandemics likely resulted from humans coming into contact with infectious microbes that had mutated in groups of domesecrated animals.[125]

The danger of new strains of influenza virus did not emerge again until the 1990s, when infections among domesecrated chickens skyrocketed and multiple bird-flu viruses began infecting people in several parts of the world. In 1998, a virus emerged and spread throughout the U.S. pig population that contained gene segments from the classic pig virus, from a bird virus, and from the human influenza virus—the first triple-hybrid influenza virus on record. The virus quickly spread to industrial pig operations throughout much of North America and was transmitted to Eurasia; by 2009, the triple-hybrid animal influenza, first discovered in the United States, also had acquired gene segments from a Eurasian pig influenza. The virus then began to infect humans, resulting in the H1N1 pandemic of 2009.

Why did these influenza virus mutations occur so rapidly in the last part of the twentieth century? Michael Greger, a physician and the director of Public Health and Animal Agriculture at the Humane Society International, maintains that the source of the increased threat to human and animal health lies in the growing number and size of industrial animal operations.

> What has been happening in recent years to trigger this kind of evolutionary fast-forward for both *swine* and chicken flu viruses? . . . Chickens raised for *meat* are typically warehoused in sheds confining tens of thousands of birds. Half of the egg-laying hens in the world are now intensively confined in battery cages, small, barren, wire enclosures extending down long rows of windowless sheds. There can be a million birds on one farm. About half of the world's pig population is also now crowded into industrial confinement operations. Old MacDonald's Farm got replaced by the new [Ronald] McDonald's farm. These intensive systems represent the most profound alteration of the human-animal relationship in ten thousand years. No surprise, perhaps, that they have been shown repeatedly to be breeding grounds for disease.[126]

The confinement of thousands or tens of thousands of domesecrated animals in CAFOs vastly increases the possibility of dangerous, mutated viruses. The novel H1N1 virus first gained attention when a community adjacent to a Smithfield-owned CAFO in Mexico began experiencing high rates of infection. However, its origins can be traced to a triple-hybrid virus discovered in North Carolina CAFOs in 1998. Michael Greger points out that CAFOs vastly increase the potential for the development of new virulent influenza strains for a number of reasons, including the fact that the operations' massive numbers of pigs and chickens, whose immune systems are weakened by the stress of being in overcrowded, intensive operations, tend to be clustered together geographically. The domesecrated animals' respiratory systems also are compromised because of the lack of fresh air and high levels of ammonia from decomposing wastes. In short, the conditions in CAFOs hardly could have been designed better as breeding grounds for influenza viruses. Infected other animals are then transported long distances in contaminated trucks and shipping containers, further multiplying the opportunities for mutation and transmission.[127]

Gregory Gray, the director of the Center for Emerging Infectious Diseases at the University of Iowa College of Public Health, notes:

> When respiratory viruses get into these confinement facilities, they have continual opportunity to replicate, mutate, reassort, and recombine into novel strains. The best surrogates we can find in the human population are prisons, military bases, ships, or schools. But respiratory viruses can run quickly through these [human] populations and then burn out, whereas in CAFOs—which often have continual introductions of [unexposed] animals—these's much greater potential for the viruses to spread and become endemic.[128]

After the 1998 discovery of the novel triple-hybrid mutant in U.S. pigs, scientists warned that CAFOs were breeding grounds for new, virulent pathogens that could infect workers and veterinarians and then spread to the general population, triggering a pandemic.[129] The animal-industrial complex did little to address this growing threat to public health, other than to begin vaccinating pigs against the virus—a strategy that kept many individual pigs from getting sick and losing profitable body weight but that did not keep the virus from infecting other animals. In fact, some scientists fear that "widespread vaccination may actually be selecting for new viral types."[130]

While the 2009 pandemic was mild in comparison to earlier epidemics—and some scientists say the danger from the H1N1 virus may not be past—the threat of more, newly evolving strains is clear. For example, in Canada a novel H4N6 virus was discovered in pigs. If such a virus were to be introduced to the general human population, the consequences "would be catastrophic, as humans have no immunity to H4 viruses."[131] According to Michael T. Osterholm, the director of the Center for Infectious Disease Research and Policy and associate director of the Department of Homeland Security's National Center for Food Protection and Defense, "An influenza pandemic of even moderate impact will result in the biggest single human disaster ever—far greater than AIDS, 9/11, all wars in the 20th century, and the recent tsunami combined. It has the potential to redirect world history as the Black Death redirected European history in the 14th century."[132]

An editorial in a 2007 edition of the *American Journal of Public Health* stated: "Inductive reasoning leads to the conclusion that an influenza epidemic *will* arise, as such epidemics have arisen many times before, including 3 times during the twentieth century. The relevant questions, therefore, are when the next one will emerge and how bad it will be."[133]

The 2008 report of the National Intelligence Council cited earlier, in addition to military plans for future water, oil, and food shortages, also considered the potential for conflict relating to a deadly influenza pandemic.

> The emergence of a novel, highly transmissible, and virulent human respiratory illness for which there are no adequate countermeasures could initiate a global pandemic. If a pandemic disease emerges by 2025, internal and cross-border tension and conflict will become more likely as nations struggle—with degraded capabilities—to control the movement of populations seeking to avoid infection or maintain access to resources. . . .
>
> The absence of an effective vaccine and near universal lack of immunity would render populations vulnerable to infection. In this worst case, tens to hundreds of millions of Americans within the U.S. Homeland would become ill and deaths would mount into the tens of millions. Outside the U.S., critical infrastructure degradation and economic loss on a global scale would result as approximately a third of the worldwide population became ill and hundreds of millions died.[134]

A joint report issued by the World Health Organization, the UN Food and Agricultural Organization, and the World Organisation for Animal Health stated, "Many of the human diseases that are new, emerging and re-emerging at the beginning of the 21st century are caused by pathogens originating from animals or from products of animal origin referred to as zoonotic diseases." The first of the risk factors listed in the report as increasing the risk for such diseases was the rising global demand for "animal protein."[135]

Threats to public health also stem from the pharmaceuticals given to other animals exploited by agribusiness in order to produce rapid growth and limit costly diseases. Throughout most of the world, antibiotics are included routinely in the feed given to intensively confined other animals in order to improve growth, although such use increases the likelihood of antibiotic-resistant bacteria. In the United States, agribusiness and pharmaceutical companies have exerted political power to resist multiple calls from public health and medical associations to stop this practice.

## The Growing Pandemic of Chronic Diseases

While public health officials and the military brace for a deadly pandemic, chronic diseases related to the consumption of products derived from domesticated animals already are prevalent and rising. Frequent patronizing of fast-food restaurants, where "meat," "dairy," and "egg" consumption is combined with high levels of salt and sugar, is linked to the high rate of obesity in the United States, where 64 percent of the population is overweight or obese. The relationship between unhealthy consumption of sugary sodas and "meat"-eating is noted by Richard Robbins: "The sugar in soft drinks serves as the perfect complement to *hamburgers* and *hot dogs* because it possesses what nutritionists call 'go-away' qualities—removing the fat coating and the *beef* aftertaste from the mouth."[136] Obesity is a major risk factor for coronary artery disease.[137] Heart disease, especially coronary artery disease, is the leading cause of death in the United States and a principal cause of disability; a person in the United States dies from a heart attack every minute.[138] Following heart disease, the second and third leading causes of death—cancer and stroke—also are linked strongly to the consumption of products derived from domesecrated animals.

As such products are sold at a rapidly increasing rate worldwide, the problem of global hunger and malnutrition is accompanied by what the World Health Organization calls "an escalating global epidemic of overweight and obesity—'globesity.'"[139] By 2015, the WHO projects 2.3 billion adults will be overweight, four hundred million will be obese, and millions will suffer from an array of serious health disorders, including diabetes, hypertension, heart disease, and cancers.[140] The "Westernization— in some circles Americanization—of the global culinary landscape no doubt contributed to the fattening of the world."[141] Colonization, motivated in many instances by the expansion of ranching operations, has been followed by "McDonaldization."[142] A joint report of the WHO and the UN Food and Agricultural Organization noted:

> Food and food products have become commodities produced and traded in a market that has expanded from an essentially local base

to an increasingly global one. Changes in the world food economy
are reflected in shifting dietary patterns, for example, increased
consumption of energy-dense diets high in fat, particularly saturated fat, and low in unrefined carbohydrates. . . .

Because of these changes . . . obesity, diabetes mellitus, cardiovascular disease, hypertension and stroke, and some forms of cancer
are becoming increasingly significant causes of disability and premature death in both developing and newly developed countries,
placing additional burdens on already overtaxed national health
budgets.[143]

"According to the WHO, such chronic (often termed 'non-communicable')
diseases are the largest cause of death in the world, led by cardiovascular
disease."[144]

This comparative historical analysis shows that the exploitation of large
numbers of domesecrated animals, a practice initially developed in Eurasia, enabled and promoted large-scale violence in many regions of the
world. The use of domesecrated animals as instruments of war, as laborers, and as rations and other resources facilitated warfare that was much
more extensive than it could have been in the absence of animal exploitation. And, as a result of crowding other animals closely together, infectious zoonotic diseases mutated, spread, and eventually caused the deaths
of countless humans and other animals while also weakening the resistance of populations who were being invaded, in many cases for the expansion of ranching operations.

While this enormous level of violence and death was *enabled* by
domesecration, it also was *driven* by this process, as the possession of large
numbers of horses, cows, pigs, sheep, goats, and other animals became
desirable as an important source of wealth. For thousands of years, male-
dominated societies violently expropriated the land and water necessary
to maintain large groups of other animals; over time, pastoralism developed into ranching, as many domesecrated animals came to be raised
primarily for sale. The violent and oppressive use of domesecrated animals was deeply entangled with the experiences of people who were conquered and had their land expropriated for pasture. This entanglement
also included the free-living animals who were displaced or killed so they
would not threaten or interfere with pastoralist or ranching operations.

Over the course of history, it was mainly the social and economic elites who possessed large numbers of domesecrated animals, as such territorial holdings required a great deal of military power to gain and keep and to stave off raiders. The violence and carnage that domesecration produced unquestionably played a role in the development of militaristic, elite-dominated, patriarchal cultures and states.

Domesecration, with its accompanying violence and culture of oppression, was forced on the Americas, with devastating consequences. The bloodshed and plunder in Latin America made possible by domesecration and the eventually resulting enclosure of the commons in Europe for sheep ranching were essential for the rise of the capitalist system and the ensuing imperialist policies and practices. Much of the violence perpetrated by leaders of industrializing capitalist nations in the nineteenth century thus was either caused by the expropriation of land for ranching or enabled by the exploitation of ranched animals. Indigenous people throughout the world suffered death, displacement, exploitation, and hunger.

In the nineteenth century, as in earlier times, the material gain generated from domesecration-related violence—wealth disproportionately controlled by the most affluent and powerful—was made possible by elites' control of the state and by ideological legitimation. The ideology supporting the large-scale violence generated by domesecration included Social Darwinist theory and religious and philosophically backed speciesism, ideas promoted at the time by such scholars as Nathaniel Southgate Shaler and Frank Wilson Blackmar, as noted in the introduction.

The general pattern of violence resulting from domesecration changed somewhat under capitalism beginning in the early twentieth century. The aggressive expropriation of huge land masses for grazing had been accomplished and, in industrialized capitalist nations, the use of other animals as instruments of war and laborers diminished. However, as these forms of oppression declined, the numbers of domesecrated animals exploited for food increased. Tens of millions of humans and other animals suffered from the deadly influenza pandemic of 1918—a disaster that would be linked to domesecrated animals only decades later.

Over the course of the twentieth century, the number and size of businesses involved in the exploitation of domesecrated animals—especially as food—grew enormously and coalesced into the animal-industrial complex, whose synergy drove a huge expansion of the domesecrated animal-based food industry. Publicly subsidized feed-grain production, emerging fast-food companies, state agricultural colleges, and related forces grew along with radio and television technology, and the public was exhorted to consume. As mass consumption of fast food and a diet based on do-mesecrated animals grew in the United States, so did the level of struc-tural violence, as people died prematurely from the chronic diseases as-sociated with eating other animals.

The production of enormous amounts of "meat" and related products created other new harms, including through the transformation of ranch-ing processes to intensive and frequently confined operations. As the sheer numbers of domesecrated animals climbed—and as their suffering increased exponentially—enormous supplies of fresh water and topsoil for feed production were needed. And in the twentieth century, profitable ranching relied not just on water and land, as it had for thousands of years, but now also became equally dependent on *oil*.

In the twentieth century, people in the United States saw little of the direct violence generated by land expropriation, such as had facilitated capitalist development in the eighteenth and nineteenth centuries. How-ever, U.S. policy in Latin America generated an enormous level of such violence there. The decision of U.S. leaders to promote capitalist expan-sion in the region, in part by increasing "beef" exports, resulted in large-scale violence and the predictable poverty and exploitation for the dis-possessed. Like countless others before them who were displaced by the expansion of ranching operations, many of the displaced in Latin Amer-ica became exploitable workers—increasingly for transnational corpora-tions. As in the past, the expansion of ranching in the region and the appropriation of farmland for pasture caused a decline in the cultivation of maize and beans in the region, which increased hunger and malnutri-tion. This decerealization also was facilitated by the increasing use of land for profitable feed-grain production.

Today, hundreds of millions of indigenous and other devalued people are landless, impoverished, exploited, and hungry, and the land they once occupied and used to feed themselves is devoted to raising domese-crated animals and producing feed grain. The multiple environmental and public health consequences of growing numbers of CAFOs also are being felt throughout the world.

Violent, domesecration-driven land expropriation continues today, al-though it is more incremental and regional than in the past and attracts relatively little international attention. When murder and genocide related to domesecration do come to the attention of the public in the West, the incidents frequently are explained as "ethnic" conflict (as in Darfur) or as merely the act of a few bad individuals (as in the murder of Dorothy Stang). The violence seldom is linked to the production of what most everyone has been socially programmed to eat.

Growing consumption of the U.S.-style diet in other areas of the world has caused an epidemic of chronic disease. Increasing numbers of people become ill or die from coronary artery disease, various forms of cancer, and other conditions linked to the consumption of domesecrated animal products. The animal-industrial complex's confinement of growing numbers of other animals also puts the world at high risk for the emergence of deadly new strains of influenza.

What is more, the demands of growing global production and consumption of products from domesecrated animals are contributing to the depletion of essential, finite resources. Enormous amounts of precious fresh water, fossil fuel, and topsoil are being used—and rainforests destroyed—to build and expand the global "hamburger culture," and the use of domesecrated animals as food is a major contributor to global warming. In the twenty-first century, the destruction caused by the exploitation of domesecrated animals as food does not take the form of plundering and burning cities, as in the days of Chinggis Khan or the conquistadors. However, the relentless quest for the land, water, and energy necessary to maintain enormous numbers of oppressed other animals plunders the environment and these life-sustaining resources. The unsustainable and destructive—not to mention horrifically violent—exploitation of growing numbers of domesecrated animals as food and resources is on course to create a scarcity of resources that will lead to international warfare. In 2008, the director-general of the World Health Organization stated that the most serious threats to international security were food shortages, climate change, and an influenza pandemic.[145] To be thorough, the director-general should have included in that list the depletion of world supplies of fresh water, topsoil, and fossil fuel. The trauma and loss of life that would be produced by scarcity-driven conflict and warfare hardly can be calculated. And it seems certain that indigenous peoples, the poor, and the devalued will suffer the most.

Deeply entangled with the violence, disease, and deprivation currently confronting the human species—and the looming risks of scarcity-driven warfare and an influenza pandemic—is the treatment of domesecrated animals around the world. Every year, more than *fifty-five billion*[146] sentient beings—cows, chickens, pigs, and other animals—experience enormous levels of deprivation and pain before they are cruelly transported and killed. In addition to the terrible treatment of domesecrated animals, countless numbers of free-living animals are displaced and killed because of the destruction of rainforests and any other area into which profitable grazing, feed-grain, and fodder production can be expanded. In addition to the distress and trauma each individual endures under the "exploitative forces of capital,"[147] more than 16,000 *entire species* of other animals are threatened with extinction, and 1,528 are critically endangered.[148] This impact on free-living animals is greatly exacerbated by the effects of global warming. As a result of climate change, a team of international scientists predicts 15 to 37 percent of all the species on the earth could become extinct by 2050.[149]

Tens of thousands of other animals also are killed each year because they are seen as interfering with the maximization of ranching profits. In just the United States, for example, in 1997 the government transferred control of the U.S. Animal Damage Control Program, created in 1931 to exterminate other animals considered to be injurious to western ranching enterprises, from the Department of the Interior to the agribusiness-promoting Department of Agriculture; the program was renamed "*Wildlife* Services." Despite its slogan "Living with *Wildlife*," in 2008 alone the agency used methods such as trapping, snaring, poisoning, and aerial gunning to kill more than five million other animals—including prairie dogs, bobcats, bears, cougars, wolves, badgers, coyotes, foxes, mountain lions, opossums, raccoons, skunks, beavers, porcupines, blackbirds, and starlings.[150]

While dreadful, domesecration-related outcomes for humanity are foreseen sometime in the not-too-distant future, for the rest of the inhabitants of the earth—especially domesecrated animals—the worst scenario is already here. Domesecrated and free-living animals were inhabitants of the earth for millions of years before their enslavement and extermination became deeply intertwined with human violence and repression just ten thousand years ago. Even if all of the harm done to the other inhabitants of the earth were not inextricably entangled with other critical global issues, the enslavement and killing of the other inhabitants of the earth is morally unacceptable. Ten thousand years of such violence and harm is enough.

The grave problems confronting the world are directly linked to the increasing exploitation of domesecrated animals under contemporary capitalism. The creation of a truly "civilized" global order and world peace and justice—that is, a path in which the human species truly would be "on its upward way"—depends on the nonviolent transcendence of capitalism and an end to domesecration.

CHAPTER NINE

# NEW WELFARISM, VEGANISM, AND CAPITALISM

> Animal liberation and capitalism are . . . not merely in tension with one another, they are mutually incompatible modes of civilizational development.
>
> —John Sanbonmatsu, *Critical Theory and Animal Liberation*

> People who pronounce themselves in favour of the method of legislative reform in place and in contradistinction to the conquest of political power and social revolution, do not really choose a more tranquil, calmer and slower road to the same goal, but a different goal. Instead of taking a stand for the establishment of a new society they take a stand for surface modifications of the old society.
>
> —Rosa Luxemburg, *Reform or Revolution*

Through the haze of the ubiquitous "meat," "dairy," and "egg" advertisements, some people in the United States and Western Europe still have been able to learn about the treatment of domesecrated animals on factory farms. Many have changed their purchasing habits, opting for free-range chickens and cows, cage-free "eggs," and other fare presented similarly as more "humanely" processed and healthier to eat. Indeed, many advocacy organizations for other animals have promoted—through corporate campaigns, legislation, and ballot initiatives—the more "humane" production of "meat," "dairy," and "eggs," ostensibly as a step toward the eventual end of animal oppression. To the contrary, this strategy—labeled the "new welfarism"[1]—actually *promotes* the continued oppression of domesecrated animals and the underlying global injustices and dangers that accompany it, for several reasons.

The first problem with these efforts to protect domesecrated animals is that the lives and deaths of most "humanely" treated animals are in fact not qualitatively different than those of their factory-farmed counterparts.[2] There are few defined standards and little government oversight of the marketing and sale of "humanely" derived products, and most of the exploited other animals still are confined in CAFO-like facilities before they are dispatched to the same slaughterhouses. Marketing "meat," "dairy," and "eggs" with the largely misleading label of "humane" makes the consumption of these commodities more acceptable among the socially or environmentally conscious.[3]

Second, regulatory reforms purportedly undertaken to improve the plight of domesecrated animals suffer from the same fundamental flaws as many other legal attempts to ameliorate injustice in capitalist society. These regulations largely are created in cooperation with the affected industries, whose enormous economic and political influence insures that such measures do not significantly undermine corporate interests—and frequently actually promote them.[4] Such tepid reforms usually are underfunded and largely unenforced, and they rarely prove to be paths to the abolition of the oppression of other animals. They primarily serve to mute calls for meaningful change by appeasing the concerns of the more conscientious citizens, thus blunting movements for more significant social transformation.[5]

Third, modest and mostly localized reforms in the name of animal welfare are profoundly eclipsed by the continuous expansion of the animal-industrial complex and the enormous increase in the sheer numbers of animals forced into CAFOs throughout the world—and by the growing numbers of humans eating them. The relatively weak welfarist reforms pursued in wealthier nations are unlikely "to transfer to animal production at a more global level";[6] indeed, the World Trade Organization does not permit countries to restrict imports of domesecrated animal products if there is a lack of animal welfare regulations in the nation of origin.[7]

Finally, it is counterproductive for opponents of factory farming to promote grass-fed, free-range, cage-free, organic solutions because the prices of such commodities are higher than those produced in factory farms, making them largely inaccessible to those without the ability to pay. The new welfarism thus reflects the historical pattern of elites consuming most of the "meat"—only now, the more affluent consume most of the chemical-free, "humanely" produced "meat," while the vast majority consume the cheapest fare that the animal-industrial complex profitably can produce. And even if the world were much more equitable, there simply is not enough land to "free range" the enormous number of individuals necessary to meet the growing, socially created demand for domesecrated animal products. If the entire population of cows raised for food in the United States were freely ranged, half the land in the country would have to be converted to pasture. This estimate does not include the land needed for pigs, chickens, turkeys, goats or sheep. It also should be noted that much of the nation's and the world's existing pasture already is seriously degraded. Moreover, while the purchase of locally grown food is desirable, and although many large populations can be fed on regionally produced plant-based food, the energy resources necessary to raise domesecrated animals for local consumption is considerably more than that required to transport plant-based food long distances.[8]

In sum, the promotion of locally produced, "humanely" raised and killed domesecrated animal products as the responsible answer to concerns over factory farms is counterproductive. Most of the urgent problems currently plaguing the world and creating the risks of future conflict and warfare—including the increasing scarcity of water, fertile topsoil, and oil; global warming; chronic disease; and violence—all still accompany the "humane" free-range, grass-fed, locally produced "solution." Even if one is not eating the particular "meat" or related commodities produced, for example, on lands acquired by genocide in Darfur—or produced in Kenya, where tens of thousands of lions have been poisoned, or raised by the ranchers who ordered the murder of Sister Dorothy Stang, or produced in Australia or the U.S. western plains, where indigenous people remain marginalized—eating any "animal product" gives tacit moral consent to such violent and repressive practices. As long as it is considered socially and morally acceptable for humans to eat and use commodities derived from the bodies of other animals, locally produced or not, the disastrous global expansion of the animal-industrial complex will continue. If the more educated, affluent, and politically influential segments of the world's population are unwilling to forgo "meat," "dairy," and "eggs," then the vast majority of the growing global population, socially engineered to desire the Western diet, will reason that they should partake as well.

## VEGANISM AS A GLOBAL IMPERATIVE

In the face of these realities, not the least of which is the exploitation and violence against growing numbers of domesecrated animals, the morally responsible position is to practice and promote global veganism.

Some may suggest the promotion of veganism is injurious for the poor and marginalized human population of the world. It is true that many people around the world continue to exploit animals for basic subsistence. The continued use of both domesecrated and free-living animals as food because of the absence of other dietary alternatives, linked to poverty, is itself an indictment of the capitalist system and the obstacles it poses for, in the words of Nathaniel Shaler, the "advancement of the race." Until nutritious, affordable plant-based food is available to all throughout the world, criticism of peoples who have no alternatives to exploiting animals for subsistence should be redirected against the capitalist system.

Millions in Latin America, Africa, and other parts of the world suffer from poverty and malnutrition after having been displaced from the land to make way for profitable ranching and feed-crop operations, and more deprivation and disaster will come as resources are depleted. If all forms of ranching of domesecrated animals came to an end and if food production was no longer under the control of giant transnational corporations pushing for ever-greater profits, enormous amounts of land could become available both for cultivation and for sanctuaries for other animals. As more people are permitted to return to the land, plant-based food could be cooperatively produced for local consumption, and precious topsoil and water supplies could be used more wisely and conserved for future generations. The impending scarcity and violence that threaten so many throughout the world, especially those with few resources, could be forestalled. In a more just, vegan global order, a genuine policy of "comparative advantage"[9] could provide nutritious plant-based food and fresh water where it is needed throughout the world, including areas where many now have few alternatives to exploiting animals. People in these regions could provide other resources, services, or fairly paid labor in return. A movement for global veganism—which necessitates the end of violence against other animals—is essential for improving the quality of life in areas of the world marginalized after several hundred years of imperialist practices.

Another often-stated objection to a proposed transformation to global veganism is that people in many regions have cultural roots in hunting, pastoralism, and other such practices and that challenging these customs would constitute a form of ethnocentrism. Certainly, just because an oppressive practice has cultural roots or significance—as do, for example, harmful practices ranging from the U.S. "hamburger" culture to whaling, ethnic segregation, and female genital mutilation—does not mean it should be immune to criticism and movements for progressive change. This is especially true when the oppressive cultural practices are linked to exploitation, environmental destruction, resource scarcity, and violent conflict. The argument that the promotion of global veganism somehow represents cultural imperialism is disingenuous, at best, considering that the erosion of diverse cultures and customs throughout the world to date has been the result of capitalist expansion and cultural hegemony. This cultural invasion, undertaken in the name of "modernization," in fact primarily serves the interests of elites in large capitalist nations. It should also be noted that not all hunting of free-living animals today actually is part of some cultural heritage; in Africa, for example, much of the hunting is carried out with automatic weapons and is motivated by the commercial market for "bush meat."[10]

Based on the ideas promoted through the dominant paradigm, many in the United States and other affluent nations might ultimately conclude that the serious domesecration-related problems facing the world do not require the move to veganism but instead will be solved by "science." However, as early as 1995 a report by an international team of scientists examining the decline of global resources noted: "Many people and governments share the mistaken belief that science, with new, ingenious devices and techniques, can rescue us from the troubles we face without having to mend our ways and change our patterns of activity. . . . On the contrary, science and technology enabled the destruction."[11]

Finally, some may feel the proposal for a global conversion to veganism is simply too *radical*. However, nothing is more radical—indeed, nothing could be more extreme and disastrous—than continuing with the violent and destructive practice of exploiting and eating domesecrated animals. Widespread promotion of a transition to global veganism is a necessary and logical strategy for a nonviolent and sustainable future.

The transition to global veganism also must include ending the use as food of other animals who live in water. While some conflict and violence over ocean territories have occurred,[12] the potential for regional and international conflict is increasing as industrialized commercial fishing fleets go beyond their own nation's ocean boundaries and trespass on the territorial waters of other countries. Large-scale commercial fishing already has dramatically reduced the population of ocean fish over the past hundred years, and the decline is exacerbated by changing water temperatures caused by global warming; dozens of species are at risk for extinction.[13]

The industrial plundering of free-living aquatic animals is driven by the socially engineered consumption of growing quantities of "seafood." Human consumption of aquatic animals as food increased from twenty pounds per person annually in 1960 to more than forty pounds in 2010; the earth's human population more than doubled during the same period, increasing the consumption of sea animals exponentially.[14] And, more and more, these other animals killed for food—consumed disproportionately by the affluent—are raised in a form of factory farming known as "aquaculture." The aquaculture industry has grown enormously over the past several decades, almost 9 percent a year between 1970 and 2007. Factory-farmed aquatic animals are confined in tanks or open-water cages, typically with fifty thousand to ninety thousand fish in enclosures only one hundred feet square.[15] Like domesecrated animals in CAFOs, fish and other animals exploited by aquaculture experience stress from confinement and overcrowding and suffer from "fin and tail injuries, disease outbreaks, blinding cataracts, deformities, abnormal behaviours, serious infestation of salmon by sea lice, and high rates of mortality."[16]

Many aquatic animals who are not considered profitable high-end "seafood" are captured and killed for use as feed for both domesecrated land and aquatic animals. A 2008 study, conducted in cooperation with the Pew Memorial Trusts, reported that 37 percent of the aquatic animals captured by commercial fishing operations do not have high value as "seafood"; of these, 90 percent are killed and used as feed for factory-farmed fish, pigs, chickens, and turkeys.[17] Producers of corn and soy also are promoting their products as feed for factory-farmed fish. Within the next few years, it is projected that almost 20 percent of the soy meal produced in the United States alone will be used as feed in aquaculture.[18]

Although aquatic factory farms are touted as the future of "seafood" production, they are environmentally unsound and unsustainable. In addition to the enormous supply of valuable fresh water required by tank-based aquatic factory farms and the associated pollution and depletion of finite resources as increasing amounts of feed grains go to fish farms, open-water cages are causing growing levels of ocean pollution. According to a report in the *Los Angeles Times*, open-water factory farms

consume a tremendous amount of highly concentrated protein pellets and they make a terrific mess. Fish wastes and uneaten feed smother the sea floor beneath these farms, generating bacteria that consume oxygen vital to shellfish and other bottom-dwelling sea creatures. Disease and parasites, which would normally exist in relatively low levels in fish scattered around the oceans, can run rampant in densely packed fish farms. Pesticides fed to the fish and toxic copper sulfate used to keep nets free of algae are building up in sea-floor sediments. Antibiotics have created resistant strains of disease that infect both wild and domesticated fish. Clouds of sea lice, incubated by captive fish on farms, swarm wild salmon as they swim past on their migration to the ocean.[19]

What is more, the eating of domesecrated aquatic animals that have been confined in large populations and treated with antibiotics is as hazardous to human health as the consumption of similarly raised domesecrated land animals. And one study of salmon raised in factory farms found they contained even higher amounts of dioxins and polychlorinated biphenyls (PCBs) and other cancer-causing agents than salmon who were captured, while containing similar amounts of methyl mercury.[20]

The capturing or raising of aquatic other animals for food or feed is a violent act that involves considerable levels of suffering and stress. At the same time, this form of violence against other animals carries with it many of the same environmental harms and risks to human health as other forms of animal exploitation and contributes to the scarcity of finite resources. As with the commercial exploitation of domesecrated animals on land, the profit-driven use for food of other animals living in water will further misdirect valuable resources and grains. While some may argue that fishing is essential for people with few resources to survive, many such people have been adversely affected by the expansion of "seafood" consumption. For example, large-scale industrial fishing operations have so depleted the numbers of aquatic animals in coastal waters that few opportunities are left for subsistence fishing activities, especially in many African regions.[21]

As we have seen, scientists, military intelligence officials, and others have foreseen truly dire consequences from the continued use of the other animals of the earth as food and resources. Only a moral and behavioral transformation toward the abolition of the use of all animals as food and resources can create change substantial enough to avert the worst possibilities for the future. Importantly, however, even if all animal and human rights activists, all environmentalists, teachers, scholars, scientists, all forward-looking politicians, and simply good global citizens promote a turn to veganism, the capitalist system stands as a formidable obstacle to change.


## Transcending the Capitalist System

As we have seen, domesecration fueled the rise of capitalism, and many of its most deplorable colonial and imperialist practices have shaped the contemporary world. Today, capitalism promotes domesecration on an enormous level. Tens of billions of animals are tortured and brutally killed every year to produce growing profits for twenty-first-century elites, who hold investments in the corporate equivalents of Chinggis Khan. These new khans are the corporate "persons" whose ranks include Tyson Foods, ConAgra, Smithfield, Pilgrim's Pride (a subsidiary of JBS "Beef"), Cargill, Archer Daniels Midland, Perdue Farms, Maple Leaf Foods, Vestey Foods, United "Egg" Producers, United "Poultry" Growers Association, National Corn Growers' Association, American Soybean Association, the National Restaurant Association, the International "Meat" Trade Association, McDonald's, Wendy's, "Burger" King, Red Lobster, and YUM! Brands (KFC, Taco Bell, Pizza Hut, Long John Silver's). They display a pathological, single-minded pursuit of profit that is often more subtle but certainly as violent, destructive, and ultimately deadly as the practices of the murderous khans of Eurasia's past.[22] These and other actors in the animal-industrial complex—including the World Bank, the U.S. Department of Agriculture, agricultural departments in major land-grant universities, the Chicago Board of Trade, innumerable advertising and marketing firms, and related enterprises—exert enormous economic, cultural, and political influence to promote the consumption of "meat," "dairy," "eggs," and "seafood" and to protect the interests of those who profit from it. Contemporary domination of the world by global capitalist elites is furthered by corporate-friendly, so-called free-trade agreements and by the World Trade Organization, which has joined the World Bank and the International Monetary Fund as a champion of corporate capitalism.

Transcending capitalism will not automatically bring about a just world and the end of all animal domesecration, but it is a *necessary precondition*, for three reasons. First, capitalists have long used mass-media technology to socially engineer the public consciousness, including the idea that humans should eat other animals. Concentrated corporate control of the mass media virtually guarantees that efforts to make citizens in nations like the United States aware of the growing risks of continued domesecration and consumption of products derived from other animals will be vastly overshadowed both by advertisements by fast-food and other companies and by unfavorable representations in entertainment programming and news reports on any substantial challenges to the system. Even today, although the animal-industrial complex already has a crushing advantage over opponents in the production and distribution of information, it continues to create and fund organizations such as the "Center for Consumer Freedom." This organization constantly conducts public relations campaigns to challenge critiques of the animal-industrial complex and its practices. Among other things, it asserts that reports about the nation's obesity epidemic are "big fat lies" and labels public health advocates as the "food police" and animal and human rights activists and other "do-gooders" as "self-appointed, haloed busybodies."[23] In its very name and many of its slogans, this organization and others like it exploit concepts of "freedom" and "consumer choice"—while attempting to shout down voices that would foster more reasonable and informed choices about diet and its impact. The industry-funded messages, lacking in substance though they may be, have the advantage over the critics, both because they are backed with far greater resources and because they are largely congruent with what Michael Parenti calls our "background assumptions."

What is more, while a small segment of the community of scientists and educators is trying to inform students and the general public about the multiple harms associated with the growing use of animals for food and resources, most teachers and scholars who even broach the issue adhere to the corporate position on the "place of animals." Many teachers happily accept "educational" videos and other materials from such organizations as the National "Cattlemen's" Association and the National "Dairy" Council and incorporate them into their instructional plans. Most colleges and universities, reliant on grants and gifts from wealthy individual and corporate donors and anxious to recruit and retain students raised on McDonald's "happy meals," permit and even invite fast-food chains to locate on campus.

The second major obstacle the capitalist system poses to the end of domesecration and the creation of a more just and sustainable global order is the power that the animal-industrial complex and other huge, profitable industries exert over government policy and decision making. While the freedom necessary for capitalism to expand may have contributed to the extension of basic civil liberties, capitalism and democracy today are largely contradictory. In the United States, for instance, economic and political power largely has remained in the hands of the nation's elite since its inception.[24] The wealthy exert a commanding influence over the state through virtually unlimited political campaign contributions, armies of lobbyists, the revolving door that shuffles former government officials into corporate jobs as consultants and lobbyists (and moves bankers into positions in financial regulatory agencies), and the aforementioned control of news and media outlets that defines both the subjects of public discourse and the range of acceptable opinion. As we have seen in this historical overview of domesecration, the ability of elites to oppress vast numbers of humans and other animals has been possible only because of their enormous influence over the state—and that power is expanding today.[25] So long as corporate elites and plutocrats control state policy and practice, welfarist efforts to ameliorate the oppression of other animals will be ineffective and most likely will be co-opted by the animal-industrial complex.

The first two obstacles capitalism poses to the end of domesecration, elite control of public consciousness and control of the state, have led to the creation of the third obstacle—the economic marginalization and financial struggles that consume the mass of the citizenry. It is important to note that over the years, masses of people in this country pressed for political rights and social and economic justice and, even in the face of fierce and violent resistance from elites, achieved some limited victories. In the United States, for instance, these victories included modest entitlement programs such as Social Security, Medicaid, and Medicare—social programs to which most powerful capitalists acquiesced, so long as their businesses could continue to expand and yield growing profits for corporate shareholders. However, in the last quarter of the twentieth century, as the potential for economic expansion declined, U.S. capitalism was advanced in no small part by policies of deregulation and tax cuts for the wealthy. For example, corporate-driven environmental deregulation increased water and air pollution from largely unfettered hydraulic fracturing for natural gas and mountaintop removal for coal. Financial deregulation characterized the last several decades of the twentieth century, culminating in the undoing of the Glass-Steagall Act of 1933, a

Depression-era law that mandated the separation of investment companies, commercial banks, and insurance companies—leading to the emergence of oversized financial powerhouses. Nefarious financial practices emerged, such as credit derivatives and credit default swaps, which in essence were potentially profitable side bets on U.S. mortgage markets and the performance of huge financial institutions. By 2008, the global economy was thrown into crisis in no small part because of the circulation of bad debt resulting from U.S. subprime mortgages—loans made to people whose limited incomes placed them at high risk for foreclosure. This irresponsible quest for expanding profit taking, an imperative of the capitalist system, eventually resulted in a global financial crisis; governments were forced to spend hundreds of billions of taxpayer dollars, euros, and other currencies to restore profitable banking and financial practices and salvage the capitalist system.

Globally, masses of humans have been impoverished by the practices and policies of more powerful capitalist nations. For instance, a UN report at the close of the twentieth century declared that "global inequities in income and living standards have reached grotesque proportions,"[26] and the World Bank recognized that more than one billion people around the world live on less than one dollar a day.[27] Now, marginally comfortable people in the more affluent nations of Western Europe and the United States saw hundreds of billions of public funds diverted to bail out huge financial institutions labeled "too big to fail," and strapped governments began to curtail hard-won entitlement programs, worker rights, and pension plans and impose the harsh austerity measures required to keep powerful capitalist institutions profitable.

State and local governments in the United States, facing budget deficits not seen since the Great Depression, responded by cutting funding for schools, health care, libraries, and other important public services, all while exhorting the public to buy lottery tickets. At the same time, millions of ordinary citizens have experienced job loss, home foreclosure, lost or reduced pensions or health care benefits, cuts in wages—and for many, increased hunger. In 2012, the political right in the United States was pressing for cuts and changes for the few hard-fought elements of the social safety net, including Social Security. Clearly, the capitalist system provides little stability or security for most individuals. Reforms and public-interest regulations are tenuous and highly vulnerable during periods of economic crisis and reactionary politics. This lesson, one now especially obvious for many of those in the European Union who thought before 2008 that capitalism could be made compatible with social needs, is an important one for contemporary animal-welfarist groups.

It is from such historical and contemporary capitalist practices that the third obstacle to ending domesecration emerges. In a world with so much poverty, deprivation, and insecurity, it is difficult for most people—who are struggling with meeting the necessities of life—to focus on challenging the oppression of devalued groups they long have been taught to disregard and exploit. As long as capitalism prevails, with its imperatives for expansion, exploitation, increasing profits, and concentrated wealth and income—and the accompanying environmental destruction and domesecration—most humans will be too preoccupied with day-to-day survival to realize the vital importance of rejecting products derived from animals and cultivating a plant-based diet. As long as the capitalist system is dominant, the people of the world will be embroiled in endless crisis, turmoil, conflict, struggle, and deprivation, conditions that will prevent the national and international discussion and cooperation necessary to achieve global justice.

Truly free and democratic discussion, planning, and policy implementation for the good of all will be possible only in a democratic socialist world order free of elite social engineering and control of the state and without consciousness-consuming economic marginalization and deprivation. Moving toward an end to domesecration and the related injurious practices would be much more likely in a societal and global order characterized by economic democracy and a democratically controlled state and mass media. Under a more egalitarian system, one with a much greater potential to inform the public about vital global issues—including their connection to domesecration—campaigns to improve the lives of other animals would be more abolitionist in nature. For example, truly democratic policymaking might seek not merely for other animals to be farmed free range but for them to range as free individuals. A global democratic socialist system would go far to ameliorate the dangers of scarcity, infectious disease, and economically driven warfare, allowing a more just and peaceful order to emerge. To create such a future, the struggle against human and animal oppression must occur in concert with efforts to transcend the capitalist system.

It is important that the movement to transcend the capitalist system and domesecration be nonviolent, for two reasons. First, it would be im-

possible to use violent means to bring about the abolition of animal oppression when the state has enormous resources (intelligence, surveillance, labor power, and weaponry) to counter successfully such a campaign.
Moreover, the corporate-controlled media unquestionably would portray
such efforts in the most negative light, undermining the necessary public
sympathy and support. More importantly, however, the use of violent
strategies would be entirely inconsistent with both moral appeals and the
pursuit of a future that is free of oppression and violence. If social justice
activists pursued a campaign of violence, they would lose their moral com-
pass. From Gandhi's approach to the independence of India to the refusal
of the people in the Soviet Union to continue to submit to the deprivations
created by a global arms race, history supports the premise that masses
joined together nonviolently—motivated by both material concerns and a
desire for justice—can force substantial system changes.

For decades, countless people in the Third World have struggled
against the harsh reality of global capitalism. At the time of this writing,
growing numbers of people now are demonstrating against undemocrati-
cally imposed austerity measures in Western Europe, and thousands in the
United States are participating in "Occupy Wall Street" actions throughout the nation. Although militarized police departments around the
nation have violently dispersed occupiers in cities from New York to
Oakland, the Occupy movement remains one of the most promising mass
efforts to resist corporate tyranny—and an inspiration for working together to press for change. It is essential for those interested in promoting
justice for other animals to work together with all those who are striving
to replace capitalism with a just and sustainable global system. Con-
versely, for everyone working for social justice and a better future for humanity, it is imperative to recognize that such a future can only be
achieved by ending domesecration. It will be through such realizations
and alliances that the momentum and power will arise for the creation of
both a democratic social and economic order and the concomitant abolition of the oppression of other animals.

## INTRODUCTION

1. Frank Wilson Blackmar, *The Story of Human Progress: A Brief History of Civilization* (Ann Arbor: University of Michigan Library, 1896), 51. Italics in this and all other quoted material are used to highlight the use of words or expressions that mask and normalize oppressive language. More explanation is provided below.

2. Nathaniel Southgate Shaler, *Domesticated Animals: Their Relation to Man and to His Advancement in Civilization* (New York: C. Scribner, 1895), 2, 4.

3. Michael Parenti, "Lies, Wars, and Empire," lecture, May 12, 2007, Antioch University, Seattle, Wash., http://www.youtube.com/watch?v=CZTrY3TQpzw.

4. For an example of the argument for the economic basis of the end of human enslavement in the United States, see Howard Zinn, *A People's History of the United States: 1492–Present* (1980; New York: HarperCollins, 1999), chap. 9.

5. Jackson J. Spielvogel, *Western Civilization*, vol. A: *To 1500*, 7th ed. (Belmont, Calif.: Wadsworth, 2008), 4.

6. Jared M. Diamond, *Guns, Germs, and Steel: The Fates of Human Societies* (New York: Norton, 1997).

7. Pat Shipman, *The Animal Connection: A New Perspective on What Makes Us Human* (New York: Norton, 2011).

8. On the issue of animal personality, see, for example, Michael Breed and Janice Moore, *Animal Behavior* (Salt Lake City, Utah: Academic Press, 2012), 172–174; Geordie Duckler, "On Redefining the Boundaries of Animal Ownership: Burdens and Benefits of Evidencing Animals' Personalities," *Animal Law* 10 (2004): 63–86; Max Wolf, "Adaptive Individual Differences: The Evolution of Animal Personalities" (Ph.D. diss., University of Groningen, 1976).

9. Thorstein Veblen, *The Higher Learning in America* (1918; New Brunswick, N.J.: Transaction, 1992), 192.

10. Robin W. Winks, "Australia, the Frontier, and the Tyranny of Distance," in *Essays on Frontiers in World History*, ed. George Wolfskill and Stanley Palmer (Arlington: Texas A&M University Press, 1983), 137.

11. Alvin W. Gouldner, "Anti-Minotaur: The Myth of a Value-Free Sociology," *Social Problems* 9, no. 3 (1962): 212.

12. Parenti, "Lies, Wars, and Empire."

13. Rosamund Young, *The Secret Life of Cows: Animal Sentience at Work* (Preston, U.K.: Farming Books and Videos Ltd., 2003), 8–9.

14. See, for example, Donald R. Griffin, *Animal Minds: Beyond Cognition to Consciousness* (Chicago: University of Chicago Press, 2001); Marc Bekoff, *The Emotional Lives of Animals* (Novato, Calif.: New World Library, 2008); Jonathan Balcombe, *Second Nature: The Inner Lives of Animals* (New York: Palgrave Macmillan, 2010).

15. Readers not familiar with this literature are encouraged to read Gary L. Francione, *Introduction to Animal Rights: Your Child or the Dog?* (Philadelphia, Penn.: Temple University Press, 2000); and Gary L. Francione, *Animals as Persons: Essays on the Abolition of Animal Exploitation* (New York: Columbia University Press, 2009).

16. This book is guided by the theory of oppression, a theoretical perspective I modified from Donald Noel's theory of ethnic stratification (*Social Problems* 16, no. 2 [1968]: 157–172), which appears in chapter 1 of *Animal Rights/Human Rights: Entanglements of Oppression and Liberation* (Lanham, Md.: Rowman & Littlefield, 2002). This framework posits that there are three basic components underlying the oppression of both humans and other animals. First, the pursuit of material gain is the primary factor that motivates oppression. Humans and other animals may be exploited as labor for another group's economic gain, or they may be displaced or killed when they are viewed as competition for desired resources, such as land and water. In the case of other animals, over the centuries billions also have been tortured and killed for the profitable use or sale of their body parts.

The second component of the theory of oppression—unequal power between groups—pertains to the actual imposition of domination and exploitation. Over the course of recorded history, the source of much of the power necessary for one group to impose its will over another, especially in the face of resistance, is the state. Those who control the state use its power and authority to institutionalize and legalize oppression while protecting and permitting the expansion of the oppressive practices.

The third component in the theory of oppression is ideological control, with ideology being defined as a set of shared beliefs that explains and justifies an existing or desired social order. To limit or minimize challenges to the status quo, the oppressive treatment of devalued groups must be presented as a natural and normal state of affairs. Explanations that denigrate devalued humans and other animals, such as racism, sexism, classism, and speciesism, are ideologies. Such beliefs are not the primary cause of oppression; rather, they legitimate and reinforce exploitation that is largely economically motivated. Prejudice, then, is an individual-level attitude that is fostered and perpetuated by elite-promoted ideology; it is a tool that supports oppression.

While the culture and social structure of societies grounded in oppressive practices teach their inhabitants to accept and support oppressive practices, not everyone in society will accept such systems uncritically. However, for such systems to continue and expand, total acceptance is not necessary. The existence of a minority who protest oppression is tolerated, especially when the economic, power, and ideological forces available to the defenders of the status quo are able thoroughly to eclipse dissenting or challenging voices. Under these circumstances, the illusion of "democracy" can be celebrated, with little actual self-governance.

Prejudice against other animals arises from socially promulgated beliefs that reflect a speciesist ideology, created to legitimate economic exploitation or elimination of a competitor. Oppressive practices have deep roots in economic and political arrangements. *Therefore, for injustices to be addressed effectively, it is not enough to try to change socially acquired prejudice or to focus only on moral change. The structure of the oppressive system itself must be challenged and changed.*

The relationship among the three factors in the theory of oppression— economic exploitation or competition, unequal power, and ideological legitimation—is dialectical in nature, with each component driving the others. However, at the core is the economic factor. This book will consider the role of the state in supporting "domestication"-related violence and the underlying ideological supports, especially racism and speciesism. However, the primary focus will be on the first element of the theory of oppression, the economic forces that underlie the large-scale, entangled oppression of humans and other animals.

17. In this work, the term "ranching" will be used generically for all commercial practices where other animals are raised to be used as food and resources.

18. For an account of other animals actively resisting oppressive treatment, see Jason Hribal, *Fear of the Animal Planet: The Hidden History of Animal Resistance* (Oakland, Calif.: AK Press, 2010).

19. Edward Palmer Thompson, "The Peculiarities of the English," in *The Poverty of Theory and Other Essays* (New York: Monthly Review, 1978), 296.

20. William Kornblum, *Sociology in a Changing World*, 8th ed. (Belmont, Calif.: Wadsworth, 2008), 59.

21. Walter Lippmann, *Public Opinion* (New York: Harcourt, Brace & Co., 1922), 81.

22. See Carol J. Adams, *The Sexual Politics of Meat: A Feminist-Vegetarian Critical Theory* (New York: Continuum, 1990).

1. NOMADIC PASTORALISM, RANCHING, AND VIOLENCE

1. James Chambers, *The Devil's Horsemen: The Mongol Invasion of Europe* (New York: Athenaeum, 1979), 6.

2. See Marshall Sahlins, *Stone Age Economics* (Chicago: Aldine, 1972).

3. Patrick Noland and Gerhard Lenski, *Human Societies: An Introduction to Macrosociology*, 10th ed. (Boulder, Colo.: Paradigm, 2006), 93.

4. See Lewis R. Binford, "Human Ancestors: Changing Views of Their Behavior," *Journal of Anthropological Archaeology* (1985): 292–327; J. F. O'Connell et al., "Male Strategies and Plio-Pleistocene Archaeology," *Journal of Human Evolution* 43, no. 6 (December 2002): 831–872.

5. Peggy Reeves Sanday, *Female Power and Male Dominance: On the Origins of Sexual Inequality* (Cambridge: Cambridge University Press, 1981), 64–68.

6. Joanna Swabe, *Animals, Disease, and Human Society: Human-Animal Relations and the Rise of Veterinary Medicine* (London: Routledge, 1999), 40.

7. See, for example, Robert L. O'Connell, *Ride of the Second Horseman: The Birth and Death of War* (Oxford: Oxford University Press, 1995), 62.

8. See, for example, Marc Bekoff, *The Emotional Lives of Animals* (Novato, Calif.: New World Library, 2007); Jonathan Balcombe, *Pleasurable Kingdom: Animals and the Nature of Feeling Good* (Hampshire: Palgrave Macmillan, 2006); Donald Redfield Griffin, *Animal Minds: Beyond Cognition to Consciousness* (Chicago: University of Chicago Press, 2001).

9. Structural violence refers to physical and psychological harm experienced by humans and other animals that results from societal economic and political policies and practices. For more on the origins of the term, see, for example: Johan Galtung, "Violence, Peace, and Peace Research," *Journal of Peace Research* 6, no. 3 (1969): 167–191.

10. Bruce Smith, *The Emergence of Agriculture* (New York: Scientific American Library, 1995), 32–33.

11. L. K. Horwitz and P. Smith. "The Contribution of Animal Domestication to the Spread of Zoonoses: A Case Study from the Southern Levant," *Ibex Journal of Mountain Ecology* 5 (2000): 80.

12. Ibid., 18.

13. Pierre Ducos, "'Domestication' Defined and Methodological Approaches to Its Recognition in Faunal Assemblages," in *Approaches to Faunal Analysis in the Middle East*, ed. R. H. Meadow and M. A. Zeder (Boston: Harvard University Peabody Museum Bulletin, 1978), 53.

14. William H. McNeill, *Plagues and Peoples* (1976; repr. New York: Anchor, 1998), 54; cited in Swabe, *Animals, Disease, and Human Society*, 48.

15. Scott Sernau, *World Apart: Social Inequalities in a Global Society* (Thousand Oaks, Calif.: Pine Forge, 2006), 75.

16. K. N. Chaudhuri, *Asia Before Europe: Economy and Civilization of the Indian Ocean from the Rise of Islam to 1750* (New York: Cambridge University Press, 1990), 276.

17. J. J. Saunders, *The History of the Mongol Conquests* (Philadelphia: University of Pennsylvania Press, 1971), 11.

18. Leo de Hartog, *Chinggis Khan: Conqueror of the World* (New York: St. Martin's, 1989), 65–66.

19. L. Luca Cavalli-Sforza, "The Spread of Agriculture in Nomadic Pastoralism: Insights from Genetics, Linguistics, and Archaeology," in *The Origins and Spread of Agriculture and Pastoralism in Eurasia*, ed. David R. Harris (Oxon: Routledge, 2004), 60.

20. V. Gordon Childe, *Man Makes Himself* (New York: New American Library, 1951), 99.

21. Kristian Kristiansen, *Europe Before History* (Cambridge: Cambridge University Press, 1998), 191.

22. Morris Rossabi, "All the Khan's Horses," *Natural History* 103, no. 10 (October 1994): 48–58.

23. Rudi Paul Lindner, "Nomadism, Horses, and Huns," *Past & Present* 92 (August 1981): 5.

24. Marija Gimbutas, "The First Wave of Eurasian Steppe Pastoralists Into Copper Age Europe," *Journal of Indo-European Studies* 5 (1977): 281.

25. See, for example, Elizabeth R. Arnold and Haskel J. Greenfield, *The Origins of Transhumant Pastoralism in Temperate Southeastern Europe: A Zooarchaeological Perspective from the Central Balkans* (Oxford: Archaeopress, 2006), chap. 3.

26. Ibid.

27. Gimbutas, "The First Wave of Eurasian Steppe Pastoralists," 311.

28. Margaret Eleanor Gonsoulin, "Women's Rights and Women's Rites: Religion at the Historical Root of Gender Stratification," *Electronic Journal of Sociology*, ISSN 1198 3655 (2005): 19.

29. Cavalli-Sforza, "The Spread of Agriculture," 58.

30. Cedric Yeo, "The Overgrazing of Ranch-Lands in Ancient Italy," *Transactions and Proceedings of the American Philological Association* 29 (1948): 284, 285.

31. Nathan Rosenstein, "Republican Rome," in *War and Society in the Ancient and Medieval Worlds: Asia, The Mediterranean, Europe, and Mesoamerica* (Washington, D.C.: Center for Hellenic Studies, Trustees for Harvard University, 1999), 206–207.

32. M. Rostovtzeff, *The Social and Economic History of the Roman Empire*, 2nd ed. (Oxford: Clarendon, 1957), 208.

33. Yeo, "The Overgrazing of Ranch-Lands in Ancient Italy," 281–282.

34. Ibid., 282.

35. *The Fontana Economic History of Europe*, vol. 1: *The Middle Ages*, ed. Carlo M. Cipolla (Sussex: Harvester, 1976) 194.

36. Zvi Yavetz, *Slaves and Slavery in Ancient Rome* (New Brunswick, N.J.: Transaction, 1991), 21.

37. K. D. White, *Roman Farming* (Ithaca, N.Y.: Cornell University Press, 1970), 281.

38. Ibid.

39. R. W. Davies, "The Roman Military Diet," *Britannia* 2 (1971): 122–142; also see Adrian Keith Goldsworthy, *The Roman Army at War: 100 BC–AD 200* (Oxford: Clarendon, 1996), 292; and Jonathan P. Roth, *The Logistics of the Roman Army at War (264 BC–AD 235)* (Boston: Brill, 1999), 213–214.

40. Paul Erdkamp, *Hunger and the Sword: Warfare and Food Supply in Roman Republic Wars (264–30 BC)* (Amsterdam: J. C. Gieben, 1998), 32.

41. Charles Wayland Towne and Edward Norris Wentworth, *Cattle and Men* (Norman: University of Oklahoma Press, 1955), 96.

42. Sing C. Chew, *The Recurring Dark Ages: Ecological Stress, Climate Changes, and System Transformation* (Lanham, Md.: Rowman & Littlefield, 2007), 127.

43. Roth, *The Logistics of the Roman Army at War*, 201.

44. Goldsworthy, *The Roman Army at War*, 294.

45. Chew, *The Recurring Dark Ages*, 126.

46. Rostovtzeff, *The Social and Economic History of the Roman Empire*, 491.

47. Ibid., 16, 17.

48. Miriam Greenblatt, *Julius Caesar and the Roman Republic* (New York: Marshall Cavendish, 2006), 73.

49. William Montgomery McGovern, *The Early Empires of Central Asia: A Study of the Scythians and the Huns and the Part They Played in World History* (Chapel Hill: University of North Carolina Press, 1939), 12.

50. Yeo, "The Overgrazing of Ranch-Lands in Ancient Italy," 275–307.

51. McGovern, *The Early Empires of Central Asia*, 12.

52. Cavalli-Sforza, "The Spread of Agriculture," 60.

53. Clive A. Spinage, *Cattle Plague: A History* (New York: Kluwer Academic/Plenum, 2003), 89.

54. Ibid.

55. René Grousset, *The Empire of the Steppes: A History of Central Asia* (New Brunswick, N.J.: Rutgers University Press, 1970), 23.

56. Ibid.

57. See Gerhard Lenski, *Ecological-Evolutionary Theory: Principles and Applications* (Boulder, Colo.: Paradigm, 2005), 102.

58. David Christian, *Maps of Time: An Introduction to Big History* (Berkeley: University of California Press, 2004), 263.

59. Chambers, *The Devil's Horsemen*, 17.

60. Robert L. O'Connell, *Of Arms and Men: A History of War, Weapons, and Aggression* (Oxford: Oxford University Press, 1989), 99.

61. Chambers, *The Devil's Horsemen*, 6.

62. de Hartog, *Chinggis Khan*, 66.

63. Archer Jones, *The Art of War in the Western World* (Chicago: University of Illinois Press, 1987), 142.

64. Chambers, *The Devil's Horsemen*, 60.

65. John Andrew Boyle, *The History of the World-Conqueror*, by 'Ala-ad-Din 'Ata-Malik Juvaini (Cambridge: Harvard University Press, 1958); reprinted in de Hartog, *Chinggis Khan*, 51.

66. William H. McNeill, *The Rise of the West: A History of the Human Community* (Chicago: University of Chicago Press, 1963), 491.

67. Alexander Monro, "Chinggis Khan," in *The Seventy Great Journeys in History*, ed. Robin Hanbury-Tenison (London: Thames and Hudson, 2006), 72.

68. Ibid.

69. Denis Sinor, "Horse and Pasture in Inner Asian History," *Oriens Extremus* 19, nos. 1–2 (1972): 181.

70. McGovern, *The Early Empires of Central Asia*, 7.

71. Chaudhuri, *Asia Before Europe*, 267.

72. Ibid.

73. Dudley Giehl, *Vegetarianism: A Way of Life* (New York: Barnes and Noble, 1979), 96.

74. Donald R. Hopkins, *The Greatest Killer: Smallpox in History* (Chicago: University of Chicago Press, 2002), 18; Basiro Davey, David Male, and Michael Gillman, *Pathogens and People* (Milton Keynes: The Open University, 2003), 12.

75. McNeill, *Plagues and Peoples*, 174.

76. BBC News, "Decoding the Black Death," October 3, 2001, http://news .bbc.co.uk/2/hi/health/1576875.stm.

77. James F. Brooks, *Captives and Cousins: Slavery, Kinship, and Community in the Southwest Borderlands* (Chapel Hill: University of North Carolina Press, 2002), 89.

78. Edward Gibbon, *The Decline and Fall of the Roman Empire* (New York: P. Fenelon Collier, 1901), 901.

79. Chambers, *The Devil's Horsemen*, 167.

80. Ibid., 167–168.

81. Alan Macfarlane, *The Savage Wars of Peace: England, Japan, and the Malthusian Trap* (Oxford: Blackwell, 1997), 50.

82. Ibid.

83. Alan Lomax and Conrad M. Arensberg, "A Worldwide Evolutionary Classification of Cultures by Subsistence Systems," *Current Anthropology* 18, no. 4 (December 1977): 676.

84. Bernard S. Bachrach, *Armies and Politics in the Early Medieval West* (Brookfield, Vt.: Ashgate, 1993), 750.

85. Ibid., 711.

86. Ibid., 712.

87. See James Graham-Campbell, *The Viking World* (London: Frances Lincoln, 1980).

88. Towne and Wentworth, *Cattle and Men*, 99.

89. Ibid., 99.

90. Denzel Ferguson and Nancy Ferguson, *Sacred Cows at the Public Trough* (Bend, Ore.: Maverick, 1983), 11.

91. J. H. Parry, "The New World: 1521–1580," in *The Reformation: 1520–1559*, 2nd ed. (Cambridge: Cambridge University Press, 1990), 2:648.

92. Giehl, *Vegetarianism*, 99–100.

93. Carlo M. Cipolla, ed., *The Fontana Economic History of Europe*, vol. 2: *The Sixteenth and Seventeenth Centuries* (Sussex: Harvester, 1977), 116.

94. Karl F. Helleiner, "The Population of Europe from the Black Death to the Eve of the Vital Revolution," in *The Cambridge Economic History of Europe*, vol. 4: *The Economy of Expanding Europe in the Sixteenth and Seventeenth Centuries*, ed. E. E. Rich and C. H. Wilson (Cambridge: Cambridge University Press, 1967), 69; cited in Immanuel Wallerstein, *The Modern World System: Capitalist Agriculture and the Origins of the European World-Economy in the Sixteenth Century* (New York: Academic Press, 1974).

95. See Helleiner, "The Population of Europe," 69.

96. See, for example, Thomas E. Emerson, "Cahokia and the Evidence for Late-Pre-Columbian War in the North American Continent" and Richard J. Chacon and Ruben G. Mendoza, "Ethical Considerations and Conclusions Regarding Indigenous Warfare and Violence in North America," both in *North American Indigenous Warfare and Ritual Violence*, ed. Richard J. Chacon and Ruben G. Mendoza (Tucson: University of Arizona Press, 2007); and Maria Ostendorf Smith, "Beyond Palisades: The Nature and Frequency of Late Prehistoric Deliberate Violent Trauma in the Chickamauga Reservoir of East Tennessee," *American Journal of Physical Anthropology* 121 (2003): 303–318.

97. Stacy Kowtko, *Nature and the Environment in Pre-Columbian American Life* (Westport, Conn.: Greenwood, 2006), 180–181.

98. Gary B. Nash, *Red, White, and Black: The Peoples of Early America* (Englewood Cliffs, N.J.: Prentice-Hall, 1982), 17.

99. Gerhard Lenski, Jean Lenski, and Patrick Nolan, *Human Societies: An Introduction to Macrosociology*, 6th ed. (New York: McGraw-Hill, 1991), 136.

100. David E. Stannard, *American Holocaust: The Conquest of the New World* (Oxford: Oxford University Press, 1992), 37.

101. Lynn V. Foster, *Handbook to Life in the Ancient Maya World* (New York: Facts on File, 2002), 143.

102. David Webster, "Ancient Mayan Warfare," in *War and Society in the Ancient and Medieval Worlds: Asia, the Mediterranean, Europe, and Mesoamerica*, ed. Kurt A. Raaflaub and Nathan Stewart Rosenstein (Washington, D.C.: Center for Hellenic Studies, 1999), 347.

103. Stannard, *American Holocaust*, 6.

104. Ibid., 3.

105. McNeill, *The Rise of the West*, 561.

106. George C. Vaillant, *Aztecs of Mexico: Origin, Rise, and Fall of the Aztec Nation* (Garden City, N.Y.: Doubleday, 1962), 277.

107. Brian M. Fagan, *The Aztecs* (New York: W. H. Freeman, 1984), 130.

108. Vaillant, *Aztecs of Mexico*, 180.

109. Ross Hassig, "The Aztec World," in *War and Society in the Ancient and Medieval Worlds: Asia, the Mediterranean, Europe, and Mesoamerica*, ed. Kurt A. Raaflaub and Nathan Stewart Rosenstein (Washington, D.C.: Center for Hellenic Studies, 1999), 376.

110. Vaillant, *Aztecs of Mexico*, 221.

111. Ibid., 183.

112. Stannard, *American Holocaust*, 41.

113. Terence N. D'Altroy, *The Incas* (Malden, Mass.: Blackwell, 2002), 207.

114. Ibid., 205.

115. Alan Kolata, "In the Realm of the Four Quarters," in *America in 1492: The World of the Indian Peoples Before the Arrival of Columbus*, ed. Alvin M. Josephy Jr. (New York: Vintage, 1991), 244.

116. John Victor Murra, *The Economic Organization of the Inca State* (Greenwich, Conn.: JAI, 1980), 52.

117. D'Altroy, *The Incas*, 225.

118. Ibid., 225.

119. Murra, *The Economic Organization of the Inca State*, 49.

## 2. Domesecration and the Americas

1. Alfred W. Crosby, "An Ecohistory of the Canary Islands: A Precursor of European Colonization in the New World and Australia," *Environmental Review* 8, no. 3 (Autumn 1984): 226.

2. Chris Harman, *A People's History of the World: From the Stone Age to the New Millennium* (London: Verso, 2008), 156.

3. Terry G. Jordan, *North American Cattle-Ranching Frontiers: Origins, Diffusion, and Differentiation* (Albuquerque: University of New Mexico Press, 1993), 15, 17.

4. John E. Rouse, *The Criollo: Spanish Cattle in the Americas* (Norman: University of Oklahoma Press, 1977), viii.

5. Ibid., 24–25.

6. Louis A. Pérez Jr., *Cuba: Between Reform and Revolution*, 3rd ed. (New York: Oxford University Press, 2006), 18–19.

7. Bartolomé de las Casas, *Tears of the Indians* (1542); and Sir Arthur Helps, K.C.B., *The Life of las Casas*, double vol. (Williamstown, Mass.: The John Lilburne Company, 1970), 11–12.

8. Richard J. Morrisey, "Colonial Agriculture in New Spain," *Agricultural History* 31, no. 3 (July 1957), 24–25.

9. Rouse, *The Criollo*, 25.

10. Ibid., 25.

11. Henry Kamen, *Empire: How Spain Became a World Power, 1492–1763* (New York: Harper Collins, 2003), 205.

12. Frank Miessner and Nancy Morrison, *Seeds of Change: Stories of IDB Innovation in Latin America* (Washington , D.C.: Inter-American Development Bank, 1991), 81.

13. Las Casas, *Tears of the Indians*, 22.

14. John Aberth, *The First Horseman: Disease in Human History* (Upper Saddle River, N.J.: Prentice Hall, 2007), 50.

15. Pérez, *Cuba*, 21.

16. G. B. Masefield, "Crops and Livestock," in *The Cambridge Economic History of Europe from the Decline of the Roman Empire*, vol. 4: *The Economy of Expanding Europe in the Sixteenth and Seventeenth Centuries*, ed. E. E. Rich and C. H. Wilson (Cambridge: Cambridge University Press, 1967), 281.

17. Robert L. O'Connell, *Of Arms and Men: A History of War, Weapons, and Aggression* (Oxford: Oxford University Press, 1989), 129.

18. Donald K. Sharpes, *Sacred Bull, Holy Cow: A Cultural Study of Civilization's Most Important Animal* (New York: Peter Lang, 2006), 141.

19. Charles Wayland Towne and Edward Norris Wentworth, *Cattle and Men* (Norman: University of Oklahoma Press, 1955), 118–119.

20. Laurie Winn Carlson, *Cattle: An Informal Social History* (Chicago: Ivan R. Dee, 2001), 78.

21. Edward Tomlinson, *The Other Americas: Our Neighbors to the South* (New York: Charles Scribner's Sons, 1943), 60–61.

22. J. H. Parry, "The New World: 1521–1580," in *The Reformation: 1520–1559*, 2nd ed. (Cambridge: Cambridge University Press, 1990), 2:645.

23. Alfred W. Crosby, *The Columbian Exchange: Biological and Cultural Consequences of 1492* (Westport, Conn.: Greenwood, 1972), 86.

24. James Lockhart and Stuart B. Schwartz, *Early Latin America: A History of Colonial Spanish America and Brazil* (Cambridge: Cambridge University Press, 1983), 213.

25. See, for example, Stuart B. Schwartz, "Plantations and Peripheries, c. 1580–c. 1750," in *Colonial Brazil*, ed. Leslie Bethell (Cambridge: Cambridge University Press, 1987), 105.

26. John Hemming, *Red Gold: The Conquest of the Brazilian Indians, 1500–1760* (Cambridge, Mass.: Harvard University Press, 1978), 38.

27. See, for example, Eugenio Matibag, *Haitian-Dominican Counterpoint: Nation, State, and Race in Hispaniola* (New York: Palgrave Macmillan, 2003), 32.

28. Jordan, *North American Cattle-Ranching Frontiers*, 73.

29. Ibid.

30. Alfred W. Crosby Jr., "The Biological Consequences of 1492," *Report on the Americas* 25, no. 2 (September 1991): 10, 87.

31. Crosby, *The Columbian Exchange*, 89.

32. Peter Bakewell, *A History of Latin America: Empires and Sequels, 1450–1930* (Malden, Mass.: Blackwell, 1997), 193.

33. Ibid., 188.

34. Geoffrey Rudolph Elton, *The New Cambridge Modern History*, vol. 2: *The Reformation, 1520–1559*, 2nd ed. (Cambridge: Cambridge University Press, 1990), 645.

35. Jordan, *North American Cattle-Ranching Frontiers*, 88.

36. Crosby, "The Biological Consequences of 1492," 10.

37. Richard H. Stekel, "Health and Nutrition in Pre-Columbian America: The Skeletal Evidence," *Journal of Interdisciplinary History* 36, no. 1 (Summer 2005): 1–32.

38. Richard J. Morrisey, "The Northward Expansion of Cattle Ranching in New Spain, 1550–1600," *Agricultural History* 25, no. 3 (July 1951): 116.

39. Albert Marrin, *Cowboys, Indians, and Gunfighters: The Story of the Cattle Kingdom* (New York: Macmillan, 1993), 9.

40. Crosby, *The Columbian Exchange*, 92.

41. Eric Wolf, "Sons of the Shaking Earth," in *Crossing Currents: Continuity and Change in Latin America*, ed. Michael B. Whiteford and Scott Whiteford (Upper Saddle River, N.J.: Prentice Hall, 1998), 60.

42. Towne and Wentworth, *Cattle and Men*, 118.

43. Edward Gaylord Bourne, *Narratives of the Career of Hernando De Soto* (London: David Nutt, 1905), 1:139.

44. Kamen, *Empire*, 252.

45. Ibid., 253.

46. Masefield, "Crops and Livestock," 282.

47. Carlos Pereyra, *La Obra de España en América* (Madrid, 1920); cited in Morrisey, "Colonial Agriculture in New Spain," 26.

48. Masefield, "Crops and Livestock," 281.

49. Richard Cooke, "The Native Peoples of Central America During Pre-columbian and Colonial Times," in *Central America: A Natural and Cultural History*, ed. Anthony G. Coates (New Haven, Conn.: Yale University Press, 1997), 172–173.

50. Wolf, "Sons of the Shaking Earth," 66.

51. Ibid., 65.

52. Lynn V. Foster, *A Brief History of Central America* (New York: Facts on File, 2000), 96.

53. Stanley Heckadon-Moreno, "Spanish Rule, Independence, and the Modern Colonization Frontiers," in *Central America: A Natural and Cultural History*, ed. Anthony G. Coates (New Haven, Conn.: Yale University Press, 1997), 181.

54. Ibid., 190–191.

55. Laura J. Enríquez, *Harvesting Change: Land and Agrarian Reform in Nicaragua, 1979–1990* (Chapel Hill: University of North Carolina Press, 1991), 21.

56. http://www.mongabay.com/reference/country_studies/nicaragua/ECON OMY.html.

57. Crosby, *The Columbian Exchange*, 86.

58. Jack Weatherford, *Indian Givers: How the Indians of the Americas Transformed the World* (New York: Fawcett Columbine, 1988), 17.

59. Crosby, *The Columbian Exchange*, 94.

60. Bakewell, *A History of Latin America*, 324.

61. Crosby, *The Columbian Exchange*, 90.

62. Ibid.

63. Lockhart and Schwartz, *Early Latin America*, 213–214.

64. Stephen Bell, *Campanha Gaúcha: A Brazilian Ranching System, 1850–1920* (Palo Alto, Calif.: Stanford University Press, 1998), 23.

65. Ibid., 25.

66. Bakewell, *A History of Latin America*, 339.

67. Schwartz, "Plantations and Peripheries," 105.

68. Bakewell, *A History of Latin America*, 325.

69. Hemming, *Red Gold*, 346.

70. Ibid.

71. Ibid., 351, 353.

72. Ibid., 366.

73. R. Brian Ferguson, "Blood of the Leviathan: Western Contact and Warfare in Amazonia," *American Ethnologist* 17, no. 2 (May 1990): 239.

74. Bakewell, *A History of Latin America*, 334.

75. Stuart Schwartz, *Slaves, Peasants, and Rebels: Reconsidering Brazilian Slavery* (Urbana: University of Illinois Press, 1992), 79.

76. Lockhart and Schwartz, *Early Latin America*, 382.

77. Ibid., 381.

78. Schwartz, *Slaves, Peasants, and Rebels*, 107.

79. Richard W. Slatta, *Cowboys of the Americas* (New Haven, Conn.: Yale University Press, 1990), 14.

80. Jeremy Rifkin, *Beyond Beef: The Rise and Fall of the Cattle Culture* (New York: Plume, 1993), 51.

81. Kamen, *Empire*, 271.

82. Lockhart and Schwartz, *Early Latin America*, 338.

83. Andre Gunder Frank, *Capitalism and Underdevelopment in Latin America: Historical Studies of Chile and Brazil* (New York: Monthly Review Press, 1967), 29.

84. Fernando Tasso Fragoso Pires, *Fazendas: The Great Houses and Plantations of Brazil* (New York: Abbeville, 1995), 17.

85. Hemming, *Red Gold*, 168.

86. Towne and Wentworth, *Cattle and Men*, 118.

87. Slatta, *Cowboys of the Americas*, 14.

88. Kamen, *Empire*, 282.

89. Ibid., 467.

90. Wolf, "Sons of the Shaking Earth," 64.

91. Carlson, *Cattle*, 85.

92. Ibid., 86.

93. Matibag, *Haitian-Dominican Counterpoint*, 44.

94. Weatherford, *Indian Givers*, 20.

95. Ibid., 15.

96. Walter Prescott Webb, *The Great Frontier* (1951; repr. Lincoln: University of Nebraska Press, 1980), 174.

97. O'Connell, *Of Arms and Men*, 134.

98. L. A. Clarkson, "The Organization of the English Leather Industry in the Late Sixteenth and Seventeenth Centuries," *Economic History Review* 13, no. 2 (1960): 245.

99. Ibid., 252.

100. Robert S. Duplessis, *Transitions to Capitalism in Early Modern Europe* (Cambridge: Cambridge University Press, 1997), 93.

101. Carlo M. Cipolla, *The Fontana Economic History of Europe* (New York: Barnes and Noble, 1977), 2:468.

102. Ibid., 2:471, 2:473–474.

103. Joe A. Akerman, *Florida Cowman: A History of Florida Cattle Raising* (Kissimmee, Fla.: Florida Cattlemen's Association, 1976), 5.

104. Kamen, *Empire*, 205.

105. Raymond Nelson, *The Philippines* (New York: Walker and Co., 1968), 38.

106. Linda A. Newson, *Conquest and Pestilence in the Early Spanish Philippines* (Honolulu: University of Hawaii Press, 2009), 251–263.

107. Robert Tignor et al., *World Together, Worlds Apart: A History of the World from the Beginnings of Humankind to the Present* (New York: Norton, 2008), 573.

3. RANCHING AND VIOLENCE IN NORTH AMERICA

1. David W. Stahle et al., "The Lost Colony and Jamestown Droughts," *Science*, n.s., 280, no. 5363 (April 24, 1998): 564–567.

2. Virginia DeJohn Anderson, *Creatures of Empire: How Domestic Animals Transformed Early America* (New York: Oxford University Press, 2004), 99.

3. Ibid., 99.

4. Donald K. Sharpes, *Sacred Bull, Holy Cow: A Cultural Study of Civilization's Most Important Animal* (New York: P. Lang, 2006), 144.

5. Ibid.

6. Anderson, *Creatures of Empire*, 91.

7. Peter O. Wacker, *Land and People: A Cultural Geography of Preindustrial New Jersey (Origins and Settlement Patterns)* (New Brunswick, N.J.: Rutgers University Press, 1975), 104.

8. Anderson, *Creatures of Empire*, 177.

9. Carol H. Behrman, *The Indian Wars (Chronicle of America's Wars)* (Minneapolis, Minn.: Lerner, 2004), 13–14.

10. Anderson, *Creatures of Empire*, 209.

11. Howard Zinn, *A People's History of the United States* (1980; repr. New York: Harper Collins, 2003), 14.

12. Anderson, *Creatures of Empire*, 182.

13. John Franklin Jameson, *Narratives of New Netherland, 1609–1664* (New York: Barnes and Noble, 1909), 273.

14. Ibid., 228.

15. Joan A. Lovisek, "Aboriginal Warfare on the Northwest Coast," in *North American Indigenous Warfare and Ritual Violence*, ed. Richard J. Chacon and Ruben G. Mendoza (Tucson: University of Arizona Press, 2007), 73.

16. Dean R. Snow, "Iroquois-Huron Warfare," in *North American Indigenous Warfare and Ritual Violence*, ed. Richard J. Chacon and Ruben G. Mendoza (Tucson: University of Arizona Press, 2007), 152.

17. Ibid., 153.

18. Rudolf Alexander Clemen, *The American Livestock and Meat Industry* (New York: The Ronald Press Company, 1923), 3.

19. Charles Wayland Towne and Edward Norris Wentworth, *Cattle and Men* (Norman: University of Oklahoma Press, 1955), 136.

20. See Anderson, *Creatures of Empire*, 225.

21. William Hand Browne et al., *Archives of Maryland, vol. 2: Proceedings and Acts of the General Assembly of Maryland, April 1666–June 1676* (Baltimore: Maryland Historical Society, 1884), 15.

22. Anderson, *Creatures of Empire*, 225.

23. Samuel Gardner Drake, *The Old Indian Chronicle; Being a Collection of Exceeding Rare Tracts, Written and Published in the Time of King Philip's War, by Persons Residing in the Country* (Boston: S. A. Drake, 1867), 102; cited in Anderson, *Creatures of Empire*, 236.

24. Anderson, *Creatures of Empire*, 237.

25. Ibid., 238.

26. Zinn, A People's History of the United States, 40.

27. Richard L. Haan, "The 'Trade Do's Not Flourish as Formerly:' The Ecological Origins of the Yamassee War of 1715," Ethnohistory 28, no. 4 (Autumn 1981): 344.

28. Ibid., 350.

29. Ibid., 342.

30. Ibid.

31. Laurie Winn Carlson, Cattle: An Informal Social History (Chicago: Ivan R. Dee, 2001), 66.

32. Terry G. Jordan, North American Cattle-Ranching Frontiers: Origins, Diffusion, and Differentiation (Albuquerque: University of New Mexico Press, 1993), 118.

33. Ibid., 120.

34. Brooks Blevins, Cattle in the Cotton Fields: A History of Cattle Raising in Alabama (Tuscaloosa: University of Alabama Press, 1998), 5.

35. Carlson, Cattle, 79.

36. Joe A. Akerman, Florida Cowman: A History of Florida Cattle Raising (Kissimmee, Fla.: Florida Cattlemen's Association, 1976), 25.

37. William H. Bergmann, "A Commercial View of This Unfortunate War: Economic Roots of an American National State in the Ohio Valley, 1775–1795," Early American Studies: An Interdisciplinary Journal 6, no. 1(Spring 2008): 159.

38. Susan Sleeper-Smith, Indian Women and French Men: Rethinking Cultural Encounter in the Western Great Lakes (Native Americans of the Northeast) (Amherst: University of Massachusetts Press, 2001), 85.

39. Clemen, The American Livestock and Meat Industry, 3–4.

40. Paul C. Henlein, Cattle Kingdom in the Ohio Valley: 1783–1860 (Lexington: University of Kentucky Press, 1959), 3.

41. Ibid., 4.

42. Jordan, North American Cattle-Ranching Frontiers, 193–194.

43. Clemen, The American Livestock and Meat Industry, 74.

44. Ibid., 71.

45. Ibid., 125.

46. William Pooley, "The Settlement of Illinois from 1830 to 1850" (Ph.D. diss., University of Wisconsin, 1908), 264.

47. Kenneth C. Davis, Don't Know Much About History: Everything You Needed to Know About American History but Never Learned (New York: Crown, 1990), 121.

48. Pooley, The Settlement of Illinois from 1830 to 1850, 310.

49. Alvin M. Josephy, The Indian Heritage of North America (New York: Houghton Mifflin, 1991), 334.

50. Richard N. Current, T. Harry Williams, and Frank Freidel, American History: A Survey, 4th ed. (New York: Knopf, 1975), 209.

51. Elizabeth L. Plummer, "White Attitudes and Their Effects on the Wyandot Indian Removal" (MA thesis, Bowling Green State University Graduate College, 1976), 54.

52. Letter by Evan Jones, 1838, printed in *The Cherokee Removal: A Brief History with Documents*, ed. Theda Perdue and Michael D. Green (Boston: Bedford Books of St. Martin's Press, 1995), 165.

53. Thomas D. Clark and John D. W. Guice, *The Old Southwest, 1795–1830: Frontiers in Conflict* (Norman: University of Oklahoma Press, 1996), 99.

54. Ibid., 100.

55. Frank L. Owsley, *Plain Folk of the Old South* (1949); cited in ibid., 100.

56. Clark and Guice, *The Old Southwest*, 110.

57. Josephy, *The Indian Heritage of North America*, 335.

58. Paul W. Gates, *Landlords and Tenants on the Prairie Frontier: Studies in American Land Policy* (Ithaca, N.Y.: Cornell University Press, 1973), 67–68.

59. Gerad Middendorf, Terrie A. Becerra, and Derrick Cline, "Transition and Resilience in the Kansas Flint Hills," *Online Journal of Rural Research and Policy* 4, no. 3 (2009): 3.

60. Ibid., 6.

61. Ibid., 123.

62. Ibid., 171.

63. Ibid., 186–187.

64. Ibid., 194, 170–171.

65. Ibid., 230.

66. Ibid., 139.

67. Clemen, *The American Livestock and Meat Industry*, 58.

68. James Parton, "Cincinnati," *Atlantic Monthly* 20 (August 1867): 241; reprinted in Edgar Allen Miller, "The Historical Development of Livestock Marketing in the Eastern Corn Belt and an Analysis of the Buyers and Sellers on the Cleveland and Cincinnati Terminal Markets" (MA thesis, Ohio State University, 1956), 8–9.

69. John Solomon Otto, "Traditional Cattle Herding Practices in Southern Florida," *Journal of American Folklore* 47, no. 385 (July–September 1984), 303.

70. Akerman, *Florida Cowman*, 82.

71. Alfred W. Crosby, *Germs, Seeds, and Animals: Studies in Ecological History* (Armonk, N.Y.: M. E. Sharpe, 1994), 26.

## 4. DOMESECRATION IN THE WESTERN PLAINS

1. Jack Weatherford, *How the Indians Transformed the World* (New York: Crown, 1989), 43.

2. Miriam Partlow, *Liberty, Liberty County, and the Atascosito District* (Austin, Tex.: The Pemberton Press of the Jenkins Publishing Company, 1974), 123–125.

3. C. Allan Jones, *Texas Roots: Agriculture and Rural Life Before the Civil War* (College Station: Texas A&M University Press, 2005), 177.

4. Albert Marrin, *Cowboys, Indians, and Gunfighters: The Story of the Cattle Kingdom* (New York: Athenaeum, 1993), 29.

5. Jones, *Texas Roots*, 178.

6. Alfredo Mirande, *Gringo Justice* (Notre Dame, Ind.: University of Notre Dame Press, 1987), 3.

7. Ibid., 3–4.

8. See Howard Zinn, *A People's History of the United States: 1492–Present* (New York: Harper Collins, 1999), chap. 8.

9. Ibid., 165.

10. Albert Gallatin, *Peace with Mexico* (New York: Bartlett and Welford, 1847), 14.

11. See Mirande, *Gringo Justice*.

12. Julian Samora and Patricia Vandel Simon, *A History of the Mexican American People* (Notre Dame, Ind.: University of Notre Dame Press, 1993), 116–117.

13. Laurie Winn Carlson, *Cattle: An Informal Social History* (Chicago: Ivan R. Dee, 2001), 86.

14. Philip S. Foner, *The Fur and Leather Workers Union* (Newark, N.J.: Nordan, 1950), 5.

15. Andrew C. Isenberg, *The Destruction of the Bison: An Environmental History, 1750–1920* (Cambridge: Cambridge University Press, 2000), 130.

16. Philip Durham and Everett L. Jones, "Slaves on Horseback," *Pacific Historical Review* 33, no. 4 (November 1964): 405–409.

17. Jon E. Lewis, *The Mammoth Book of the West: The Making of the American West* (New York: Carroll and Graf, 1996), 185.

18. Ibid., 183–184.

19. William Cronon, *Nature's Metropolis: Chicago and the Great West* (New York: Norton, 1990), 208.

20. Isenberg, *The Destruction of the Bison*, 21–25.

21. Russell Thornton, *American Indian Holocaust and Survival: A Population History Since 1492* (Norman: University of Oklahoma Press, 1987), 42.

22. Richard A. Barrett, *Culture and Conflict: An Excursion in Anthropology* (Belmont, Calif.: Wadsworth, 1984), 89.

23. Ibid., 87–88.

24. James F. Brooks, "Served Well by Plunder: La Gran Ladronería and Producers of History Astride the Río Grande," *American Quarterly* 52, no. 1 (March 2000): 36.

25. Pekka Hämäläinen, *The Comanche Empire* (New Haven, Conn.: Yale University Press, 2008), 333.

26. Gerald Friesen, *The Canadian Prairies: A History* (Toronto: University of Toronto Press, 1990), 39.

27. Hämäläinen, *The Comanche Empire*, 296.

28. Ibid.

29. Philip Katcher, *U.S. Cavalry on the Plains: 1850–90* (Oxford: Osprey, 1985), 23.

30. Alvin M. Josephy, *The Indian Heritage of North America* (New York: Houghton Mifflin, 1991), 336.

31. Richard White, *"It's Your Misfortune and None of My Own": A New History of the American West* (Norman: University of Oklahoma Press, 1993), 108.

32. Robert V. Hine and John Mack Faragher, *The American West: A New Interpretive History* (New Haven, Conn.: Yale University Press, 2000), 228.

33. Peter Cozzens, *Eyewitnesses to the Indian Wars: 1865–1890: Conquering the Southern Plains* (Mechanicsburg, Penn.: Stackpole, 2003), xxii.

34. Dee Brown, *Bury My Heart at Wounded Knee: An Indian History of the American West* (New York: Holt, 2007), 90.

35. Ibid., 89–90.

36. James Welch and Paul Stekler, *Killing Custer: The Battle of Little Bighorn and the Fate of the Plains Indians* (New York: Penguin, 1995), 30.

37. Ibid., 31.

38. Cronon, *Nature's Metropolis*, 216.

39. Brian Schofield, *Selling Your Father's Bones: America's 140-Year War Against the Nez Perce Tribe* (New York: Simon & Schuster, 2009), 224.

40. Ernest Staples Osgood, *The Day of the Cattleman: The Legend of the Wild West Viewed Against the Truth of History* (1929; repr. Toronto: University of Toronto Press, 1968), 79.

41. Denzel Ferguson and Nancy Ferguson, *Sacred Cows at the Public Trough* (Bend, Ore.: Maverick, 1983), 13.

42. Lewis Atherton, *The Cattle Kings* (Bloomington: Indiana University Press, 1961), 13.

43. Carlson, *Cattle*, 110.

44. Theodore Roosevelt, "Ranch Life in the Far West: In the Cattle Country," *Century Magazine* (February 1888); cited in T. J. Stiles, *Warriors and Pioneers* (New York: Berkley, 1996), 214–220.

45. David D. Smits, "The Frontier Army and the Destruction of the Buffalo, 1865–1883," *Western Historical Quarterly* 25, no. 3 (Autumn, 1994): 337.

46. Ferguson and Ferguson, *Sacred Cows at the Public Trough*, 15.

47. Joseph M. Petulla, *American Environmental History: The Exploitation and Conservation of Natural Resources* (San Francisco: Boyd & Fraser, 1977), 212.

48. Ferguson and Ferguson, *Sacred Cows at the Public Trough*, 15.

49. Ibid., 30.

50. Carey McWilliams, *Factories in the Field: The Story of Migratory Farm Labor in California* (1935; repr. Salt Lake City, Utah: Peregrine Smith, 1971), 30.

51. Gerald D. Nash. "A Veritable Revolution: The Global Economic Significance of the California Gold Rush," *California History* 77, no. 4 (Winter 1998): 279.

52. Schofield, *Selling Your Father's Bones*, 227.

53. Carlson, *Cattle*, 110–111.

54. Ibid., 112.

55. *Annual Report of the Commissioners of the General Land Office, Report to the Secretary of the Interior*, prepared by William A. Sparks (1883); cited in Sharpes, *Sacred Bull, Holy Cow*, 118–119.

56. Ferguson and Ferguson, *Sacred Cows at the Public Trough*, 26.

57. Bill Walker and D. F. Baber, *The Longest Rope: The Truth About the Johnson County Cattle War* (Caldwell, Idaho: The Caxton Printers, Ltd., 1940), 18.

58. John Upton Terrell, *Land Grab: The Truth About "The Winning of the West"* (New York: Dial, 1972), 181.

59. Ferguson and Ferguson, *Sacred Cows at the Public Trough*, 15–16.

60. Ibid., 27.

61. Ibid., 27–28.

62. Tim Ingold, *Hunters, Pastoralists, and Ranchers: Reindeer Economies and Their Transformations* (Cambridge: Cambridge University Press, 1980), 254.

63. John W. Bennett, *Northern Plainsmen: Adaptive Strategy and Agrarian Life* (Chicago: Aldine, 1969), 90.

64. Peter Coates, "Unusually Cunning, Vicious, and Treacherous: The Extermination of the Wolf in United States History," in *The Massacre in History*, ed. Mark Levene and Penny Roberts (New York: Berghahn, 1999), 169.

65. Ibid., 169.

66. Ibid., 171.

67. Ibid., 172.

68. Barry Holstun Lopez, *Of Wolves and Men* (New York: Scribner, 1978), 167; cited in ibid., 17.

69. *Report of the Massachusetts Railroad Commissioners* (1871), 31; cited in Rudolf Alexander Clemen, *The American Livestock and Meat Industry* (New York: Johnson Reprint Corp., 1966), 195.

70. George T. Angell, *Cattle Transportation: An Essay* (Boston: Massachusetts Society for the Prevention of Cruelty to Animals, 1875), 1–8.

71. Clemen, *The American Livestock and Meat Industry*, 198.

72. Cronon, *Nature's Metropolis*, 208.

73. Ibid.

74. Ibid., 212.

75. Ibid., 208.

76. J'Nell L. Pate, *America's Historic Stockyards: Livestock Hotels* (Forth Worth, Tex.: TCU Press, 2005), 3.

77. Edith Abbott and S. P. Breckinridge, "Women in Industry: The Chicago Stockyards," *Journal of Political Economy* 19, no. 8 (October 1911): 633.

78. Sidney Lens, *Labor Wars: From the Molly Maguires to the Sitdowns* (Garden City, N.Y.: Anchor Press/Doubleday, 1974), 222.

79. James R. Barrett, *Work and Community in the Jungle: Chicago's Packinghouse Workers, 1894–1922* (Chicago: University of Illinois Press, 1987), 17.

80. Lens, *Labor Wars*, 222.

81. Barrett, *Work and Community in the Jungle*, 57. This quotation contains two sentences from Upton Sinclair's *The Jungle*, published by Upton Sinclair (1920), 20.

82. Richard Halpern and Roger Horowitz, *Meatpackers: An Oral History of Black Packinghouse Workers and Their Struggle for Racial and Economic Equality* (New York: Monthly Review Press, 1999), 6.

83. Margaret Garb, "Health, Morality, and Housing: The 'Tenement Problem' in Chicago," *American Journal of Public Health* 93, no. 9 (September 2003): 1.

84. Edward G. Roddy, *Mills, Mansions, and Mergers: The Life of William M. Wood* (North Andover, Mass.: Merrimack Valley Textile Museum, 1982), 71.

85. Alex Carey, *Taking the Risk Out of Democracy* (Urbana: University of Illinois Press, 1997), 42.

86. Roddy, *Mills, Mansions, and Mergers*, 71.

87. Ibid., 100.

88. Cited in Petulla, *American Environmental History*, 189.

89. See, for example, Nick Fiddes, *Meat: A Natural Symbol* (London: Routledge, 1991), 24.

90. Jeremy Rifkin, *Beyond Beef: The Rise and Fall of the Cattle Culture* (New York: Plume, 1992), 54.

91. Maurice Frink, W. Turrentine Jackson, and Agnes Wright Spring, *When Grass Was King: Contributions to the Western Range Cattle Industry Study* (Boulder: University of Colorado Press, 1956), 160.

92. Rifkin, *Beyond Beef*, 89.

93. Ferguson and Ferguson, *Sacred Cows at the Public Trough*, 29.

94. Osgood, *The Day of the Cattleman*, 192.

95. Chip Carlson, *Tom Horn: Killing Men Is My Specialty* (Cheyenne, Wyo.: Beartooth Corral, 1976), 234.

96. Frink, Jackson, and Spring, *When Grass Was King*, 197.

97. Paul W. Gates, *Landlords and Tenants on the Prairie Frontier: Studies in American Land Policy* (Ithaca, N.Y.: Cornell University Press, 1973), 295.

98. Frink, Jackson, and Spring, *When Grass Was King*, 289.

99. Samuel Plimsoll, *Cattle Ships: The Fifth Chapter of Mr. Plimsoll's Second Appeal for Our Seamen* (London: Kegan, Paul, Trench, Trubner and Co. Ltd, 1890), 65.

100. Ibid., 72–75.

101. Ibid., 4.

102. Ibid., 9.

103. Ibid., 76–77.

104. Ibid., 2.

105. Ibid., 87.

106. Josephy, *The Indian Heritage of North America*, 342.

107. Marian C. McKenna, "Across the Blue Line: Policing the Frontier in the Canadian and American West, 1870–1900," in *The Borderlands of the American and Canadian Wests: Essays on Regional History of the Forty-ninth Parallel*, ed. Sterling Evans (Lincoln: University of Nebraska Press, 2006), 102.

108. Paul F. Sharp, *Whoop-Up Country: The Canadian-American West, 1865–1885* (Helena: Historical Society of Montana, 1955), 233.

109. McKenna, "Across the Blue Line," 98.

110. *Fort Macleod Gazette* (May 14, 1883); cited in McKenna, "Across the Blue Line," 97.

111. Martha Harroun Foster, *We Know Who We Are: Métis Identity in a Montana Community* (Norman: University of Oklahoma Press, 2006), 132.

112. Ibid., 166.

113. Warren M. Elofson, "The Untamed Canadian Ranching Frontier, 1874–1914," in *Cowboys, Ranchers, and the Cattle Business: Cross-Border Perspectives on Ranching History*, ed. Simon M. Carter, Sarah Carter, and Bill Yoo (Calgary, Alberta: University of Calgary Press, 2000), 84.

114. Friesen, *The Canadian Prairies*, 236–237.

115. Mary Beth Norton et al., *A People and a Nation: A History of the United States* (Boston: Houghton Mifflin, 2008), 279.

116. Jim Downs, *Sick from Freedom: African-American Illness and Suffering During the Civil War and Reconstruction* (Oxford: Oxford University Press, 2012).

## 5. Capitalist Colonialism and Ranching Violence

1. Joel Mokyr, *The Economics of the Industrial Revolution* (Lanham, Md.: Rowman and Littlefield, 1989), 141.

2. See, for example, Barbara Lewis Solow and Stanley L. Engerman, *British Capitalism and Caribbean Slavery: The Legacy of Eric Williams* (Cambridge: Cambridge University Press, 2004).

3. Mark Kurlansky, *Salt: A World History* (New York: Penguin, 2003), 125.

4. Bertie Mandelblatt, "A Transatlantic Commodity: Irish Salt Beef in the French Atlantic World," *History Workshop Journal* 63, no. 1 (2007): 19.

5. S. J. Connolly, "The Houghers: Agrarian Protest in Early Eighteenth-Century Connacht," in *Nationalism and Popular Protest in Ireland*, ed. C. H. E. Philpin (Cambridge: Cambridge University Press, 1987), 145.

6. Donald E. Jordan Jr., *Land and Popular Politics in Ireland: County Mayo from the Plantation to the Land War* (Cambridge: Cambridge University Press, 1994), 39.

7. Ibid., 43.

8. Anonymous, *The Groans of the Irish* (1741); reprinted in Augustus J. Thébaud and John Habberton, *Ireland: Past and Present* (New York: P. F. Collier, 1878), 309.

9. Eric B. Ross, "An Overview of Trends in Dietary Variation from Hunter-Gatherer to Modern Capitalist Societies," in *Food and Evolution: Toward a Theory of Human Food Habits*, ed. Marvin Harris and Eric B. Ross (Philadelphia, Penn.: Temple University Press, 1987), 30.

10. James Connolly, *Labour in Irish History* (Dublin: New Books, 1973), 15.

11. Ibid., 15–16.

12. Ronald Takaki, *A Different Mirror: A History of Multicultural America* (Boston: Little, Brown, 1993), 141.

13. Susan Campbell Bartoletti, *Black Potatoes: The Story of the Great Irish Famine, 1845–1850* (Boston: Houghton Mifflin, 2001), 168.

14. Ibid., 94, 55.

15. Jeremy Rifkin, *Beyond Beef: The Rise and Fall of the Cattle Culture* (New York: Penguin, 1992), 57.

16. Donald Macleod, *The Stonemason: Donald Macleod's Chronicle of Scotland's Highland Clearances*, ed. Douglas MacGowan (1841; repr. Westport, Conn.: Praeger, 2001), 8–9.

17. Ibid., 9.

18. Ibid., 24.

19. Ross, "An Overview of Trends in Dietary Variation," 29.

20. Eric R. Wolf, *Europe and the People Without History* (Berkeley: University of California Press, 1982), 364.

21. *Australia: The Complete Encyclopedia* (New York: Firefly, 2001), 110.

22. Stuart Macintyre, *A Concise History of Australia* (Cambridge: Cambridge University Press, 1999), 59.

23. Ian D. Clark and Toby Heydon, *A Bend in the Yarra: A History of the Merri Creek Protectorate Station Merri Creek Aboriginal School, 1841–1851* (Canberra: Aboriginal Studies Press, 2004), 13.

24. John Maynard, *Aboriginal Stars of the Turf: Jockeys of Australian Racing History* (Canberra: Aboriginal Studies Press, 2002), 2.

25. Henry Reynolds, "The Breaking of the Great Australian Silence: Aborigines in Australian Historiography," lecture given at the University of London, 1984, http://www.kcl.ac.uk/content/1/c6/01/65/70/Reynolds1.pdf.

26. *Australia: The Complete Encyclopedia*, 95.

27. Ian D. Clark, *Scars in the Landscape: A Register of Massacre Sites in Western Victoria, 1803–1859* (Canberra: Aboriginal Studies Press for the Australian Institute of Aboriginal and Torres Strait Islander Studies, 1995), 1.

28. Ibid., 2.

29. Erinn Banting, *Australia: The People* (New York: Crabtree, 2003), 9.

30. Malcolm D. Prentis, *A Study in Black and White: The Aborigines in Australian History*, 2nd ed. (Sydney: Rosenberg, 1988), 70.

31. Wolf, *Europe and the People Without History*, 323.

32. Ibid.

33. Macintyre, *A Concise History of Australia*, 41–42.

34. Donald Denoon, Philippa Mein-Smith, and Marivic Wyndham, *A History of Australia, New Zealand, and the Pacific* (Oxford: Blackwell, 2000), 171.

35. Ibid., 75.

36. A. J. Marshall, "On the Disadvantages of Wearing Fur," in *The Great Extermination: A Guide to Anglo-Australian Cupidity, Wickedness, and Waste*, ed. A. J. Marshall (London: William Heinemann, 1966), 18.

37. James Jupp, *The Australian People: An Encyclopedia of the Nation, Its People and Their Origins* (Cambridge: Cambridge University Press, 2002), 112.

38. Henry Ling Roth, Marion E. Butler, and John George Garson, *The Aborigines of Tasmania* (1923; repr. Berlin: Nabu, 2010), 168.

39. Jupp, *The Australian People*, 113.

40. Denoon, Mein-Smith, and Wyndham, *History of Australia, New Zealand, and the Pacific*, 171.

41. Thalia Anthony, "Reconciliation and Conciliation: The Irreconcilable Dilemma of the 1965 'Equal' Wage Case for Aboriginal Station Workers," *Labour History* 93 (November 2007): 15.

42. Phillip Knightley, *The Vestey Affair* (London: Macdonald Futura, 1981), 133.

43. Ibid., 138–139.

44. J. W. Bleakley, *The Aboriginals and Half-Castes of Central Australia and North Australia*, report to the parliament of the Commonwealth of Australia (1928), 6, 7.

45. Ibid., 9.

46. Knightley, *The Vestey Affair*, 141–142.

47. Ibid., 144.

48. J. C. Byrne, *Twelve Years' Wanderings in the British Colonies: From 1835 to 1847* (London: Richard Bentley, 1848), 48.

49. Keith Sinclair, A History of New Zealand (London: Allen Lane, 1980), 93.

50. Statement by Te Kemara, chief of the Ngatikawa in 1840; cited in Maori Is My Name: Historical Maori Writings in Translation, ed. John Caselberg (Dunedin: John McIndoe, 1975), 44–45.

51. Dom Felice Vaggioli, History of New Zealand and Its Inhabitants, trans. by John Crocket (1896; repr. Dunedin: University of Otago Press, 2001), 49.

52. James Belich, Making Peoples: A History of the New Zealanders, from Polynesian Settlement to the End of the Nineteenth Century (Honolulu: University of Hawaii Press, 2002), 249.

53. Denoon, Mein-Smith, and Wyndham, History of Australia, New Zealand, and the Pacific, 173.

54. R. Ogilvie Buchanan, The Pastoral Industries of New Zealand (London: George Philip and Son, 1935), 4.

55. Ibid., 5.

56. Ibid.

57. William Woodruff, "The Emergence of an International Economy: 1700–1914," in The Fontana Economic History of Europe: The Emergence of Industrial Societies, ed. Carlo M. Cipolla (Glasgow: William Collins Sons, 1973), 2:659.

58. Benjamin Keen and Mark Wassermann, A Short History of Latin America (Boston: Houghton Mifflin, 1984), 162.

59. Ibid., 181.

60. Silvio R. Duncan Baretta and John Markoff, "Civilization and Barbarism: Cattle Frontiers in Latin America," Comparative Studies in Society and History 20, no. 4 (October 1978): 600, 607.

61. See, for example, Hector Perez-Brignoli, A Brief History of Central America (Berkeley: University of California Press, 1989).

62. Baretta and Markoff, "Civilization and Barbarism," 588.

63. Ibid., 602.

64. George V. Rauch, Conflict in the Southern Cone: The Argentine Military and the Boundary Dispute with Chile, 1870–1902 (Westport, Conn.: Prager, 1999), 58.

65. Philip D. Curtain, "Location in History: Argentina and South Africa in the Nineteenth Century," Journal of World History 10, no. 1 (Spring 1999): 76.

66. Rauch, Conflict in the Southern Cone, 10.

67. John H. Bodley, Victims of Progress, 4th ed. (Mountain View, Calif.: Mayfield, 1999), 50.

68. Samuel Amaral, The Rise of Capitalism on the Pampas: The Estancias of Buenos Aires, 1785–1870 (Cambridge: Cambridge University Press, 1998), 108.

69. Ibid., 108.

70. John Lynch, "The River Plate Republics from Independence to the Paraguayan War," in The Cambridge History of Latin America, vol. 3: From Indepen-

*dence to c. 1870,* ed. Leslie Bethell (Cambridge: Cambridge University Press, 1985), 659.

71. Alida C. Metcalf, *Family and Frontiers in Colonial Brazil: Santana de Parnaíba* (Berkeley: University of California Press, 1992), 4

72. Joseph L. Love, *Rio Grande do Sul and Brazilian Regionalism, 1882–1930* (Palo Alto, Calif.: Stanford University Press, 1971), 12.

73. Charles Darwin, *The Voyage of the Beagle* (New York: P. F. Collier and Son, 1909), 138.

74. C. B. Mansfield, *Paraguay, Brazil, and the Plate: Letters Written in 1852–1853* (1856; repr. New York: AMS Press, 1971), 228–229, 159–160, 146–147.

75. Stephen Bell, *Campanha Gaúcha: A Brazilian Ranching System, 1850–1920* (Palo Alto, Calif.: Stanford University Press, 1998), 68.

76. Love, *Rio Grande do Sul and Brazilian Regionalism,* 11.

77. Simon G. Hanson, *Argentine Meat and the British Meat Market: Chapters in the History of the Argentine Meat Industry* (Palo Alto, Calif.: Stanford University Press, 1938), 18.

78. Lynch, "The River Plate Republics from Independence to the Paraguayan War," 662.

79. Kenneth C. Ferris, "The War of the Triple Alliance (1864–1870): A Historical Case Study on the Causes of Regional Conflict" (MA thesis, U.S. Army Command and General Staff College, 2009).

80. Keen and Wasserman, *A Short History of Latin America,* 185.

81. David Rock, *Argentina, 1516–1987: From Spanish Colonialism to Alfonsín* (Berkeley: University of California Press, 1985), 129.

82. Keen and Wasserman, *A Short History of Latin America,* 112.

83. Bell, *Campanha Gaúcha,* 4.

84. Ibid., 139, 247–248.

85. Robert B. Kent, *Latin America: Regions and People* (New York: Guilford, 2006), 311.

86. Carson I. A. Ritchie, *Food in Civilization: How History Has Been Affected by Human Tastes* (New York: Beaufort, 1981), 186.

87. Kent, *Latin America,* 319.

88. Alfred Hasbrouck, "The Conquest of the Desert," *Hispanic American Historical Review* 15, no. 2 (1935): 205.

89. Ibid., 205–206.

90. See Glyn Williams and Julia Garlant, "The Impact of the 'Conquest of the Desert' Upon the Tehuelche of Chubut: From Hunters and Gathers to Peasants," paper presented at the Symposium on Landlord and Peasant in Latin America and the Caribbean, Cambridge (1972), 1, 11, 50.

91. Hasbrouck, "The Conquest of the Desert," 222–223.

92. Williams and Garlant, "The Impact of the 'Conquest of the Desert,'" 1, 11, 50.

93. Hasbrouck, "The Conquest of the Desert," 228.

94. Kent, *Latin America*, 319.

95. Ibid., 313.

96. Rauch, *Conflict in the Southern Cone*, 57.

97. John Charles Chasteen, "Background to Civil War: The Process of Land Tenure in Brazil's Southern Borderland, 1801–1893," *Hispanic American Historical Review* 71, no. 4 (November 1991): 758.

98. Love, *Rio Grande do Sul and Brazilian Regionalism*, 57–58.

99. Ibid., 75.

100. Ibid., 3.

101. Shawn Van Ausdal, "Pasture, Profit, and Power: An Environmental History of Cattle Ranching in Colombia, 1850–1950," *Geoforum* 40 (2009): 707–719.

102. James R. Barrett, *Work and Community in the Jungle: Chicago's Packinghouse Workers, 1894–1922* (Chicago: University of Illinois Press, 1987), 18.

103. Doug Yarrington, "The Vestey Cattle Enterprise and the Regime of Juan Vicente Gómez, 1908–1935," *Journal of Latin American Studies* 35, no. 1 (February 2003): 92.

104. Raymond E. Crist, "Land Tenure Problems in Venezuela," *American Journal of Economics and Sociology* 1, no. 2 (January 1942): 147.

105. Rauch, *Conflict in the Southern Cone*, 57.

106. C. Reginald Enock, *The Republics of Central and South America: Their Resources, Industries, Sociology, and Future* (London: J. M. Dent and Sons, 1913), 151, 152.

107. See, for example, Azar Gat, *War in Human Civilization* (Oxford: Oxford University Press, 2006).

108. John Lamphear, *The Scattering Time: Turkana Response to Colonial Rule* (Oxford: Oxford University Press, 1992), 24–25.

109. George Peter Murdoch, *Africa: Its Peoples and Their Culture History* (New York: McGraw-Hill, 1959), 393.

110. Gerhard Lenski and Jean Lenski, *Human Societies: An Introduction to Macrosociology*, 5th ed. (New York: McGraw-Hill, 1987), 213.

111. See, for example: W. G. Clarence-Smith, *The Economics of the Indian Ocean Slave Trade in the Nineteenth Century* (London: Frank Cass and Company, 1989); Catherine Lowe Besteman, *Unraveling Somalia: Race, Violence, and the Legacy of Slavery* (Philadelphia, Penn.: University of Pennsylvania Press, 1999); Susan Charnley, "Pastoralism and Property Rights: The Evolution of Communal Property on the Usabgu Plains, Tanzania," *African Economic History* 25 (1997): 97–119; Martin A. Klein, *Slavery and Colonial Rule in French West Africa* (Toronto: University of Toronto, 1998).

112. Clare Janaki Holden and Ruth Mace, "Spread of Cattle Led to the Loss of Matrilineal Descent in Africa: A Coevolutionary Analysis," *Biological Sciences* 270, no. 1532 (December 7, 2003): 2425–2433.

113. John Lewis Burckhardt, *Travels in Nubia* (1822; repr. New York: AMS Press, 1978), 290.

114. Ibid., 294–295.

115. Ibid., 92, 301–302.

116. Robert Lacour-Gayet, *A History of South Africa*, trans. Stephen Hardman (London: Cassell, 1977), 25.

117. Leonard Guelke, "Frontier Settlement in Early Dutch South Africa," *Annals of the Association of American Geographers* 66, no. 1 (March 1976): 25–42.

118. Leonard Monteath Thompson, *A History of South Africa* (New Haven, Conn.: Yale University Press, 2000), 39.

119. Robert Ross, "Capitalism, Expansion, and Incorporation on the Southern African Frontier," in *The Frontier in History: North American and Southern Africa Compared*, ed. Howard Lamar and Leonard Thompson (New Haven, Conn.: Yale University Press, 1981), 213.

120. Lacour-Gayet, *A History of South Africa*, 30–31.

121. Eric A. Walker, *A History of Southern Africa* (London: Longmans, Green and Company, 1956), 116.

122. J. F. Ade Ajayi, "Africa at the Beginning of the Nineteenth Century: Issues and Prospects," in *General History of Africa*, vol. 6: *Africa in the Nineteenth Century Until the 1880s*, abridged ed. (Berkeley: University of California Press, 1998), 7.

123. Robert Tignor et al., *Worlds Together, Worlds Apart: A History of the World*, 2nd ed. (New York: Norton, 2008), 770.

124. Gregory Fremont-Barnes, *The Boer War, 1899–1902* (Oxford: Osprey, 2003), 86.

125. Ibid., 86.

126. Writers' Program of the WPA, *Wyoming: A Guide to Its History, Highways, and People* (London: Oxford University Press, 1941), 270.

127. Hanson, *Argentine Meat and the British Meat Market*, 123.

128. Ibid., 122–143.

129. Department of Information and Publicity, SWAPO of Namibia, *To Be Born a Nation: The Liberation Struggle for Namibia* (London: Zed, 1981), 17.

130. Ibid., 18.

131. Jeremy Swift, "Sahelian Pastoralists: Underdevelopment, Desertification, and Famine," *Annual Review of Anthropology* 6 (1977): 471.

132. Virginia Thompson and Richard Adloff, *French West Africa* (Palo Alto, Calif.: Stanford University Press, 1957), 337.

133. William Harper Dean, "The Livestock Tangle in France," *Country Gentleman* 83 (July 6, 1918): 9.

134. Swift, "Sahelian Pastoralists," 474.

135. I. N. Kimambo, "The East African Coast and Hinterland: 1845–80," in *General History of Africa*, vol. 6: *Africa in the Nineteenth Century Until the 1880s*, abridged ed. (Berkeley: University of California Press, 1998), 96.

136. Lamphear, *The Scattering Time*, 3.

137. Tom Lithgow and Hugo van Lawick, *The Ngorongoro Story* (Nairobi: Camerapix, 2004), 54.

138. William Beinart, "The Night of the Jackal: Pastures and Predators in the Cape," *Past & Present* 158 (February 1998): 201.

139. Bartle Bull, *Safari: A Chronicle of Adventure* (New York: Penguin, 1988), 192.

140. Lithgow and van Lawick, *The Ngforongoro Story*, 65.

141. Bull, *Safari*, 197.

142. Roualeyn Gordon Cumming, *Five Years' Adventures in the Far Interior of South Africa, with Notices of the Native Tribes and Savage Animals* (1850; repr. London: John Murray, 1904), 362.

143. John Berger, "Why Look at Animals?" in *The Animals Reader: The Essential Classic and Contemporary Writings*, ed. Linda Kalof and Amy Fitzgerald (1980; repr. New York: Berg, 2007), 259.

144. Social Darwinism was a popular pseudoscientific theory in the late nineteenth and early twentieth centuries that explained and justified European dominance as a natural evolutionary result of the alleged biological superiority of the "white race."

## 6. Social Construction of the "Hamburger" Culture

1. Willard F. Williams and Thomas T. Stout, *Economics of the Livestock-Meat Industry* (New York: MacMillan, 1964), 17.

2. Joint Commission of Agricultural Inquiry, *The Agricultural Crisis and Its Causes, Part One.* (Washington, D.C.: Government Printing Office, 1921), 86.

3. John Wesley Powell, *Report on the Lands of the Arid Region of the United States* (Washington, D.C.: U.S. Government Printing Office, 1879).

4. Lynn Jacobs, *Waste of the West: Public Land Ranching*, (Tucson, Ariz.: Lynn Jacobs, 1991), 17.

5. Sidney Lens, *The Labor Wars: From the Molly Maguires to the Sitdowns* (New York: Anchor, 1974), 224.

6. Howard Zinn, *A People's History of the United States: 1492–Present*, rev. ed. (New York: Harper Perennial, 1995), 359.

7. Ibid., 301–302.

8. Lens, *The Labor Wars*, 223.

9. James E. Downing, *The Breeders' Gazette* (August 25, 1921); cited in Rudolph Alexander Clemen, *The American Livestock and Meat Industry* (1923; repr. New York: Johnson Reprint Corp., 1966), 196–197.

10. David Gerard Hogan, *Selling 'Em by the Sack: White Castle and the Creation of American Food* (New York: New York University Press, 1997), 28.

11. Ibid., 30.

12. See, for example, Edwin Palmer Hoyt, *The Palmer Raids, 1919–1920: An Attempt to Suppress Dissent* (New York: Seabury, 1969); Christopher Finan, *From the Palmer Raids to the Patriot Act: A History of the Fight for Free Speech in America* (Boston: Beacon, 2007).

13. See, for example, David Nibert, "The Political Economy of Developmental Disability," *Critical Sociology* 21, no. 1 (1995): 59–80.

14. Richard H. Robbins, *Global Problems and the Culture of Capitalism*, 3rd ed. (Boston: Pearson Education, 2005), 19.

15. Ibid., 23.

16. Stuart Ewen, *Captains of Consciousness: Advertising and the Social Roots of Consumer Culture* (New York: McGraw-Hill, 1976), 19.

17. Edward Bernays, *Propaganda* (1928; repr. Brooklyn: Ig, 2004), 73.

18. Larry Tye, *The Father of Spin: Edward L. Bernays and the Birth of Public Relations* (New York: Henry Holt and Company, 2002), 51–52.

19. See Robert W. McChesney, *Rich Media, Poor Democracy: Communications Politics in Dubious Times* (New York: The New Press, 1999), 189–225.

20. Carolyn Wyman, *SPAM: A Biography* (New York: Harcourt, Brace and Company, 1999), 61.

21. Hogan, *Selling 'Em by the Sack*, 79.

22. Ibid., 90.

23. Jeffrey Tennyson, *Hamburger Heaven: The Illustrated History of the Hamburger* (New York: Hyperion, 1993), 24.

24. Arthur Kallet and F. J. Schlink, *100,000,000 Guinea Pigs: Dangers in Everyday Foods, Drugs, and Cosmetics* (New York: Vanguard, 1933), 38–39.

25. Ronald L. McDonald, *The Complete Hamburger: The History of America's Favorite Sandwich* (Secaucus, N.J.: Carol, 1997), 19.

26. Hogan, *Selling 'Em by the Sack*, 33.

27. Ibid., 57–58, 80.

28. See, for example, John M. Murrin et al., *Liberty, Equality, Power: Enhanced Concise Edition*, 4th ed. (Belmont, Calif.: Wadsworth, 1999), 838–840.

29. Bill Winders and David Nibert, "Consuming the Surplus: Expanding 'Meat' Consumption and Animal Oppression," *International Journal of Sociology and Social Policy* 24, no. 9 (2004): 78.

30. Arturo Warman, *Corn and Capitalism: How a Botanical Bastard Grew to Global Dominance* (Chapel Hill: University of North Carolina Press, 2003), 181.

31. Office of Price Administration pamphlet, cited in Amy Bentley, *Eating for Victory: Food Rationing and the Politics of Domesticity* (Chicago: University of Illinois Press, 1998), 85.

32. Bentley, *Eating for Victory*, 94.

33. Charles A. Beard and Mary R. Beard, *The Beards' New Basic History of the United States* (Garden City, N.Y.: Doubleday, 1968), 440.

34. See, for example, Richard Breitman, *Official Secrets: What the Nazis Planned, What the British and Americans Knew* (New York: Hill & Wang, 1999); Richard Breitman and Alan M. Kraut, *American Refugee Policy and European Jewry, 1933–1945* (Bloomington: Indiana University Press, 1987).

35. See, for example, Zinn, *A People's History of the United States*, 423–425.

36. C. Wright Mills, *White Collar: The American Middle Class* (New York: Oxford University Press, 1951), 63.

37. Harold R. Kerbo, *Social Stratification and Inequality: Class Conflict in Historical and Comparative Perspective*, 2nd ed. (New York: McGraw-Hill, 1991), 33.

38. See, for example, J. Allen Whitt and Glenn Yago, "Corporate Strategies and the Decline of Transit in U.S. Cities," *Urban Affairs Review* 21, no. 1 (1985): 37–65.

39. Louis A. Sposa, *Television Primer of Production and Direction* (New York: McGraw-Hill, 1947), 145.

40. Reynold Kraft, "Television Advertising," in John F. Royal, *Television Production Problems* (New York: McGraw-Hill, 1948), 150.

41. See, for example, Michael Parenti, *Make-Believe Media: The Politics of Entertainment* (Belmont, Calif.: Wadsworth, 1992).

42. Ray Kroc and Robert Anderson, *Grinding It Out: The Making of McDonald's* (New York: St. Martin's, 1977), 123.

43. Hogan, *Selling 'Em by the Sack*, 141–142.

44. Eric Schlosser, *Fast Food Nation: The Dark Side of the All-American Meal* (Boston: Houghton Mifflin, 2001), 40–41.

45. Kroc and Anderson, *Grinding It Out*, 160.

46. Tennyson, *Hamburger Heaven*, 77.

47. James W. McLamore, *The Burger King: Jim McLamore and the Building of an Empire* (New York: McGraw-Hill, 1998), 57, 59, 62.

48. See, for example, Philip Mattera, *USDA INC.: How Agribusiness Has Hijacked Regulatory Policy at the U.S. Department of Agriculture* (Washington. D.C.: Corporate Research Project of Good Jobs First, 2004), http://www.nffc.net /Issues/Corporate%20Control/USDA%20INC.pdf.

49. Ruth Harrison, *Animal Machines: The New Factory Farming Industry* (New York: Ballantine, 1966), 176.

50. Barbara Noske, *Beyond Boundaries: Humans and Animals* (Montreal: Black Rose, 1997).

51. Ibid., 14.

52. Ray E. Bolz and George Lewis Tuve, *CRC Handbook of Tables for Applied Engineering Science* (Boca Raton, Fla.: CRC, 1973), 744.

53. Faith McNulty, *Must They Die? The Strange Case of the Prairie Dog and the Black-Footed Ferret* (New York: Doubleday, 1971), 11.

54. Denzel Ferguson and Nancy Ferguson, *Sacred Cows at the Public Trough* (Bend, Ore.: Maverick, 1983), 136.

55. Ann E. Weiss, *Save the Mustangs* (New York: Simon and Schuster, 1974), 44.

56. Ferguson and Ferguson, *Sacred Cows at the Public Trough*, 113.

57. See Johan Galtung, "Cultural Violence," *Journal of Peace Research* 27, no. 3 (August 1990): 291–305.

58. Warman, *Corn and Capitalism*, 189.

59. Manning Feinleib, "Trends in Heart Disease in the United States," *American Journal of the Medical Sciences* 310, no. 6 (1995): 8–14.

60. Polly Walker et al., "Public Health Implications of Meat Production and Consumption," *Public Health Nutrition* 8, no. 4 (2005): 349.

61. U.S. Public Health Service, *Vital Statistics of the United States: 1900–1970*, http://www.infoplease.com/ipa/A0922292.html.

62. See, for example, National Research Council, *Diet and Health: Implications for Reducing Chronic Disease Risk* (Washington, D.C.: National Academies Press, 1989).

63. U.S. Public Health Service, *Vital Statistics of the United States*.

64. See, for example, Debra Kain, "How Eating Red Meat Can Spur Cancer Progression: New Mechanism Identified," *Science Daily* (November 28, 2008), http://www.sciencedaily.com/releases/2008/11/081113181428.htm; T. Colin Campbell, *The China Study* (Dallas, Tex.: BenBella, 2006).

65. Bill Winders, *The Politics of Food Supply: U.S. Agricultural Policy in the World Economy* (New Haven, Conn.: Yale University Press, 2009), 187.

66. See, for example, Ward Churchill and Jim Vander Wall, *Agents of Repression* (Cambridge, Mass.: South End Press, 2002).

7. THE "HAMBURGER" CULTURE AND LATIN AMERICA

1. James D. Nations and Daniel I. Komer, "Rainforests and the Hamburger Society," *Environment* 25, no. 3 (1983): 17.

2. Howard Handelman, "Economic Policy and Elite Pressures," in *Military Government and the Movement Toward Democracy in South America*, ed. Howard Handelman and Thomas G. Saunders (Bloomington: University of Indiana Press, 1979), 243–244.

3. Jeremy Rifkin, *Beyond Beef: The Rise and Fall of the Cattle Culture* (New York: Penguin, 1992), 51.

4. Patricia Howard-Borjas, *Cattle and Crisis: The Genesis of Unsustainable Development in Central America: Land Reform, Land Settlement, and Cooperatives* (Rome: U.N. Food and Agricultural Organization, 1995), 4, http://www.fao.org/docrep/V9828T/v9828t10.html.

5. Tom Barry, *Roots of Rebellion: Land and Hunger in Central America* (Boston: South End Press, 1987), 30.

6. See William Blum, *Killing Hope: U.S. Military and CIA Interventions Since World War II* (Monroe, Maine: Common Courage, 1995), 232.

7. Samuel Shapiro, *Invisible Latin America* (1963; repr. Freeport, N.Y.: Books for Libraries, 1971), 84.

8. Michael Parenti, *Against Empire* (San Francisco: City Lights, 1995), 28–29.

9. Teresa Hayter and Catherine Watson, *Aid: Rhetoric and Reality* (London: Pluto, 1985).

10. Richard H. Robbins, *Global Problems and the Culture of Capitalism* (Needham, Mass.: Allyn and Bacon, 2002), 215.

11. Douglas R. Shane, *Hoofprints in the Forest: Cattle Ranching and the Destruction of Latin America's Tropical Forests* (Philadelphia, Penn.: Institute for the Study of Human Issues, 1986), 45.

12. Hayter and Watson, *Aid: Rhetoric and Reality*, 51.

13. Shane, *Hoofprints in the Forest*, 36.

14. Ibid., 40.

15. Charles D. Brockett, *Land, Power, and Poverty: Agrarian Transformation and Political Conflict in Central America* (Boston: Unwin Hyman, 1990), 48.

16. David Kaimowitz, *Livestock and Deforestation in Central America in the 1980s and 1990s: A Policy Perspective* (Jakarta: Center for International Forestry Research, 1996), 25–26.

17. Ibid., 26.

18. Daniel Faber, "Imperialism, Revolution, and the Ecological Crisis of Central America," *Latin American Perspectives* 19, no. 1 (1992): 25.

19. Kaimowitz, *Livestock and Deforestation in Central America*, 27.

20. *World Bank Annual Reports* (Washington, D.C.: World Bank, 1970–1987).

21. National Research Council, *Sustainable Agriculture and the Environment in the Humid Tropics* (Washington, D.C.: National Academy Press, 1993), 88.

22. Frances Moore Lappé, *Diet for a Small Planet* (New York: Ballantine, 1982), 50.

23. Philip McMichael, *Food and Agrarian Orders in the World Economy* (Westport, Conn.: Praeger, 1995), 108.

24. David Barkin, Rosemary L. Blatt, and Bille R. DeWalt, *Feed Crops Versus Food Crops: Global Substitution of Grains in Production* (Boulder, Colo.: Lynne Rienner, 1990), 30.

25. Quevedo Martin Morgan and J. Phillip Rourk, *The Beef and Cattle Industries of Central America and Panama* (Washington, D.C.: U.S. Department of Agriculture, 1973), 22.

26. E. Bradford Burns, *Latin America: Conflict and Creation* (Englewood Cliffs, N.J.: Prentice Hall, 1993), 6.

27. Faber, "Imperialism, Revolution, and the Ecological Crisis of Central America," 25.

28. Barry, *Roots of Rebellion*, xiv.

29. Walden Bello, "Cows Eat Better Than People Do," *Time* (November 8, 1999): 5.

30. James D. Nations, "Terrestrial Impacts in Mexico and Central America," in *Development or Destruction: The Conversion of Tropical Forest to Pasture in Latin America*, ed. Theodore E. Downing et al. (Boulder, Colo.: Westview, 1992), 195.

31. Faber, "Imperialism, Revolution, and the Ecological Crisis of Central America," 20.

32. David Kaimowitz, "Policies Affecting Deforestation for Cattle in Central America," in *Sustainable Agriculture in Central America*, ed. Jan P. de Groot and Ruerd Ruben (New York: St. Martin's, 1997).

33. George Ledec, "New Directions for Livestock Policy: An Environmental Perspective," in *Development or Destruction: The Conversion of Tropical Forest to Pasture in Latin America*, ed. Theodore E. Downing et al. (Boulder, Colo.: Westview, 1992), 28.

34. Christopher Uhl and Geoffrey Parker, "Our Steak in the Jungle," *BioScience* 36, no. 10 (November 1986): 642.

35. Hayter and Watson, *Aid: Rhetoric and Reality*, 152.

36. Neoliberalism is a philosophy that promotes increased market control of trade and resources while reducing governmental regulation.

37. Hayter and Watson, *Aid: Rhetoric and Reality*, 160.

38. Ibid., 162.

39. Ibid., 159.

40. Ibid., 174.

41. Robert G. Williams, *Export Agriculture and the Crisis in Central America* (Chapel Hill: University of North Carolina Press, 1986), 160.

42. Ibid., 151.

43. Sue Branford and Oriel Glock, *The Last Frontier: Fighting Over Land in the Amazon* (London: Zed, 1985), 126.

44. Howard-Borjas, *Cattle and Crisis*, 2.

45. Ibid., 1.

46. After years of protests by concerned people in the United States and amid increasing public awareness of the philosophy and practices of the School of the

Americas (SOA) and its graduates, the government changed the name of the school to the Western Hemisphere Institute for Security Cooperation. For more information, see http://www.soaw.org.

47. Barry, *Roots of Rebellion*, 123.

48. Williams, *Export Agriculture and the Crisis in Central America*, 134.

49. Norman Myers, *The Primary Source: Tropical Forests and Our Future* (New York: Norton, 1992), 133.

50. John Stockwell, *The Praetorian Guard: The U.S. Role in the New World Order* (Boston: South End Press, 1991), 65.

51. Williams, *Export Agriculture and the Crisis in Central America*, 126.

52. Ibid., 170.

53. Ibid.

54. Ibid.

55. Ibid., 171.

56. Robert E. White, "Preliminary Assessment of the Situation in El Salvador," classified memo prepared for the U.S. State Department (March 19, 1980), http://foia.state.gov/documents/elsalvad/738d.PDF.

57. Elisabeth Jean Wood, *Insurgent Collective Action and Civil War in El Salvador* (Cambridge: Cambridge University Press, 2003), 8.

58. Williams, *Export Agriculture and the Crisis in Central America*, 138.

59. Barry, *Roots of Rebellion*, 139–140.

60. Brockett, *Land, Power, and Poverty*, 99–100.

61. Guatemalan Death Squad Dossier, National Security Archive Electronic Briefing Book no. 15, http://www.gwu.edu/~nsarchiv/NSAEBB/NSAEBB15/press.html.

62. Myers, *The Primary Source*, 132.

63. Jack A. Nelson, *Hunger for Justice: The Politics of Food and Faith* (Maryknoll, N.Y.: Orbis, 1980), 43.

64. Blum, *Killing Hope*, 163.

65. Chico Mendes, *Fight for the Forest: Chico Mendes in His Own Words*, 2nd ed. (London: Latin American Bureau, 1992), 65–67.

66. Aaron Sachs, *Eco-Justice: Linking Human Rights and the Environment* (Washington, D.C.: Worldwatch Institute, 1995), 5–6.

67. Renée González-Montagut, "Factors That Contributed to the Expansion of Cattle Ranching in Veracruz, Mexico," *Estudios Mexicanos* 15, no. 1 (Winter 1999): 110.

68. Ibid., 111.

69. Aaron Bobrow-Strain, *Intimate Enemies: Landowners, Power, and Violence in Chiapas* (Durham, N.C.: Duke University Press, 2007), 109.

70. Ibid., 110.

71. Frans J. Schryer, *Ethnicity and Class Conflict in Rural Mexico* (Princeton, N.J.: Princeton University Press, 1990).

72. Nations, "Terrestrial Impacts in Mexico and Central America," 195.

73. Joseph M. Whitmeyer and Rosemary L. Hopcroft, "Community, Capitalism, and Rebellion in Chiapas," *Sociological Perspectives* 39, no. 4 (1996): 523.

74. George A. Collier with Elizabeth Lowery Quaratiello, *Basta! Land and the Zapatista Rebellion in Chiapas* (Oakland, Calif.: Food First, 1994); cited in ibid.

75. Branford and Glock, *The Last Frontier*, 205.

76. Ibid., 194.

77. Ibid., 208.

78. Ibid., 203.

79. Ibid., 213.

80. Patricia Louise Howard Ballard, "From Banana Republic to Cattle Republic: Agrarian Roots of the Crisis in Honduras" (Ph.D. thesis, University of Wisconsin, 1987), 501–502, 589–590.

81. MADRE: An International Women's Human Rights Organization, "Violence Against Women In Latin America," http://www.madre.org/articles/int/b10/violence.html.

82. Branford and Glock, *The Last Frontier*, 126–127.

83. MADRE, "Violence Against Women In Latin America," 2.

84. McMichael, *Food and Agrarian Orders in the World Economy*, 223.

85. Ibid., 225.

86. Barry, *Roots of Rebellion*, 11.

87. Branford and Glock, *The Last Frontier*, 185.

88. See David E. Guinn and Elissa Steglich, *In Modern Bondage: Sex Trafficking in the Americas* (Ardsley, N.Y.: Transnational, 2003), 41–43.

89. Barry, *Roots of Rebellion*, 4, xiv.

90. World Bank, *Atlas of Global Development* (Washington, D.C.: World Bank, 2007), 92.

91. Jim Yong Kim and Joyce V. Millen, *Dying for Growth: Global Inequality and the Health of the Poor* (Monroe, Maine: Common Courage, 2002), 432.

92. Faber, "Imperialism, Revolution, and the Ecological Crisis of Central America," 19.

93. Rifkin, *Beyond Beef*, 216–217.

94. Ibid., 216.

95. Ibid.

96. Marcus Linear, *Zapping the Third World* (London: Pluto, 1985), 46.

97. Ibid., 62.

98. Robbins, *Global Problems and the Culture of Capitalism*, 271.

99. Ibid., 273.

100. See, for example, Abiodun Alao, *Natural Resources and Conflict in Africa: The Tragedy of Endowment* (Rochester, N.Y.: University of Rochester Press, 2007).

101. Michelé Pickover, *Animal Rights in South Africa* (Cape Town: Double Storey, 2005), 157–158.

## 8. DOMESECRATION AND IMPENDING CATASTROPHE

1. 2011 World Hunger and Poverty Facts and Statistics, http://www.worldhun ger.org/articles/Learn/world%20hunger%20facts%202002.htm#Number_of _hungry_people_in_the_world.

2. Julian Rubinstein, "They Call It Suicide," *Rolling Stone* 842 (June 8, 2002): 75–78.

3. Simon Romero, "Violence Hits Brazil Tribes in Scramble for Land," *New York Times* (June 10, 2012).

4. Erin C. Heil, "The Brazilian Landless Movement, Resistance, and Violence," *Critical Criminology* 18 (2009): 85.

5. Juliana Barbassa, "Brazil to Protect Environmental Activists as Murders Increase Over Illegal Logging," *Huffington Post* (May 30, 2011), http://www.huff ingtonpost.com/2011/05/31/brazil-environmental-activist-murders-logging _n_869206.html.

6. http://www.u.tv/News/Brazilian-police-arrest-suspects-in-Amazon-murders -of-environmentalists/3bd616f0-f565-4647-a52b-74dae3c9e2a1.

7. "Brazil: Environmental Rights Defender Murdered," *The Argentina Independent* (October 22, 2011), http://www.argentinaindependent.com/tag/murder/.

8. Binka Le Breton, *Trapped: Modern-Day Slavery in the Brazilian Amazon* (Bloomfield, Conn.: Kumarian, 2003).

9. Greenpeace, *State of Conflict: An Investigation Into the Landgrabbers, Loggers, and Lawless Frontiers in Pará State* (Washington, D.C.: Greenpeace, 2004), 16.

10. George Monbiot, "The Price of Cheap Beef: Disease, Deforestation, Slavery, and Murder," *The Guardian* (November 18, 2005), http://www.globalpolicy .org/component/content/article/212/45250.html.

11. Simon Romero, "Clash of Hope and Fear as Venezuela Seizes Land," *New York Times* (May 17, 2007).

12. See, for example, Nikolas Kozloff, *Hugo Chávez: Oil, Politics, and the Challenge to the United States* (New York: Palgrave Macmillan, 2006).

13. "Chavez Plan Rattles Venezuelan Ranchers," *Washington Times* (February 23, 2010), http://www.washingtontimes.com/news/2010/feb/23/chavez-plan-rattles -venezuelan-ranchers/.

14. Blake Schmidt, "Ranchers and Drug Barons Threaten Rain Forest Once Ruled by the Maya," *New York Times* (July 18, 2010).

15. Ginger Thompson, "In Guatemalan Town Buried by Mud, Unyielding Hope for a Little Girl," *New York Times* (October 9, 2005).

16. Jerome Taylor, "El Salvador Flood Disaster Worsened by Deforestation," *The Independent* (October 9, 2005), http://www.independent.co.uk/environment /el-salvador-flood-disaster-worsened-by-deforestation-509617.html.

17. Blake Schmidt, "Guatemala Struggles to Recover After Storm," *New York Times* (June 1, 2010), http://www.nytimes.com/2010/06/02/world/americas/02gua temala.html?ref=landslides_and_mudslides.

18. See, for example, Jennifer Dillard, "Slaughterhouse Nightmare: Psychological Harm Suffered by Slaughterhouse Employees and the Possibility of Redress Through Legal Reform," *Georgetown Journal on Poverty Law and Policy* 15, no. 391 (Summer 2008).

19. Spencer S. Hsu, "Immigration Raid Jars a Small Town: Critics Say Employers Should Be Targeted," *Washington Post* (May 18, 2008), http://www.washingtonpost .com/wp-dyn/content/article/2008/05/17/AR2008051702474.html. The manager of the Postville operation was tried and convicted; however, the charges centered on acts of financial fraud unrelated to the undocumented workers. Prosecutors did conclude that the manager loaned funds to immigrant workers so they could purchase fake identity documents; see Julia Preston, "27-Year Sentence for Slaughterhouse Manager in Financial Fraud Case," *New York Times* (June 22, 2010).

20. Randal C. Archibold, "Arizona Enacts Stringent Law on Immigration," *New York Times* (April 23, 2010), http://www.nytimes.com/2010/04/24/us /politics/24immig.html.

21. Paula Hammon, *The Atlas of Endangered Animals: Wildlife Under Threat Around the World* (New York: Marshall Cavendish, 2010), 160.

22. Greenpeace, "How KFC Is Junking the Jungle by Driving Rainforest Destruction in Indonesia" (May 2012), http://www.greenpeace.org/usa/en/media -center/reports/Junking-the-Jungle.

23. Chris McGreal, "US Should Return Stolen Land to Indian Tribes, says United Nations," *The Guardian* (May 4, 2012).

24. *Yearbook Australian, 2004* (Canberra: Australian Bureau of Statistics, 2004), 203.

25. Craig Hilton-Taylor et al., "State of the World's Species," in *Wildlife in a Changing World: An Analysis of the 2008 IUCN Red List of Threatened Species* (Gland: International Union for the Conservation of Nature, 2009), 30.

26. James Bevan, *Between a Rock and a Hard Place: Armed Violence in African Pastoralist Communities* (New York: United Nations Development Program, 2007).

27. Ibid., 5.

28. Karen E. Lange, "Desperate Measure: The Grim Practice of Culling Elephants May Resume," *National Geographic* 214, no. 3 (2008): 64–69; http://www

.intracen.org/Appli2/Leather/AfricanPlatform/CountryProfile.aspx?info=LiveSt
ock&countryid=47&countryname=South%20Africa&kk=.

29. Lange, "Desperate Measure," 69.

30. "Poison Takes Toll on Africa's Lions," 60 Minutes CBS News Broadcast
(July 26, 2009).

31. Karen Klein, "Going Global: From Georgia to Tanzania," Bloomberg Business Week (October 10, 2007), http://www.businessweek.com/smallbiz/content/
oct2007/sb20071010_810304.htm.

32. Human Rights Watch, Darfur Destroyed: Ethnic Cleansing by Government
and Militia Forces in Western Sudan, vol. 16, no. 6A (New York: Human Rights
Watch, 2004), 31.

33. Olivier Degomme and Debarati Guha-Sapir, "Patterns of Mortality Rates
in Darfur Conflict," Lancet 375, no. 9711 (January 23, 2010): 294–300.

34. Human Rights Watch, World Report, 2010 (New York: Human Rights
Watch, 2010), 171.

35. Jehron Muhammad, "Scarce Water the Source of Darfur Conflict?" Final
Call (March 9, 2010), http://www.finalcall.com/artman/publish/World_News_3
/article_6808.shtml.

36. Christopher W. Tatlock, Water Stress in Saharan Africa (Washington, D.C.:
Council on Foreign Relations, 2006), http://www.cfr.org/publication/11240/.

37. Lawrence A. Kuznar and Robert Sedlmeyer, "Collective Violence in Darfur: An Agent-Based Model of Pastoral Nomad/Sedentary Peasant Interaction,"
Mathematical Anthropology and Cultural Theory: An International Journal 1, no. 4
(2005): 1.

38. Josh Kron, "Death Toll Passes 600 From Raid in South Sudan," New York
Times (August 22, 2011), http://www.nytimes.com/2011/08/23/world/africa/23sudan
.html.

39. Mark Jenkins, "Who Killed the Virunga Gorillas?" National Geographic
(July 2008), http://ngm.nationalgeographic.com/2008/07/virunga/jenkins-text.

40. David Pimentel and Marcia H. Pimentel, Food, Energy, and Society, 3rd
ed. (New York: CRC, 2008), 67 (revised numbers estimate using same estimates
based on 2010 world population).

41. Peter Dauvergne, The Shadows of Consumption: Consequences for the Global
Environment (Cambridge, Mass.: The MIT Press, 2010), 140; Agriculture and
Food—Meat Consumption: Per capita, http://earthtrends.wri.org/text/agriculture
-food/variable-193.html.

42. Judy Putnam and Jane Allshouse, "Trends in U.S. per Capita Consumption of Dairy Products, 1909 to 2001," Amber Waves: The Economics of Food,
Farming, Natural Resources and Rural America (June 2003), http://www.ers.usda
.gov/amberwaves/june03/datafeature/; Rosanna Mentzer Morrison, Jean C. Buzby,
and Hodan Farah Wells, "Guess Who's Turning 100? Tracking a Century of

American Eating," *Amber Waves: The Economics of Food, Farming, Natural Resources and Rural America* (March 2010), http://www.ers.usda.gov/amberwaves/march10/features/trackingacentury.htm; U.S. Poultry and Egg Association, *U.S. Egg per Capita Consumption*, http://www.poultryegg.org/economic_data/.

43. World Watch Institute, *Vital Signs 2005: The Trends That Are Shaping Our Future* (New York: Norton, 2005), 25; United Nations Food and Agricultural Organization, *Food Outlook: Global Market Analysis*, http://www.fao.org/docrep/012/ak341e/ak341e09.htm.

44. Dan Morgan, *Merchants of Grain* (New York: Penguin, 1980), 182; cited in Bill Winders, *The Politics of Food Supply: U.S. Agricultural Policy in the World Economy* (New Haven, Conn.: Yale University Press, 2009), 156.

45. Winders, *The Politics of Food Supply*, 183.

46. Ibid., 2.

47. William Neuman, "Farmers Facing Loss of Subsidy May Get New One," *New York Times* (October 18, 2011).

48. Elanor Starmer and Timothy A. Wise, *Feeding at the Trough: Industrial Livestock Firms Saved $35 Billion From Low Feed Prices*, Policy Brief no. 07-03 (Medford, Mass.: Tufts University's Global Development and Environment Institute, December, 2007), http://www.ase.tufts.edu/gdae/Pubs/rp/PB07-03Feeding AtTroughDec07.pdf.

49. Neal D. Bernard, "Pushing Beef in China," *New York Times* (December 28, 1999), http://www.nytimes.com/1999/12/28/opinion/world-bank-s-aim-beef-for-china.html.

50. Food and Agricultural Organization of the United Nations, 2006, 15; Michael Parenti, *Against Empire* (San Francisco: City Lights, 1995), chap. 1.

51. http://beefmagazine.com/mag/beef_global_snapshot/ June 1, 2006.

52. *Big Mac: Inside the McDonald's Empire*, broadcast on July 30, 2007 on CNBC.

53. Ibid.

54. Miriam Marcus, *McDonald's Super Sizes Globally*, 2008, http://www.forbes.com/2008/04/22/mcdonalds-international-update-markets-equities-cx_mlm_0422markets31.html.

55. ScienceDaily, "Environmental and Social Impact of the 'Livestock Revolution'" (March 17, 2010), http://www.sciencedaily.com/releases/2010/03/100316101703.htm.

56. S. Kilman and S. Gray, "Fast Food Seeks Influence in WTO," *Wall Street Journal* (April 19, 2005).

57. Yee Haung, *Spotlight on CAFOs: EPA Settlement Requires More Info on CA-FOs*, Center for Progressive Reform (June 3, 2010), http://www.progressivereform.org/CPRBlog.cfm?idBlog=FE27276F-C4D0-9305-DC9870FC87A261F4; Thomas Gordon Field and Robert E. Taylor, *Beef Production and Management Decisions*

(Upper Saddle River, N.J.: Prentice Hall, 2003), 221; Lynn Jacobs, *Waste of the West: Public Lands Ranching* (Tucson, Ariz.: Lynn Jacobs, 1991), 350.

58. Mark Bittman, "Rethinking the Meat-Guzzler," *New York Times* (January 27, 2008), http://www.nytimes.com/2008/01/27/weekinreview/27bittman.html.

59. Maryn McKenna, *Superbug: The Fatal Menace of MRSA* (New York: The Free Press, 2010), 153.

60. Sierra Club, *The Rap Sheet on Animal Factories*, 2002, http://www.mid westadvocates.org/archive/dvorakbeef/rapsheet.pdf.

61. American Public Health Association, *Precautionary Moratorium on New Concentrated Animal Feed Operations* (November 18, 2003), policy no. 20037, http://www.apha.org/advocacy/policy/policysearch/default.htm?id=1243.

62. Ibid.

63. Pew Commission on Industrial Farm Animal Production, *Putting Meat on the Table: Industrial Farm Animal Production in America, Executive Summary* (Baltimore, Md.: The Johns Hopkins Bloomberg School of Public Health, 2008), 5.

64. Ibid., 33.

65. Doug Gurian-Sherman, *CAFOs Uncovered: The Untold Costs of Confined Animal Feeding Operations* (Cambridge, Mass.: Union of Concerned Scientists, 2008), 5, http://www.ucsusa.org/assets/documents/food_and_agriculture/cafos -uncovered.pdf.

66. Mike Wagner and Dale Dempsey, "Nasty Turf Wars Erupt," *Dayton Daily News* (December 4, 2002).

67. Roger Bybee, "The Fight Against Factory Farms in Wisconsin," *Isthmus: The Daily Page* (August 14, 2009), http://www.thedailypage.com/isthmus/article. php?article=26640.

68. "Missouri Jury Returns $4.5 Million Verdict, 2006," http://www.globen ewswire.com/newsroom/news.html?d=105761.

69. Food and Agriculture Organisation of the United Nations, *Livestock's Long Shadow—Environmental Issues and Options* (2006), 278, http://www.fao.org /docrep/010/a0701e/a0701e00.HTM.

70. Danielle Nierenberg, "Factory Farming in the Developing World," *World Watch Magazine* 16, no. 3 (May/June 2003).

71. Ibid.

72. Ibid.

73. Richard Manning, "The Oil We Eat," *Harper's Magazine* (February 2004): 45.

74. Jack Santa Barbara, *The False Promise of Biofuels* (San Francisco: International Forum on Globalization, 2007), 9.

75. Stephen Leahy, "Peak Soil: The Silent Global Crisis," *Earth Island Journal*, http://www.earthisland.org/journal/index.php/eij/article/peak_soil/.

76. Jason Clay, *World Agriculture and the Environment* (Washington, D.C.: Island, 2004), 478.

77. See, for example, ibid., 411; and Santa Barbara, *The False Promise*, 10.

78. Charles C. Mann, "Our Good Earth: The Future Rests on Soil," *National Geographic* 214, no. 3 (September 2008): 88.

79. *World Day to Combat Desertification*, 2009 Statement of the UN Convention to Combat Desertification, http://www.unccd.int/publicinfo/june17/2009/menu.php; see also Juliette Jowit, "UN Says Eat Less Meat to Curb Global Warming," *Observer* (September 7, 2008), http://www.guardian.co.uk/environment/2008/sep/07/food.foodanddrink.

80. Jowit, "UN Says Eat Less Meat," 1.

81. Manning, "The Oil We Eat," 39–40, 45.

82. Pimentel and Pimentel, *Food, Energy, and Society*, 68–70.

83. Manning, "The Oil We Eat," 42.

84. Richard H. Robbins, *Global Problems and the Culture of Capitalism*, 4th ed. (Boston, Mass.: Allyn and Bacon, 2008), 224.

85. David Pimentel et al., "Water Resources, Agriculture, and the Environment," *Bioscience* 54, no. 10 (2004): 911.

86. Jerry Adler et al., "The Browning of America," *Newsweek* (February 23, 1981): 26.

87. Food and Agricultural Organization of the United Nations, *The State of Food Insecurity in the World* (ROME: FAO, 2011), 126, http://www.fao.org/docrep/014/i2330e/i2330e00.htm.

88. Vandana Shiva, *Water Wars: Privatization, Pollution, and Profit* (London: Pluto, 2002), ix.

89. Ibid., ix.

90. See, for example, Jon R. Luoma, "Water for Profit," *Mother Jones* 27, no. 6 (November–December 2002): 35–45.

91. Food and Agriculture Organisation of the United Nations, xxii.

92. Ibid., xx.

93. Ibid., xxi.

94. David Tilman et al., "Forecasting Agriculturally Driven Global Environmental Change," *Science* 292 (April 13, 2002): 283.

95. Thomas F. Homer-Dixon, Jeffrey H. Boutwell, and George W. Rathjens, "Environmental Change and Violent Conflict," *Scientific American* (February 1993): 38.

96. Klaus Deininger and Derek Byerlee, *Rising Global Interest in Farmland* (Washington, D.C.: World Bank, 2011), 14.

97. Oxfam, "Land and Power: The Growing Scandal Surrounding the New Wave of Investment in Land" (2011), http://www.oxfam.org/sites/www.oxfam.org/files/bp151-land-power-rights-acquisitions-220911-en.pdf.

98. GRAIN, "Big Meat Is Growing in the South," *Seedling* (October 2010), http://www.grain.org/article/entries/4044-big-meat-is-growing-in-the-south.

99. See, for example, United Nations International Panel on Climate Change, *Special Report on Managing the Risks of Extreme Events and Disasters to Advance Climate Change Adaptation* (November 18, 2001), http://ipcc-wg2.gov/SREX/images/uploads/SREX-SPM_Approved-HiRes_opt.pdf.

100. Christina Nellemann, *The Environmental Food Crisis* (Arendal: United Nations Environmental Programme, 2009).

101. Justin Gillis, "Global Warming Reduces Expected Yields of Harvests in Some Countries, Study Says," *New York Times* (May 6, 2011).

102. http://www.telegraph.co.uk/news/worldnews/africaandindianocean/ethiopia/8628735/Climate-change-is-cause-of-Ethiopian-drought.html; http://www.huffingtonpost.com/2011/08/19/somalia-famine-climate-change-global-warming_n_930935.html.

103. See, for example, Jeffrey Mazo, *Climate Conflict: How Global Warming Threatens Security and What to Do About It* (London: International Institute for Strategic Studies, 2010).

104. David D. Zhang et al., "Global Climate Change, War, and Population Decline in Recent Human History," *Proceedings of the National Academy of Sciences in the United States of America* 104, no. 49 (2007): 19214–19219.

105. Robin Mearns and Andrew Norton, *Social Dimensions of Climate Change: Equity and Vulnerability in a Warming World* (Washington, D.C.: The World Bank, 2010), chap. 1.

106. Mazo, *Climate Conflict*, chap. 4.

107. CIA, *A Study of Climatological Research as it Pertains to Intelligence Problems* (Central Intelligence Agency, 1974), 31, http://www.climatemonitor.it/wp-content/uploads/2009/12/1974.pdf.

108. Marcus Linear, *Zapping the Third World: The Disaster of Development Aid* (London: Pluto, 1985), 32.

109. Peter Schwartz and Doug Randall, *An Abrupt Climate Change Scenario and Its Implications for United States National Security* (U.S. Department of Defense 2007), http://www.gbn.com/articles/pdfs/Abrupt%20Climate%20Change%20February%202004.pdf.

110. CNA Corporation, *National Security and the Threat of Climate Change* (Alexandria, Va.: CNA Corporation, 2007), 7, http://securityandclimate.cna.org/report/.

111. Enid Schoettle, interview on ABC News' *Nightline*, broadcast January 18, 2001.

112. National Intelligence Council, *Global Trends 2025: A Transformed World* (Washington, D.C.: U.S. Government Printing Office, 2008), 41, 51–52.

113. Ibid., 51.

114. Ibid., 41.

115. Ibid., 63, 54.

116. Tom Gjelten, "Pentagon, CIA Eye New Threat: Climate Change," *National Public Radio: Morning Edition*, broadcast May 28, 2010.

117. "CIA Opens Center on Climate Change and National Security" (2009), https://www.cia.gov/news-information/press-releases-statements/center-on -climate-change-and-national-security.html.

118. CNA Corporation, *National Security and the Threat of Climate Change*.

119. U.S. Department of Defense, *Quadrennial Defense Review Report* (February 2010), http://www.defense.gov/QDR/QDR%20as%20of%2029JAN10%201600.pdf.

120. Bruno Waterfield, "Climate Change Will Spark Global Conflict," *The Telegraph* (March 10, 2008), http://www.telegraph.co.uk/earth/earthnews/3335483 /Climate-change-will-spark-global-conflict.html.

121. Jonathan Pearlman and Bob Cubby, "Defense Warns of Climate Conflict," *Sydney Morning Herald* (January 7, 2009), http://www.smh.com.au/news/ environment/global-warming/defence-warns-of-climate-conflict/2009/01 /06/1231004021036.html.

122. Jeffery K. Taubenberger and David M. Morens, *1918 Influenza: The Mother of All Pandemics* (Rockville, Md.: Department of Molecular Pathology, Armed Forces Institute of Pathology, January, 2006), http://www.cdc.gov/ncidod /eid/vol12no01/05-0979.htm; also see Bernice Wuethrich, "Chasing the Fickle Swine Flu," *Science* 299, no. 5612 (March 7, 2003): 1502–1505.

123. E. Fuller Torrey and Robert H. Yolken, *Beasts of the Earth: Animals, Humans, and Disease* (New Brunswick, N.J.: Rutgers University Press, 2005), 117.

124. See, for example, John M. Barry, *The Great Influenza: The Epic Story of the Deadliest Plague In History* (New York: Penguin, 2004).

125. World Health Organization, *Ten Concerns If Avian Influenza Becomes a Pandemic* (2005), http://www.who.int/csr/disease/influenza/pandemic10things/en/.

126. Michael Greger, *Flu Factories: Tracing the Origins of the Swine Flu Pandemic* (DVD) (Washington, D.C.: Humane Society of the United States, 2009).

127. Greger, *Flu Factories*.

128. Cited in Charles W. Schmidt, "Swine CAFOs & Novel H1N1 Flu: Separating Facts from Fears," *Environmental Health Perspectives* 117, no. 9 (2009): A395–396.

129. See, for example, Deborah MacKenzie, "Scientists Have Warned About Swine Flu for Last Decade," *New Scientist* 202, no. 2706 (2009): 6–7.

130. Wuethrich, "Chasing the Fickle Swine Flu," 1503.

131. Ibid., 1505.

132. "Bird Flu Could Kill Millions," *The Gazette* (Montreal) (March 9, 2005); cited in Greger, *Flu Factories*.

133. Avid Benatar, "The Chickens Come Home to Roost," *American Journal of Public Health* 97, no. 9 (September 2007): 1545.

134. National Intelligence Council, *Global Trends 2025*, 75.

135. *Report of The WHO/FAO/OIE Joint Consultation on Emerging Zoonotic Disease* (Geneva, Switzerland: World Health Organisation, 2004), 7, http://whqlibdoc.who.int/hq/2004/WHO_CDS_CPE_ZFK_2004.9.pdf; cited in Greger, *Flu Factories*.

136. Richard H. Robbins, *Global Problems and the Culture of Capitalism*, 4th ed. (Boston: Allyn and Bacon, 2008), 223.

137. Simon A. French, Lisa Harnack, and Robert W. Jeffery, "Fast Food Restaurant Use Among Women in the Pound of Prevention Study: Dietary, Behavioral, and Demographic Correlates," *International Journal of Obesity and Related Metabolic Disorders* 24, no. 10 (October 2000): 1353; U.S. Department of Health and Human Services, *Healthy People Report, 2010,* http://www.healthypeople.gov/Publications/Cornerstone.pdf.

138. See http://www.cdc.gov/DHDSP/announcements/american_heart_month.htm.

139. World Health Organization, *Controlling the Global Obesity Epidemic* (2000), http://www.who.int/nutrition/topics/obesity/en/index.html.

140. World Health Organization, *Obesity and Overweight Factsheet*, http://www.who.int/mediacentre/factsheets/fs311/en/index.html.

141. J. M. Hirsh, "U.S. Contributes to Global Obesity, but Can't Take All the Blame, Experts Say," *Dayton Daily News* (May 9, 2004).

142. Chantil Blouin et al., "Trade, Health, and Dietary Change," in *Trade, Food, Diet, and Health: Perspectives and Policy Options,* ed. Corinna Hawkes et al. (Oxford: Wiley-Blackwell), 7.

143. World Health Organization and the United Nations Food and Agricultural Organization, *Diet, Nutrition, and the Prevention of Chronic Diseases* (Geneva: World Health Organization, 2003), 1–2.

144. Blouin, "Trade, Health, and Dietary Change," 8.

145. "World Warned About Three Major Threats to Human Health," News-Medical.net (May 20, 2008), http://www.news-medical.net/news/2008/05/20/38472.aspx.

146. Food and Agriculture Organisation of the United Nations, *Livestock's Long Shadow*, xxi.

147. Torres, *Making a Killing*, 39.

148. Food and Agriculture Organisation of the United Nations, *Livestock's Long Shadow*, 186.

149. Carl Zimmer, "Multitude of Species Face Threat of Warming," *New York Times* (April 5, 2011).

150. *Petition for Executive Order and Rulemaking Banning Aerial Gunning and Poisoning Activities of Native Wild Carnivores on Federal Public Lands,* submitted to President Barack Obama by WildEarth Guardians (Broomfield, Colorado, 2009), http://wildearthguardians.org/Portals/0/legal/petition_APA_11-23-09.pdf.

## 9. New Welfarism, Veganism, and Capitalism

1. Gary L. Francione, *Rain Without Thunder: The Ideology of the Animal Rights Movement* (Philadelphia: Temple University Press, 1996).

2. See, for example, Norma E. Bubier and R. Harry Bradshaw, "Movement of Flocks of Laying Hens in and out of the Hen House in Four Free Range Systems," *British Poultry Science* 39, suppl. 1 (1998): 5–6; Marian Stamp Dawkins et al., "What Makes Free-Range Broiler Chickens Range? In Situ Measurement of Habitat Preference," *Animal Behavior* 66, no. 1 (2003): 151–160; Isabelle Veissier et al., "European Approaches to Ensure Good Animal Welfare," *Applied Animal Behaviour Science* 113 (2008): 279–297; Tracye Lynn McQuirter, *By Any Greens Necessary* (Chicago: Lawrence Hill, 2010), 39.

3. See, for example, Sibyl Anwander Phan-Huy and Ruth Badertscher Fawaz, "Swiss Market for Meat from Animal Friendly Production—Responses of Public and Private Actors in Switzerland," *Journal of Agricultural and Environmental Ethics* 16, no. 2 (2003): 119–136.

4. For example, one writer promoting welfarist regulations based on the economic benefits they bring to the industry states that "more humane transport, handling and slaughter of animals . . . is likely to reduce monetary losses caused by *carcass* shrinkage, bruising of *meat*, and damage to *hides*." David Fraser, "Toward a Global Perspective on Farm Animal Welfare," *Applied Animal Behaviour Science* 111 (2008): 334; also see Gary L. Francione and Robert Garner, *The Animal Rights Debate: Abolition or Regulation*, chap. 1 (New York: Columbia University Press, 2010).

5. See, for example, David Nibert, *Animal Rights/Human Rights: Entanglements of Oppression and Liberation* (Lanham, Md.: Rowman & Littlefield, 2002), 142–194.

6. Fraser, "Toward a Global Perspective on Farm Animal Welfare," 333.

7. See, for example, Lori Wallach and Patrick Woodall, *Whose Trade Organization?* (New York: The New Press, 1991), chap. 1; Global Justice for Animals and the Environment, *World Trade Organization: Undermining Animal Protection*, http://wetlands-preserve.org/phpUpload/uploads/WTO%20and%20Animals.pdf.

8. See James E. McWilliams, "The Myth of Sustainable Meat," *New York Times* (April 12, 2012); and Vasile Stănescu, "Green Eggs and Ham? The Myth of Sustainable Meat and the Danger of the Local," in *Critical Theory and Animal Liberation*, ed. John Sanbonmatsu (Lanham, Md.: Rowman & Littlefield, 2011), 239–251.

9. Comparative advantage is an economic term that refers to the capacity of a good to be produced more efficiently and with less cost in one region compared to others. Comparative advantage has frequently been used to legitimate

the promotion of export crops from areas that have been exploited by powerful capitalist nations. For example, the promotion of the expansion of "beef" production in many areas of Central America—a practice that proved to be disastrous for the majority of humans and other animals in the region and that caused extensive environmental damage—was promoted using the idea of comparative advantage.

10. See, for example, Alexander Wood, Pamela Stedman-Edwards, and Johanna Mang, *The Root Causes of Biodiversity Loss* (London: Earthscan, 2000).

11. Henry W. Kendall et al., *Meeting the Challenges of Population, Environment, and Resources: The Costs of Inaction*, a report co-sponsored by the Union of Concerned Scientists and the World Bank (Washington, D.C.: World Bank, 1995), 37, 38.

12. See, for example, John Richard Thackrah, *The Routledge Companion to Military Conflict Since 1945* (New York: Routledge, 2009), 44–45.

13. See, for example, Robert Gough, "Stress on Stress: Global Warming and Aquatic Resource Depletion," *Native Americas* 16, no. 3–4 (1999): 46.

14. Vazhiyil Venugopal, *Marine Products for Health Care: Functional and Bioactive Nutraceutical Compounds from the Ocean* (Boca Raton, Fla.: Taylor Francis Group, 2009), 33.

15. Kenneth R. Weiss, "Fish Farms Become Feedlots of the Seas," *Los Angeles Times* (December 9, 2002), http://www.latimes.com/news/nationworld/nation/la-me-salmon9dec09,0,2475812.story.

16. Philip Lymbery, *In Too Deep: The Welfare of Intensively Farmed Fish* (Hampshire: A Report for Compassion in World Farming Trust, 2002), 4, http://www.ciwf.org.uk/includes/documents/cm_docs/2008/i/in_too_deep_summary_2001.pdf; also see T. Ellis et al., "The Relationships Between Stocking Density and Welfare in Farmed Rainbow Trout," *Journal of Fish Biology* (2002): 61, 493–531.

17. Jacqueline Alder et al., "Forage Fish: From Ecosystems to Markets," *Annual Review of Environment and Resources* 33 (2008): 153–166.

18. Corn and Soybean Digest, *Soy Makes a Splash* (February 15, 2006), http://cornandsoybeandigest.com/mag/soybean_soy_makes_splash.

19. Weiss, "Fish Farms Become Feedlots of the Seas."

20. Ronald A. Hites et al., "Global Assessment of Organic Contaminants in Farmed Salmon," *Science* 303 (January 9, 2004): 226–229.

21. Daniel Pauly, Reg Watson, and Jackie Alder, "Global Trends in World Fisheries: Impacts on Marine Ecosystems and Food Security Source," *Philosophical Transactions of the Royal Society: Biological Sciences* 360, no. 1453 (January 29, 2005): 5–12.

22. For a discussion of the pathological nature of corporate "persons," see Joel Bakan, *The Corporation: The Pathological Pursuit of Profit and Power* (New York: The Free Press, 2004).

23. See, for example, Stephanie Storm, "Nonprofit Advocate Carves Out an Unusual For-Profit Niche," *New York Times* (June 18, 2010); http://www.consumer freedom.com.

24. See, for example, Howard Zinn, *A People's History of the United States* (1980; repr. New York: Harper Collins, 2010); Michael Parenti, *Democracy for the Few*, 9th ed. (Boston: Wadsworth, 2011).

25. See Parenti, *Democracy for the Few*, chap. 18.

26. See United Nations Development Program (UNDP), *Human Development Report 1999* (Oxford: Oxford University Press, 1999).

27. World Bank, *Atlas of Global Development* (Washington, D.C.: World Bank, 2007), 18.

# INDEX

Aborigines, 133–39, 143, 216–17, 230
absent referents, 6
Adams, Carol, 6
advertising and marketing, 177–80,
    182–85, 234–35, 266; to children,
    186–88, 195, 235
Africa: "cattle" raiding in, 219, 231–33;
    domesecration in, 154–70; European
    invasion in, 154–70, 217–18; gold in,
    159–60; killing of free-living animals
    in, 164–66, 230–31; nomadic
    pastoralism in, 154–58, 162–63,
    167–68; Scramble for, 161, 168, 218;
    slavery and, 55, 64. See also specific
    countries and peoples
Afrikaners, 160, 168
agrarian societies: military use of
    domesecrated animals in, 18–24;
    practices of, 12–13
agribusiness, 182, 193, 211, 228, 239, 251
agriculture: history of, 10–13;
    "livestock," 176; New Deal policy for,

181–82, 234; nomadic pastoralism
    and, 27–28
AIM. See American Indian Movement
Akerren, Bo, 212
Alliance for Progress, 198–99
alpacas, 34, 39–40, 55
amaXhosa people, 158–59
American Indian Movement (AIM),
    195
American Journal of Public Health,
    250–51
American Public Health Association,
    237
American "Woolen" Company, 114–15
Americas: animal oppression and
    invasion of, 45–50; Portuguese
    invasion of, 6, 45, 56, 67–69;
    Spanish invasion of, 6, 45–50,
    67–69; violence and warfare in
    pre-Columbian, 34–42
Anaya, James, 229–30
Anderson, J. Walter, 174, 179–80

Angell, George T., 110–11
*Animal Connection, The* (Shipman), 3
Animal Damage Control Program,
U.S., 257
animal exploitation: capitalism and,
2–3, 5, 247; history of, 10–12,
253–57; impacts of, 40, 224. *See also*
domesecrated animals;
domesecration; "domestication"
animal "husbandry," 33
animal-industrial complex, 189;
expansion of, 260, 261; influence of,
192–94, 213, 219, 221, 238–39, 254–55,
267–68; participants in, 234, 235,
266
*Animal Machines: The New Factory
Farming Industry* (Harrison, R.),
171, 189
animal oppression: growing levels of,
108–20; invasion of Americas and,
45–50; views on, 5–6, 12
animal plagues, 23
animals. *See* other animals
antelope, 164
antibiotics, 193, 251, 265
Apache people, 97
APP. *See* Asia Pulp and Paper
aquaculture industry, 264–65
aquatic animals, 264–65
Arana Osorio, Carlos, 209
Argentina, 143–45, 147–53
aristocracy, 15
armies: Argentina, 149; Aztec, 38;
Cortés's, 52; El Salvador, 208; Incan,
40; Mexico, 99, 211; Mongol, 24–29;
Roman, 20–21; United States, 79, 83,
99, 213; Venezuela, 227. *See also*
militaries
Armour, Philip, 113
Armour "Meat" Packing Company,
182–83
Asia Pulp and Paper (APP), 229
Atherton, Lewis, 103
Attila the Hun, 23

Austin, Stephen, 93
Australia, 133–39, 167, 216–17,
229–30
automobiles, 183–84
Aztecs, 36–38, 49

Bachrach, Bernard, 31
background assumptions, 4, 267
Bacon, Nathaniel, 75
Baker, E. M., 101–2
Bakewell, Peter, 58
Ballard, Patricia, 213
Barry, Tom, 197, 214
Battle of Fallen Timbers, 80
battue (hunting), 25–26
beaver, 71
Beaver Wars, 73
"beef": butchering differences in Britain
and United States, 119; Central
America and, 55; ground, 196, 220;
from Latin America, 196, 198–201,
203–7, 209, 211–12, 215, 220–21, 255;
quotas on imports of, 215. *See also*
*charque*
Berger, John, 166
Berle, Adolphe, 92, 114–15
Bernays, Edward L., 177
*Between a Rock and a Hard Place:
Armed Violence in African Pastoralist
Communities* (UN), 230
*Big Mac: Inside the McDonald's Empire*,
235
biomachines, 189
bison. *See* buffalo
Black Death, 29–30
Blackfeet people, 101–2
Blackmar, Frank Wilson, 1–2, 41,
120, 254
Bleakley, John William, 138–39
*Bloomberg Business Week*, 231
bluebuck, 164
Boers, 157–60
bovine diseases, 98
Branco, Castello, 209–10

branding and castrating calves, 96
Branford, Sue, 204, 212
Brazil: "cattlemen" in, 56; rainforests in, 225–26, 229; ranching in, 56–61, 144–45, 147–48, 199, 209–10, 212–13
breakfast, "bacon" and "eggs" for, 177
*Breeders' Gazette, The*, 173–74
bridewealth, 156
Britain: Australia and New Zealand invaded by, 133–41, 167; "beef" butchering differences in United States and, 119; "Cattle" Acts, 126–27, 129; "cattle" companies and, 115–19; "cattle" diseases in, 128; colonialism and, 71–75, 158–61, 163, 165, 167–68; enclosure movement in, 63; factory farming in, 189; Florida and, 79; immigrants from, 78–79, 132; Latin America and, 147–48, 150–53; relations with Ireland, 126–30, 167; relations with Scotland, 130–32, 167
British "cavalries," 126, 130
Brown, Dee, 100–101
bubonic plague, 29–30
"buckskin," 76
buffalo: diseases and, 98; massacre of, 102–3; Native Americans and, 96–98, 102–3, 121
Buffalo Bill. *See* Cody, William F.
Burckhardt, John Lewis, 156–57
Bureau of Land Management, 190–91
"Burger" King, 187, 199, 235
Burns, E. Bradford, 200–201

Caffa siege, 29
CAFOs. *See* concentrated animal feeding operations
*CAFOs Uncovered: The Untold Costs of Confined Animal Feeding Operations* (Union of Concerned Scientists), 238
California, 94

calves. *See* "cattle"
camels, 136, 156
*campesinos* (subsistence farmers), 205
Canada: racism in, 121; ranching in, 120–25
Canary Islands, 43–44, 47
cancer, 193–94, 252
capitalism: animal exploitation and, 2–3, 5, 247; domesecration, human oppression, and, 61–65; economic and political control in, 87, 176; growth of, 7, 44, 45, 90, 124, 167, 169, 171; impacts of, 193–94; transcending, 266–71; World War II and, 183
Caribbean, 48, 127, 132
castration, 96, 156
Catholic Church, 60–61, 142–43
"cattle": amaXhosa people's killing of, 158–59; attitudes toward, 108–9; branding and castrating calves, 96; British "cattle" companies, 115–19; calf capture and, 77; corn for, 85; diseases, 128, 217; driven to market, 80–81; free-living cows as public property, 95; free-range, 71–72, 74–75; grain-fed compared to grass-fed, 220; "herds" of, 18–22; "hide" hunters and, 50; insurance for, 119–20; murder of, 81; overpopulation and deaths of, 107; raiding, 219, 231–33; on railroads, 110–11, 115, 150–51; reasons for losses of, 109–10, 121; in Roman Empire, 18–22, 32; on ships, 117–20; torture of, 118; whips for driving, 77, 81. *See also* "beef"; "oxen"
"Cattle" Acts (Britain), 126–27, 129
"cattle" barons, 61, 105–6
"cattle" culture, 86
"cattle" kings, 86–91, 92
"cattlemen": in Brazil, 56; inhumanity of, 107–8; sheep ranching conflict with, 106; superiority of, 104

"cattle" ranching: in Australia, 133–38, 216–17; in New Zealand, 141; number of "cattle" on ranches, 52, 104; Spain and, 49, 51–52, 55, 56
"Cattle" Ships (Plimsoll), 117–20
caudillos (military strong men), 142
"cavalries": British, 126, 130; Colorado, 100; military, 99, 101–2; Roman, 20–21; Turkish Ottoman, 45; U.S., 79–80, 93, 101–2
Center for Consumer Freedom, 267
Central Intelligence Agency (CIA), 197, 206, 245
Chaliand, Gérard, 9
Chambers, James, 30
Champlain, Samuel de, 52
Charlemagne, 23
charque (salted "beef"), 144–45
charqui (salted llama and alpaca), 40
Chávez, César, 195
Chávez, Hugo, 226–27
"cheese," 233
Cherokee people, 83–84, 143
Cheyenne people, 100–101
Chicago Exchange Building, 112
Chicago "stockyards" and slaughterhouses, 111–14, 172–73, 174
chickens: consumption of, 188; diseases and, 248–49; factory farms and, 193
Childe, V. Gordon, 15, 16
children, advertising to, 186–88, 195, 235
Chile, 196–97
China: corn and, 234; land grabs and, 243; McDonald's in, 235; Mongol violence in, 24–27, 30; nomadic pastoralists' invasion of, 17
Chinggis Khan, 24–27
Chivington, John, 100
Cholmondeley, Hugh. See Delamere, Lord
Christian, David, 24
chronic diseases, 193–94, 252–53, 256
CIA. See Central Intelligence Agency

Civil War, 111–12, 124
Clark, Ian D., 134–35
Clark, R. D., 180
climate change and global warming, 202–3, 231, 243–47, 263
Coates, Peter, 109–10
Cody, William F. (Buffalo Bill), 102
coffee, 218
Colombia, 151
colonialism: Britain and, 71–75, 158–61, 163, 165, 167–68; Dutch, 71, 72–73, 157–59; French, 77, 162, 218; German, 161–62, 164, 218; in New England, 70–71; ranching and, 7; Spanish invasion of Philippines, 65–69
Columbus, Christopher, 45–46, 70
Columella, Lucius Iunius Moderatus, 20
Comanches, 98
commercial ranching: expansion of, 51–55, 68, 91; violence and, 76–82
commodities: animals' parts and body fluids as, 6, 51, 68; consumption of, 176–77
commons (shared land), 63, 68
comparative advantage, 262, 317n9
concentrated animal feeding operations (CAFOs), 194, 236–40, 249–50, 260
Conquest of the Desert, 149–50
Control Methods Research Laboratory, 173
corn: China and, 234; as feed, 85, 86, 87; soil erosion and, 240; surpluses, 181–82, 194, 234
Coronado, Francisco Vásquez, 53
corporations: in Latin America, 197, 200, 203, 213, 225; list of, 266; public consciousness and, 175–80, 266–68
Cortés, Hernando, 48–49, 209
cottage system, putting-out or, 63
counterinsurgency warfare, 203, 205–6, 208–9
"cowboys," 61, 96, 105, 142, 144–45

cows. *See* "cattle"
coyotes, 190
Crees, 121–22
Cronon, William, 112–13
crop-based plantations, 78, 84
crop damage conflict, warfare and,
71–75, 90
Crosby, Alfred, 91
Cuba, 197, 220
culture: "cattle" culture, 86;
"hamburger" culture, 7, 188–95, 233,
256; impacts of, 262–63
Cuzco (Inca city), 39

Damophilus, 19
Darfur, 231–32, 256
Dark Ages, 23
Darwin, Charles, 145. *See also* Social
Darwinism
Dean, William Harper, 162
Debs, Eugene V., 176
debt bondage, 226
decerealization, 33, 42, 221
deer, 71, 76
degola, 151
Delamere, Lord, 163–64, 165
democratic social change, 176, 270–71
Denoon, Donald, 126, 135–36
Department of Agriculture, U.S., 172,
188, 207, 257, 266
Department of Commerce, U.S., 176
Department of Defense, U.S., 247
Department of Homeland Security,
U.S., 228
Department of Interior, U.S., 257
desertification from overgrazing, 14, 180,
217, 231
de Soto, Hernando, 53
devalued humans: blamed for plagues,
23; domesecration and, 212–16;
terminology used for, 6; violence
against, 2, 5
Diamond, Jared, 2–3
diamonds, 159

diet: of humans, 192–94; "meat,"
compared to plant-based, 233;
U.S.-style, 245–46, 256; veganism,
261–66
dingoes, 136
Dinka people, 167, 233
Dinor, Denis, 27
diseases: bovine, 98; buffalo and, 98;
"cattle," 128, 217; chickens and,
248–49; chronic, 193–94, 252–53,
256; from crowding other animals,
6–7, 12, 23, 41, 166–67, 193, 253;
domesecration and pandemic,
247–52; indigenous peoples and,
48, 52, 67, 73–74, 97, 137; pigs and,
248–50; spread of, 52, 54, 66;
transmission to humans, 12, 23,
248–51; zoonotic, 5, 48, 67, 122,
136, 167. *See also* plagues; *specific
diseases*
Dodd, George, 126
domesecrated animals: agrarian
societies' military use of, 18–24;
embedding together large numbers
of, 145; growing global consumption
of, 233–35; mining and, 50; in
Netherlands, 64; in Roman Empire,
40–41; torture of, 75; treatment of,
153, 257, 259; in West Indies, 47
domesecration: in Africa, 154–70;
definition of, 12; devalued humans
and, 212–16; human oppression,
capitalism and, 61–65; Mongol
violence and, 24–31; pandemic
and, 247–52; power and status
regarding, 13–14; as replacement for
"domestication," 6; transcending
capitalism and ending, 266–71
"domestication": definitions of, 11–12;
domesecration as replacement for, 6;
views on, 1–5; violence and, 4–5
"draft animals," 71
Ducos, Pierre, 11
Dust Bowl, 180–81

Dutch colonialism, 71, 72–73, 157–59
Dutch East India Company, 66–67, 157
Dutch "stockmen" (*trekboeren*), 157

*E. coli*, 240
East African Hunting Bureau, 165
economic crisis, 269
economic marginalization, 268, 270
educational videos, 267
elephants, 166, 230
El Salvador, 206–8
enclosure movement, 63
*engenhos* (sugar mills), 50, 56
English Civil War, 74
Enock, C. Reginald, 153
enslavement. *See* slavery
environment: environmental
    deregulation, 268; hunger and
    environmental degradation,
    200–203; impacts on, 172, 193,
    240–42
Equator Ranch, 164
Eradication Methods Laboratory. *See*
    Control Methods Research
    Laboratory
Espírito Santo, Maria do, 225
ethanol, 234
ethnocentrism, 262
European invasion in Africa, 154–70,
    217–18
European Union, 247, 270
Ewen, Stuart, 177

Faber, Daniel, 201
factory farming: aquatic animals and,
    264–65; birth of, 188–89; in Britain,
    189; chickens and, 193; impacts of,
    2, 5, 193–95, 236–37, 259–60; prices
    and, 234, 260. *See also* concentrated
    animal feeding operations
FAO. *See* Food and Agricultural
    Organization
"farm animals," 4, 190
Farm Bill (1996), 234

farming: fattening farms, 81; subsistence,
    203–7; tenant, 86–87. *See also*
    agriculture; factory farming
Farm Security and Rural Reinvestment
    Act (2002), 234
fast-food industry, 7, 185–88, 195, 216,
    234–35, 252, 267. *See also*
    "hamburgers"
fattening farms, 81
Fein, Helen, 223
Ferguson, Denzel, 191
Ferguson, Nancy, 191
Fernandez, Carlos, 227
fertilizers, 241
feudal economy, 44, 45
financial deregulation, 268–69
fish and fishing, 263–65
Florida: Britain and, 79; Spain and, 53,
    64–65, 76, 82
food: locally grown, 261; shortages,
    244–45
Food and Agricultural Organization
    (FAO), 200, 217, 240, 242, 251,
    252–53
food surpluses: corn, 181–82, 194, 234;
    impacts of, 2, 10; protection of, 13
Food Trade Alliance, U.S., 235
forests, destruction of, 151, 201–2, 221,
    227–28. *See also* rainforests
Forest Service, United States, 172, 173
*Fort Benton River Press*, 122
Fort Laramie, 99
Fort Leavenworth, Kansas, 99–100
Frank, Andre Gunder, 60
Franks, 31
free-living animals: cows as public
    property, 95; hunting of, 25–26, 35,
    61, 164–67, 169, 263; killing of,
    109–10, 144, 164–66, 173, 190–91,
    230–31, 257; in rainforests, 215–16,
    229, 257; types of, 71, 73; in zoos,
    166, 216. *See also specific animals*
free-range animals, 260–61; cows and
    pigs, 71–72, 74–75

free-trade policies, 203, 266
French colonialism, 77, 162, 218
Friedman, Thomas, 223
Frink, Maurice, 115–16
frontier, 62
Fulani, 154, 156

*ganaderización* ("livestock" expansion), 213
Gandhi, 271
Garlant, Julia, 150
Gates, Paul, 86–87
*gauchos* ("cowboys"), 142, 144–45
General Land Office, U.S., 106, 116
genetically manipulated animals, 189
genocide, 34, 161–62, 232–33
German East African Company, 164
Germany: colonialism and, 161–62, 164, 218; World War II and, 182
getter (cyanide device), 190
Gimbutas, Marija, 16
Glass-Steagall Act (1933), 268–69
global warming. *See* climate change and global warming
Glock, Oriel, 204, 212
gold: in Africa, 159–60; mining, 49, 57, 60, 99; supply of, 61, 63, 68
Goldman, Emma, 176
Gómez, Juan Vicente, 152
Gorotire people, 213
Goths, 17, 22
Goulart, Joao, 209
Gouldner, Alvin, 3
grains, 182, 194–95, 200, 220, 234
grass-fed compared to grain-fed "cattle," 220
Gray, Gregory, 250
grazing: damage from overgrazing, 28, 32, 44, 96, 162; desertification from overgrazing, 14, 180, 217, 231; regulations, 172, 182
Great Depression, 181, 269
Greger, Michael, 249
ground "beef," 196, 220

Guanches, 43–44
Guarani people, 225
Guatemala, 197, 208–9, 227
Guerra Grande (Big War, Uruguay), 144
guns: manufacturers, 62; other animals traded for ammunition and, 98, 121
*Guns, Germs, and Steel* (Diamond), 2–3

"hamburger" culture, 7, 233, 256; violence and, 188–95
"hamburgers," 174–75, 178–79, 186, 220
Harrison, Ruth, 171, 189
Harrison, William Henry, 82–83
Harvey, W. S., 99
heart disease, 192, 252
Helleiner, Karl F., 33
Hemming, John, 43, 58, 60
Henlein, Paul, 80
"herding" societies, 13–14
"herds" of "cattle," 18–22
hereditary slavery, 24, 156
"hides": exportation of, 51, 56, 59–60; "hide" hunters and "cattle," 50; uses for, 21
highways, 184
Hispaniola Island, 46–48
Honduras, 206–7
Los Horcones ranch, 206
Hormel, Jay, 177
Horn, Tom, 116
horses: as instruments of war, 14, 20–21, 31, 53, 79–80, 90, 157, 160, 167; Native Americans and, 97–98, 121–23; nomadic pastoralism and, 14–16, 155. *See also* "cavalries"; "wild" mustangs
horticulture: history of, 10, 12; in pre-Columbian Americas, 35–36
houghing, 127
Howard-Borjas, Patricia, 196
human oppression: domesecration, capitalism and, 61–65; revolts and uprisings from, 44

humans: diet of, 192–94, 233–34; disease
transmission to, 12, 23, 248–51;
exploitation of, 124; impacts on
advancement of, 3; other animals
relationship with, 4, 10–13, 223, 257;
transition from foraging to hunting,
6, 10–11. *See also* devalued humans
hunger and malnutrition, 252; and
environmental degradation in Latin
America, 200–203; poverty and, 148,
226, 244, 255, 262; Spanish "cattle"
ranching and, 51–52; and violence
in Middle Ages, 31–33
Huns, 17, 22, 23, 24
hunting: of free-living animals, 25–26,
35, 61, 164–67, 169, 263; humans'
transition from foraging to, 6,
10–11
Hutu people, 218–19, 233

ideology, 274n16
IMF. *See* International Monetary Fund
immigrants: from Britain, 78–79, 132;
laws against, 228–29;
undocumented, 228–29
Incas, 38–40, 52
*Independent*, 227
"Indian" Removal Act (1830), 83
"Indians." *See* indigenous peoples;
Native Americans
indigenous peoples: diseases and, 48, 52,
67, 73–74, 97, 137; displacement of,
82–86, 148–49, 216–17, 224, 229–30;
in Latin America, 209, 212–13;
warfare among, 73, 98, 122–23, 159,
168. *See also* Native Americans;
*specific peoples*
Indonesia, 229
influenza, 248–51, 254
Ingram, Edgar Waldo "Billy," 171,
174–75, 178–80
insurance for "cattle," 119–20
Inter-American Development Bank,
198, 199

Intergovernmental Panel on Climate
Change, 241
International Bank for Reconstruction
and Development. *See* World Bank
International Development Association,
199
International Finance Corporation,
199
International Human Rights Law
Institute, 215
International Monetary Fund (IMF),
210, 215, 218, 266
Ireland: Britain, relations with, 126–30,
167; potato famine in, 127–29
Iroquois Confederation, 73–74

Jackson, Andrew, 82–83
Jackson, W. Turrentine, 115–16
Jakarta, Indonesia, 66–67
Jamestown, 70
Janaweed, 231–32
Janibeg, Kipchak Khan, 29
Japan, 182, 183
Jews, 182, 183
Johns Hopkins Bloomberg School of
Public Health, 237–38
Johnson County, Wyoming, 105
Jordan, Terry, 77
Joseph, Chief, 99
*Jungle, The* (Sinclair, U.), 174

Kallet, Arthur, 178–79
kangaroos, 136
Kendrick, John R., 109
Kennedy administration, 198
Kentucky Fried Chicken (KFC), 188,
229
Kenya, 154, 163–65, 231
Kenya Cooperative Creameries, 164
KFC. *See* Kentucky Fried Chicken
Khan, Chinggis, 24–27
Khan, Ghazan, 28
Khan, Möngke, 29
Khoikhoi people, 157–58

King, Richard, 104
King Philip's War, 75
Kino, Father, 61
Kipling, Rudyard, 112
Kornblum, William, 6
Kroc, Ray, 171, 185–87
Kurgans, 16
Kuznar, Lawrence, 223

Lacandón rainforest, 211–12
Lacour-Gayet, Robert, 126, 158
Lake of the Moon, 37
land: borrowing of, 139; competition
    for, 98; control of, 18–19, 30, 67–68,
    123; conversion from communal
    to private, 63; displacement of
    indigenous peoples and, 82–86,
    148–49, 216–17, 224, 229–30;
    expropriation, 30, 51, 59, 68, 75,
    79–80, 96–103, 254–56; grabs, 141,
    243–44; in Mexico, 93–95; ranchers
    acquiring, 104–8; restrictions on
    foreign ownership of, 117. See also
    commons; grazing
land-grant universities, 176, 188
Las Casas, Bartolomé de, 46–48
late Neolithic crisis, 16
Latin America: "beef" from, 196,
    198–201, 203–7, 209, 211–12, 215,
    220–21, 255; Britain and, 147–48,
    150–53; corporations in, 197, 200,
    203, 213, 225; domesecration and
    devalued humans in, 212–16; hunger
    and environmental degradation in,
    200–203; indigenous peoples in,
    209, 212–13; ranching in, 7, 142–53,
    196–216, 220–21; repression and
    poverty in, 203–5; slaughterhouses
    in, 146; women in, 213–15. See also
    specific countries
"leather" industry, 63, 95, 115
Legazpi, López de, 65
Lemarchand, René, 218
Linear, Marcus, 244–45

lions, 164–66, 231, 261
Lippmann, Walter, 6
"livestock" agriculture, 176
"livestock" expansion (ganaderización),
    213
"livestock" industry, 103
Living with "Wildlife" slogan, 257
llamas, 34, 39–40, 55
lobbying, 173, 215
locally grown food, 261
Lopez, Barry, 110
López, Francisco Solano, 147
Los Angeles Times, 264–65
low-intensity warfare, 197–98
Lugo, Fernando, 246
Luxemburg, Rosa, 259
Lymbery, Philip, 239
lynching, 94–95, 105, 122

Maasai people, 154, 163–64, 231
Machu Picchu (Inca city), 39
Macintyre, Stuart, 133
Macleod, Donald, 130–32
MADRE (women's organization), 214
Magellan, Ferdinand, 65
Malacca, sacking of, 66
Malheur "Wildlife" Refuge, Oregon,
    191–92
malnutrition. See hunger and
    malnutrition
Manchus, 17, 30
Mansfield, C. B., 145–46
manure, 239–40, 242
Maori, 139–41, 217
Marshall, A. J., 136
Mauritius, 159
Mayans, 36, 212
McDonald, Maurice "Mac," 185
McDonald, Richard, 185
McDonald, Ronald, 187
McDonaldization, 252
McDonald's restaurants, 185–88, 235
McLamore, Jim, 187
McMichael, Philip, 214

McNeill, William H., 9, 26, 29, 43

"meat": compared to plant-based diet, 233; consumption of, 115, 123, 172, 182–83, 185, 188, 194; federal policy and production of, 180–85; health consequences from consumption of, 179–80, 192–94; industry, 172, 173, 180, 228; price of, 220; as rations, 90, 99, 103, 124, 160, 167, 182; salted, 67, 68, 71, 90–91, 124, 127, 132, 143, 148, 159, 167; spoiled, 173, 179. *See also* "beef"

"meatpacking" firms and plants, 152, 199

media, control of, 267–68, 270–71

Mein-Smith, Philippa, 126, 135–36

men: "meat" consumption by, 182–83; status and role of, 10, 156

Mencken, H. L., 115

Mendes, Chico, 210

mercantilism, 68

methane gas, 203

Mexican American Legal Defense and Education Fund, 229

Mexico: grain production in, 200; land in, 93–95; racism in, 93–94; ranching in, 210–11; United States war with, 93–94. *See also* Texas

Mfecane people, 159, 168

Middle Ages, 31–33

Middle East, 243–44, 247

militaries: "cavalries," 99, 101–2; domesecrated animals' use by, 18–24; warrior or military class, 13. *See also* armies

military strong men (*caudillos*), 142

Miller, Henry, 104–5

mining: gold, 49, 57, 60, 99; silver, 49–50, 55

missions and missionaries, 60–61, 66, 139–40

modernization, 263

Moncrieffe, Malcolm, 160

Moncrieffe, William, 160

Mongol violence, 17; in China, 24–27, 30; domesecration and, 24–31; examples of, 23; Riazan massacre, 9, 27, 40

Monro, Alexander, 26

Montezuma II, 49

Moors, 32

Morris, Nelson, 113

mules, 59, 160

Murdock, George, 155

Murle people, 233

Myall Creek Massacre, 135, 143

Nambikwara people, 212

Nanticoke society, 70, 74

Napoleon, 142

NASA. *See* National Aeronautics and Space Administration

Nash, Gary, 35–36

National Aeronautics and Space Administration (NASA), 245

National Animal Damage Control Act (1931), 180

National "Cattlemen's" Association, 267

National Council on Foreign Relations, 232

National "Dairy" Council, 267

National Intelligence Council, 245–46, 251

Nations, James, 201

Native Americans: at Battle of Fallen Timbers, 80; buffalo and, 96–98, 102–3, 121; conflicts and displacement of, 99–103, 107–8, 120–22, 143–44; Conquest of the Desert and, 149–50; crop damage conflict and warfare with, 71–75, 90; decimation of, 58–59; horrific treatment of, 47–50, 53–55; horses and, 97–98, 121–23; Northwest Ordinance and, 79; raiding, slavery and trade by, 97–98; on reservations, 85, 99–100, 103, 108, 122; resistance of, 57–58; women, 48, 59, 76, 97, 122. *See also* *specific peoples*

Navarro, Manuel, 59
Nelson, Jack, 209
Neolithic revolution, 13
Netherlands, 64
New Deal policy, 181–82, 234
New England, 70–71, 74–75
New Mexico, 94
New Netherland, 73
New Spain, 49–52, 55, 60–61
*Newsweek*, 241
new welfarism, 259–61, 317n4
New Zealand, 139–41, 167, 216–17, 229
Nez Percé people, 99–100
Nicaragua, 197, 205–6
nomadic pastoralism: in Africa, 154–58,
    162–63, 167–68; agriculture and,
    27–28; communities destroyed by,
    16–17; fall of Roman Empire and
    invasions by, 22–23; horses and,
    14–16, 155; invasions and raids,
    14–17, 22–24; rise of, 13–18; social
    organization and cultural practices
    of, 24; social stratification in, 17,
    26, 156
Northwest Ordinance, 79
Noske, Barbara, 189–90
Nuer people, 167, 233

obesity, 252, 267
Occupy movement, 271
oil, 242, 246, 255
Oñate, Juan de, 53
oppression: contemporary ranching
    and, 224–33; Parenti on, 1; terminol-
    ogy used for, 6; three components in
    theory of, 274n16. *See also* animal
    oppression; human oppression
Oregon Trail, 99
Osgood, Ernest Staples, 102–3
Osterholm, Michael T., 250
other animals: consequences of
    confinement of, 189–90; diseases
    from crowding, 6–7, 12, 23, 41,
    166–67, 193, 253; genetically

manipulated, 189; "humanely"
    raised, 259–61; humans' relationship
    with, 4, 10–13, 223, 257; parts and
    body fluids as commodities, 6, 51,
    68; poisoning of, 106, 109, 136, 144,
    164, 180, 190, 231, 261; role of, 1;
    sentience, consciousness and
    mindedness of, 4, 11, 189; on ships,
    70–71, 110–11, 117–20; as term, 6;
    traded for ammunition and guns,
    98, 121. *See also* animal exploitation;
    animal oppression; aquatic animals;
    domesecrated animals; "domestica-
    tion"; "farm animals"; free-living
    animals; free-range animals; "hides";
    "pack animals"; skins; *specific
    animals*
Owl Child (Blackfeet warrior), 101
"oxen" (mature, castrated cows), 20
Oxfam, 243–44

Pachauri, Rajendra, 241
"pack animals," 21
"packinghouses," 114, 207; arrests and
    deportation at Postville, Iowa, 228,
    309n19
Paiacú people, 59
Panzós massacre, 209
Paraguay, 147–48, 246
Parenti, Michael: on background
    assumptions, 4, 267; on low-intensity
    warfare, 197–98; on oppression, 1
Parton, James, 70
pastoralism: as term, 30; transhumant,
    16; violence of, 5, 24. *See also*
    nomadic pastoralism
Patagonia, 148–49
patriarchal societies, 13, 156, 167,
    254
"peasants": defiance of, 31–32;
    tributes, 15
Pequots, 72
Pereyra, Carlos, 53
Persians, 21

Pew Charitable Trusts, 237–38
Pew Memorial Trusts, 264
Philippines, 239–40; Spanish invasion of, 65–69
Pickover, Michelé, 219
pigs, 53–54; consumption of, 177–78; corn for, 87; diseases and, 248–50; free-range, 71–72, 74–75; at slaughterhouses, 88
Pizarro, Gonzalo, 54
plagues: animal plagues, 23; devalued humans blamed for, 23; spread of, 28–30, 33
plantations: crop-based, 78, 84; sugar, 44, 50, 61, 74, 127, 159
Plimsoll, Samuel, 117–20
plows: "oxen" forced to pull, 20; use of, 12–13
poisoning of other animals, 106, 109, 136, 144, 164, 180, 190, 231, 261
Polk, President, 93, 94
pollution, 242, 268
Porkopolis (Cincinnati), 88
Portugal: invasion of Americas, 6, 45, 56, 67–69; sacking of Malacca, 66
Postville, Iowa, 228, 309n19
potato famine in Ireland, 127–29
Potosí mines, 55, 62
poverty: hunger and malnutrition and, 148, 226, 244, 255, 262; Latin American repression and, 203–5; reports on, 269
Powhatan, 72
pre-Columbian Americas: horticulture in, 35–36; trade and, 35; violence and warfare in, 34–42
priests, 10, 60–61
Primo, João, 226
prod pole, 174
Propaganda (Bernays), 177
public consciousness and corporations, 175–80, 266–68
purchasing habits, 259–60
putting-out or cottage system, 63

Quadrennial Defense Review Report (Department of Defense), 247
quagga, 164

racism: in Canada, 121; impacts of, 171; in Mexico, 93–94; Social Darwinism and, 169, 176, 300n144
radio, 177–78
railroads, 121; buffalo killing and, 102; "cattle" on, 110–11, 115, 150–51; sheep on, 110–11, 150–51; for transportation to slaughterhouses, 110–11, 173–74
rainforests: in Brazil, 225–26, 229; conservation of, 210; diversity of, 202; free-living animals in, 215–16, 229, 257; Lacandón, 211–12
rancher associations, 105–6, 109, 207
ranching, 5; in Brazil, 56–61, 144–45, 147–48, 199, 209–10, 212–13; in Canada, 120–25; Catholic Church and, 60–61, 142–43; "cattle" kings and, 86–91; colonialism and, 7; definition of, 275n17; expansion of, 82–86, 103–8, 168; in Latin America, 7, 142–53, 196–216, 220–21; lobbying and, 173, 215; in Mexico, 210–11; oppression and contemporary, 224–33; ranchers acquiring land, 104–8; range improvements, 191; range wars between ranchers, 105; in Roman Empire, 18–20; Roosevelt, T., on, 103; Spain and, 32, 49, 51–52, 54–55; in Texas, 7, 92–95, 104. See also "cattle" ranching; commercial ranching; sheep ranching
rations: llamas and alpacas as "pack animals" and, 39–40; "meat" as, 90, 99, 103, 124, 160, 167, 182
Reagan, Ronald, 206
reconquista, 32
refrigeration, 117, 141, 150–52, 168
regional and international conflict, 242–47, 263

resources: competition as explanation
    for warfare, 34–35; depletion and
    scarcity of, 243–47, 256, 263, 265;
    misuse of finite, 240–42
Revolutionary War, 79
Riazan massacre, 9, 27, 40
Ribeiro da Silva, José Cláudio, 225
Rifkin, Jeremy, 116
rinderpest, 23, 160, 167
Robbins, Richard, 252
Roca, Julio, 149–50
Rocky Mountain News, 106
Roman "cavalries," 20–21
Roman Empire: booty in, 21; "cattle"
    in, 18–22, 32; domesecrated animals
    in, 40–41; fall of, 22–23; gluttony
    and scarcity in, 33; military use of
    domesecrated animals in, 18–22;
    ranching in, 18–20; slavery in, 18–22
Romero, Óscar, 208
Romero, Sílvio, 151
Roosevelt, Franklin, 181, 182
Roosevelt, Theodore, 103, 109
Rosas, Juan Manuel de, 143–44, 203
rubber tappers, 203, 210
rustling, 122
Rwanda, 218, 222, 233

salted "meat," 67, 71; slavery and, 68,
    90–91, 124, 127, 143, 148, 159, 167.
    See also charque; charqui
Sanbonmatsu, John, 259
Sand Creek, Colorado, 100–101
Sanders, Colonel Harlan, 188
Sandinista Revolution, 206
Sandino, Augusto Nicolás Calderón,
    197, 206
Scars in the Landscape: A Register of
    Massacre Sites in Western Victoria
    (Clark, I.), 134–35
Schlink, F. J., 178–79
School of the Americas, 205
Schwartz, Jeff, 235
Scientific American, 243

Scotland, 130–32, 167
Scramble for Africa, 161, 168, 218
Scully, Alfred, 101–2
Scythians, 17, 24
"seafood," 264–65
Second Boer War, 160
Sedlmeyer, Robert, 223
Seminole people, 82, 89
Serpell, James, 9
Shaler, Nathaniel Southgate, 1–2, 120,
    254, 262
sharecroppers, 181
sheep: murder of, 106; on railroads,
    110–11, 150–51; textile industry
    and, 63, 82, 114, 130–32, 148
sheep ranching, 32, 52; in Australia,
    133–37; "cattlemen" conflict with,
    106; in New Zealand, 140–41;
    number of sheep on ranches, 104
Sheridan, Philip, 101–2
Sherman, William Tecumseh, 92, 104
Shipman, Pat, 3
ships, 70–71, 110–11, 117–20
Shiva, Vandana, 241
Siedentopf, Adolph, 164, 165
Siedentopf, Friedrich, 164, 165
Sierra Club, 236–37
"silent global crisis," 240
silver: mining, 49–50, 55; supply of,
    61–63, 68
Sinclair, Keith, 140
Sinclair, Upton, 174
Sinopec, 235
Sioux people, 99, 230
skins, 71, 73, 76, 90. See also "hides"
slaughterhouses: Chicago, 111–14,
    172–73, 174; conditions in, 113–14,
    172–73, 219, 228; in Latin America,
    146; mammals killed annually in,
    172; pigs at, 88; railroads for
    transportation to, 110–11, 173–74
slavery: Africa and, 55, 64; Franks
    and, 31; gold mining and, 57, 60;
    hereditary, 24, 156; Native American

slavery (*continued*)
    raiding, trade and, 97–98; in Roman
    Empire, 18–22; salted "meat" and,
    68, 90–91, 124, 127, 132, 143, 148,
    159, 167; "slave" trade, 68, 96, 156–57;
    sugar plantations and, 50, 61, 159
smallpox, 28–29, 48, 52, 67, 74, 124, 157
Social Darwinism, 169, 176, 254,
    300n144
social programs, 268, 269
Social Progress Trust Fund, 198
soil erosion, 240–41
Somalia famine, 244
Somoza, President, 205
Somoza family, 197, 206
sorghum, 211
soy meal, 264
Spain: "cattle" ranching and, 49, 51–52,
    55, 56; conquest of Canary Islands
    by, 43–44; Florida and, 53, 64–65,
    76, 82; invasion of Americas by, 6,
    45–50, 67–69; invasion of
    Philippines by, 65–69; ranching and,
    32, 49, 51–52, 54–55
Spam, 177–78
Spanish-American War, 173
Sparks, William A., 92
speciesism, 124, 171, 275n16
spice trade, 66–67
Spring, Agnes Wright, 115–16
Stang, Dorothy, 225, 256, 261
state: influence on, 268, 270; role of,
    124, 194, 271, 275n16
steamers. *See* ships
"stock breeding," 61
"stockyards," Chicago, 111–14
stress and bone deformities, 11
structural violence, 11, 276n9
strychnine, 109, 180, 190
Stull, Don, 238
subsistence farming, 203–7
Sudan, 231–33, 256
sugar companies, 197
sugar mills (*engenhos*), 50, 56

sugar plantations, 44, 50, 61, 74, 127,
    159
Swan Land and "Cattle" Company, 116
Swift, Gustavus, 113

Tamerlane, 23
"tanneries," 95, 242
Tanzania, 231
Tapuia, 58–59
Tasmania, 137
Taylor, Edward, 182
Taylor Grazing Act, 182
Te Kemara (Maori leader), 140
television, 184–85
tenant farming, 86–87
Tenochtitlán (Aztec city), 36–37, 49
terminology, 6
Terrell, John Upton, 106
Texas, 7, 92–95, 104
textile industry, 91; sheep and, 63, 82,
    114, 130–32, 148; working conditions
    in, 114–15
Thailand, 239–40
Thala siege, 21
Thompson, E. P., 5
Tikal (Mayan city), 36
Torres, Bob, 223
torture, 75, 118
Towne, Charles Wayland, 32
trade: free-trade policies, 203, 266;
    horses for women, 97; Native
    American raiding, slavery and,
    97–98; other animals for ammu-
    nition and guns, 98, 121; pre-
    Columbian Americas and, 35;
    search for trade routes, 45–46; in
    skins, 71, 73, 76, 90; "slave" trade, 68,
    96, 156–57; spice, 66–67
Trail of Tears, 83
transhumant pastoralism, 16
*trekboeren* (Dutch "stockmen"), 157
tsetse flies, 167, 217
Tuareg people, 162–63
Turkana people, 154, 163

Turkish Ottoman "cavalries," 45
Turks, 17
Tutsi people, 217–18, 233

Union Cold Storage Company, 138
Union of Concerned Scientists, 238
United Nations (UN), 242;
Development Program, 232; Food
and Agricultural Organization, 200,
217, 241, 242, 251, 252–53;
Intergovernmental Panel on Climate
Change, 241; on poverty, 269;
*Between a Rock and a Hard Place:
Armed Violence in African Pastoralist
Communities,* 230
United States (U.S.): "beef" butchering
differences in Britain and, 119;
Forest Service, 172, 173; Mexico
war with, 93–94; -style diet, 245–46,
256
Urquiza, Justo José de, 147–48
Uruguay, 144, 147, 152, 196
U.S. *See* United States
U.S. Agency for International
Development (U.S. AID), 198–99,
217
U.S. Export-Import Bank, 198
USDA, 200, 234

Vaggioli, Dom Felice, 140–41
*vaqueros* ("cowboys"), 61
Veblen, Thorstein, 3
veganism, 261–66
Venezuela, 143, 152, 226–27
Vernam, Glenn, 43
Vestey Brothers, 138–39, 152, 170, 216
Vikings, 31
violence: commercial ranching and,
76–82; against devalued humans, 2,
5; "domestication" and, 4–5; factors
promoting, 41; "hamburger" culture
and, 188–95; and hunger in Middle
Ages, 31–33; nonviolence compared
to, 270–71; of pastoralism, 5, 24;

structural, 11, 276n9; and warfare in
pre-Columbian Americas, 34–42.
*See also* domesecration; Mongol
violence

wage laborers, 63, 68
Wampanoag Nation, 75
warfare: counterinsurgency, 203, 205–6,
208–9; crop damage conflict and,
71–75, 90; horses as instruments of,
14, 20–21, 31, 53, 79–80, 90, 157,
160, 167; among indigenous peoples,
73, 98, 122–23, 159, 168; low-
intensity, 197–98; pre-Columbian
Americas violence and, 34–42;
problems creating risks of, 261;
resource competition as explanation
for, 34–35; timing of, 36, 37
Warman, Arturo, 192
War of Flowers, 38
War of the Triple Alliance, 147–48
warrification, 59, 121
warrior or military class, 13
Washington, George, 79
water: control of, 18, 28, 30, 67, 105,
123; deep wells, 217; depletion and
shortages of, 172, 241–42, 244–45,
256, 264; disputes over, 232, 241–42,
245, 246; impacts on, 172, 193;
pollution, 237, 242, 264, 268
Wayne, "Mad" Anthony, 79–80, 99
Webb, Walter Prescott, 62
Wendy's, 235
Wentworth, Edward Norris, 32
Western land expropriation, 96–103
West Indies, 46, 47, 74
westward expansionism, 75
Whiskey Rebellion, 80
White, James Taylor, 92–93
White, Robert, 208
White Castle "hamburgers," 175,
178–79, 186
White Guards, 210
WHO. *See* World Health Organization

"Wild Animal" Poisoning Congresses, 164
"Wildlife" Services, 257
"wild" mustangs, 191
Williams, Glyn, 150
Williams, Robert G., 196, 203–4
Winders, Bill, 181
Winks, Robin W., 3
Wisconsin, 238–39
Wolf, Eric, 135
wolves, 109–10
women: labor exploitation, 63, 114, 141, 214; in Latin America, 213–15; Native Americans, 48, 59, 76, 97, 122; as possessions, 14, 24, 53, 97, 135, 154; status and role of, 10, 14, 156; violence against and sexual exploitation of, 9, 47–48, 59, 76, 101–2, 121–22, 135–36, 138–39, 213–15, 232, 233
Wood, William Madison, 114
World Bank, 221, 223, 266; on food shortages, 246; on land grabs, 243; loans from, 198–99, 203, 210, 211, 217, 234; on poverty, 269; on water disputes, 241–42
World Health Organization (WHO), 251, 252–53, 256
World Organisation for Animal Health, 251
World Trade Organization, 235, 260, 266
World War I, 173, 176, 218
World War II, 182–83
Wyatt, Francis, 72
Wyndham, Marivic, 126, 135–36

Yale Crowd, 86
Yamassee Nation, 76

Zaire (now Democratic Republic of the Congo), 233
Zapatista movement, 211
Zimbabwe, 230
zoonotic diseases, 5, 48, 67, 122, 136, 167
zoos, 166, 216
Zulu people, 159, 168

CPSIA information can be obtained
at www.ICGtesting.com
Printed in the USA
LVOW10s1431141217
559723LV00023B/842/P